Living a Supernatural Life

Volume 2

Pastor M. F. Olumbo
Foreword written by Pastor E. A. Adeboye
General Overseer RCCG

LIVING A SUPERNATURAL LIFE
VOLUME 2

Copyright © 2008 by:

PASTOR MICHAEL F. OLUMBO

ISBN No
978-083-504-0

First Published in Nigeria by:
EXTRA TIME COMMUNICATIONS LTD.

All rights reserved.
No portion of this book may be reproduced or transmitted in any form or by any means, electronics or mechanical, including photocopy, recording, or any information storage and retrieval system, without the written permission of the author
michaeolumbo@outlook.com

For further information or permission address:
Pastor Michael F Olumbo, The Apostolic Church,
Olorunda Ketu, Lagos, Nigeria.
Tel +234 816 526 5668
Tel +234 802 310 3275
First Print April 2008

Foreword written by Pastor E. A. Adeboye General Overseer
Redeemed Christian Church of God
All Scripture quotations are from the King James Version of the Bible, except otherwise stated

DEDICATION

To God who ordered me to write the two book series titled *"Living a Supernatural life"* and *"You are a New Creature"* even when I knew next to nothing in the Word. It was He who stood by me, taught me and encouraged me throughout the course of writing the eight volumes that make up these two books series. Whenever it looked like I could no longer go forward with the writing because of my lack of enough knowledge of the Word, He would point me to the right Word in the Scriptures and give me the necessary revelation of the Word to fire me on. He has used the writing of these books to build up my faith in Him and in His Word.

CONTENTS

ACKNOWLEDGEMENTS	7
PREFACE	11
FOREWORD BY PASTOR E. A. ADEBOYE	13
INTRODUCTION	15
1 YOU ARE A SUPERNATURAL BEING	33
2 RELEASING THE SUPERNATURAL	83
3 THE NAME OF JESUS (A key of the kingdom)	105
4 HOW TO USE THE NAME OF JESUS	147
5 YOUR MOUTH IS THE VEHICLE	221
6 FULFILLMENT IS IMMEDIATE	283
7 PRACTICING SUPERNATURAL LIVING	299

The next seven chapters give some of the things that you have to do or be if you want to practice living in the supernatural. You must:

8 SEE BEYOND THE NATURAL	319
9 ABIDE IN CHRIST	355
10 HAVE NO SIN-COMPLEX	383
11 BE SENSITIVE TO THE HOLY SPIRIT	403
12 BE VIOLENT AGAINST THE DEVIL	411
13 BE BOLD	449
14 BE PATIENT	465

15 YOU ARE GOD'S BATTLE AXE	495
16 PULLING DOWN SATAN'S STRONG HOLDS	533
17 YOU MUST BE BORN AGAIN	589
REFERENCES	605
INDEX	607

ACKNOWLEDGEMENTS

I am thankful to God for giving me the opportunity to write these book series. He alone should take whatever glory accrues from the writing of these books.

I thank late Pastor S. S. Jemigbon who is the third Chairman of The Apostolic Church in the Lagos and Western/Northern Areas (LAWNA) Territory and the Vice President of The Apostolic Church, Nigeria for reviewing the book and passing it to the Chairman of the Literature Committee of the Church.

I also thank Pastor A. M. O. Oshinowo who is the Chairman of the Literature Committee of The Apostolic Church in the LAWNA Territory and also the Superintendent of the Abeokuta Area of The Apostolic Church in the LAWNA Territory for agreeing to review the book and sending it to Pastor G. A. Oyetunji, the LAWNA literature Committee Secretary.

My thanks also go to late Pastor E. O. Arokodare who is the Superintendent of the Agege Area of The Apostolic Church in the LAWNA Territory for the useful advice that he gave me concerning the publishing of these book series. Thanks to Pastor G. A. Oyetunji of the Literature Department of The Apostolic Church LAWNA Territory who is also the District Apostle of Coker District in Apapa Area of The Apostolic Church in the LAWNA Territory for patiently reading this book series and making some very useful observations and corrections, which have been incorporated into the book series.

I owe a debt of gratitude to Pastor E. A. Adeboye who is the General Overseer of the Redeemed Christian Church of God worldwide who despite his very busy schedule accepted to review this book and write the Foreword, which he has done very beautifully. His revision of the book and his prayers for me on various occasions has encouraged me to pursue the publication of these book series.

I owe a big thank you to my precious friend late Elder Francis O. Aisida of The Apostolic Church Surulere Area of the LAWNA Territory for his encouragement throughout the period of the writing of these book series. He keeps reminding me that these books need to be published as quickly as possible as they are written as a result of an injunction from the Lord. He even took me to a printer in Ibadan two years ago to explore the possibility of getting the printer to print and publish the books. He not only encouraged me throughout the period of the writing of these books but has joined me several times to pray concerning these books and other issues. He was the one who suggested the breaking up of the books into volumes for easy reading and so as to make them more appealing to readers.

I also thank all my friends and worshippers in the various Churches or Assemblies in which I have preached sermons based on some of the topics discussed in these books who have ceaselessly been asking me to get the printed version of the sermons published. This has encouraged me.

My thanks also go to my wife, Grace who keeps nudging me asking when the books will be published. She felt so concerned that the books were getting too big for easy reading and kept advising me to make them short.

Finally I thank my children Foluso, Foluke, Ayodeji and Feyisayo who during the preparation for and writing of these books having observed that they always see me studying the Scriptures and jotting down notes for long periods day after day spanning several years kept asking me if I was writing a Bible Commentary. I thank them for their patience in bearing with me and for their encouragement.

PREFACE

LIVING A SUPERNATURAL LIFE

You can live above sickness and disease. You can live above failure. You can live above poverty and lack. You can live above every afflictions of life. God created man to be a spirit being housed in a physical body and man is a supernatural being like Him. He made man in His own image. You are a spirit being, a supernatural being and you can live a supernatural life here on earth. You don't have to get to heaven before you start living a supernatural life. When you are born-again, you are given a new invisible nature in Christ. With that new invisible nature, living a supernatural life here on earth becomes easy. Basically supernatural living involves practicing the release of this your new invisible nature in Christ into your visible human nature. It is the application of the **TRUTH** to **FACTS**, where the **TRUTH** is what the Word of God says, and the **FACTS** are what your natural situations say. How then do you live a supernatural life above sicknesses, above diseases, above failure, above lack, above poverty and above all the afflictions of life? The answer to that question is what this book series is all about. To live in the supernatural you must be convinced that you are what God says that you are, that you are who God says that you are, that you have what God says that you have, that you can do what God says that you can do and that you are where God says that you are.

Once you are convinced of these truths and you live your life in the light of the truths, supernatural living then becomes very cheap for you.

You must note that you have been sent to this world just as Jesus was sent. You are an ambassador of heaven here on earth. You have been given the powers to do the same supernatural works that Jesus did when He came to this earth. You have been given the power to do even greater works than He did. You have been made a god to your enemies and to all the situations and circumstances around you. This must be your mentality all the time and if it is, then you must live your life like someone who is reigning over and on top of all the circumstances and situations of life. Nothing should be daunting to you. The greater One than he that is in the world now lives in you. Therefore stop seeing yourself as an ordinary human being. You are a spirit being and you are supposed to live conscious of this truth as a spirit being. Once you can do these and realize that it is not you who will be doing the supernatural acts, but the greater One who lives in you without whom you can do nothing then living in the supernatural realm will become very cheap and even ordinary for you.

This book series, *"Living a supernatural life" Volumes 1, 2, 3 and 4* have been written to help you do all of these and much more.

FOREWORD

You can live a supernatural life here on earth. If we have no expectation or hope of enjoying the supernatural here on earth, then heaven is to that extent irrelevant to us. The truth however is that there is a constant interaction between the physical and the spiritual. Jacob saw the angels ascending and descending, taking things up – be they prayers, worship, self-sacrifice or wickedness and bringing the answers or consequences (of things sowed) in the flesh back. We need help to send the appropriate things up and empowerment to overcome the pull and power of our carnal nature.

"But you shall receive power after the Holy Ghost is come upon you." This proclamation admits no equivocation. The immediate and direct consequence of the presence of the Holy Spirit in a man's life is endowment of enormous power – to live the supernatural here on earth. Olumbo summarizes this beautifully "Supernatural living is therefore your heritage in Christ".

The reality on the ground however, is that Christians are seeking out other Christians; searching every nook and corner for "powerful men of God". Every Christian is a powerhouse in Christ Jesus. Worse some search for the power outside Christ.

The battle is won or lost even before the first shot is fired – in the mind. What we believe, our faith, determines how much power flows through our lives.

But then faith without works is dead. Living faith will produce dynamic words, which leads to action, reaction and release of spiritual power from on high. The book is interlaced, copiously, with the living Word for the proper instruction of the reader.

The author is not dealing in the realm of precepts but in the reality of applied principles so ably set out in this book. The spiritual battle with the ganglion on his wrist, for example, though protracted, ended in a resounding and permanent victory of the power of God over the unnatural growth. Flesh cannot of course understand the matter of the spirit. You need to tap into the source of all power in heaven and earth by accepting the Lord Jesus Christ as your personal Lord and Saviour and then you can receive power.

Find out how in the last chapter of this wonderful book.

Read on. God bless and empower you to do exploits – here on earth.

PASTOR E. A. ADEBOYE
General Overseer
Redeemed Christian Church of God

INTRODUCTION

Just before Jesus left this earth, He promised that those who believe in Him would be empowered to do supernatural acts. He said that they would live supernatural lives as supernatural beings here on earth. He said that supernatural power would be flowing out of them. He said that following them in their paths would be miracles, signs and wonders. He also said in Mark 16:17-18 that signs and wonders would follow them, that they would cast out devils in His Name, that they would speak with new tongues in His Name, that they would take up serpents in His Name, that if they drink any deadly thing it will not hurt them, that they would lay hands on the sick in His Name and they shall recover. He said in Acts 1:8 that they would receive the power to do these after the Holy Ghost has come upon them.

> *And these signs shall follow them that believe; In my name shall they cast out devils; they shall speak with new tongues;*
>
> *They shall take up serpents; and if they drink any deadly thing, it shall not hurt them; they shall lay hands on the sick, and they shall recover.* **Mark 16:17-18**
>
> *But ye shall receive power, after that the Holy Ghost is come upon you: and ye shall be witnesses unto me both in Jerusalem, and in all Judaea, and in Samaria, and unto the uttermost part of the earth.*
> **Acts 1:8**

He had said earlier in John 7:38 that once they receive this power, which He called rivers of living water, it would be flowing out of them. In John 14:12 He also said that equipped with this power, they would do the same works that He did and that they would even do greater works than He did.

> *He that believeth on me, as the scripture hath said, out of his belly shall flow rivers of living water.*
>
> **John 7:38**

> *Verily, verily, I say unto you, He that believeth on me, the works that I do shall he do also; and greater works than these shall he do; because I go unto my Father.*
>
> **John 14:12**

Now look at the works that He did as described by Him in Luke 4:18-19. Then you will see there what you are supposed to do as a believer in Christ. You would realize that you need power in order to be able to do these. Among the things that you are supposed to be doing are healing the sick, setting the captives free, restoring eyes to the blind and of course preaching the gospel of Christ to the poor to make them rich. You have been given the power of God in order that you may be able to do these.

> *The Spirit of the Lord is upon me, because he hath anointed me to preach the gospel to the poor; he hath sent me to heal the brokenhearted, to preach deliverance to the captives, and recovering of sight to the blind, to set at liberty them that are bruised,*

Introduction

To preach the acceptable year of the Lord.
                               Luke 4:18-19

But the sad thing is that most Christians who are believers in Christ are not mindful of this power that they are supposed to have and demonstrate to the world. Even most of those that are mindful of it are unable to demonstrate this power in their lives. They keep praying that God should empower them by sending down His power to them. But God had already sent down the Holy Spirit and He, the Holy Spirit, is supposed to be living inside every believer in Christ. It is the believer who now has to give the Holy Spirit the room to operate in His life. God has promised that if we want the Holy Spirit all we have to do is ask God for Him with a sincere heart and we shall have Him. Secondly, Jesus Christ who is the power of God is also supposed to be living inside every believer in Christ.

That is what Jesus Christ Himself told us in John 14:20. God also made us to understand this through Apostle John in 1 John 4:13 and also through Apostle Paul as written in 1 Corinthians 1:24. Therefore as a believer in Christ, you are supposed to be loaded with the power of God. You are a carrier of the power of God. The power of God is living inside you. It is already inside you.

At that day ye shall know that I am in my Father, and ye in me, and I in you.
                                   John 14:20

Hereby know we that we dwell in him, and he in us, because he hath given us of his Spirit.
                                   1 John 4:13

Living a Supernatural Life (Volume 2)

> *But unto them which are called, both Jews and Greeks, Christ the power of God, and the wisdom of God.*
>
> **1 Corinthians 1:24**

As a believer in Christ, the rivers of living water, which is also the virtue and the power to work miracles, signs and wonders are supposed to be flowing out of you. If you are a true believer in Christ therefore, then this power of God is truly living inside you. ***Supernatural living is therefore your heritage in Christ.***

You need to be able to demonstrate this power of God in your life. This is so because the world is moving perilously towards the end-time. As a believer in Christ in this end-time, you will be required to demonstrate this power of God that is now residing in you. We are now in the last days that God described vividly for us in Micah 4:1-8 through Prophet Micah and through Prophet Joel in Joel 2:28 and, which God told us through Apostle Peter in Acts 2:16-17 had already started on the day of Pentecost.

> *But in the last days it shall come to pass, that the mountain of the house of the LORD shall be established in the top of the mountains, and it shall be exalted above the hills; and people shall flow unto it.*
>
> *And many nations shall come, and say, Come, and let us go up to the mountain of the LORD, and to the house of the God of Jacob; and he will teach us of his ways, and we will walk in his paths: for the law shall go forth of Zion, and the word of the LORD from Jerusalem.*

Introduction

And he shall judge among many people, and rebuke strong nations afar off; and they shall beat their swords into plowshares, and their spears into pruning hooks: nation shall not lift up a sword against nation, neither shall they learn war any more.

But they shall sit every man under his vine and under his fig tree; and none shall make them afraid: for the mouth of the LORD of hosts hath spoken it.

For all people will walk every one in the name of his god, and we will walk in the name of the LORD our God for ever and ever.

In that day, saith the LORD, will I assemble her that halteth, and I will gather her that is driven out, and her that I have afflicted;

And I will make her that halted a remnant, and her that was cast far off a strong nation: and the LORD shall reign over them in mount Zion from henceforth, even for ever.

And thou, O tower of the flock, the strong hold of the daughter of Zion, unto thee shall it come, even the first dominion; the kingdom shall come to the daughter of Jerusalem.
Micah 4:1-8

Living a Supernatural Life (Volume 2)

> *And it shall come to pass afterward, that I will pour out my spirit upon all flesh; and your sons and your daughters shall prophesy, your old men shall dream dreams, your young men shall see visions:*
> **Joel 2:28**

> *But this is that which was spoken by the prophet Joel;*

> *And it shall come to pass in the last days, saith God, I will pour out of my Spirit upon all flesh: and your sons and your daughters shall prophesy, and your young men shall see visions, and your old men shall dream dreams:*
> **Acts 2:16-17**

If the last days started on the day of Pentecost, then we must be in the thick of the last days now. If you are truly a believer in Christ in these last days, then as a last day saint, the power of God should be flowing out of you without any inhibitions at all. You should be living a supernatural life here on earth.

Take a look at the description of the last day saints that God gave us through Prophet Micah in Micah 4:1-8 written above and through Prophet Joel in Joel 2:1-11 written below and you will see just how much of the power of God should be oozing out of you as a last day saint.

> *Blow ye the trumpet in Zion, and sound an alarm in my holy mountain: let all the inhabitants of the land tremble: for the day of the LORD cometh, for it is nigh at hand;*

Introduction

A day of darkness and of gloominess, a day of clouds and of thick darkness, as the morning spread upon the mountains: a great people and a strong; there hath not been ever the like, neither shall be any more after it, even to the years of many generations.

A fire devoureth before them; and behind them a flame burneth: the land is as the garden of Eden before them, and behind them a desolate wilderness; yea, and nothing shall escape them.

The appearance of them is as the appearance of horses; and as horsemen, so shall they run.

Like the noise of chariots on the tops of mountains shall they leap, like the noise of a flame of fire that devoureth the stubble, as a strong people set in battle array.

Before their face the people shall be much pained: all faces shall gather blackness.

They shall run like mighty men; they shall climb the wall like men of war; and they shall march every one on his ways, and they shall not break their ranks:

Neither shall one thrust another; they shall walk every one in his path: and when they fall upon the sword, they shall not be wounded.

> *They shall run to and fro in the city; they shall run upon the wall, they shall climb up upon the houses; they shall enter in at the windows like a thief.*
>
> *The earth shall quake before them; the heavens shall tremble: the sun and the moon shall be dark, and the stars shall withdraw their shining:*
>
> *And the LORD shall utter his voice before his army: for his camp is very great: for he is strong that executeth his word: for the day of the LORD is great and very terrible; and who can abide it?*
>
> **Joel 2:1-11**

He said that the last day saints would be strong and great. The world has never seen anything that looks like them in greatness and in strength before. This means that as a last day saint you should be greater than Solomon and stronger than Samson.

Anything that comes against the last day saints would be devoured and destroyed. No evil shall escape them unpunished. No devil can hide anywhere and escape them. They will run like horses and like mighty horsemen, they will leap and jump over walls and they will not be tired. Nothing shall escape them. Yet they will not break their ranks so the enemy cannot tempt them into breaching the commands of God. Neither will they thrust one another. Every one of them will walk in his own path, which means that all the artificial denominational divides and traditions will not be an obstacle to their unity and strength.

Introduction

This is because they will all see themselves as one army of the Lord. When they fall they will not be wounded. The whole earth shall quake before them. Even the heavens shall tremble. Nothing shall make them afraid. They would be filled with the Holy Spirit and it is the Holy Spirit inside them that would lift up a standard against any opposition that comes against them. So, all oppositions would dissolve before them. Miracles, signs and wonders will be following them for as the army of the Lord, they shall be executing the Word of the Lord. This is a description of what you are supposed to be as a last day saint. This is your heritage as a last day believer in Christ. If you are a believer in Christ, you are supposed to be in Christ and you are supposed to be a member of this last day army of the Lord. If you are not experiencing that surge in the power of God flowing through your life then you need to examine your life to look at what you are doing or not doing that has not allowed this power of God to be manifested through you and, which has not allowed you to live the supernatural life that you are supposed to live right here on earth as a believer in Christ.

Don't look at your position. It does not matter whether you are a Pastor, a Reverend, a Bishop, a Prophet, an Evangelist, an Apostle, an Elder, an Overseer or just an ordinary member of the Church without a title. As long as you are a believer in Christ in these last days, you are supposed to be demonstrating this Power of God in your life. Living in the miraculous is supposed to be a normal thing for you as a last day saint. It should be your way of life. If you are not living such a life then you need to find out why you are not doing so. **That is what this** *"Living a supernatural life"* **book series is all about.**

Living a Supernatural Life (Volume 2)

But if you want to live this supernatural type of life, which is accompanied by miracles, signs and wonders, then note what we have been told by God in Acts 2:22 that it was God that approved Jesus Christ such that miracles, signs and wonders could be done by Him. It is God that will also approve you such that miracles, signs and wonders could be done by you.

> *Ye men of Israel, hear these words; Jesus of Nazareth, a man approved of God among you by miracles and wonders and signs, which God did by him in the midst of you, as ye yourselves also know:*
>
> **Acts 2:22**

But how do you get this approval of God? What do you need to do to get God's approval so that you could do miracles, signs and wonders? God has given us the answer to these questions in 2 Timothy 2:15 through Apostle Paul. He said,

> *"Study to shew thyself approved unto God, a workman that needeth not to be ashamed, rightly dividing the word of truth."*
>
> **2 Timothy 2:15**

It means that what you need to do is to study, to get the necessary knowledge so as to be approved of God. Whatever is currently blocking your way so that you have not received this approval of God it is knowledge that will deliver you from it. Whatever is stopping you from flowing in the supernatural so that miracles, signs and wonders cannot flow out or be done through you it is knowledge that would deliver you from it.

Introduction

This is so because as a believer in Christ, God has now justified you He has imputed His own righteousness to you so that you are as righteous as anybody else therefore you are now "The Just". But as the just, it is through knowledge that you would be delivered. That is what God told us through Solomon in Proverbs 11:9.

> *An hypocrite with his mouth destroyeth his neighbour: but through knowledge shall the just be delivered.*
>
> **Proverbs 11:9**

This book has been written to give you some basic knowledge that you require to live as a last day saint and believer in Christ.

Once you gain this knowledge, armed with it you can be delivered from whatever has held you down and you will be able to live the supernatural life that you have been ordained and destined to live as a believer in Christ.

The lack of knowledge is the bane of the problem that most Christians have, which is not allowing them to live the power-packed life that has been ordained for them. God himself had seen this and He has sent two of His prophets to us to let us know this. Through Prophet Isaiah in Isaiah 5:13 He said,

> *"Therefore my people are gone into captivity, because they have no knowledge: and their honourable men are famished, and their multitude dried up with thirst."*
>
> **Isaiah 5:13**

Living a Supernatural Life (Volume 2)

And through Prophet Hosea in Hosea 4:6, He said,

> *"My people are destroyed for lack of knowledge: because thou hast rejected knowledge, I will also reject thee, that thou shalt be no priest to me: seeing thou hast forgotten the law of thy God, I will also forget thy children."*
>
> **Hosea 4:6**

Therefore it is the lack of knowledge that has not allowed many of the believers in Christ who are sons of God to actually demonstrate the power of God in their lives. Knowing the truth will set you free. There are various categories of this lack of knowledge and I will give here a few of these.

Firstly, there are those who are not really born-again. I have emphasized in this book that it is the born-again Christian that can claim the rights to live the supernatural life that we are talking about in this book. There are many people who call themselves Christians, who go to Church regularly but who are not really born-again. Such people not only lack the knowledge but also lack the power that they require to live a supernatural power-packed life here on earth.

In the last Chapter of this book I have listed what it takes to become a born-again Christian. If you know that you are not a born-again Christian or you are not convinced of your status in Christ and you will like to live a supernatural life with miracles, signs and wonders following you then I will advise that you first go through that last Chapter so as to make your standing in Christ sure. **That is fundamental.**

Introduction

Secondly, there are those people who are really born-again Christians but who do not know that they are supposed to have this power flowing out of them. Such Christians go through life being tossed about and oppressed by all types of trials and tribulations of life because they are not aware that they can live in a realm, which is far above the oppressions of the devil.

Thirdly, there are those people who are born-again Christians, who know that this power is available to them either through reading or having been told this. So, they know and they believe it is possible for them to have this power but at the same time they believe that it is most improbable that they would have the power. This is so because they believe that the power is meant for those people who are righteous enough before God and whom God had given the special gifts required for the working of miracles.

They don't know that the righteousness of God has been imputed to them, and that they are as righteous as anybody else before God. They don't know how to make this power of God flow out of them so that through them God can demonstrate this power to the world. So, they keep praying that God should send down His power to work miracles in their lives.

This book series has been written to prove to you that if you are born-again then you are in Christ and supernatural living is your heritage. It is also written to show you what you have to do to attain this supernatural living and thus have the power of God flowing freely through you.

Living a Supernatural Life (Volume 2)

In order to show you these effectively we explained to you in *Volume 1* what the make-up of man is. We showed that man is basically created as a spirit being and therefore ought to be more sensitive to the spiritual things, which are unseen than he is to the physical things that are seen. Then we talked about a law of the spirit, which is operating in man's life on a continuous basis and, which most men have not taken cognizance of. This law is very important in the scheme of things and any man that wants to live a supernatural life here on earth must not only be very conversant with the law but must also make use of it. We tried to show you that it is not only possible but also essential to live a supernatural life right now here on earth and we believe that to a great extent we were able to do this.

Specifically in this *Volume 2* as you will see we showed with proof the truth that as a born-again Christian you are really a supernatural being. We then looked at how as a supernatural being you can release the supernatural into your life. We discussed the role that the Name of Jesus plays in the release of the supernatural and showed that the Name of Jesus is the major key for the release of the supernatural. We then showed that there are specific instructions left by Jesus Christ as to how to use His Name for the release of the supernatural and we showed that these instructions have been misinterpreted by many modern day Christians. We looked at the power that is in that Name of Jesus Christ and showed how that power can best be harnessed for the release of the supernatural by looking at the specific instructions given by Jesus as to how to use His Name. From His instructions we saw that His Name can be used to ask and receive from the Father and to get miracles done by Jesus Himself.

Introduction

Even though the Father and Jesus are One and the same (Just two different manifestations of the same God), the method of using the Name of Jesus to receive from God manifesting as the Father is different from the method of using it to get God manifesting as Jesus Christ to do miracles, signs and wonders. We discussed how to use the two methods as well as the mistakes in our current approach. We again showed in this *Volume 2* that the supernatural is in your mouth because your mouth is the vehicle through which the supernatural is delivered. One of the major reasons why many Christians fail in their effort to live the supernatural life is that they expect that whatever commands they give to have immediate manifestation. We showed that it is the fulfillment that is immediate but the manifestation may take some time.

Further in this *Volume 2* we also listed some of the things that you must be and that you must do if you want to successfully live a supernatural life. Those things that we have listed here are not by any means all that you have to do but these will go a long way to getting you there. One major requirement for any Christian wanting to live in the supernatural is that such a Christian must know how to pull down the strong holds that Satan will try to build in his mind from time to time. Satan will bombard the mind of such a Christian with all kinds of thoughts that can become strong holds if they are not pulled down.

You must pull down Satan's thoughts that he attempts to establish as strong holds in your mind before they can take root. How to do this is discussed in detail with examples in this *Volume 2*

Living a Supernatural Life (Volume 2)

In *Volume 3* we showed how Jesus lived for the brief period that He came down to live here on earth as an example of how we are supposed to live our lives also. If we want to do the works that Jesus did and get the results that Jesus got then we must do them the way that Jesus did them. We must follow the footsteps of Jesus. If we follow His footsteps then the miracles, signs and wonders that followed Him will also follow us. Many so-called Christians who claim to be born-again mock other Christians when they see them attempting to heal the sick or do the miraculous. When they see fellow Christians doing miracles they quickly say it must have been done by some devilish power. To them the devil can do miracles in this end time but God is no longer disposed to doing so. After reading through this book I am sure you will not only be convinced that you too can do miracles, you will actually start to do them. It is time for us born-again Christians to wake up and be what we are meant to be here on earth. We are not meant to be like everyone else. We are supposed to be walking in the miraculous. When we speak we must do so like the oracle of God because the wisdom of God should answer to us. We are supposed to be the light of the world and we should be shining here on earth.

Finally you will note that in this book practically every Scripture verse quoted is also boldly written out. This is to make the reading of the book and referencing easier for you the reader. **Happy reading!**

CHAPTER 1

YOU ARE A SUPERNATURAL BEING

When you actually know the truth about your New Birth's invisible nature in Christ, you will be totally convinced that you are a supernatural being, that your victory is already guaranteed and that supernatural living is your heritage in Christ. You will know that nothing can paralyze your destiny anymore. You will also know that your inadequacy has been turned into sufficiency in every aspect of your life, and that in any struggle in life your victory is now fully guaranteed. That your victory is already guaranteed can be seen from what God told us through John in 1 John 4:1-4.

> *Beloved, believe not every spirit, but try the spirits whether they are of God: because many false prophets are gone out into the world.*
>
> *Hereby know ye the Spirit of God: Every spirit that confesseth that Jesus Christ is come in the flesh is of God:*

> *And every spirit that confesseth not that Jesus Christ is come in the flesh is not of God: and this is that spirit of antichrist, whereof ye have heard that it should come; and even now already is it in the world.*
>
> *Ye are of God, little children, and have overcome them: because greater is he that is in you, than he that is in the world.*
>
> **1 John 4:1-4**

God said that *you have overcome them* not that *you will overcome them*. Therefore you already have the victory. You have the victory as a result of your new birth in Christ. If you have already overcome them why are you still struggling with them? You do not have to struggle with them if you use the authority that you now have in Christ. Get the right Scriptural perspective of who you are in Christ and your struggle with them will be over. I want you to note in particular the following seven points about your New Birth nature in Christ. These will help to give you the right Scriptural image and inner confidence concerning who you are – *You are a supernatural being.*

1. YOU ARE A SPIRIT BEING. JOHN 3:5-8

We have proved that you are a spirit being in Chapter One of *Volume 1* of this *"Living a supernatural life"* book series. Since you are a spirit being, then you should see yourself as such not as an ordinary human being because if you continue to see yourself as an ordinary human being, you will not be able to achieve the supernatural potential that you now have with your new invisible nature in Christ.

You are a Supernatural being

You have the potential to live a supernatural life but you must recognize who you are. Your **new birth** is a spiritual rebirth, which means that you are born of the Spirit. Therefore you are a spirit being since anything that is born of the Spirit is spirit. Jesus Himself said this as written by John in John 3:5-8.

> *Jesus answered, Verily, verily, I say unto thee, Except a man be born of water and of the Spirit, he cannot enter into the kingdom of God.*
>
> *That which is born of the flesh is flesh; and that which is born of the Spirit is spirit.*
>
> *Marvel not that I said unto thee, Ye must be born again.*
>
> *The wind bloweth where it listeth, and thou hearest the sound thereof, but canst not tell whence it cometh and whither it goeth: so is every one that is born of the Spirit.*
> **John 3:5-8**

Like begets like, God is a Spirit. You are now born of God therefore you are a spirit being. But from what is written in Proverbs 23:7 you can see that it is as you think in your mind that you will be.

> *For as he thinketh in his heart, so is he: Eat and drink, saith he to thee; but his heart is not with thee.*
> **Proverbs 23:7**

So, if you think that you are just an ordinary human physical being, then that will be the limit of the potential that you can exhibit. But if you think in your heart that you are a spirit being with the capabilities of a spirit being, you will start to act it and that is what you will be. It is that consciousness that you will have. You will therefore be more conscious of spiritual things than physical things in this physical realm. This is because a spirit being is more conscious and more sensitive to spiritual things than the things in the physical realm. Spiritual things are eternal because spirits don't die. Set your mind on things that are eternal and not on temporary things. That is why you are told by God through Apostle Paul in 2 Corinthians 4:18 that you should not look at the things which are seen but look at the things which are not seen for the things which are seen are temporal but the things which are not seen are eternal.

> *While we look not at the things which are seen, but at the things which are not seen: for the things which are seen are temporal; but the things which are not seen are eternal.*
> **2 Corinthians 4:18**

LIVE AND WALK IN THE SPIRIT

You are a spirit being, therefore live in the Spirit and walk in the Spirit. That is what God advised you to do through Apostle Paul in Galatians 5:25.

> *If we live in the Spirit, let us also walk in the Spirit.*
> **Galatians 5:25**

You are a Supernatural being

Walking in the Spirit means that one's actions are not dictated by the physical senses or symptoms but by what the Word of God says. This means that they are not dictated by or based on what you see, hear, taste, smell or feel but by the Spirit's leading. When you walk in the Spirit it will lead to your having a strong faith. Living in the Spirit means to act under the guidance, direction and influence of the Holy Spirit. It is the Holy Spirit that will influence such a person's decisions and actions. When you live in the Spirit it will show in your deeds and it will lead you to holiness, which will result in your living a holy and sanctified life. You can see this in verse five of Romans 8:1-9 written below. It is when you walk after the Spirit that you can be said to be in Christ and a child of God. It is then that God will be pleased with you. That is what God said in Romans 8:1-9.

> *There is therefore now no condemnation to them which are in Christ Jesus, who walk not after the flesh, but after the Spirit.*
>
> *For the law of the Spirit of life in Christ Jesus hath made me free from the law of sin and death.*
>
> *For what the law could not do, in that it was weak through the flesh, God sending his own Son in the likeness of sinful flesh, and for sin, condemned sin in the flesh:*
>
> *That the righteousness of the law might be fulfilled in us, who walk not after the flesh, but after the Spirit.*

For they that are after the flesh do mind the things of the flesh; but they that are after the Spirit the things of the Spirit.

For to be carnally minded is death; but to be spiritually minded is life and peace.

Because the carnal mind is enmity against God: for it is not subject to the law of God, neither indeed can be.

So then they that are in the flesh cannot please God.

But ye are not in the flesh, but in the Spirit, if so be that the Spirit of God dwell in you. Now if any man have not the Spirit of Christ, he is none of his.
Romans 8:1-9

It is only when you delight yourself in God and let everything that is of God be pleasing to you that God will be pleased with you and we also know that it is when God is pleased with you that He will give you the desires of your heart. That is what He made us to see through David in Psalm 37:4. Therefore you must be spiritually minded if you want to be able to receive whatever you ask from the Father. It is when you walk in the Spirit that you can know that the Spirit of God dwells in you. It is only then that you will have life and peace.

Delight thyself also in the LORD; and he shall give thee the desires of thine heart.
Psalm 37:4

You are a Supernatural being

That is what God further told us in Romans 8:6 through Apostle Paul.

For to be carnally minded is death; but to be spiritually minded is life and peace.
Romans 8:6

Because you are a spirit being, you are not supposed to walk as carnal men walk anymore. That is the essence of what God is telling you in 1 Corinthians 3:3.

For ye are yet carnal: for whereas there is among you envying, and strife, and divisions, are ye not carnal, and walk as men?
1 Corinthians 3:3

If you walk as carnal men walk, you will fall like their princes fall. But if you walk as a spirit-being, your victory is sure. All this may look like Greek to you but when you walk in the Spirit, it is then that what you are reading in this book now will not look stupid to you, because if you are carnally minded, what you are now reading in this book will be foolishness to you.

You will not be able to comprehend it because it is only with your regenerated spirit that you can comprehend it. This is so because the Words of God are Spirit and they are life and there is no way that a carnal mind can comprehend it. It will be foolishness to him.

This is true because we can only comprehend such Words of God spiritually. That is what God said to us through Apostle Paul in 1 Corinthians 2:14.

Living a Supernatural Life (Volume 2)

> *But the natural man receiveth not the things of the Spirit of God: for they are foolishness unto him: neither can he know them, because they are spiritually discerned.*
> **1 Corinthians 2:14**

As a spirit-being, if you walk in the Spirit and not after the flesh you will respond positively all the time to the things of the Spirit. If you are walking in the Spirit, whenever the Holy Spirit, which is living in you, gives you any information either by speaking to you from the Word of God (Scriptures) that you read or hear, or by throwing the information directly into your conscience, your mind will readily accept it.

As a spirit-being, if you are spiritually minded then your spirit is directly connected to God who is the source of life and peace and who now lives in you as the Holy Spirit. This confirms what we have said previously that when you are spiritually minded, you will have life and peace.

You will be at peace because you will no longer be in any bondage to fear since you no longer have the spirit of fear in you but that of power, of love and of a sound mind.

If you want to know the various characteristics that you now have with your new nature in Christ and you're your true Scriptural image then you should read the **Volume 3** of this *"Living a supernatural life"* book series written by the same author.

2. YOU ARE A GOD

Once you are born-again then God immediately adopts you as His son. That is what God told us through Apostle Paul in Galatians 4:5. You then have to live according to the Spirit.

> *To redeem them that were under the law, that we might receive the adoption of sons.*
> **Galatians 4:5**

Not only that, He actually gives you the power to become His son. That is what God told us through John in John 1:12.

> *But as many as received him, to them gave he power to become the sons of God, even to them that believe on his name:*
> **John 1:12**

What this means is that God adopts you to be His son and then empowers you to become His son. This means that God gives you everything that you need to become and operate as His son. If God merely adopts you without empowering you to become His son you will not be able to live like a son of God.

Like begets like, the son of a dog is a dog. You are a son of God. Therefore you are a kind of god also. This was what God also revealed to us through King David in Psalm 82:5-8.

> *They know not, neither will they understand; they walk on in darkness: all the foundations of the earth are out of course.*

> *I have said, Ye are gods; and all of you are children of the most High.*
>
> *But ye shall die like men, and fall like one of the princes.*
>
> *Arise, O God, judge the earth: for thou shalt inherit all nations.*
> **Psalms 82:5-8**

So, if you are a child of God, you are a god because everything produces after its kind. *You are now born of God. God can only give birth to gods or beget gods.* Therefore you are a god and therefore a supernatural being. God created you in His image to act exactly like Him. That is what we are told in Genesis 1:26.

> *And God said, Let us make man in our image, after our likeness: and let them have dominion over the fish of the sea, and over the fowl of the air, and over the cattle, and over all the earth, and over every creeping thing that creepeth upon the earth.*
> **Genesis 1:26**

Jesus Christ also confirmed this truth that you are a god by what He said in John 10:34-35.

> *Jesus answered them, Is it not written in your law, I said, Ye are gods?*
>
> *If he called them gods, unto whom the word of God came, and the scripture cannot be broken;*
> **John 10:34-35**

You are a Supernatural being

But many do not know this truth so they continue to walk on in darkness, and fall like ordinary carnal men. God created you to be a god and to have dominion over every other thing that He created, in particular over those enemies of yours that you are so frightened of. Those enemies should be frightened of you.

If you can only have the correct Scriptural perspective of yourself as to whom you are, where you are, and what you are capable of, you will realize that those enemies should be running away from you. But if you don't know what you are capable of the enemy will take advantage of you. That is why Satan fights so much to make sure that people do not get to know the truth about their capabilities and new divine nature in Christ. When God was sending Moses to Pharaoh, God said that He had made Moses a god unto Pharaoh. That is what God said in Exodus 7:1.

> *And the LORD said unto Moses, See, I have made thee a god to Pharaoh: and Aaron thy brother shall be thy prophet.*
> **Exodus 7:1**

Just as God made Moses a god unto Pharaoh, so also He has now made you a god unto your enemies. But like God said through David in the Psalm 82:5-8 previously referred to above, if you are not conscious of this truth that you are a god, and have been made a god to your enemies then you will still die like a man, you will still fall like the princes and your enemies will lord it over you. You are supposed to have dominion over your enemies. You have been made a god to them and you are supposed to be a god to them. Therefore think like a god and act like a god

Living a Supernatural Life (Volume 2)

Your enemies are not supposed to have any power over you at all because you have been given power that is far above that of your enemies no matter who they are. That is what Jesus said in Luke 10:19.

> *Behold, I give unto you power to tread on serpents and scorpions, and over all the power of the enemy: and nothing shall by any means hurt you.*
>
> **Luke 10:19**

But it all depends on what you decide or choose to believe and what you are conscious of in your heart. Your belief dictates your thoughts, and your thoughts dictate what you confess with your mouth and this will in turn dictate what you do, which determines what happens to you in life and therefore what you become. You have power if you choose to believe this.

3. YOU ARE PECULIAR

That is exactly what God told us through Apostle Peter in 1 Peter 2:9

> *But ye are a chosen generation, a royal priesthood, an holy nation, a peculiar people; that ye should shew forth the praises of him who hath called you out of darkness into his marvellous light:*
>
> **1 Peter 2:9**

You are a peculiar person. You are a member of the chosen generation, of the royal priesthood, of an holy nation, of a peculiar people.

You are a Supernatural being

You are holy unto the Lord. God has put you above all His other creatures. He created you to have dominion over all His other creatures. By now, you should know that once you are born again, you are different from any ordinary human being.

Your spirit has been regenerated so you are a new creature, who should now be more conscious of the spirit realm than the physical realm. In short you should be conscious of being a spirit being and not just an ordinary human being.

You should be more conscious of your spirituality than your humanity. You are not like everyone else anymore. You are a son of God. You are not like them of the world anymore. Unto you Christ is now the power of God. Unto you Christ is now the wisdom of God.

You are a peculiar being because as a born-again Christian, you have now been washed, sanctified and set apart by God. That is what God tells us through Paul in 1 Corinthians 6:11.

> *And such were some of you: but ye are washed, but ye are sanctified, but ye are justified in the name of the Lord Jesus, and by the Spirit of our God.*
> **1 Corinthians 6:11**

You are peculiar because the Blood of Jesus Christ, which He shed for you, has purged your conscience from dead works to serve the Living God. That is what God also told us through Apostle Paul in Hebrews 9:14.

Living a Supernatural Life (Volume 2)

> *How much more shall the blood of Christ, who through the eternal Spirit offered himself without spot to God, purge your conscience from dead works to serve the living God?*
> **Hebrews 9:14**

So you no longer have the same conscience that they of this world have. You must be peculiar if you no longer have the same conscience as them. You are also peculiar because you have overcome the devil. You are no longer under the devil's dominion. Instead you are now supposed to dominate and rule over all the circumstances and situations surrounding you. You are supposed to reign over them. Not only that, you are also supposed to have dominion over Satan and his demons.

You must know this truth and exercise your dominion over them. Even though you have dominion over them, if you do not exercise your dominion over them, they will establish their own dominion and authority over you.

If you want to know just how peculiar you are supposed to be after you are born again then read *Volume 3* of this *"Living a supernatural life"* book series and the companion series to this book series written by this same author and titled, *"You are a New Creature" Volumes 1,2, 3 and 4.*

If as Jesus said that in His Name, you can cast out devils, take up serpents, drink deadly poison and not get hurt, lay hands on the sick and have them recover then you must be peculiar. An ordinary carnal human being cannot do such things.

4. YOU ARE AN AMBASSADOR FOR CHRIST

You are really not one of them in this world so don't join them. You now represent the Kingdom of God here on earth. You are an ambassador for Christ here on earth. You should realize that once you are born-again you no longer belong to this earthly kingdom. You now belong to a Kingdom that is not of this earth. Therefore rather than seeing yourself as one of them you should see yourself as a representative of your own Kingdom here on earth. That is what God tells us through Apostle Paul in 2 Corinthians 5:20.

> *Now then we are ambassadors for Christ, as though God did beseech you by us: we pray you in Christ's stead, be ye reconciled to God.*
> **2 Corinthians 5:20**

If you are an ambassador for Christ, then you ought to note what God said through King Solomon about ambassadors in Proverbs 13:17. He said, "A faithful ambassador is health". So if God says that you are an ambassador, and says that a faithful ambassador is health, then it means that if you are faithful to your calling as an ambassador for Christ, you are health personified. This is very significant. This is a truth that you must allow to sink into your mind and imbibe. If you are faithful to your calling in Christ, then you are health.

> *A wicked messenger falleth into mischief: but a faithful ambassador is health.*
> **Proverbs 13:17**

Living a Supernatural Life (Volume 2)

This means that you are health personified. Can health be sick? NO! That will be contradictory. ***This means that you cannot be sick, for how can health be sick?*** So you see, as a faithful ambassador for Christ, you are not supposed to be sick.

I know that some people will say that this is far-fetched. Some will even say that it is blasphemy. Some have even said that the wisdom books of the Bible, Job, Proverbs and Ecclesiastes are Old Testament wisdom and that these are not necessarily the wisdom of God. They say that even though God inspired the writings, He did not inspire them as absolute truths and therefore we cannot claim them to be God's promises. What I know is what God said to us through the Apostle Paul in his Epistle to Timothy in 2 Timothy 3:16. He said,

"All scripture is given by inspiration of God, and is profitable for doctrine, for reproof, for correction, for instruction in righteousness:"
2 Timothy 3:16

He said ***ALL*** Scripture not *some* Scriptures. But you must remember that it is as you think in your heart that you will be. Remember also that you are not an ordinary human being. You are a spirit being. Sickness is not for you anymore. If you believe that you cannot be sick, that is what you will confess out with your lips. Whatever you confess out with your lips is what is really dominating your inner being, because you unconsciously confess what you believe and what you confess is what you will get. You may not know it but that is what you do every day. Therefore if you talk sickness, it is what you will eventually get.

You are a Supernatural being

There are people who have held to this believe that they cannot be sick and who have lived in divine health for many years. If only you can believe this and start confessing it into your life on a regular basis that you cannot be sick, you will see that sickness actually has no power over you.

You must realize that you will never rise above your thoughts and confessions. So if you believe that you are an ambassador for Christ here on earth and that if you are faithful to your calling as an ambassador, then you are health and therefore cannot be sick. That is what you would confess all the time. The confession, *"I cannot be sick"* will be what will be coming out of your mouth all the time and that is what you will get.

5. YOU ARE FOR SIGNS AND WONDERS

God gave Moses a rod with which to do signs and wonders when He was sending him to Pharaoh. That is what He said in Exodus 4:17, 21.

> *And thou shalt take this rod in thine hand, wherewith thou shalt do signs.*
>
> *And the LORD said unto Moses, When thou goest to return into Egypt, see that thou do all those wonders before Pharaoh, which I have put in thine hand: but I will harden his heart, that he shall not let the people go.*
> **Exodus 4:17, 21**

The rod was used by Moses to perform all types of miracles signs and wonders.

Living a Supernatural Life (Volume 2)

The rod was given to Moses by God for him to do great signs and wonders and with the rod many signs and wonders were wrought by Moses. Among the signs and wonders wrought by Moses with the rod are the case of the rod becoming a snake which swallowed the snakes of the Egyptian magicians, the case of the rod turning the waters of the streams and rivers of Egypt into blood and the case of the rod stretched forth over the streams to bring forth frogs all over the land of Egypt. Remember also that it was the rod that was pointed at the Red sea to create a pathway for the Children of Israel to cross the sea. Now Jesus Christ has also said that signs and wonders are supposed to follow you when you believe and get born-again. He said this in Mark 16:17-18, which is written below.

And these signs shall follow them that believe; In my name shall they cast out devils; they shall speak with new tongues;

They shall take up serpents; and if they drink any deadly thing, it shall not hurt them; they shall lay hands on the sick, and they shall recover.
                                            Mark 16:17-18

YOU HAVE A ROD FOR DOING SIGNS AND WONDERS

Just like He did for Moses, God has also given you a rod with which you are to do signs and wonders. The rod that God has given you in this dispensation is Jesus Christ and it is the Name of Jesus Christ that you will use to do the signs and wonders.

You are a Supernatural being

This is so because if you look at Mark 16:17-18 as previously written, you will see there that the signs and wonders that Jesus mentioned above are to be done using His Name. Also the miracles, signs and wonders that Jesus was talking about in that passage are meant to confirm the Word of God that you speak out. That was what happened to the Apostles as we are told by Mark in Mark 16:20.

And they went forth, and preached every where, the Lord working with them, and confirming the word with signs following. Amen

Mark 16:20

Therefore it is when you speak the Word of God using the Name of Jesus Christ as the rod that He confirms it with signs and wonders. If you are not speaking out the Word of God, then there is nothing that He can confirm with signs and wonders. Jesus Christ who was the Word that was living in the Father and, which the Father spoke out to create all things is now living in you. This means that it is the Jesus Christ who was the Word that was in God whom God used to create all things is the same Jesus that is now also living in you. That same Jesus Christ who lives in the Father is now living in you just like Paul wrote in Galatians 2:20 shown below that He was living in him. Jesus Himself confirmed that He lives in the Father as written by John in John 14:11.below.

I am crucified with Christ: nevertheless I live; yet not I, but Christ liveth in me: and the life which I now live in the flesh I live by the faith of the Son of God, who loved me, and gave himself for me.

Galatians 2:20

Living a Supernatural Life (Volume 2)

> *Believe me that I am in the Father, and the Father in me: or else believe me for the very works' sake.*
> **John 14:11**

Therefore the same Jesus Christ that was living in the Father as the Word whom He used to create all things is also now living in you as the Word with which you can do miracles, signs and wonders. I wish you can get a revelation of this truth because if you can get it that should provoke you into the supernatural realm. The Name of Jesus Christ has miraculous and creative powers when spoken out.

It is when you use that Name that the signs and wonders will be following you. To further show you that Jesus Christ is *the Rod* that God has given you in this dispensation as a born-again Christian with which to do signs and wonders, look at what God said through Isaiah in Isaiah 11:1 in his prophecy concerning Jesus Christ.

> *And there shall come forth a rod out of the stem of Jesse, and a Branch shall grow out of his roots:*
> **Isaiah 11:1**

God called Jesus Christ here a rod out of the stem of Jesse. So Jesus Christ is the rod and He Himself has said that it is in His name that miracles, signs and wonders will be done.

Jesus Christ is the rod and His Name together with faith in the Name are the two prerequisite for doing the signs and wonders as confirmed by Peter in Acts 3 16.

You are a Supernatural being

And his name through faith in his name hath made this man strong, whom ye see and know: yea, the faith which is by him hath given him this perfect soundness in the presence of you all.

Acts 3:16

As stated the Name of Jesus Christ is the rod that you now have with which you can do miracles, signs and wonders in this dispensation.

The signs and wonders are meant to confirm the Word of God that you speak out in the Name of Jesus Christ. But the Word is now living inside you if you are a born-again Christian. You are supposed to speak the Word forth from your mouth and give your commands in the Name of Jesus in order that the miracles, signs and wonders may be done to confirm the Word of God and the commands that you speak out. So, if you are not speaking the Word and giving commands in the Name of Jesus, you cannot get the signs and wonders to follow you. Even in the Old Testament before Jesus physically came to the world, when the people needed deliverance, it was the Word that God sent to heal them as recorded in Psalm 107:17-20.

Fools because of their transgression, and because of their iniquities, are afflicted.

Their soul abhorreth all manner of meat; and they draw near unto the gates of death.

Then they cry unto the LORD in their trouble, and he saveth them out of their distresses.

Living a Supernatural Life (Volume 2)

> *He sent his word, and healed them, and delivered them from their destructions.*
> **Psalm 107:17-20**

I want to prove conclusively to you that the miracles, signs and wonders that Jesus Christ said will be following you are meant to confirm the Word of God that you speak. Now we know that genuine signs and wonders from above only follow those people who are approved of God. It is with signs and wonders following you that God shows that you are approved of Him. We all know that Jesus Christ was approved of God when He came to the world. It was said of Him in Acts 2:22 that He was approved of God by miracles and signs and wonders. He did many miracles, signs and wonders for all to see.

> *Ye men of Israel, hear these words; Jesus of Nazareth, a man approved of God among you by miracles and wonders and signs, which God did by him in the midst of you, as ye yourselves also know:*
> **Acts 2:22**

So if you are approved of God, miracles, signs and wonders will follow you. How then do you get the approval of God so that signs and wonders can follow you? The answer to this question is given by God through Paul in 2 Timothy 2:15. He said,

> *"Study to shew thyself approved unto God, a workman that needeth not to be ashamed, rightly dividing the word of truth."*
> **2 Timothy 2:15**

You are a Supernatural being

We can see from this that what we need to do to get the approval of God is to study His Word. As a result of your New Birth, you are now meant for miracles, signs and wonder because all believers are meant to do miracles, signs and wonders in the Name of Jesus Christ. This means that signs and wonders are supposed to be following you.

But if you must have the signs and wonders following you, then you must study the Word. This is so because as we have said it is the Word that you speak out that the signs and wonders will confirm. We have seen in Mark 16:20 earlier that it was the Word of God that the disciples spoke that the signs and wonders confirmed.

Therefore the depth and level of the miraculous that you can have following you in your life is dependent on the level of revelation that you have in the Word of God and in the revelation that you have of the power that is in the Name of Jesus Christ, which you are supposed to use as the rod in this dispensation to effect the miracles, signs and wonders..

Like Prophet Isaiah said of himself and his children in Isaiah 8:18, you are also for miracles, signs and wonders. But it is the words that come out of your mouth that will determine whether these will follow you.

> *Behold, I and the children whom the LORD hath given me are for signs and for wonders in Israel from the LORD of hosts, which dwelleth in mount Zion.*
> **Isaiah 8:18**

Note that it is the level of the depth in the Word of God that you have and the level of the depth of insight that you have about the power that is in that Name of Jesus that will decide whether you will do miracles. Also the insight that you have of the Word of God and how much of the Word comes out of your mouth as well as the level of the revelation that you have in applying the Word will decide the level of the manifestation of miracles, signs and wonders that you will have in your life.

6. YOU ARE SENT AS JESUS WAS SENT

Jesus said that it is as His Father had sent Him that He is now sending you. He made this statement on two different occasions as recorded in John 17:18 as well as in John 20 21. If you are now sent as Jesus was sent then you should be able to do what Jesus did when He was on earth. Jesus has promised you this.

> *As thou hast sent me into the world, even so have I also sent them into the world.*
> *John 17:18*

> *Then said Jesus to them again, Peace be unto you: as my Father hath sent me, even so send I you.*
> *John 20:21*

Since you are sent as Jesus was sent, if you want to know how you have been sent into this world then you must first find out how Jesus was sent into the world by the Father.

You are a Supernatural being

What Jesus is really saying to you here is that the same power that supported Him while He was here on earth is now supporting you. Jesus sent you as His ambassador just as He was sent by God. This means that you are now drawing unction from the same source that Jesus Christ drew unction from while He was here physically on earth.

Because Apostle John was with Jesus when He made these statements, and was one of the closest to Him of His disciples, he was able to understand the significance of what Jesus was saying here. Hence God was able to confirm these statements through him as written in 1 John 4:17, where he said, *"As Jesus is, so are we in this world."*

> *Herein is our love made perfect, that we may have boldness in the day of judgment: because as he is, so are we in this world.*
> **1 John 4:17**

This is also confirmed by what God said through Apostle Paul in Romans 8:11, where God said that it is the same Spirit that raised Jesus up from the dead, that is now dwelling in you if you are born-again.

> *But if the Spirit of him that raised up Jesus from the dead dwell in you, he that raised up Christ from the dead shall also quicken your mortal bodies by his Spirit that dwelleth in you.*
> **Romans 8:11**

Jesus Christ was put to death but His body was quickened by the Holy Spirit and made alive again. That same Holy Spirit is now living in you.

What the Scripture above is making us to understand is that if that same Holy Spirit is the One that is now in you, then it means that you are drawing power from the same source that Jesus drew power from. Therefore whatever He could do when He came you too can now do because the Spirit that supported Him when He was here on earth is now supporting you.

Whatever helped Him when He was here on earth can now help you also. You can have the capabilities that He had. Since you are drawing power from the same source that Jesus drew power from, you now have the potential to do the works that Jesus did. This was what Jesus Himself confirmed as you will see in the next section.

7. YOU TOO CAN DO WHAT JESUS DID

You have the potential to do what Jesus did. Jesus Himself made this assertion in John 14:12. He said that whoever believes in Him, will also do the works that he did. He said that he will not only do the works that He did but that whosoever believes in Him will even do greater works than He did.

> *Verily, verily, I say unto you, He that believeth on me, the works that I do shall he do also; and greater works than these shall he do; because I go unto my Father.*
> **John 14:12**

This means that if you believe in Jesus, you can operate at the same level of anointing that He operated in while He was here on earth. There is a condition though that you must note here.

You are a Supernatural being

If you believe on Him and have accepted Him as your Saviour then you are born of the Spirit. That is what is referred to as being born-again. But God also told us through John in 1 John 5:18 that *whosoever is born of God sinneth not.*

> *We know that whosoever is born of God sinneth not; but he that is begotten of God keepeth himself, and that wicked one toucheth him not.*
>
> **1 John 5:18**

If you are born of God you will no longer be sinning as a habit. You will no longer be sinning deliberately because you will have power over sin. If you want to operate at the level of anointing that will make you do the same works that Jesus did, you must live a consecrated life. You must live a highly spiritual life minding the things of the Spirit. Depending on how consecrated a life you are willing to live, you can even operate at a higher level of anointing. Jesus Himself made this statement in John 14:12. I did not make it and we have discussed this on the previous page. He said that you will do the works that He did and even greater works than He did. You can choose to believe Him and live your life conscious of this truth, which will then manifest in your life or you can choose not to believe Him and live a tormented and subdued life.

If you choose not to believe Him you will live through your life struggling under the oppression of the enemy from time to time and have an epileptic "hot today cold tomorrow" type of unction on your life unable to manifest fully the power of God to achieve the destiny that God has ordained for you.

Living a Supernatural Life (Volume 2)

What are the works that Jesus did? He performed miracles, healed the sick, opened blind eyes, cast out devils and evil spirits, raised the dead and many other such works. These were all supernatural acts. You are supposed to do these also. If you know the God that now lives in you, it will not be difficult for you to realize that you are potentially a supernatural being. When you know your God, you will be strong and you will do exploits and you will realize that you can do all things through Christ. That is what God has made us to know through Daniel in Daniel 11:32 and through Paul in Philippians 4:13.

And such as do wickedly against the covenant shall he corrupt by flatteries: but the people that do know their God shall be strong, and do exploits.
Daniel 11:32

I can do all things through Christ which strengtheneth me.
Philippians 4:13

Every believer in Christ who is living in the will of God and who knows how powerful his God is can live a potentially very strong and supernatural life here on earth. Potentially, he should be capable of doing great exploits. That is the promise of Jesus to all believers. **But remember that what you say is what you get and what you think is what you become.** It is by your words and in particular the Words of God spoken through your mouth that you can bring forth the supernatural. And it is as you think in your mind that you will be.

You are a Supernatural being

This is so because it is what you have in your mind that will come out from your mouth and this will determine your actions and therefore your destiny.

You will ask, "What has what I say got to do with my not being sick or my health?" What has it got to do with my prosperity? What has it got to do with my living a triumphant life here on earth now? But I am sure that if you have read *Volume 1* of this *"Living a supernatural life"* book series written by the same author you would have known that it has everything to do with it. God Himself even told us through Isaiah in Isaiah 33:24 not to confess negative things with our mouths. He said,

> *"And the inhabitant shall not say, I am sick: the people that dwell therein shall be forgiven their iniquity."*
> **Isaiah 33:24**

And through Prophet Joel in Joel 3:10 He said,

> *"Beat your plowshares into swords, and your pruninghooks into spears: let the weak say, I am strong."*
> **Joel 3:10**

What God is saying in these two verses is that you should not follow your five natural senses to speak, but your sixth sense, which is faith. Do not speak by what the body sees, hears, tastes, smells or feels. That is, you should say or speak out what you want to happen to you in faith, not what is happening to you. This is because what you say is what you get. If you are weak, that is what the body is feeling so do not confess that. Instead if you say that you are strong, you will be strong.

Living a Supernatural Life (Volume 2)

This is so because from what is written by Apostle Paul in Philippians 4:13 Christ is now your strength and this strength of Christ that you now have is made perfect in weakness. That is what we are told through the same Apostle Paul in 2 Corinthians 12:9.

> *I can do all things through Christ which strengtheneth me.*
> **Philippians 4:13**

> *And he said unto me, My grace is sufficient for thee: for my strength is made perfect in weakness. Most gladly therefore will I rather glory in my infirmities, that the power of Christ may rest upon me.*
> **2 Corinthians 12:9**

Therefore it is when you are weak that you are really strong in Christ. That is what we are told by God through Paul in 2 Corinthians 12:10.

> *Therefore I take pleasure in infirmities, in reproaches, in necessities, in persecutions, in distresses for Christ's sake: for when I am weak, then am I strong.*
> **2 Corinthians 12:10**

When you are sick, say I am healed and in good health because the Bible says in 1 Peter 2:24 that you have already been healed by the stripes that Jesus took on the Cross at Calvary. And if you have already been healed then you cannot be sick. That sickness is merely pretending to have the authority to stay in your body. It does not and you should command it to get out of your body in the Name of Jesus.

You are a Supernatural being

Who his own self bare our sins in his own body on the tree, that we, being dead to sins, should live unto righteousness: by whose stripes ye were healed.
1 Peter 2:24

When you are poor, say I am rich because according to what is written in Ephesians 1:3 God has already given you all things in the spiritual realm.

Blessed be the God and Father of our Lord Jesus Christ, who hath blessed us with all spiritual blessings in heavenly places in Christ:
Ephesians. 1:3

When you have failed, say I am a success. This means that you don't go by what you can see, hear, smell, taste, feel or understand by your carnal mind. Don't let the symptoms that you see or your natural senses control you. Go by the Word.

Let your actions be based on what the Word of God says not on what your natural senses, symptoms or conditions are saying to you. These are mere facts. Whatever the Word of God says, that is the truth. Do not speak or make your confessions based on the circumstances around you or what is happening to you. Make your confessions based only on what the Word of God says. Try this for a change: *For the next six months, don't even say, "I am sick." "I have a cold." "I have a headache."* Do not acknowledge any sickness. Do not acknowledge failure. Do not acknowledge poverty. Do not acknowledge any contrary symptoms. Do not acknowledge any situation that runs contrary to what the Word of God says that should be happening to you.

Living a Supernatural Life (Volume 2)

Do not acknowledge any problem; see every problem as a mere challenge. Don't say what your enemies are doing to you. Say that you have victory over your enemies. Say, *"I am full of health. In fact I am health personified. There is no strain or pain in my body."* Do not acknowledge failure. Say, *"I am a success. I cannot fail."* Why don't you start by making these confessions using the Word of God from today?

In **Chapters 2-6** of **Volume 3** of this *"Living a Supernatural Life"* book series written by the same author you will see the type of confessions that should be coming out of your mouth. Choose from these the confessions that are most appropriate for you and make it a duty to confess them several times daily. It is what you believe in your heart and say with your mouth that you will get. It is by hearing these Words of God over and over again that your faith in them will develop because faith comes by hearing, and hearing by the Word of God. That is what we are told by God in Romans 10:17 through Paul.

> *So then faith cometh by hearing, and hearing by the word of God.*
> **Romans 10:17**

Therefore read the Word of God written in the Bible verses given to support those confessions in *Volume 3* and meditate on them daily so that you can also believe them from your heart. All the promises that God made to you are only potential provisions. Once you believe them in your heart, you have to take hold of them spiritually by faith and bring them into physical reality by confessing them continually and boldly with your mouth.

You are a Supernatural being

For it is by your bold declaration with your mouth that you are to make the confession unto your salvation. That is what we are told by God in Romans 10:10 through Apostle Paul as written below. As we have seen earlier when you use the Word of God, you can cast down and bring into captivity to the obedience of ***Christ, (i.e. the Word)*** every thought and imagination that exalts itself against the knowledge of the Word. That is how powerful the Word of God is as we can see from what God said through Apostle Paul in 2 Corinthians 10:4-6, which is written below.

> *For with the heart man believeth unto righteousness; and with the mouth confession is made unto salvation.*
> **Romans 10:10**

> *For the weapons of our warfare are not carnal, but mighty through God to the pulling down of strong holds;*

> *Casting down imaginations, and every high thing that exalteth itself against the knowledge of God, and bringing into captivity every thought to the obedience of Christ;*

> *And having in a readiness to revenge all disobedience, when your obedience is fulfilled.*
> **2 Corinthians 10:4-6**

The Word of God is God as stated by God through Apostle John in John 1:1, and by inference from what is stated by God through Apostle John in John 1:14 the Word of God is Jesus Christ.

Living a Supernatural Life (Volume 2)

In the beginning was the Word, and the Word was with God, and the Word was God.
John 1:1

And the Word was made flesh, and dwelt among us, and we beheld his glory, the glory as of the only begotten of the Father, full of grace and truth.
John 1:14

I want to emphasize here the truth that Jesus Christ is the Word of God and is God once again because until you can see the truth that the Word of God is God you will lack the power. Therefore this Scripture written in 2 Corinthians 10:4-6 above can be read as, "Casting down imaginations, and every high thing that exalteth itself against the knowledge of the **Word of God** and bringing into captivity every thought to the obedience of **the Word**."

This means that any negative imagination or thought that comes into your mind you can cast it down using the Word and bring it into subjection to the Word. What God is telling us in that Scripture through Paul is that when we come across any situation or circumstance that runs contrary to what the Word of God says, we have the necessary weapons at our disposal that we can use to bring the situation captive and thereby bring it into subjection to and in line with what the Word of God says about the situation or circumstance. This means that the situation can be forced and made to fall in line with and be subjected to what the Word of God says. You have what it takes to do this.

You are a Supernatural being

Therefore no situation that you come across should give you any sleepless night. You are far above every situation. You should be able to bring any situation under the control of the Word. The reason why you are unable to bring such situations under the control of, and subject them to, what the Word of God says is because you probably have not taken into consideration the condition attached to your doing so.

This is written by Apostle Paul in verse six of that Scripture in 2 Corinthians 10:6, which says that your own obedience of the Word must be fulfilled before you can force such thoughts and imaginations to obey and be subject to your commands which is based on what the Word of God says about the situation. You must subject yourself to God's authority if you are to exercise such authority.

And having in a readiness to revenge all disobedience, when your obedience is fulfilled.
2 Corinthians 10:6

For any situation that you come across if you are to command the thoughts and imaginations that you have about the situation to come in line with what the Word of God says about the situation then your own obedience of the Word of God must first be in place. God attaches a lot of importance to His Word that you speak because as far as God is concerned, it is His Words that you speak that determines, or that God uses to judge, whether you have light in you or not. That is what He said through the Prophet Isaiah in Isaiah 8:20. He said if you do not speak according to His Word then there is no light in you.

Living a Supernatural Life (Volume 2)

> *"To the law and to the testimony: if they speak not according to this word, it is because there is no light in them."*
>
> **Isaiah 8:20**

Remember also that the words that you speak are the fruits of your mouth that you eat or get. Therefore begin to release the Word of God from your mouth to every situation in your life.

The Word is in your heart, but it is when you release it through your mouth that it becomes fruit for you and the fire that will devour your adversaries and bring every situation under the control of what the Word of God says.

It will also bring deliverance to you. Therefore speak out boldly what the Word of God says to every situation of your life. People may say you are self-esteeming yourself or boasting, but to God you are not boasting. You are only glorying in what the Almighty God in you can do.

You can always boast in the Lord. You can always glory in what God can do, not what you can do. So you don't have to be afraid to speak out what God can do to your adversaries. Do not be afraid to pronounce God's judgment on any situation that comes your way, which is contrary to what the Word of God says that should be happening to you. Remember that its death is in your mouth.

Many people are afraid of witches and the wicked forces of this world. They glorify them by ascribing power to them.

You are a Supernatural being

But as for you it is clear that you no longer need to be afraid of them. If death and life are in the power of your tongue as stated in Proverbs 18:21, how can you be afraid of a witch or anybody at all and think that he can do anything against you when even his death is in your mouth?

Death and life are in the power of the tongue: and they that love it shall eat the fruit thereof.
Proverbs 18:21

How can any occult force come against you when it is in your power to pronounce its death through your tongue? I am not saying that you should go about killing witches or declaring their death, but I am telling you that you have the power to do so if the need arises. You can pronounce death to and kill all their plans, intrigues, plotting, maneuverings, machinations and actions. You don't have to be afraid of them. You have the power to free yourself from their clutches.

YOU ARE STRONGER THAN A WITCH

By the way, what makes a witch a witch? Is it not the human blood that he or she drinks? If that is what makes a witch then you know that you are the stronger witch because the Blood of Jesus that you take in Communion regularly is far stronger than any human blood that any witch can drink. This verse above should show you how much power you now have over your adversaries if you are willing to give the command with your mouth. Jesus said in Luke 21:15 that He will give you a mouth and wisdom, which none of your adversaries will be able to gainsay or resist.

> *For I will give you a mouth and wisdom, which all your adversaries shall not be able to gainsay nor resist.*
>
> **Luke 21:15**

Therefore whatever you say concerning any situation none of your adversaries has any power that is capable of resisting what your mouth speaks when you speak out what the wisdom of God, which is the Word of God, says about it. This is an awesome power that you now have. That is why you are a supernatural being. Say the good Words every day that God has said about you.

Speak God's Word to your situations and your future. Declare whatever you want God to confirm for you because until you say it, you won't see it and the louder you say it, the faster you will get it. If you are willing to declare what you want, its fulfillment is immediate, but its manifestation may not be immediate. It may take some time before you see the physical manifestation of your declaration.

YOU NOW PARTAKE OF GOD'S DIVINE NATURE

So that you may be able to live the supernatural life as a son of God, He has also made you a partaker of His divine nature. That is what we are told in 2 Peter 1:4. This means that you are now a partaker of the nature of God. This is another very important point that you must take cognizance of because if you partake of the nature of God then you must learn to act like God and do things like God does them.

You are a Supernatural being

Whereby are given unto us exceeding great and precious promises: that by these ye might be partakers of the divine nature, having escaped the corruption that is in the world through lust.
2 Peter 1:4

This means that you now have or partake of the attributes of that divine nature among which are the following six attributes of God:

1. GOD IS A SPIRIT

That is what we are made to understand by what we are told in John 4:24

God is a Spirit: and they that worship him must worship him in spirit and in truth.
John 4:24

From John 3:6 you can see that when you become born again, you are born of the Spirit and your spirit-being is activated. You are therefore a spirit-being. The divine nature of God that you have should make you more conscious of the spiritual realm than the physical realm.

That which is born of the flesh is flesh; and that which is born of the Spirit is spirit.
John 3:6

2. GOD IS ETERNAL

He is an eternal God. That is what we can see from what is written in Deuteronomy 33:27.

> *The eternal God is thy refuge, and underneath are the everlasting arms: and he shall thrust out the enemy from before thee; and shall say, Destroy them.*
>
> **Deuteronomy 33:27**

Once you are born again another part of the divine nature of God that you are given is eternal life. That is what Jesus Himself made us to see from what He said in John 5:24. We are not talking here of your physical body but your spirit, which is quickened to become alive unto God.

> *Verily, verily, I say unto you, He that heareth my word, and believeth on him that sent me, hath everlasting life, and shall not come into condemnation; but is passed from death unto life.*
>
> **John 5:24**

3. GOD IS OMNIPOTENT

This means that God is all powerful. He can do all things. Nothing is impossible for Him. That is what we can see from what Job said in Job 42:2.

> *I know that thou canst do every thing, and that no thought can be withholden from thee.*
>
> **Job 42:2**

Once you become born-again this absolute power of God is made available to you also through Christ. That is what Jesus said in Luke 10:19.

You are a Supernatural being

Behold, I give unto you power to tread on serpents and scorpions, and over all the power of the enemy: and nothing shall by any means hurt you.
Luke 10:19

This is so because as a born-again Christian you can also do all things through Christ, the One who now strengthens you. That is what we are made to see from what Apostle Paul said in Philippians 4:13.

I can do all things through Christ which strengtheneth me.
Philippians 4:13

This means that Christ who is the power of God as we told by Apostle Paul in 1 Corinthians 1:24 now becomes your strength.

But unto them which are called, both Jews and Greeks, Christ the power of God, and the wisdom of God.
1 Corinthians 1:24

4. GOD IS OMNISCIENT

This means that God knows all things. That is what we are made to know from what we are told by John the Apostle in 1 John 3:20.

For if our heart condemn us, God is greater than our heart, and knoweth all things.
1 John 3:20

Living a Supernatural Life (Volume 2)

It will surprise you if I say that this is also part of the divine nature of God that you acquire when you become born again. If you will only believe you can also know all things. I say this because we are made to understand that when you get born again you receive the Holy Spirit of God. Your body becomes a temple for that Spirit of God as we are told by Apostle Paul in 1 Corinthians 3:16. This Spirit of God will teach you *all things.* That is what we are told in John 14:26.

> *Know ye not that ye are the temple of God, and that the Spirit of God dwelleth in you?*
> **1 Corinthians 3:16**

> *But the Comforter, which is the Holy Ghost, whom the Father will send in my name, he shall teach you all things, and bring all things to your remembrance, whatsoever I have said unto you.*
> **John 14:26**

To make sure that you have the capability to know all things when you get born again God puts in you the mind of Christ. That is what we are told through Paul the Apostle in 1 Corinthians 2:16.

> *For who hath known the mind of the Lord, that he may instruct him? But we have the mind of Christ.*
> **1 Corinthians 2:16**

This mind of Christ that you now have is the mind that made all things. Without this mind was not anything made that was made. That is what we are made to understand by what is written by John in John 1:1-3, 14.

You are a Supernatural being

In the beginning was the Word, and the Word was with God, and the Word was God.

The same was in the beginning with God.

All things were made by him; and without him was not any thing made that was made.

And the Word was made flesh, and dwelt among us, and we beheld his glory, the glory as of the only begotten of the Father, full of grace and truth.

John 1:1-3, 14

It is obvious that the mind that made all things must by deduction know all things. Therefore we can say that this mind of Christ knows all things. Therefore whoever harbours this mind has the potential to know all things. Another thing to note from the Scriptures is that this mind of Christ that you now have also harbors the wisdom of God because Christ who owns this mind is actually the wisdom of God as we are told by Apostle Paul in 1 Corinthians 1:24. The mind is the seat of wisdom therefore His mind must harbor this wisdom of God. That same Christ has now been made wisdom to you as we are also told by Paul in 1 Corinthians 1:30.

But unto them which are called, both Jews and Greeks, Christ the power of God, and the wisdom of God.

1 Corinthians 1:24

But of him are ye in Christ Jesus, who of God is made unto us wisdom, and righteousness, and sanctification, and redemption:

1 Corinthians 1:30

What this means is that the wisdom of God is now available to you if you will only tap into it. Therefore you have the potential to be omniscient once you are born again.

5. GOD IS HOLY

God is holy as seen from what King David said in Psalm 22:3. He repeated this in Psalm 99:5, 9. The holiness of our God is one of His attributes that separates Him from all other gods

> *But thou art holy, O thou that inhabitest the praises of Israel.*
> **Psalm 22:3**

> *Exalt ye the LORD our God, and worship at his footstool; for he is holy.*

> *Exalt the LORD our God, and worship at his holy hill; for the LORD our God is holy.*
> **Psalm 99:5, 9**

You are also given the power to be holy when you become born again. This is done through Christ because once you are redeemed you are spiritually grafted into the Body of Christ. As a result of being grafted into the Body of Christ you become a member of the Body of Christ. Christ is the vine; you are a branch of the vine. That is what Jesus said in John 15:5.

> *I am the vine, ye are the branches: He that abideth in me, and I in him, the same bringeth forth much fruit: for without me ye can do nothing.*
> **John 15:5**

You are a Supernatural being

Now the Scriptures say in Romans 11:16 that if the firstfruit be holy then the lump is also holy and if the root be holy then the branches are also holy. Therefore if Christ who is the vine is holy then you the branch are supposed to be holy.

For if the firstfruit be holy, the lump is also holy: and if the root be holy, so are the branches.
Romans 11:16

God has also made you His temple and His temple is supposed to be holy. That is what He said through Apostle Paul as written in 1 Corinthians 3:16-17. It is so that His temple, which you are now, can be holy that He has now made you a partaker of His holiness as we are told in Hebrews 12:10. He even told us through Apostle Paul in Hebrews 12:14 that without holiness it will be impossible for us to see God. Therefore holiness is an essential attribute that we must have. Don't let the devil deceive you by telling you that you cannot live a holy life. You can do so because God said so.

Know ye not that ye are the temple of God, and that the Spirit of God dwelleth in you?

If any man defile the temple of God, him shall God destroy; for the temple of God is holy, which temple ye are.
1 Corinthians 3:16-17

For they verily for a few days chastened us after their own pleasure; but he for our profit, that we might be partakers of his holiness.
Hebrews 12:10

> *Follow peace with all men, and holiness, without which no man shall see the Lord:*
> **Hebrews 12:14**

As you can see you are a partaker of God's holiness. He has made you a member of a nation of priests unto Himself according to what is written by John in Revelation 5:10. That is why He has referred to you as a member of a holy priesthood and a holy nation as written in 1 Peter 2:5, 9.

> *And hast made us unto our God kings and priests: and we shall reign on the earth.*
> **Revelation 5:10**

> *Ye also, as lively stones, are built up a spiritual house, an holy priesthood, to offer up spiritual sacrifices, acceptable to God by Jesus Christ.*

> *But ye are a chosen generation, a royal priesthood, an holy nation, a peculiar people; that ye should shew forth the praises of him who hath called you out of darkness into his marvellous light:*
> **1 Peter 2:5, 9**

6. GOD IS RIGHTEOUS

This is one of the major attributes of God. God is a righteous God. That is what we are made to know from Ezra 9:15, from Psalm 145:17, from Jeremiah 12:1 and from Daniel 9:14. The Lord is righteous in His ways, in all His works, which He doeth and in all His judgments.

You are a Supernatural being

God is so morally upright and virtuous that no evil can be found in Him.

O LORD God of Israel, thou art righteous: for we remain yet escaped, as it is this day: behold, we are before thee in our trespasses: for we cannot stand before thee because of this.
Ezra 9:15

The LORD is righteous in all his ways, and holy in all his works.
Psalm 145:17

Righteous art thou, O LORD, when I plead with thee: yet let me talk with thee of thy judgments: Wherefore doth the way of the wicked prosper? wherefore are all they happy that deal very treacherously?
Jeremiah 12:1

Therefore hath the LORD watched upon the evil, and brought it upon us: for the LORD our God is righteous in all his works which he doeth: for we obeyed not his voice.
Daniel 9:14

As a born-again Christian you have also been given the righteousness of God as a gift so that you too can be righteous. That is what we are told in Romans 5:17. It is a gift which you have not worked for. It is a free gift. All you have to do is just accept the gift by faith and the righteousness of God is yours through Christ.

> *For if by one man's offence death reigned by one; much more they which receive abundance of grace and of the gift of righteousness shall reign in life by one, Jesus Christ.*
> **Romans 5:17**

You have been given the righteousness of God through Christ and Christ who is the Sun of righteousness as we can infer from Malachi 4:2 has now been made righteousness unto you as written in 1 Corinthians 1:30 as shown earlier.

> *But unto you that fear my name shall the Sun of righteousness arise with healing in his wings; and ye shall go forth, and grow up as calves of the stall.*
> **Malachi 4:2**

> *But of him are ye in Christ Jesus, who of God is made unto us wisdom, and righteousness, and sanctification, and redemption:*
> **1 Corinthians 1:30**

You reflect the righteousness of Christ Jesus who is the Sun of righteousness just as the moon reflects the light of the sun to the earth. God created the sun to rule the day and the moon to rule the night. The moon has no light of its own but because of its alignment to the sun it is able to reflect the light of the sun to the earth thereby ruling the earth by night. Similarly you have no righteousness of your own but God has made Christ righteousness to you and given you His righteousness as a gift. Therefore from that point on when you approach God you must be conscious of one truth.

You are a Supernatural being

The truth is that you are approaching Him not with your own righteousness but with the righteousness of Christ, which you are reflecting. This is so because when you align yourself properly with Christ who is the Sun of righteousness you can reflect His righteousness. By so doing God sees you as righteous. Not only just righteous but as righteous as anybody else can be since it is the righteousness of Jesus Christ that you are reflecting. Therefore nobody is more righteous than you are before God. From what we have discussed so far in this Chapter definitely you must have seen that you are a supernatural being with supernatural potential.

This is one of the most important and central doctrines of Christianity. It is the doctrine that says that the righteousness of God can be imputed to a man by just believing in the sacrificial death and resurrection of Jesus Christ. God made this known to us firstly through Abraham. The Scripture says Abraham believed God and it was imputed unto him for righteousness. That is what we are told by James in James 2:23 and also by Paul in Romans 4:20-22. Paul also made us to know that what God did for Abraham He has also done for us by what he wrote in Romans 4:23-24

> *And the scripture was fulfilled which saith, Abraham believed God, and it was imputed unto him for righteousness: and he was called the Friend of God.*
> **James 2:23**

> *He staggered not at the promise of God through unbelief; but was strong in faith, giving glory to God;*

Living a Supernatural Life (Volume 2)

And being fully persuaded that, what he had promised, he was able also to perform.

And therefore it was imputed to him for righteousness.
Romans 4:20-22

Now it was not written for his sake alone, that it was imputed to him;

But for us also, to whom it shall be imputed, if we believe on him that raised up Jesus our Lord from the dead;
Romans 4:23-24

However if you want to get a more detailed discussion on the truth that you are a supernatural being I will advise you to read the *Volume 3* of this *"Living a supernatural life"* book series which is written by the same author. When you can get a revelation of the truths recorded in that volume it will become too obvious to you that you are actually a supernatural being and you will know that through the Christ that lives in you nothing is no longer impossible to you any longer.

How then do you release the supernatural in your life? The answer to that question is what we shall discuss in the next Chapter.

CHAPTER 2

RELEASING THE SUPERNATURAL

The supernatural life power is in your tongue, for that is what God told us through King Solomon as written in Proverbs 18:20-21. He said, "Death and life are in the power of the tongue".

> *A man's belly shall be satisfied with the fruit of his mouth; and with the increase of his lips shall he be filled.*
>
> *Death and life are in the power of the tongue: and they that love it shall eat the fruit thereof.*
> **Proverbs 18:20-21**

So, death and life are in the power of your tongue, but it is only if you love to use that your tongue that you can reap the benefit, which is referred to here as the fruit. You can actually live a supernatural life now if you are willing to speak supernatural things out with your mouth. It is with the increase of your lips that your life will increase; and it is the fruit of your mouth that will satisfy you. So use your mouth to say positive things into your life if you want to be satisfied. Then you will reap the benefits.

Living a Supernatural Life (Volume 2)

The release of the supernatural is through bold talking with your mouth. The story of Job gives us a good example of how one can eat the fruit of his mouth.

Remember that God had put a hedge of protection about Job, about his house, and about everything that he had, on every side. That is what we are told in Job 1:10.

> *Hast not thou made an hedge about him, and about his house, and about all that he hath on every side? thou hast blessed the work of his hands, and his substance is increased in the land.*
>
> **Job 1:10**

It was even Satan himself who said this to God. Obviously Satan must have tried to attack Job or his possessions from all angles on many occasions and failed, hence that statement. However, despite the hedge of protection around Job, he lived in fear. He feared that the worst would come upon him. He probably was not even aware of the hedge of protection, which God had made about him. He made several statements based on his fears. Look at what he said in Job 3:25-26. He said,

> *"For the thing which I greatly feared is come upon me, and that which I was afraid of is come unto me.*
>
> *I was not in safety, neither had I rest, neither was I quiet; yet trouble came."*
>
> **Job 3:25-26**

NEVER CONFESS ANYTHING OUT OF FEAR

As a result of Job's fear, he confessed so many bad things unto his own life. He said that he was not in safety as written above. He said that he had no rest and these became true in his life. Among the many bad confessions that he made was the one where he even said that it was God Himself that was taking his things away. That's in Job 1:21. Look at what he said below.

> *And said, Naked came I out of my mother's womb, and naked shall I return thither: the LORD gave, and the LORD hath taken away; blessed be the name of the LORD.*
> **Job 1:21**

But we all know from the story that it was Satan that was taking his things away, and not God. However, God gave Satan the permission to do so. That should teach us that whenever we have any affliction, we should not say anything in anger or fear because of the affliction that we are going through since we may end up saying the wrong things with our mouth. Job had the hedge of God's protection around him all right, but he used his own mouth to break the hedge by confessing that he was not in safety, and did not have rest.

He confessed these because he was not aware of God's hedge of protection around him and all that he had. So it is with most Christians today; many of the things that they confess with their mouths are not necessarily true but they speak them out because they are not fully aware of what God is really doing in their lives.

Living a Supernatural Life (Volume 2)

They have the wrong Scriptural perspective or image of themselves. Whenever we are going through any affliction we should remember that as born-again Christians we are quite capable of carrying whatever burdens the affliction brings. God has promised that He will not suffer us to be tempted above that, which we are able to cope with. He also promised that no matter what temptation if it becomes necessary, He would make a way of escape for us according to what He said in 1 Corinthians 10:13. So, when you go through any affliction you should know that a way of escape is bound to come because God's Word will not fail. You should have the confidence that you will sail over it.

> *There hath no temptation taken you but such as is common to man: but God is faithful, who will not suffer you to be tempted above that ye are able; but will with the temptation also make a way to escape, that ye may be able to bear it.*
> **1 Corinthians 10:13**

EXPUNGE BITTERNESS

One more thing that we ought to note concerning Job's case is that when we are going through afflictions we should not hold any bitterness, malice or grudge against anybody

We should not base our reactions to afflictions on such negative thoughts thinking that some people are responsible for the afflictions that we are going through. If we do so it may prolong the route of our escape from the affliction.

The case of Job is a good example of this. Remember the three friends of Job, Eliphaz the Temanite, Bildad the Shuhite and Zophar the Naamathite? These friends on the pretense of mourning with Job mocked him. Job must have been very angry with them. But it was not until Job prayed for them that the Lord turned Job's captivity and brought him out of his afflictions. That is what we are told in Job 42:10.

And the LORD turned the captivity of Job, when he prayed for his friends: also the LORD gave Job twice as much as he had before.
Job 42:10

That man who has offended you whom you are so bitter against and have refused to forgive may be the reason why your captivity has not been turned yet. Therefore if there is such unforgiveness or bitterness in your life expunge it today so that the good promises of God can be made effective in your life. Unforgiveness and its consequences are discussed in detail in the book by the same author titled, *"Why many are not healed"*.

GOD'S PROMISES ARE THE HEDGE OF PROTECTION AROUND YOU

If you are a believer in Christ and you are living your life in the will of God, then just like God had an hedge of protection about Job, about his house and about everything that he had on every side, so also has God built a hedge of protection about you, about your house and about everything that you have on every side. This is true because God has also made several promises of protection for you in the Scriptures.

Living a Supernatural Life (Volume 2)

All of God's promises to you as well as the attributes of your new nature are God's hedge of protection around you. These include His promises of protection, blessings, favour, good health, fruitfulness, healing and many others, which you must agree with so as to enjoy this hedge of protection. You must have this revelation of your security.

When you confess or speak words into your life that are against those promises then you are breaking the hedge of protection that God has built around you. The serpent (the devil) will come in and bite you because God has told us through King Solomon in Ecclesiastes 10:8 that whosoever breaks an hedge a serpent will bite him. Satan took permission from God, Yes! But it was Job's confessions that opened the hedge for him.

> *He that diggeth a pit shall fall into it; and whoso breaketh an hedge, a serpent shall bite him.*
> **Ecclesiastes 10:8**

As a born-again Christian, if you live your life in the will of God, Satan has no power over you anymore to do anything to you. It is what you say into your life with your own mouth, or what you allow other people to speak into your life with their mouths, which you fail to reject or challenge that Satan uses against you. That is why he brings fear so that when you fear, you will say some negative things into your life out of fear, which he can then go ahead and effect. You know that where fear begins faith ends and where faith begins fear ends. So Satan knows that you cannot have fear and have faith at the same time. That is why he tries to fill your mind with fear and doubt.

Therefore stop confessing out of fear and doubt. Stop confessing or talking of failure, defeat, loss, weakness, poverty, sickness and any other type of affliction. Stop confessing these into your life. God has made us to know in Proverbs 6:2 through Solomon that our mouths can snare us and put us under bondage.

> *Thou art snared with the words of thy mouth, thou art taken with the words of thy mouth.*
> **Proverbs 6:2**

Therefore confess positive things into your life with your mouth. In particular, confess the Word of God especially all His good promises, into your life. God has said, *"Let the weak say I am strong."* Therefore never confess weakness.

Never confess with your mouth the negative situations that you are going through. Instead see and confess with your mouth the positive situations that you would rather want. What you see physically may be totally contrary to what you are confessing but do not let that deter you from making your positive confessions in faith.

God has said that you should fight the good fight of faith by holding fast to your confession of faith. That is the essence of what God is telling us through Apostle Paul in 1 Timothy 6:12, Hebrews 4:14 as well as in Hebrews 10:23.

> *Fight the good fight of faith, lay hold on eternal life, whereunto thou art also called, and hast professed a good profession before many witnesses.*
> **1 Timothy 6:12**

> *Seeing then that we have a great high priest, that is passed into the heavens, Jesus the Son of God, let us hold fast our confession.*
> **Hebrews 4:14 NKJV**

> *Let us hold fast the confession of our faith without wavering; for he is faithful that promised;*
> **Hebrews 10:23 NKJV**

YOUR MOUTH CREATES YOUR FUTURE

If you think deeply, you will know that what you are confessing is what you actually believe and accept as the truth. Therefore whatever you confess is what you will eventually get since Christ said that it is to you according to your faith. Therefore say what you want and it shall be so with you. In Proverbs 13:2 God said through Solomon that,

> *"A man shall eat good by the fruit of his mouth: but the soul of the transgressors shall eat violence."*
> **Proverbs 13:2**

This means that it is what you say with your mouth that creates your future. Many times we believe what God says in His Word but we just find it impossible to speak them out with our mouth or act on them. But it is what you say with your mouth that will produce the fruits that will be seen in your life. Whatever you now have in your life today is mainly the result of what you have confessed into your life in the past.

Releasing the Supernatural

It is true that there are some happenings in our lives that may be as a result of God's own divine acts or will in our lives, but for most part God has given man the will to take decisions and choose what becomes of his life. God has put before you life and death, blessings and curses. He has given you the right to choose whichever ones of these you want. That is what He said in Deuteronomy 30:19 to the Children of Israel. We Christians are now the spiritual Israelites of God and He is saying the same thing to us today. Therefore you also have to make that choice today.

I call heaven and earth to record this day against you, that I have set before you life and death, blessing and cursing: therefore choose life, that both thou and thy seed may live:
Deuteronomy 30:19

You are eating today for the most part the fruit of what you have used your mouth to sow into your life as well as what others have used their mouths to sow into your life in the past. Your words are what have germinated to bear the fruits. You will ask, *"What about children that do fall sick, have they confessed sickness into their lives too?"*

Jesus Himself has given us the answer to that question in John 9:1-3. He did this when He came across a man that was blind from birth and His disciples asked Him whether it was the sin of the man or that of his parents that led to his being born-blind. Jesus told them that the reason was neither because the man nor his parents had sinned but it was so that the works of God should be made manifest in the man that he was made blind from birth. Therefore not all sickness comes from sin.

And as Jesus passed by, he saw a man which was blind from his birth.

And his disciples asked him, saying, Master, who did sin, this man, or his parents, that he was born blind?

Jesus answered, Neither hath this man sinned, nor his parents: but that the works of God should be made manifest in him.
John 9:1-3

There are times therefore when we have not sinned nor confessed a bad thing into our lives but God allows Satan to afflict us with the bad thing and bring suffering on us so that His works might be made manifest in us. But this is in fact the exception and not the norm.

FRAME YOUR WORLD WITH YOUR WORDS

As written in Hebrews 11:3 God framed His own worlds by the Words that came out of His mouth.

Through faith we understand that the worlds were framed by the word of God, so that things which are seen were not made of things which do appear.
Hebrews 11:3

You are created in God's image. This means that God created you so that you will act like Him. He said so in Genesis 1:26. You are supposed to imitate Him in everything that you do.

> *And God said, Let us make man in our image, after our likeness: and let them have dominion over the fish of the sea, and over the fowl of the air, and over the cattle, and over all the earth, and over every creeping thing that creepeth upon the earth.*
>
> **Genesis 1:26**

He said, "Let us make man in our image, after our likeness." That statement *after our likeness* means *to act like us, to be similar to us and to reproduce similar characteristics to us.* Therefore He created you to act like Him, to do what He does.

God framed His own world with His Words spoken out with His mouth. God created you a spirit-being to act like Him, so you better start framing your own world with your own words and in particular with the positive Words of God spoken with your mouth. Start that from today. In truth, God not only framed His worlds by His Words. We are told in Hebrews 1:3 that He is sustaining and upholding them by the Word of His Power.

> *Who being the brightness of his glory, and the express image of his person, and upholding all things by the word of his power, when he had by himself purged our sins, sat down on the right hand of the Majesty on high;*
>
> **Hebrews 1:3**

Therefore start sustaining and upholding your own world by the words that you speak, in particular by speaking God's Words to your world. What you say will determine how your world will be.

Don't let your world crumble, collapse or disintegrate around you. Start proclaiming what you want in your world. You will get what you say. You share God's Spirit and you can create things by faith. The way you create things is to call forth into view by faith whatever you have believed in your heart. That is the way that God created you to function. Even though you may not be aware of it that is the way you are actually functioning. All those things that are presently in your life, you have consciously or unconsciously called them into being in your life either with your own mouth or allowed them to be called into your life through the mouth of other people. Others have also spoken words into your life and you have consciously or unconsciously allowed such words into your life unchallenged. You must believe that whatever you say or is said into your life, which is not rejected, is what you will get because your life functions by faith. Your mouth releases the supernatural yes! But faith is the medium through which the supernatural operates. You are therefore to function by faith. Many Christians want to live by miracles but God' instruction to us is that we should live by faith.

YOU ARE TO FUNCTION BY FAITH

God functions by faith. You are created in His likeness. Therefore you are also supposed to function by faith. That is why it is so written in 2 Corinthians 5:7 that you are to walk by faith and not by sight, which are your natural senses.

For we walk by faith, not by sight:
2 Corinthians 5:7

You are not only to walk by faith; you are actually supposed to live by faith that means by the Word. That is what God told us in Romans 1:17. He said, *"Shall live by faith!"* That is a decree. It is not a choice.

For therein is the righteousness of God revealed from faith to faith: as it is written, The just shall live by faith.
Romans 1:17

When you operate by faith as God does, you will be able to *call those things that are not as though they were.* Because of your faith, those things that are not, which you called will appear or manifest and you will see them. That is what God does. He told us this through Apostle Paul in Romans 4:17.

As it is written, I have made thee a father of many nations, before him whom he believed, even God, who quickeneth the dead, and calleth those things which be not as though they were.
Romans 4:17

The way to live a supernatural life and live above the natural realm therefore is by calling the invisible things and letting them become visible. That is the way God operates by faith. When you operate by faith as God does, that is, walk by faith and live by faith, you can release your new invisible nature in Christ into your visible human nature.

Hence supernatural Living can be described as the releasing of your new invisible nature in Christ into your visible human nature.

Living a Supernatural Life (Volume 2)

What then is this your new invisible nature in Christ? When you accept Christ as your Saviour and you become born-again, then it follows that you have been:

Called, elected and chosen,
Cleansed and reconciled to God,
Justified and declared righteous,
Sanctified and set apart,
Redeemed and healed,
Completely protected and insulated from all oppression,
Sealed with Heavenly citizenship,
Enfranchised and made an heir of God,
Enthroned and empowered to become a son of God,
Blessed with all things,
Made a savior,

Note that these are not promises. We are not talking about promises here. They are what you now are, who you now are, what you now have and where you now are in Christ if you are born-again. They are what you automatically become in Christ when you are born-again. These are not what you will be, not who you will be, not what you will have or where you will be but who you now are, what you now are, what you now have and where you now are if you are born-again. They are not things that will happen for you to enjoy only when you get to heaven. No! They have already happened in the main and they are characteristics that you are supposed to have now in Christ, which you are supposed to be enjoying starting right here on earth.

But for you to enjoy these you must exercise faith because even though they are already deposited into your heavenly account it is through faith that you will draw them out of the account.

Releasing the Supernatural

Your invisible nature in Christ is discussed in detail in *Volume 3* of this *"Living a supernatural life"* book series. If you want to know more about these also read the companion book series written by this same author and titled, *"You are a New Creature" Volumes 1,2,3 and 4.* As soon as you become born-again, you are entitled to these characteristics. You can have all of them while you are still here on this earth, and you can be all those things right now.

You don't have to get to Heaven before you start enjoying these privileges, powers and attributes that are now yours in Christ even though there may be no physical manifestation of some of these yet. If you are conscious of all these and you start to confess them and start to exhibit by faith the power, authority and attributes, which God says that you now possess with the new invisible nature that you now have in Christ, then you can live a supernatural life here on earth. When you hold on to what God says and stand on it regardless of what the circumstances around you say, then you are walking by faith.

To walk by faith means that you walk by faith in what the Word of God says and not by faith in what your senses or the circumstances around you are telling you. This means that you do not base your decisions over any issue on what you hear, what you see, what you taste, what you smell, what you feel or on what any symptom may be saying but on what the Word of God says. You speak out only what the Word of God says concerning any situation that you may find yourself and not what your senses are telling you concerning the situation. Don't speak out by what you are experiencing if it does not agree with the Word of God.

Living a Supernatural Life (Volume 2)

Don't speak out your fears. Don't speak out your doubts. Don't speak out your pains. Don't speak out the symptoms. Instead speak out the words of faith that you can get from the Word of God. A secret of walking by faith is that when you pray you must believe that you received what you asked for at the time that you asked for it. That is what Jesus said in Mark 11:24.

> ***Therefore I say unto you, What things soever ye desire, when ye pray, believe that ye receive them, and ye shall have them.***
> **Mark 11:24**

Note that Jesus did not say, *"Believe that ye will receive them"* No! He said, *"Believe that ye receive them"* If you believe *that you will receive* them then you are not asking in faith; you are asking in hope. And if you believe *that you received* them when you asked for them then it is obvious that you won't go back to ask for them again. If you believe that you received them when you asked for them your actions must show that you did.

For example, if you have been tagged barren and you have been fighting the problem of barrenness, then praying in faith will mean that once you prayed for a child, if you believe that you received your child when you prayed then you will throw away all the things that you normally use for taking care of your periodic menstruation. When you should normally expect the menstruation you will go out with boldness without putting on any of the normal tissues that you wear to absorb blood during such periods. You will do this because you believe that you are pregnant therefore you will not have any blood flowing out of you that month.

Releasing the Supernatural

Not only for that month but for the next nine months. It is then you can really be said to have prayed in faith. If after your prayer you still go back to wearing such protective tissues in anticipation of menstruation then you did not ask in faith for your child. You only asked in hope that you will be given a child and not that you received a child. ***You've got to believe that you've got your answer before you get it.*** Note that it is not that you will get your answer. This really is the crux of the problem that most Christians have with the receiving of the baptism of the Holy Spirit. They pray and pray and pray yet they don't receive the baptism of the Holy Spirit. It is because they pray in hope and not in faith. You have to believe that you receive the baptism when you pray for the baptism of the Holy Spirit and not that you will receive the baptism. If you believe that you receive the Holy Spirit baptism when you pray you will immediately start to speak in tongues. But as we have referenced before Proverbs 23:7 says that it is as you think in your mind that you will be.

> *For as he thinketh in his heart, so is he: Eat and drink, saith he to thee; but his heart is not with thee.*
> **Proverbs 23:7**

Therefore no matter what God says that you now are in Christ, and no matter what powers and authorities God says that you now have in Christ, if you do not have it in your mind and agree in your mind with what God says, then those things that God said cannot be fulfilled in your life. Unless you have these truths in your mind you will not be able to live in the reality of those truths. You will just live an ordinary life. You will not be able to live a supernatural life.

PRACTICE IS THE MAIN ISSUE

You can live a supernatural life here on earth *by practicing the release of your invisible nature in Christ into your visible human nature through your confessions.* Note that I said practicing because practice is the main issue here, since it is possible for you to have supernatural powers or supernatural capabilities and not use them. When you have supernatural powers but do not use them, the supernatural will not manifest in your life. The potential may be there but you need to practice it if it is to manifest. That was why God told Moses what He said in Exodus 4:21 when He sent him to Pharaoh.

> *And the LORD said unto Moses, When thou goeth to return into Egypt, see that thou do all those wonders before Pharaoh which I have put in thine hand: but I will harden his heart that he shall not let the people go.*
> **Exodus 4:21**

You see, God knew that it was quite possible for Moses to get to Pharaoh and have all the wonders with him, but not do them before Pharaoh. It is the same with you today. Potentially, as a Christian you have supernatural capabilities. Your new invisible nature in Christ carries immense and supernatural potential. But it will only manifest or materialize if you use it by practicing it. You have to practice the use of those capabilities by speaking positive and supernatural things into existence in your life. Instead of doing this however, what most Christians do is that they are unconsciously speaking negative things into existence in their lives.

Releasing the Supernatural

As believers in Christ in whom the Spirit of God is living, many of the things that we are supposed to speak out and command into existence are the things that we pray to God about begging Him to do for us. We do these despite the truth that God has already given us the power and authority to command them into existence in the Name of Jesus. We do these most of the time as a result of our lack of faith in what God has said and also as a result of our lack of boldness. But if you will not do so, you will not be able to experience supernatural living. You must apply the truth of the Word to the facts of your life. ***Supernatural living can be defined as the application of Truth to Facts, where Truth is the Word of God and Facts are your natural situations. Facts then are natural, and Truth is supernatural.*** This means that you can achieve a supernatural life by the application of the Word, which as stated by Jesus in John 17:17 is the ***truth,*** to your natural situations, which are the *facts*.

> ***Sanctify them through thy truth: thy word is truth.***
> **John 17:17**

So when a ***"fact"*** occurs from a natural situation, you speak out the ***"Truth",*** from the Word of God, to bring the supernatural into existence. You must see in line with what the Word of God, which is the truth, says and not in line with what the facts of your natural situation are saying.

Supernatural living can therefore also be defined as the superimposing of the TRUTH of our invisible heavenly nature over the FACTS of our visible earthly life. Therefore see beyond the natural.

Living a Supernatural Life (Volume 2)

When Christ was here on earth He promised in Matthew 16:19 that He would give us the keys of the Kingdom of heaven with which we can bind and loose anything. In John 14:13-14, He also told us that whatever we ask in His Name He would do it.

> *And I will give unto thee the keys of the kingdom of heaven: and whatsoever thou shalt bind on earth shall be bound in heaven: and whatsoever thou shalt loose on earth shall be loosed in heaven.*
> **Matthew 16:19**

> *And whatsoever ye shall ask in my name, that will I do, that the Father may be glorified in the Son.*
>
> *If ye shall ask any thing in my name, I will do it.*
> **John 14:13-14**

He further said in John 15:16 and John 16:23 that whatever we ask the Father in His Name the Father will give it to us. It is obvious therefore that the Name of Jesus is one of the keys of the Kingdom of heaven that Jesus was referring to.

> *Ye have not chosen me, but I have chosen you, and ordained you, that ye should go and bring forth fruit, and that your fruit should remain: that whatsoever ye shall ask of the Father in my name, he may give it you.*
> **John 15:16**

Releasing the Supernatural

And in that day ye shall ask me nothing. Verily, verily, I say unto you, Whatsoever ye shall ask the Father in my name, he will give it you.

John 16:23

God wants us to bear fruit and what this means is to win souls into the Kingdom and a major way to do this is to show signs and wonder wrought in the Name of Jesus Christ to the unbelievers. The Scriptures said that when they see the signs and wonders they will believe. That is what Jesus Himself said in the story written by John the Apostle in John 4:45-52. He said unless they see signs and wonders they will not believe.

Then when he was come into Galilee, the Galilaeans received him, having seen all the things that he did at Jerusalem at the feast: for they also went unto the feast.

So Jesus came again into Cana of Galilee, where he made the water wine. And there was a certain nobleman, whose son was sick at Capernaum.

When he heard that Jesus was come out of Judaea into Galilee, he went unto him, and besought him that he would come down, and heal his son: for he was at the point of death.

Then said Jesus unto him, Except ye see signs and wonders, ye will not believe.

The nobleman saith unto him, Sir, come down ere my child die.

Living a Supernatural Life (Volume 2)

> *Jesus saith unto him, Go thy way; thy son liveth. And the man believed the word that Jesus had spoken unto him, and he went his way.*
>
> *And as he was now going down, his servants met him, and told him, saying, Thy son liveth.*
>
> *Then enquired he of them the hour when he began to amend. And they said unto him, Yesterday at the seventh hour the fever left him.*
>
> **John 4:45-52**

The Name of Jesus is not only a key of the Kingdom of Heaven given to us to do signs and wonders with. It is the major key that you need to use for the release of the supernatural.

In the next two chapters we shall look at the Name of Jesus as a key for the release of the supernatural and how to correctly use the Name for achieving that goal.

We shall also look at some of the wrong ways that Christians are currently making use of that Name, which constitute the major obstacles to their receiving the answers to their prayers and manifesting the supernatural in their lives.

CHAPTER 3

THE NAME OF JESUS
A MAJOR KEY OF THE KINGDOM

Jesus said that He will give you the keys of the Kingdom of Heaven and with these keys whatever you bind on earth shall be bound in Heaven and whatever you loose on earth shall be loosed in Heaven. One of these keys of the Kingdom of Heaven is the Name of Jesus. By the time you finish reading this Chapter you will agree that the Name of Jesus is a major key of the Kingdom with which you can do the supernatural. To do so you will also need to believe in the power that is in that Name. Look at what Peter said in Acts 3:16 below about that Name after the healing of the lame man at the Beautiful gate. He said,

> *"And his name through faith in his name hath made this man strong, whom ye see and know: yea, the faith which is by him hath given him this perfect soundness in the presence of you all."*
>
> **Acts 3:16**

He said that it was the Name of Jesus and through faith in that Name that healed the lame man. So the Name of Jesus can heal if you have faith in the Name.

If you can only see the weight of that statement by Peter and you can have a revelation of that statement you will surmount every encounter that you have with the forces of darkness in life with ease. The Name was used to lose the bounds of the lame man. The Name can be used to get loosed from all bondages. The Name is very powerful because at the call of the Name every knee must bow.

No matter what force you may be facing and no matter what strength it has whether it is a force based in earth that is of human origin; or it is a force based under the earth that is of demonic origin; it must bow at the call of that Name. Even if it is a force based in heaven that is of spiritual origin it must bow at the call of that Name.

WHAT MAKES THE NAME UNIQUE?

The Name Jesus is unique because it is full of power and authority. There is authority in the Name. Why do I say this? You will see why I said that there is authority in the Name when you look at the following fifteen points concerning the Name that make the Name very unique indeed. After looking at the points you will agree with me that there is authority in the Name.

1. IT IS A STRONG TOWER OF PROTECTION

The Name is unique because the Name is a strong tower, which when the righteous runs into he is saved. No matter what may be the problem that he is running away from when he runs to that Name he will be saved.

The Name of Jesus

That is what we are made to understand by what is written by King Solomon in Proverbs 18:10. You are now *"the righteous"* because you have been given the righteousness of Christ as a gift as we have explained earlier. Once you receive this righteousness of Christ by faith then you are the one that God is referring to as the righteous.

> *The name of the LORD is a strong tower: the righteous runneth into it, and is safe.*
> **Proverbs 18:10**

The righteous is saved when he runs into the tower of that Name because that is where he will find help in times of need. That is why the Word of God says in Psalm 124:8 that our help is in the Name of the Lord who made heaven and earth. But the Lord who made heaven and earth was Jesus Christ, the Word. That is what is written in John 1:1-3,14.

> *Our help is in the name of the LORD, who made heaven and earth.*
> **Psalm 128:4**

> *In the beginning was the Word, and the Word was with God, and the Word was God.*
> *The same was in the beginning with God.*
>
> *All things were made by him; and without him was not any thing made that was made.*
>
> *And the Word was made flesh, and dwelt among us, and we beheld his glory, the glory as of the only begotten of the Father, full of grace and truth.*
> **John 1:1-3, 14**

Living a Supernatural Life (Volume 2)

Therefore we can say that our help is in the Name of Jesus. Now, the word "help" covers practically everything that you need assistance for. For example you may need help for deliverance, for protection, for success, for healing, for fruitfulness, etc. You can therefore say our deliverance is in the Name of the Lord, our protection is in the Name of the Lord, our success is in the Name of the Lord, our healing is in the Name of the Lord, our justification is in the Name of the Lord, etc. You can use the Name to get whatever help you want at any time. Just believe in the power that is in that Name and use it to ask for whatever you want. That is why the Name is such a strong tower. He said the righteous run into it and is saved.

We have shown in *Volume 1* of this *"Living a supernatural life"* book series that you are now made righteous because you have been freely given the righteousness of Christ as a gift therefore **the righteous** referred to in that Scripture is you. That is why even though some trust in chariots and some trust in horses you should remember to put your trust in the Name of the Lord just as written in Psalm 20:7.

> *Some trust in chariots, and some in horses: but we will remember the name of the LORD our God.*
> **Psalm 20:7**

Right from the beginning God has been revealing Himself to mankind through His Name. That is why Solomon talked in 1 Kings 8:43 of knowing God's Name instead of knowing God. It is through knowing the Name of God that we can know God. You cannot know Him fully unless you know His Name.

The Name of Jesus

> *Hear thou in heaven thy dwelling place, and do according to all that the stranger calleth to thee for: that all people of the earth may know thy name, to fear thee, as do thy people Israel; and that they may know that this house, which I have builded, is called by thy name.*
>
> **1 Kings 8:43**

We can see in Exodus 15:26 that when the children of Israel needed healing, God revealed Himself to them through His Name as **Jehovah-Rapha, the Lord our healer** and this is just a revelation of an aspect or part of God's nature.

> *And said, If thou wilt diligently hearken to the voice of the LORD thy God, and wilt do that which is right in his sight, and wilt give ear to his commandments, and keep all his statutes, I will put none of these diseases upon thee, which I have brought upon the Egyptians: for I am the LORD that healeth thee.*
>
> **Exodus 15:26**

At some point in Judges 6:23-24, when they needed peace He also revealed Himself to them as **Jehovah-Shalom, the Lord our peace,** a revelation of another part of God's nature.

> *And the LORD said unto him, Peace be unto thee; fear not: thou shalt not die.*

> *Then Gideon built an altar there unto the LORD, and called it Jehovahshalom: unto this day it is yet in Ophrah of the Abiezrites.*
>
> **Judges 6:23-24**

Living a Supernatural Life (Volume 2)

God had progressively revealed His nature to man through His Names but all the Names thus revealed to man only revealed a part of God's nature. However God promised through Prophet Isaiah in Isaiah 52:6 that the time will come when He would fully reveal His Name to man. He said that His Name will be fully revealed in due time and all shall know His Name.

> *Therefore my people shall know my name: therefore they shall know in that day that I am he that doth speak: behold, it is I.*
> **Isaiah 52:6**

That time came when Jesus Christ came to this world for He said of Himself in John 5:43 that He came to reveal the Name of God to mankind because He came in that Name. Not only that, the Scriptures also revealed to us in Hebrews 1:4 that He actually inherited that Name, which is a more excellent Name than any angel has.

> *I am come in my Father's name, and ye receive me not: if another shall come in his own name, him ye will receive.*
> **John 5:43**

> *Being made so much better than the angels, as he hath by inheritance obtained a more excellent name than they.*
> **Hebrews 1:4**

In Psalm 22:22 it was prophetically said that the Messiah to come will declare the Name of the Lord. We now know from what the Scriptures says in Luke 22:70 that Jesus Christ is the Messiah that was been expected.

The Name of Jesus

I will declare thy name unto my brethren: in the midst of the congregation will I praise thee.
Psalm 22:22

Then said they all, Art thou then the Son of God? And he said unto them, Ye say that I am.
Luke 22:70

Therefore whatever Name Jesus Christ revealed must be the Name of God that God has promised to reveal through the Messiah.

Finally Jesus Christ Himself also said that He manifested the Name of the Father when He came to this world. That was what He said in John 17:6.

I have manifested thy name unto the men which thou gavest me out of the world: thine they were, and thou gavest them me; and they have kept thy word.
John 17:6

What then is this Name of God that the Messiah came to reveal and manifest to man? The Bible also gave us the answer to this question.

The Name of God that He has promised to reveal to man is **JESUS,** which means *Jehovah our salvation* because we are told that all the fullness of the Godhead dwells bodily in Jesus Christ. That is what God made us to know through Paul in Colossians 2:9 We can therefore say that **JESUS** is the Name of God that totally reveals God's nature to man.

Living a Supernatural Life (Volume 2)

> *For in him dwelleth all the fulness of the Godhead bodily.*
>
> **Colossians 2:9**

These Names of God reveal the nature and character of God therefore we can say that the Name of God represents God. His Name represents His power; His Name represents His authority and His Name represents His presence. Therefore as you call the Name of God you invoke His power, His authority and His presence. That is why Jesus said that whenever you gather in His Name He is there. You can therefore see why we are advised in Colossians 3:17 to do all things in that Name.

> *And whatsoever ye do in word or deed, do all in the name of the Lord Jesus, giving thanks to God and the Father by him.*
>
> **Colossians 3:17**

If you look at what the Scripture says in Isaiah 35:4-6 about what Jehovah God is supposed to do and compare this with what is written in Luke 7:21-22 concerning what Jesus Christ was doing when He came to this world you will realize that the Jehovah that the Scripture talked about in the Old Testament is the same as the Jesus of the New Testament. Jesus Christ is therefore God manifested in the flesh.

> *Say to them that are of a fearful heart, Be strong, fear not: behold, your God will come with vengeance, even God with a recompence; he will come and save you.*

The Name of Jesus

Then the eyes of the blind shall be opened, and the ears of the deaf shall be unstopped.

Then shall the lame man leap as an hart, and the tongue of the dumb sing: for in the wilderness shall waters break out, and streams in the desert.
Isaiah 35:4-6

And in that same hour he cured many of their infirmities and plagues, and of evil spirits; and unto many that were blind he gave sight.

Then Jesus answering said unto them, Go your way, and tell John what things ye have seen and heard; how that the blind see, the lame walk, the lepers are cleansed, the deaf hear, the dead are raised, to the poor the gospel is preached.
Luke 7:21-22

Therefore we can say that the Name **JESUS** is the Name of God Jehovah that He has promised to reveal to mankind through the Messiah. It is this Name that gives us the full revelation of Jehovah God. The character of God, the presence of God, the power of God, the authority of God and all the attributes of God exist in and are all represented by this Name. Now God has said in Psalm 138:2 that He magnified His Word above all His Name

I will worship toward thy holy temple, and praise thy name for thy lovingkindness and for thy truth: for thou hast magnified thy word above all thy name.
Psalms 138:2

2. IT IS ABOVE EVERY OTHER NAME

The Name of Jesus is unique because the Name is above every other Name, in heaven where angels are, in the earth where the humans are and under the earth where the demons are. Therefore everybody whether angels, humans or demons must bow at the call of that Name. That is what we are told by God through Paul in Philippians 2:9-10.

> *Wherefore God also hath highly exalted him, and given him a name which is above every name:*
>
> *That at the name of Jesus every knee should bow, of things in heaven, and things in earth, and things under the earth;*
> **Philippians 2:9-10**

We should take cognizance of the truth that the Name Jesus, which belongs to Christ, has been exalted above every other name as shown in the above passage. As we have seen previously **Jesus Christ is the Word and is God.**

Now in 2 Corinthians 10:4-6 we have also been told that using the weapons of warfare now at our disposal we can subject and bring into obedience every thought and imagination that exalts itself against the knowledge of God *(knowledge of the Word).* I believe that the Name of Jesus is one of the weapons that God is talking about here.

For the weapons of our warfare are not carnal, but mighty through God to the pulling down of strong holds;

Casting down imaginations, and every high thing that exalteth itself against the knowledge of God, and bringing into captivity every thought to the obedience of Christ;

And having in a readiness to revenge all disobedience, when your obedience is fulfilled.
2 Corinthians 10:4-6

Since Jesus Christ is the Word of God and is also God then the knowledge of God mentioned in verse 5 above is equivalent to saying the knowledge of the Word of God. Also obedience of Christ mentioned in that same verse is equivalent to saying obedience of the Word of God. Therefore what the Scripture above really means is that any high thing or imagination that exalts itself against the knowledge of what the Word of God says we can bring it into subjection in obedience to what the Word of God says.

We can also bring every thought into captivity to obey what the Word of God says. A major weapon of our warfare that we can use to do these is the Name of Jesus. Therefore using that Name of Jesus in any situation that we come across we can bring every high thing that exalts itself against what the Word of God says as well as every thought and imaginations into captivity to obey whatever the Word of God says about the situation. It follows therefore that we can bring any situation under control with the Name of Jesus.

3. HE IS HEIR OF ALL THINGS

The Name is unique because Jesus Christ to whom the Name has been given has also been appointed heir of all things and we are now joint-heirs with Him. That is what we are made to understand in Hebrews 1:2 and Romans 8:17.

> *Hath in these last days spoken unto us by his Son, whom he hath appointed heir of all things, by whom also he made the worlds;*
> **Hebrews 1:2**

> *And if children, then heirs; heirs of God, and joint-heirs with Christ; if so be that we suffer with him, that we may be also glorified together.*
> **Romans 8:17**

If He is heir of all things then it follows that using His Name you can get anything that you want once it is His will to give it to you because you are now actually joint-heirs with Him as stated above.

The Name makes all things available to you now. You don't have to struggle for anything. Just ask for it in the Name of Jesus. The Name is your cheque book with which you can withdraw anything you want from the heavenly bank. Once you know that what you want is available in the heavenly bank then all you need is to use your cheque book, which is the Name of Jesus to draw it out from your heavenly bank account. He said ***whatsoever*** you ask the Father in His Name He will give you. Just believe in the Name and you will get it.

4. HIS NAME IS MORE EXCELLENT THAN ANY ANGEL'S NAME

The Name is unique because it is an inherited Name, and it is a more excellent Name than that of any angel. That is what we are told in Hebrews 1:4.

> *Being made so much better than the angels, as he hath by inheritance obtained a more excellent name than they.*
> **Hebrews 1:4**

5. EVERYTHING IS PUT UNDER HIS FEET

The Name is unique because Jesus Christ to whom the Name has been given has been made the head over all things to the Church and He has been set far above all principality, all power, all might, all dominion and everything that is named not only in this world but even in the world to come. This means that the Name Jesus is above every other name no matter whose name it is. Every other name including that of the affliction that you are so afraid of must bow before this Name Jesus. Everything has also been put under His feet. That is what is written in Ephesians 1:19-23.

> *And what is the exceeding greatness of his power to us-ward who believe, according to the working of his mighty power,*
>
> *Which he wrought in Christ, when he raised him from the dead, and set him at his own right hand in the heavenly places,*

Living a Supernatural Life (Volume 2)

> *Far above all principality, and power, and might, and dominion, and every name that is named, not only in this world, but also in that which is to come:*
>
> *And hath put all things under his feet, and gave him to be the head over all things to the church,*
>
> *Which is his body, the fulness of him that filleth all in all.*
> **Ephesians 1:19-23**

Do you know that your life is now hidden with Christ in God and that you have been raised to seat together with Him in the heavenly and highly exalted place where He now sits? That is what we are told in Colossians 3:3 and Ephesians 2:6. If you are in Him then it follows that you are also far above all principality and power and might and dominion and anything that has a name including that affliction you are so afraid of.

> *For ye are dead, and your life is hid with Christ in God.*
> **Colossians 3:3**
>
> *And hath raised us up together, and made us sit together in heavenly places in Christ Jesus:*
> **Ephesians 2:6**

Since you are now in Him and everything has been put under His feet it follows therefore that no matter what part of His Body you may be, everything will also be under your feet.

The Name of Jesus

There are various functions and gifts for different categories of people in the Body of Christ. Some are Apostles, some are Prophets, some are Evangelists and some are Teachers. But no matter what you are in the Body of Christ and where you are in that Body you are far above all principality and powers and might and dominion and everything that has a name. Everything has also been put under your feet. We can infer this from Ephesians 1:19-23 written on the previous page.

6. SATAN AND HIS DEMONS TREMBLE AT THE CALL OF THE NAME

The Name is unique because whenever Satan and his demons hear that Name they must tremble. They must tremble because they once had an encounter with Jesus when He died as our substitute and Jesus conquered them. He not only conquered them He actually spoiled them by seizing everything that they had including the power of death, which was formally with Satan as we are told in Hebrews 2:14.

> *Forasmuch then as the children are partakers of flesh and blood, he also himself likewise took part of the same; that through death he might destroy him that had the power of death, that is, the devil;*
> **Hebrews 2:14**

Since that encounter Satan has lost the power of death. Therefore the power of death is no longer with Satan but it is now with Jesus Christ as we are told in Revelation 1:18. Therefore death should no longer frighten you.

> *I am he that liveth, and was dead; and, behold, I am alive for evermore, Amen; and have the keys of hell and of death.*
> **Revelation 1:18**

When Jesus Christ conquered Satan and his forces He made an open show of them disgracing them in the process. That is what we are told by God through Paul in Colossians 2:15. By making an open show of them He did what conquering armies normally do with any army that they have defeated in battle and taken captive. They normally line such a conquered army up behind the leader in this case the devil and parade the captives openly with their hands tied to show that they have been defeated and conquered so that all who see them will realize and know that they are a conquered army. This has been done to the devil and his team in the spiritual realm.

> *And having spoiled principalities and powers, he made a shew of them openly, triumphing over them in it.*
> **Colossians 2:15**

That is why they must tremble whenever they hear that Name of Jesus Christ their conqueror.

7. MIRACLES ARE WROUGHT THROUGH FAITH IN THE NAME

The Name is unique because when you have faith in the Name it can make you whole and strong no matter what affliction you may be going through.

The Name of Jesus

The mere call of that Name Jesus can wrought miracles that can lift any afflicted person out of his affliction. That is the essence of what Peter said in Acts 3:16.

And his name through faith in his name hath made this man strong, whom ye see and know: yea, the faith which is by him hath given him this perfect soundness in the presence of you all.

Acts 3:16

There are so many cases in the Bible of people healed, miracles done and signs and wonders wrought by that Name. Many of these are recorded in the Book of Acts of the Apostles and these are discussed later on in this book in the next Chapter where we talk of how to use the Name of Jesus.

Even people who are not followers of Jesus Christ use the Name to cast out devils as you can see as written in Mark 9:38-39. The Name is not a magic wand but a key of the Kingdom of Heaven, which God has given us in this end time to use to bind and to loose. You only need faith in that Name to use it.

And John answered him, saying, Master, we saw one casting out devils in thy name, and he followeth not us: and we forbad him, because he followeth not us.

But Jesus said, Forbid him not: for there is no man which shall do a miracle in my name, that can lightly speak evil of me.

Mark 9:38-39

8. IT IS THE ONLY NAME WHEREBY WE CAN BE SAVED

The Name is unique because it is the only Name under heaven given among men by which you must be saved. No other name will save you. That is what we are told in Acts 4:12. No matter what you may be going through the Name will save you from it. Salvation unto eternal life comes only through that Name.

> *Neither is there salvation in any other: for there is none other name under heaven given among men, whereby we must be saved.*
> **Acts 4:12**

9. YOU MUST BELIEVE ON THE NAME AND BELIEVE IN THE NAME

There is a difference between *believing on the Name of Jesus* and *believing in the Name of Jesus*. You become saved by *believing on* His Name. That is what we are made to understand by John the Apostle in John 1:12.

> *But as many as received him, to them gave he power to become the sons of God, even to them that believe on his name:*
> **John 1:12**

But after you have been saved you get all the benefits of your salvation by *believing in* His Name. That is what Jesus said in John 14:13-14, John 16:23-24 as well as in Mark 16:17-18 and in Mark 9:38-39. Believe on His Name to receive your salvation and in Name to get the benefits of your salvation.

And whatsoever ye shall ask in my name, that will I do, that the Father may be glorified in the Son.

If ye shall ask any thing in my name, I will do it.
John 14:13-14

And in that day ye shall ask me nothing. Verily, verily, I say unto you, Whatsoever ye shall ask the Father in my name, he will give it you.

Hitherto have ye asked nothing in my name: ask, and ye shall receive, that your joy may be full.
John 16:23-24

And these signs shall follow them that believe; In my name shall they cast out devils; they shall speak with new tongues;

They shall take up serpents; and if they drink any deadly thing, it shall not hurt them; they shall lay hands on the sick, and they shall recover.
Mark 16:17-18

And John answered him, saying, Master, we saw one casting out devils in thy name, and he followeth not us: and we forbad him, because he followeth not us.

Living a Supernatural Life (Volume 2)

> *But Jesus said, Forbid him not: for there is no man which shall do a miracle in my name, that can lightly speak evil of me.*
>   **Mark 9:38-39**

But you need to get this difference between *believing on* the Name and *believing in* the Name. You believe on the Name to get saved but believe in the Name for your resources.

As you can see from the above Scriptures all miracles, signs and wonders are to be done in the Name of Jesus. The resources that you need are to be asked for from the Father in the Name of Jesus. There is a difference between the prayers that you pray to the Father in Jesus Name asking for resources and the commands that you give in Jesus' Name asking for miracles, signs and wonders to be performed when you want to do the works that Jesus did.

We have two different instructions for asking for things in the Name of Jesus but they are to be used in different situations and we must take cognizance of this. But most Christians today confuse these two different ways of getting things in the Name of Jesus. They tend to ask for all things from the Father in the Name of Jesus. Jesus had taught His disciples and also shown them before He left that miracles, signs and wonders will be done in His Name not by asking the Father to do them in the Name of Jesus Christ. But no matter which of the two methods you are using at any time something that you must note is that contrary to general beliefs no proviso of faith is attached to any of the promises except faith in His Name.

You just need faith in the power that is in the Name of Jesus Christ to get what you want. Whether you are getting the resources that you need or you are doing the works that Jesus did what you are doing can be likened to what Prophet Isaiah referred to in Isaiah 12:3 as drawing water out of the wells of salvation and you need joy to do this.

> *Therefore with joy shall ye draw water out of the wells of salvation.*
> **Isaiah 12:3**

All you have to do is just know the power that is in that Name and use it. As we have explained earlier the Name is your spiritual cheque book with which you draw what you need from the resources in the bank of Heaven. The bank of Heaven has all that you can ever ask for or need. Just write the cheque for whatever you want by using the Name of Jesus Christ. But you must take cognizance of the two different approaches to the use of the Name. The difference between the two methods of approach for using the Name of Jesus Christ is discussed in greater detail later in this book in the next Chapter titled, "How to use the Name".

10. THE NAME GIVES YOU POWER TO BECOME A SON OF GOD

The Name is unique because if you believe on that Name you become saved and if you are saved and you believe on His Name you are given the power to become a son of God. That is what we are told by John the Apostle in John 1:12.

Living a Supernatural Life (Volume 2)

> *'But as many as received him, to them gave he power to become the sons of God, even to them that believe on his name:*
>
> **John 1:12**

The power to become the son of God is what the Name gives you because you need the power to be able to demonstrate your sonship.

You know that when you adopt a son it is possible for you to call him your son and make him your son but you may not empower him to be a son. Making him a son or calling him a son does not necessarily empower him to be your son. You may call him a son but not give him the full powers of a son or the full privileges of a son.

It is for the avoidance of any doubt as to your status that God made sure that once you are born again you are not only adopted and made His son but you are actually empowered to become one. That empowerment comes through your belief on the Name of Jesus.

11. YOU HAVE LIFE THROUGH THE NAME

The Name is unique because when you believe that Jesus, who is the one that inherited that Name, is the Christ then through that Name you have life. That is what we are told by God through John in John 20:31.

> *But these are written, that ye might believe that Jesus is the Christ, the Son of God; and that believing ye might have life through his name.*
>
> **John 20:31**.

12. DEVILS ARE SUBJECT TO YOU THROUGH THE NAME

The Name is unique because once you believe in that Name if you command in that Name you can cast out devils, you can lay hands on the sick and they shall recover. In that Name if you drink any deadly thing it shall not hurt you. In that Name you can take up serpents and they cannot hurt you. This means that devils are subjected to you at the call of that Name. That is what Jesus said in Mark 16:17-18.

> *And these signs shall follow them that believe; In my name shall they cast out devils; they shall speak with new tongues;*
>
> *They shall take up serpents; and if they drink any deadly thing, it shall not hurt them; they shall lay hands on the sick, and they shall recover.*
> **Mark 16:17-18**

Through that Name you can make the devils or demons to be subject to your authority. This is confirmed by what the seventy disciples of Jesus that He sent out to try what He has taught them said in Luke 10:17 when they returned. That is a spiritual power that even the devils and demons and all forces of darkness cannot withstand or resist successfully.

> *And the seventy returned again with joy, saying, Lord, even the devils are subject unto us through thy name.*
> **Luke 10:17**

Just like God's enemies are subjected to Him through the greatness of His powers as written in Psalm 66:3 so it is with you because you now also have the power of God.

> *Say unto God, How terrible art thou in thy works! through the greatness of thy power shall thine enemies submit themselves unto thee.*
>
> **Psalm 66:3**

It is through the greatness of the power of God, which you can demonstrate that your enemies will submit themselves to you and the great key that you have for releasing that power is the Name of Jesus. Therefore the major weapon that you have to make your enemies and adversaries to be subject to you is the Name of Jesus. It is only through that Name that your enemies will subject themselves unto you. If you want them to be subject to you then you must demonstrate the power of God to them by commanding them in that Name.

13. GATHERING IN THAT NAME BRINGS CHRIST'S PRESENCE

The Name is unique because whenever two or three people are gathered together in that Name, whether they know it or not, Jesus Christ the owner of the Name who is God will be there with them. That is the promise that He made in Matthew 18:20. It is a big surprise therefore when some Christians meet and they are still praying that God should come and join them.

For where two or three are gathered together in my name, there am I in the midst of them.
Matthew 18:20

14. YOU HAVE REMISSION OF SIN THROUGH THE NAME

The Name is unique because even when you believe in Jesus and believe that He is the Christ and that He died for your sins to save you, it is only through His Name that you will receive remission for your sins. That is what we are told in Acts 10:43.

To him give all the prophets witness, that through his name whosoever believeth in him shall receive remission of sins.
Acts 10:43

15. THE HOLY SPIRIT WAS SENT IN THAT NAME

The Name is unique because the Holy Spirit who was sent on the day of Pentecost was sent in that Name. That was the promise that Jesus gave in John 14:26 and it was fulfilled on the day of Pentecost. He came down on the day of Pentecost and has since been working among us to supplicate for us as well as regenerate, baptize, anoint and dwell in us. He has been living with us here on earth to comfort, guide and instruct those who are His and who will listen to His instruction.

> *But the Comforter, which is the Holy Ghost, whom the Father will send in my name, he shall teach you all things, and bring all things to your remembrance, whatsoever I have said unto you.*
>
> **John 14:26**

YOUR RIGHTS TO THAT NAME

We have discussed the authority and the power that is in the Name of Jesus Christ and the many things that the Name can do. However you must like to know what rights and authority you have to use the Name. You have a five-fold right to that Name as we will explain in the following pages.

1. YOU ARE A MEMBER OF HIS BODY

The Name of Jesus is now yours because you have been grafted into the Body of Christ to become a member of His Body. That is what we are made to know in Ephesians 5:30. Your flesh is now part of the His flesh and your bones are now part of His bones. Therefore we are not talking of something that is hypothetical here. We are talking of something that is tangible, which you can spiritually take hold of. Surely if you are a member of His Body then His Name must also be your Name. So the Name belongs to you also.

> *For we are members of his body, of his flesh, and of his bones.*
>
> **Ephesians 5:30**

The Name of Jesus

My arm is part of me? So the Name Olumbo also belongs to my arm, my hand, my head, etc. Any part of me bears the name Olumbo. If you see my hand for example you will say that is Olumbo's hand. Every part of my body bears my name. Your hands, feet etc all have your name.

But you are now a part of the Body of Christ therefore whatever part of the Body of Christ you may be as long as you belong to the Body the Name Jesus Christ now belongs to you too.

That was why Peter was able to tell the lame man at the Beautiful Gate, *"...What I have I give unto you."* Then He used the Name of Jesus. That Name of Jesus was what he had. You also have the Name now. The Name also belongs to you now. So just like Peter claimed the Name you also can now claim the Name. Just like he used the Name to heal you too can now use the Name to heal. Only just know and believe that this Name of Jesus, which is now yours to use has great powers and have faith in it. Every power that is in that Name now belongs to you and is now available to you. That Name is a key that can open any door. In truth it is a major one of the keys of the kingdom of Heaven that Jesus promised to give us in Matthew 16:19.

> *And I will give unto thee the keys of the kingdom of heaven: and whatsoever thou shalt bind on earth shall be bound in heaven: and whatsoever thou shalt loose on earth shall be loosed in heaven.*
> **Matthew 16:19**

2. YOU ARE BORN INTO THE FAMILY OF GOD

You are now born into the family of God therefore the Name has become your spiritual family name. You now bear the Name as of right. You have the Name as your birthright now therefore the Name now belongs to you. This gives you a **new-birth right** to the Name as your **spiritual family Name.** To show you that you are now born into the family of God, look at John 1:12-13 and also 1 John 5:4 as well as 1 Thessalonians 5:5 and Psalm 82:6.

> *But as many as received him, to them gave he power to become the sons of God, even to them that believe on his name:*
>
> *Which were born, not of blood, nor of the will of the flesh, nor of the will of man, but of God.*
> **John 1:12-13**
>
> *For whatsoever is born of God overcometh the world: and this is the victory that overcometh the world, even our faith.*
> **1 John 5:4**
>
> *Ye are all the children of light, and the children of the day: we are not of the night, nor of darkness.*
> **1 Thessalonians 5:5**
>
> *I have said, Ye are gods; and all of you are children of the most High.*
> **Psalm 82:6**

The Name of Jesus

From these Scriptures you will see and know that you are now born of God. You are now a son of God and therefore you now belong to the family of the Most High God.

In the natural when you are born into a family that family's name is given to you. So it is in the spiritual realm also. If you belong to the family of God then that Name Jesus Christ becomes your **spiritual family Name.** If that Name is your spiritual family Name then the Name belongs to you and you have every right to use the Name. You obviously do not need any permission to use a Name that belongs to you. Using the Name should come naturally to you. Once you know that you can have all things through that Name and you also know that the Name has the power to make them available to you all you need do then is just have faith in the Name and use the Name to get them.

The Name is your spiritual cheque book for drawing whatever you need from the Heavenly bank where all the resources are kept. With your normal earthly bank account, you use a cheque book. Once you know that you have money deposited in your account and you believe in the power of your cheque book to draw it out you then don't need any further faith to write a cheque to withdraw any money from your account.

Similarly once you know the resources and benefits available to you through your salvation and you believe and have faith in the power that is in the Name of Jesus to draw out these benefits and resources, then you don't need any further assurance to use the Name to draw out such benefits and resources.

Just use the Name to draw out the benefits and resources that you want. The unfortunate thing though with most Christians is that many use the Name of Jesus Christ without really knowing the power that is vested in that Name. To them using the Name is just a routine or customary practice whose purpose is not quite clear. They just do it because it is customary to do so.

3. YOU ARE BAPTIZED INTO THAT NAME

In the physical realm when you are baptized you receive a *baptismal name.* You are now spiritually baptized into Christ. This means that you are baptized into that Name. That Name therefore becomes your *spiritual baptismal name.* That you have been baptized into that Name can be seen or inferred from what is written in the following Scriptures, in Romans 6:3, also in 1 Corinthians 12:13 and in Galatians 3:27. Your spiritual baptismal name belongs to you.

> *Know ye not, that so many of us as were baptized into Jesus Christ were baptized into his death?*
> **Romans 6:3**

> *For by one Spirit are we all baptized into one body, whether we be Jews or Gentiles, whether we be bond or free; and have been all made to drink into one Spirit.*
> **1 Corinthians 12:13**

> *For as many of you as have been baptized into Christ have put on Christ.*
> **Galatians 3:27**

It is obvious from the above Scriptures that when you are born again and baptized you are baptized into Jesus Christ and therefore from that point on you can say that your ***spiritual baptismal name*** now is Jesus Christ. Therefore that Name now belongs to you through baptism. Note also that once you are baptized into Christ you have put on Christ as stated in the verse above. If you have put on Christ then you have also put on the Name of Christ. Therefore the Name of Jesus Christ also belongs to you from that point on. When you are baptized into Jesus Christ you are regenerated and given a new nature in Christ. Your baptism into Jesus Christ acts as your initiation into the family of God and your public identification with Jesus Christ and in particular with the Name of Jesus Christ.

4. JESUS CHRIST AUTHORIZED YOU TO USE THE NAME

Many Christians do not know or believe that they have the Name as a result of being members of the Body of Christ. Many also do not know or believe that they have the Name of Jesus Christ as a result of being born into the family of God. There are also many Christians who are not aware of the truth that they have been baptized into the Name of Jesus Christ. However most Christians know and believe that they have been authorized to use the Name by Jesus Christ the owner of the Name Himself. Jesus Christ Himself has given you ***the power of attorney to use His Name*** to get anything that you want. As we said earlier the Name has now become your spiritual cheque book with which you can draw out whatever you want.

Living a Supernatural Life (Volume 2)

When you require any miracle whether it is healing, success, fruitfulness, prosperity, power, victory or any other type of miracle you can use the Name of Jesus Christ to draw it out. You can get whatever you want provided that you draw it out using that Name as your cheque. That is the essence of what Jesus was saying to us as written in John 14:13-14 and in John 16:23-24. What Jesus has done is to give you a *legal right* to the use of that Name. You must have the consciousness that you have a legal right to the Name.

> *And whatsoever ye shall ask in my name, that will I do, that the Father may be glorified in the Son.*
>
> *If ye shall ask any thing in my name, I will do it.*
> **John 14:13-14**
>
> *And in that day ye shall ask me nothing. Verily, verily, I say unto you, Whatsoever ye shall ask the Father in my name, he will give it you.*
>
> *Hitherto have ye asked nothing in my name: ask, and ye shall receive, that your joy may be full.*
> **John 16:23-24**

The ability that is vested in that Name now belongs to you also. The power and authority in that Name has now been made available to you. Whenever you call on that Name for any situation it is as if you have called Jesus Christ Himself into the situation.

After all He promised that when you call on His Name He will be there with you. You should therefore realize that whenever you call the Name concerning any situation you have called Jesus personally into that situation. Therefore enter into that right without any element of doubt as to the power that is in the Name and use the Name with faith believing that whatever God can do, that Name can get it done. The authority and legal right to use that Name is one of the fruits of the finished work of Christ that you have.

5. YOU ARE AN AMBASSADOR OF THE NAME

You have been commissioned as an ambassador to take that Name to all nations of the world. You now represent that Name wherever you go.

You are now a representative of that Name. That is the meaning of what we are told through Paul the Apostle in 2 Corinthians 5:20. This means that you have a *proxy right* (stand-in right) to the Name. You have been commissioned to take that Name to the entire world and preach Christ to the world doing miracles with it. That command of Christ in Matthew 28:19 is known as the Great Commission. You have been commissioned to bring more people into the family of God by preaching the Gospel of Christ to them.

> *Now then we are ambassadors for Christ, as though God did beseech you by us: we pray you in Christ's stead, be ye reconciled to God.*
> **2 Corinthians 5:20**

Living a Supernatural Life (Volume 2)

> *Go ye therefore, and teach all nations, baptizing them in the name of the Father, and of the Son, and of the Holy Ghost:*
> **Matthew 28:19**

Because of these five-fold rights that you have to the Name of Jesus you now know that the Name is yours. Therefore no matter how you decide to look at it you will see that you do not need any permission to use the Name. Just be conscious of your rights to the Name and the power that is in the Name.

You don't need any struggle to use what belongs to you. The Name is something that you now have personally. The Name now belongs to you. You therefore know that you have every right (whether legal, birth, proxy or baptismal) to use the Name. Just like Peter said in Acts 3:6 that what he had to give the lame man was the Name of Jesus, you also now have the Name of Jesus to use to get what you want and to help all other people around you. You only need to know the power in that Name and have faith in it.

> *Then Peter said, Silver and gold have I none; but such as I have give I thee: In the name of Jesus Christ of Nazareth rise up and walk.*
> **Acts 3:6**

Peter knew that the Name belonged to him to use and he used it to help the lame man. You should also know that the Name belongs to you and you should use it to help others. The Name has power and will perform miracles, signs and wonders.

The Name of Jesus

The Name is a medium for supernatural power and it is available to every believer. It is you who have to know and be aware of the power that is in that Name. Once you know the power that is in the Name, when you call upon the Name He will answer you.

EVERYTHING YOU WANT IS IN THAT NAME

There is power in that Name. The enemy knows this. That is why the enemy first and foremost seeks to take the Name away from you. You can see this from the case of the Apostles when the leaders arrested them in Acts 4:17-18 they instructed them not to preach in the Name again. That Name was their target.

> *But that it spread no further among the people, let us straitly threaten them, that they speak henceforth to no man in this name.*
>
> *And they called them, and commanded them not to speak at all nor teach in the name of Jesus.*
>
> **Acts 4:17-18**

They were not worried about Jesus Himself they were worried about His Name. Why? This is because as Peter told them it was that Name and faith in the Name that performed the miracle. He also told them that it is only through that Name that they can be saved. People are trying to get salvation through many other Names but the Name Jesus is the only Name that can give you salvation.

Living a Supernatural Life (Volume 2)

It is obvious that Jesus had taught and shown the disciples before He left that miracles, signs and wonders would be done by His Name. That was why they prayed the prayer found in Acts 4:29-30 shown below.

> *And now, Lord, behold their threatenings: and grant unto thy servants, that with all boldness they may speak thy word,*
>
> *By stretching forth thine hand to heal; and that signs and wonders may be done by the name of thy holy child Jesus.*
> **Acts 4:29-30**

The disciples knew the power in that Name even before Jesus left them because when He sent seventy of them out to go and preach His gospel they came back to tell Him that it was in His Name that they cast out devils. They told Him in Luke 10:17 that through His Name even the devils were subjected to them.

> *And the seventy returned again with joy, saying, Lord, even the devils are subject unto us through thy name.*
> **Luke 10:17**

You should note this because the only way that your enemies and adversaries will be subjected to you is through the Name of Jesus Christ. All that you will ever need has been deposited for you in your account in heaven and it is by using that Name as your cheque book that you will draw out your requirements and much more.

There is nothing that you need that is not covered by that Name. It is therefore imperative that you must know how to use that Name to get what you want. That is what we shall discuss in the next Chapter. Whatever you need, you can get it through the Name of Jesus Christ.

Are you under the bondage of sickness and diseases? There is healing in that Name. Are you struggling in your battles against your enemies? There is victory in that Name. Are you suffering from lack or poverty? There is prosperity in that Name. Are you failing in all or most of your endeavours? There is success in that Name. Are you weighed down by the affliction of barrenness? There is fruitfulness in that Name. Do you lack the power with which to move the mountains of your life? There is power in that Name. Do you require a miracle to straighten things in your life? There is the miracle working power in that Name. Therefore use the Name.

REPETITIVE CALL OF THE NAME IS NOT NECESSARY

Many times when people pray they call on the Name of Jesus saying, "In the Name of Jesus" three times, seven times, twenty one times or even many more times thinking that the more the times they call on the Name the more the power that is invoked in their prayer. However if you really look at what they are doing you will come to the conclusion that they do this because of their lack of knowledge about, and their lack of faith in, the power that is in the Name of Jesus.

Living a Supernatural Life (Volume 2)

The Name of Jesus called just once will do anything. If you call the Name once and it doesn't work, calling it over and over will not make it work any faster. It is your own faith in the Name that you must check to see if it is there. If you look at the Apostles' use of that Name you will see that they just use the Name once in all cases. Calling the Name of Jesus once is powerful enough to move any mountain. The Scriptures say, "At the Name of Jesus *every* knee shall bow." *Every* knee covers *all* knees. Many believe that when they call the Name only once the knee will not bow enough so they have to call the Name again and again to give more power to the Name. People who do this are just following their emotions and feelings. They are interacting with God through their emotions and feelings. But the Bible says in John 4:24 and Philippians 3:3, God is a Spirit and we who worship Him must worship Him in spirit and in truth. I know that if I call for anything just once in that Name concerning any situation; the matter is settled. That should be your stand too concerning the Name of Jesus.

> *God is a Spirit: and they that worship him must worship him in spirit and in truth.*
> **John 4:24**
>
> *For we are the circumcision, which worship God in the spirit, and rejoice in Christ Jesus, and have no confidence in the flesh.*
> **Philippians 3:3**

This may offend some people who are used to calling the Name multiple times thinking wrongly that they are backing up their prayer with more power.

The Name of Jesus

But let us look at it in another way so that you can see the faithlessness involved in that kind of prayer. Suppose that a king gives you authority to use his name to get some things or to give a command to some people in his kingdom. When you get to where you have to collect the things or give the command will you have to say, "In the name of the king, in the name of the king" two, three, four or more times before they recognize that the order that you are giving them comes from their king? I don't think so. Will you have to mention the king's name many times before they obey the order of their king? No! Yet we are talking of the King of kings here. It is a sign of our lack of faith in, or lack of knowledge of, the power that is in the Name of Jesus when we call the Name multiple times in support of our prayers believing that will make our prayer more effective.. Satan and his hosts in the kingdom of darkness know the power that is in the Name. You only need to call it once for them to start trembling once they know that you have faith in the Name.

Contrary to our expectation that when we call the Name several times such prayers will receive very quick and immediate answers they may not even be answered because Satan who already knows the power that is in the Name will realize that you don't know the power that is in the Name and he will therefore not obey your command. That Name is so awesome and so powerful that you only need to call it once and every knee should bow. When Satan hears the Name confusion comes into his camp and everybody runs helter skater to find cover. You don't need to help the Name to work. Let me give you another illustration that will help you to understand what I am saying.

Living a Supernatural Life (Volume 2)

When you are sick and you go to a doctor, he will prescribe some drugs. In his prescription he will give you the dosage. If you decide that you want a quick solution to your problem and because of that you decide to overdose yourself the effect of that over dosage will be harmful. You may end up with some other problems rather than solve your problem. The important thing is to know the power that is in the Name and have faith in the Name. Look again at what God said about the Name in Philippians 2:9-10.

> *Wherefore God also hath highly exalted him, and given him a name which is above every name:*
>
> *That at the name of Jesus every knee should bow, of things in heaven, and things in earth, and things under the earth;*
> **Philippians 2:9-10**

There is power in that Name. If you can recognize and have faith in the power that is in that Name and also know that you have been given the authority to use the Name then whenever you command in that Name your command will be obeyed. It is not how many times you call the Name that is important. It is your faith in the Name that determines whether your command will be obeyed or not. I know that it has become the custom of some Christians to call the Name of Jesus three times, seven times or more in support of their prayers. Not only that they even believe that they can give support to the Name so as to get it to work faster by calling the Holy Spirit or the Blood of Jesus several times to support their prayers.

The Name of Jesus

They think that by so doing they are invoking more power. There is no truth in that. The Blood of Jesus has its own work and the Holy Spirit has His work of helping you to pray. But He does not give any additional power to the Name of Jesus. The Name of Jesus on its own called just once will solve any problem provided that you have faith in the Name and in the power that is vested in the Name. If you believe in the power that is in the Name and you have faith in the Name's capabilities then you will know that when you call the Name just once into any situation that situation is settled. You don't need to help the Name to work. It will work on its own. Only just have faith in the Name. What is important is the faith that you have in the power that is in the Name. Once that is in place you can get anything that you want or want done through the Name because as Jesus made us to see from what He said in Matthew 17:20 nothing is impossible to you any longer. The Name of Jesus is what gives you access and the route to getting what you want.

And Jesus said unto them, Because of your unbelief: for verily I say unto you, If ye have faith as a grain of mustard seed, ye shall say unto this mountain, Remove hence to yonder place; and it shall remove; and nothing shall be impossible unto you.
Matthew 17:20

What most Christians do not realize is that the powers that be in the kingdom of darkness know the power that is in the Name of Jesus. They know that when that Name is called with faith in the Name and faith in the power that is in the Name they must bow.

Living a Supernatural Life (Volume 2)

Even Satan their leader knows this. But when they hear you calling the Name three, seven or more times or calling some additional things to aid the Name such s the Holy Spirit and the Blood of Jesus it gives you away. They then know that you don't really know the power that is in that Name and that your strength of faith in the Name is weak. Therefore they refuse to bow to the commands that you made in that Name and you start wondering why. Now you know the reason why. Your knowledge of that Name and your faith in the Name is absolutely necessary. The disciples have come to know the power that is in this Name of Jesus and they made use of that Name to achieve great and mighty works in their own time. Now it is our time to do the miracles, signs and wonders with that Name.

Now we have seen the power and authority that is in the Name of Jesus Christ. We are now going to look at how to use the Name in such a way that the enemy will obey our commands in the Name. That is what we shall discuss in the next Chapter.

CHAPTER 4

HOW TO USE THE NAME JESUS

THE TWO INSTRUCTIONS

We now know that we have the *Name of Jesus* for our use and that the Name, which now belongs to us, is very powerful. The Name of Jesus is a major weapon in our hand for living a supernatural life here on earth. However if you must live the supernatural life then you must know how to use that Name of Jesus correctly and effectively because there is a lot of misuse of that Name by the Christians of today. How do we use the Name?

To know how to effectively make use of the Name, we must study the two promises that Jesus gave to us concerning the use of His Name. Jesus gave us two major instructions and promises concerning the use of His Name to get whatsoever we desire. If we must know how to use His Name to get whatsoever we desire then we must take cognizance of the two instructions and promises and realize that the two instructions are different from one another. Therefore let us look carefully at the two instructions.

Living a Supernatural Life (Volume 2)

Firstly, He said in John 14:13-14 that whatsoever you ask in His Name, He Jesus *will do it*. This is the instruction that most of the Christians of today tend to ignore but as we shall see in this write-up this instruction has its own use, which is very important and should not be ignored but should be used if we want to live a supernatural life here on earth.

> *And whatsoever ye shall ask in my name, that will I do, that the Father may be glorified in the Son.*
>
> *If ye shall ask any thing in my name, I will do it.*
>
> **John 14:13-14**

Secondly, He also said in John 15:16 and John 16:23 that whatsoever you ask the Father in His Name the Father *will give it* you.

> *Ye have not chosen me, but I have chosen you, and ordained you, that ye should go and bring forth fruit, and that your fruit should remain: that whatsoever ye shall ask of the Father in my name, he may give it you.*
>
> **John 15:16**

> *And in that day ye shall ask me nothing. Verily, verily, I say unto you, Whatsoever ye shall ask the Father in my name, he will give it you.*
>
> **John 16:23**

Note that these are two different promises concerning the use of the Name of Jesus Christ to obtain our needs.

How to use the Name Jesus

Therefore we can say that He gave us two different approaches for making our requests in His Name as summarized below.

1. Just *Ask* in Jesus' Name – *Jesus will do it.*
2. *Ask the Father* in Jesus' Name –*The Father will give it.*

Why are these two promises different? What things do we ask directly in Jesus' Name? What things do we ask of the Father in Jesus' Name? When do we use each of these instructions? How do we ask in each case? We know from what Jesus said in John 10:30 that Jesus Christ and the Father are One.

I and my Father are one.
John 10:30

Some people tend to use the above verse to explain that the two different instructions that Jesus gave us above are in effect the same since Jesus and the Father are One. They therefore say that whether you ask the Father or you ask Jesus Christ you are asking the same One. But we ought to know that if Jesus meant the two promises to be the same He would not have given us two separate instructions. *It is not only the "who-you-ask" really whether the Father or Jesus Christ that is the issue here but "how-you-ask" and what you ask for.* We shall see this as we study and analyze the instructions. In any case how did the disciples to whom He spoke the Words directly treat each instruction?

Living a Supernatural Life (Volume 2)

Did they differentiate them or did they treat them as the same as we do today? Jesus Christ has given us the power of attorney to use His Name. But as you can see from the two promises above there are some things that you will ask in that Name from God manifesting as the Father and God as the Father will be the One *to give them* to you. On the other hand, there are some other things that you will ask to be done in that Name and God manifesting as Jesus Christ will be the one *to do them*. This means that God manifesting as the Father *will give* you the things that you asked for and God manifesting as Jesus Christ Himself *will do* the things that you want done.

Giving is different from *doing* therefore the two approaches must be different. However no matter which one of the two methods you are using it is important that you note that you must ask in the Name of Jesus. This means that as we have said earlier the Name of Jesus is the cheque book that you have with which to draw out your needs and requests. You have a Deposit Account with God manifesting as Father from where you can draw your needs. On the other hand you have a Current Account with God manifesting as Jesus Christ from where you can draw works of miracles, signs and wonders. Even though Jesus gave to us two different instructions, methods or accounts for drawing from the Bank of Heaven, most Christians want both their needs and works of miracles from only their deposit account, which involves asking from the Father in Jesus Name even for the things that Jesus has said that He is the One who will do for them. We ask the Father for everything in Jesus' Name.

How to use the Name Jesus

If you are asking God the Father to *do* for you what Jesus has said that it is God manifesting as Jesus Christ who will be the One to *do* then the reply to your request may not come. On the other hand if you are asking God manifesting as Jesus Christ to *give* you what He has said that it is God manifesting as the Father who will *give* then you may never get what you are asking for.

It is expedient therefore to find out the differences between the two methods of approach, how and when to use each one of them and what things you can request for with each method. We must know what the Father *gives* and what Jesus *does*. It is the Father that *gives* but it is Jesus that *does*.

Because the second instruction, which says we should ask the Father is what most Christians use for every request that they make of God we shall discuss that instruction first to see what our approach to it should be. We shall first find out the things that God manifesting as the Father will give so that you can know that God as the Father is the One that we ought to approach to ask for such things. We shall also look at what our method of approach should be in order that we may receive what we ask for in that situation.

After that we shall then find out the things that God manifesting as Jesus Christ Himself will do so that we can ask for these according to how Jesus has instructed us to ask for them. Because Jesus has said that He will be the One to do these we do not have to ask God manifesting as Father to do such things for us. Let us look at the two instructions in detail.

Living a Supernatural Life (Volume 2)

So what do we ask of God in His capacity as the Father in the Name of Jesus, which He will give to us? What do we ask God in His capacity as Jesus Christ to do for us directly?

These are the two questions that we must first answer. We need to know the answers to these questions if we are to get whatever we want from God with ease. To know the answers to these two questions, we must go back into the Scriptures and look at the discourses that led to Jesus making each of the statements and the context in which each statement was made.

ASK THE FATHER IN MY NAME AND THE FATHER WILL GIVE.
WHAT LED TO THIS INSTRUCTION?

This discourse came about when He was telling them that He was the vine and they were the branches, and they were supposed to bring forth fruit and that their fruit might remain. If you look at John 15:16 as written below you will see that He was saying there that they can ask from God as Father whatsoever resources they may need to bring forth fruits and God manifesting as the Father *will give* it to them. That is the essence of what Christ said as is written in John 14:16, as well as John 15:16 and John 16:23.

> *And I will pray the Father, and he shall give you another Comforter, that he may abide with you for ever;*
>
> **John 14:16**

How to use the Name Jesus

> *Ye have not chosen me, but I have chosen you, and ordained you, that ye should go and bring forth fruit, and that your fruit should remain: that whatsoever ye shall ask of the Father in my name, he may give it you.*
>
> **John 15:16**

> *And in that day ye shall ask me nothing. Verily, verily, I say unto you, Whatsoever ye shall ask the Father in my name, he will give it you.*
>
> **John 16:23**

Whatsoever things that you need in order to bear fruit are the things that you should ask of God as your Father to give you. The Holy Spirit whom Jesus called the Comforter is the greatest resource that you need in order to be able to bear fruit and from what Jesus said above God as your Father is the One who **will give** the Holy Spirit to you in the Name of Jesus.

This is confirmed by what Jesus also said in John 14:26 that the Holy Spirit who is the major requirement that you need to bear fruit and do the work will be sent by God in His capacity as the Father in the Name of Jesus. He is the greatest resource that you require to be able to live a successful Christian life.

> *But the Comforter, which is the Holy Ghost, whom the Father will send in my name, he shall teach you all things, and bring all things to your remembrance, whatsoever I have said unto you.*
>
> **John 14:26**

Living a Supernatural Life (Volume 2)

If you look at the Lord's Prayer that Jesus gave as an example in Matthew 6:9-15 of how we should pray to God as Father you will see the type of things that you can ask of God as your Father.

> *After this manner therefore pray ye: Our Father which art in heaven, Hallowed be thy name.*
>
> *Thy kingdom come. Thy will be done in earth, as it is in heaven.*
>
> *Give us this day our daily bread.*
>
> *And forgive us our debts, as we forgive our debtors.*
>
> *And lead us not into temptation, but deliver us from evil: For thine is the kingdom, and the power, and the glory, for ever. Amen.*
>
> *For if ye forgive men their trespasses, your heavenly Father will also forgive you:*
>
> *But if ye forgive not men their trespasses, neither will your Father forgive your trespasses.*
>
> **Matthew 6:9-15**

You will notice that in this prayer to God as the Father most of what Jesus did was to praise and thank the Father. He also asked for the coming of the Kingdom of God. He asked for the forgiveness of sins committed.

He also asked for deliverance from evil as well as guidance from God. The only other request that He made was for the daily bread. These are all things to be given to us by God as our Father. They are not things that we are supposed to do of ourselves by asking it to be done in the Name of Jesus. These then are the sort of things that we should be asking the Father.

ASK IN MY NAME AND I WILL DO IT
WHAT LED TO THIS INSTRUCTION?

The discourse leading to the instruction which is written in John 14:13-14, which we have written on a previous page, came about as a result of what Jesus said in John 14:12 the previous verse as written below where He said that those who believe in Him shall do the works that He did and even greater works than He did. Jesus as God and the Father as God are just two different manifestations and personalities of the same one God. In fact when we study the Scripture it is easy to come to the conclusion that the Jehovah God of the Old Covenant is One and the same with Jesus Christ of the New Covenant

> *Verily, verily, I say unto you, He that believeth on me, the works that I do shall he do also; and greater works than these shall he do; because I go unto my Father.*
> **John 14:12**

It was immediately after this promise that He said that whatsoever you ask in His Name He would do. This instruction to the disciples therefore has to do with how to ask when they want to do the works that Jesus did.

Living a Supernatural Life (Volume 2)

What He is saying here is that whenever we want to do the works that He did we should just ask for it to be done in His Name and it is God manifesting in His capacity as Jesus who will do it. To do the works that He did therefore whatsoever we ask in His Name He would do it. Jesus Christ is the Word of God so command using the Word.

He was not talking of resources to do the work here; He was talking of the *doing* of the work itself. You should know and note the difference between the two cases. When you want to do the works that Jesus did, just command in the Name of Jesus for the work to be done and God manifesting in His capacity as Jesus *will do* it. You do not have to ask God as the Father to do the work because it is the manifestation of God in as Jesus Christ who will do the work. The important thing to note here is that you must know that you are not the one doing the work. God manifesting as Jesus Christ Himself is the One to do the work. All you have to do is just command in the Name of Jesus that it should be done and Jesus will do it. Once you know this you should not have to worry yourself as to whether what you commanded to be done will be done. You should also not feel ashamed that you gave the command and it was not done. Also you should not seek any glory for yourself since you know that you are not the one doing the work. The doing is not your responsibility. Yours is to command for it to be done in the Name of Jesus and leave the rest to God for He is the One to do the work in His manifestation as Jesus Christ. This should be differentiated from the situation where you are asking for the resources to do the works, which are to be given by God manifesting as the Father.

How to use the Name Jesus

WHAT ARE THE WORKS THAT JESUS DID?

Since we said that when you want to do the works that Jesus did you don't have to ask God as Father to do these but you just command that they be done in the Name of Jesus Christ and Jesus will do the works, it is therefore imperative that you must know the works that Jesus did. What then are the works that Jesus did? The works that He did are listed in Acts 10:38

> *How God anointed Jesus of Nazareth with the Holy Ghost and with power: who went about doing good, and healing all that were oppressed of the devil; for God was with him.*
> **Acts 10:38**

Among the works that He did therefore are doing good, healing the sick and healing all that were oppressed of the devil. Additionally you will find His other works listed on the next page. You can see therefore that whenever you want to heal anyone that is oppressed of the devil, you are doing the works that Jesus did. Therefore you just ask that it be done in His Name and God manifesting as Jesus will be the One to do it.

However there is a particular way to ask for these works to be done, which we shall see when we discuss how the disciples used the Name of Jesus Christ. We shall see that *to ask that the Work be done in the Name of Jesus means to command that it be done in His Name.* Some of the other works that Jesus came to do are listed in Luke 4:18-19 below.

Living a Supernatural Life (Volume 2)

> *The Spirit of the Lord is upon me, because he hath anointed me to preach the gospel to the poor; he hath sent me to heal the brokenhearted, to preach deliverance to the captives, and recovering of sight to the blind, to set at liberty them that are bruised,*
>
> *To preach the acceptable year of the Lord.*
> **Luke 4:18-19**

So then, here are the other works that Jesus came to do and from the Scriptures we do know that He actually did them. Therefore the following are also works that we are supposed to be doing too. They are:

Doing good
Healing all that are oppressed of the devil
Preaching the gospel to the poor (***i.e. making the poor rich***)
Healing the brokenhearted
Deliverance of the captives
Giving the recovery of sight to the blind
Setting at liberty them that are bruised
Preaching the acceptable year of the Lord

Therefore when you want to heal the oppressed just command that it be done in the Name of Jesus and Jesus will do it. You don't have to ask God in His capacity as the Father to do this.

When you want to heal the brokenhearted just command that it be done in Jesus' Name and God as Jesus will do it. You don't have to ask God as the Father to do this.

How to use the Name Jesus

When you want to deliver them that have been taken captives just command that it be done in Jesus' Name and God as Jesus will do it. You don't have to ask God as the Father to do this.

When you want to give recovery of sight to the blind just command that it be done in the Name of Jesus and God as Jesus will do it. You don't have to ask God as the Father to do this.

When you want to set people that are bruised at liberty just command that it be done in the Name of Jesus and God as Jesus will do it. You don't have to ask God as the Father to do this.

When you want to preach the Gospel of Christ to the poor to make him rich also do this in the Name of Jesus and God as Jesus will be the One to effect this. You should know that no one can come to Him unless He called them.

Jesus also gave us a list of what He expects us to do as believers in Mark. 16:15-18

> *And he said unto them, Go ye into all the world, and preach the gospel to every creature.*
>
> *He that believeth and is baptized shall be saved; but he that believeth not shall be damned.*
>
> *And these signs shall follow them that believe; In my name shall they cast out devils; they shall speak with new tongues;*

Living a Supernatural Life (Volume 2)

> *They shall take up serpents; and if they drink any deadly thing, it shall not hurt them; they shall lay hands on the sick, and they shall recover.*
>
> **Mark 16:15-18**

These are also some of the works that you are supposed to do. If you want to cast out devils just command that it is done in the Name of Jesus and God as Jesus will do it. Note that the way you ask for things from the Father in the Name of Jesus is different from the way you ask for things to be done by Jesus.

You don't have to ask God as the Father to cast out devils. You command that they be cast out in the Name of Jesus. If you take up serpents or drink any deadly thing just know and believe that in Jesus' Name they will not hurt you and they will not hurt you unless you did so just to boast or to test God.

You don't have to ask God as the Father for these. If you want to heal the sick just lay hands on that sick person and command in the Name of Jesus that he stands up because Jesus has made him whole. You don't have to ask God as the Father to do that. God has already healed him even before he fell sick.

Note that Jesus did not say "In my Name they will ask the Father and He will cast out devils" He did not say "In my Name they will lay hands on the sick and ask the Father to heal him and the Father shall make the sick recover." No!

So why are we doing just that today? Why are we not following His instruction explicitly?

How to use the Name Jesus

In John 14:13 Jesus Himself gave us the reason why He manifesting as Jesus would be the One to do the signs and wonders for you rather than God as the Father. He said that He will do these so that the Father may be glorified in the Son. The NIV version of that Scripture gave a clearer interpretation to what He said. Using the NIV version He said that He will do these so that the Son may bring glory to the Father. Therefore when God in His manifestation as Jesus does these things for you then the glory is going to God as the Father through Jesus Christ. God manifesting as Jesus is the One to do these things for you so that He can take the glory to the Father. Since Jesus said that He and the Father are One, we should realize therefore that Jesus and the Father are just two different manifestations of the same God acting in two different capacities.

And whatsoever ye shall ask in my name, that will I do, that the Father may be glorified in the Son.
John 14:13

And I will do whatever you ask in my name, so that the Son may bring glory to the Father.
John 14:13 NIV

But what most Christians do today is ask God as the Father to do all things in the Name of Jesus even though Jesus has said that it is God manifesting as Jesus who will be the One to do them. There is a major difference in the way we ask for resources from God as the Father and the way we ask when we want to do the works that Jesus did and we should note this difference because your success or failure depends on this.

Living a Supernatural Life (Volume 2)

It is the same God that will answer both requests. He answers your requests for resources in His capacity as God the Father (God manifesting as God the Father). He answers your requests to do the works of miracles, signs and wonders in His capacity as Jesus Christ (God manifesting as Jesus Christ the Son). Therefore we should take cognizance of the differences in the approach for the claiming of these two promises of Jesus. One promise concerns asking for resources required to do the works which the Father *will give* while the other promise concerns asking that the works *be done* by Jesus.

But now from the above you can see why it is wrong to ask God as the Father to do those things that Jesus said that He will do. When you ask God the Father to do them, then what you are doing in effect is that you are not recognizing the truth that God has manifested Himself to us as Jesus who has been made to us the power and the wisdom of God. You are therefore not recognizing the power of God to bring glory to God. Indirectly what that amounts to is that you are the one trying to bring the glory to God yourself. You are not allowing God to use His power to bring glory to Himself.

Therefore it is imperative that you do all these not by asking that God as the Father should do them but by commanding that they be done in Jesus' Name and it is Jesus who is the power of God who will do them. Note again what Peter said in Acts 3:16. He said His Name through faith in His Name was what made the lame man to walk. It was not the God as the Father that made the lame man to walk.

How to use the Name Jesus

And his name through faith in his name hath made this man strong, whom ye see and know: yea, the faith which is by him hath given him this perfect soundness in the presence of you all.

Acts 3:16

Therefore, as you can see, the Name of Jesus has miracle working powers. Jesus Christ is the miracle worker but His Name is the medium for doing the miracle. Peter said that *it was the Name of Jesus Christ and through faith in the Name that healed the lame man at the Beautiful Gate.* It is also the Name of Jesus Christ and through your faith in the Name which comes as a result of your having the knowledge of the great power that is vested in the Name that the miracles will be done whenever you ask for it to be done. *NOTE again, it is His Name and through faith in His Name (NOT THE FATHER) that gets the type of miracles listed above done.*

Jesus said, *"In My Name you will...."* Therefore, you must have faith in that Name of Jesus that whatever you ask to be done in that Name will be done. There is power vested in the Name of Jesus. You must believe this.

Faith in His Name releases the power that can change any situation and you can change the life of anybody through it. This is so because to pray or minister in His Name means to ask and act on His authority so that whatever gets done He alone who is the power of God takes the glory for God.

Living a Supernatural Life (Volume 2)

From the instructions that Jesus Himself gave us in Matthew 28:18-20, which is generally known as the Great Commission you can see that as you obey this command to go and teach all nations He is with you to confirm whatever you say and effect whatever you command with miracles, signs and wonders.

> *And Jesus came and spake unto them, saying, All power is given unto me in heaven and in earth.*
>
> *Go ye therefore, and teach all nations, baptizing them in the name of the Father, and of the Son, and of the Holy Ghost:*
>
> *Teaching them to observe all things whatsoever I have commanded you: and, lo, I am with you alway, even unto the end of the world. Amen.*
>
> **Matthew 28:18-20**

We know that He was with the Apostles and disciples as He promised here because after He left they started following His instructions as He had commanded before He left. We are told in Mark 16:20 that He was working with them confirming the words that they spoke with signs (miracles and wonders). So will He work with you to confirm your words with signs.

> *And they went forth, and preached every where, the Lord working with them, and confirming the word with signs following. Amen.*
>
> **Mark 16:20**

You know just like all laws and commands are made in the Kings Name but it is an officer of the law that executes them, so it is with these instructions that Jesus gave. For every command that you give in the Name of Jesus you must know that the Authority and power to do it is vested in the Name of Jesus Christ even though you are the one giving the commands.

It is you that gives the command but it will be executed through the Name of Jesus. If what you command is to be successfully executed then you must have faith in the authority that is in the Name of Jesus Christ in which the power to execute the command is vested.

HOW DID THE DISCIPLES OBEY THE COMMANDS?

Now that we have looked at the discourse that led to each of the two instructions that Jesus gave concerning the use of His Name we should also now look at what the disciples to whom Jesus gave the two instructions did after He left to see whether they agree with our reasoning above or not. That is we should find out how they followed these two instructions. This means that we must answer the following two questions.

- What things did the disciples ask God the Father to give them in the Name of Jesus and how did they ask for them?

- What did the disciples ask to be done in the Name of Jesus and how did they ask for these to be done?

Living a Supernatural Life (Volume 2)

Let us now look at ten examples from the Book of The Acts of the Apostles, which recounts what the Apostles did after Jesus left. These will show us the way the Apostles executed these two instructions that Jesus gave them. The Apostles were given the instructions directly by Jesus therefore we can assume that whatever they did was according to the instructions that Jesus gave them.

So how did they follow these two instructions of Jesus Christ? If we follow after their footsteps then we cannot go wrong because Jesus must have explained these to them. Here then are some of the various acts of the Apostles below.

1. HEALING A LAME MAN (ACTS 3:1-8)

Now Peter and John went up together into the temple at the hour of prayer, being the ninth hour.

And a certain man lame from his mother's womb was carried, whom they laid daily at the gate of the temple which is called Beautiful, to ask alms of them that entered into the temple;

Who seeing Peter and John about to go into the temple asked an alms.

And Peter, fastening his eyes upon him with John, said, Look on us.

And he gave heed unto them, expecting to receive something of them.

How to use the Name Jesus

Then Peter said, Silver and gold have I none; but such as I have give I thee: In the name of Jesus Christ of Nazareth rise up and walk.

And he took him by the right hand, and lifted him up: and immediately his feet and ankle bones received strength.

And he leaping up stood, and walked, and entered with them into the temple, walking, and leaping, and praising God.
Acts 3:1-8

Peter and John wanted to heal a lame man here. This amounts to doing one of *the works that Jesus did, which is healing the sick.* Peter gave the command, "In the Name of Jesus rise up and walk" This then must be the interpretation of the instruction that Jesus gave concerning asking in His Name and He will do it. Note that Peter did not pray to God asking Him to come and heal the lame man. He just gave a command in the Name of Jesus that the lame man be healed. Therefore to execute that instruction where Jesus said that we should ask in His Name and He would do it, what Peter did was to command in Jesus' Name for what he wanted done.

Giving such a command is equivalent to asking that it be done in the Name of Jesus by Jesus Himself. *We can therefore see that when we want to ask that Jesus do something as we are given in His second instruction we just command that it be done in the Name of Jesus.* When you do that then Jesus Christ Himself will be the One to do the work

2. PRAYING FOR BOLDNESS (ACTS 4:24-31)

And when they heard that, they lifted up their voice to God with one accord, and said, Lord, thou art God, which hast made heaven, and earth, and the sea, and all that in them is:

Who by the mouth of thy servant David hast said, Why did the heathen rage, and the people imagine vain things?

The kings of the earth stood up, and the rulers were gathered together against the Lord, and against his Christ.

For of a truth against thy holy child Jesus, whom thou hast anointed, both Herod, and Pontius Pilate, with the Gentiles, and the people of Israel, were gathered together,

For to do whatsoever thy hand and thy counsel determined before to be done.

And now, Lord, behold their threatenings: and grant unto thy servants, that with all boldness they may speak thy word,

By stretching forth thine hand to heal; and that signs and wonders may be done by the name of thy holy child Jesus.

How to use the Name Jesus

And when they had prayed, the place was shaken where they were assembled together; and they were all filled with the Holy Ghost, and they spake the word of God with boldness.
Acts 4:24-31

The Apostles were not at the point of doing the works that Jesus did here. Instead this was a prayer asking for boldness to be able to do the works whenever they came face to face with situations that warranted doing such works. They wanted to have the boldness to command that the work be done. Boldness is one of the resources that we need to be able to do the work. They also wanted God to stretch forth His hand to heal the sick whenever they call for it to be done in the Name of Jesus. After the arrest and release of the Apostles, *the disciples wanted boldness, a resource that they will require to do the work that Jesus did. (Verse 29)* For this they directed their request to God as their Father. Note that they said that the Lord should also stretch forth his hand to heal and that signs and wonders may be done by the Name of Jesus. God is the healer but the medium that God uses in which the healing power is vested is the Name of Jesus.

That Name of Jesus Christ again is what they said would do the signs and wonders (Verse 30) Therefore by now we know that the Apostles have definite understanding that it is the Name of Jesus that does the miracles, signs and wonders. It is important that you have this understanding also because it will help you to understand how to get the work done. You must have faith in the power that is in the Name of Jesus.

By now you should be getting a picture of what you are supposed to do as a believer when you want to do the works that Jesus did. You should also be getting a picture of what you are supposed to do as a believer when you are not really at the point of doing the works that Jesus did but you are arming yourself with the resources that you will need to do the work when the time comes for you to do so. We have shown that there is a major difference between the prayers for the two cases and that God as the Father is the One that provides what you need to do the work but it is God as Jesus Christ, Himself the power of God, who does the work.

3. CASTING OUT A SPIRIT OF DIVINATION (ACTS 16:16-18)

And it came to pass, as we went to prayer, a certain damsel possessed with a spirit of divination met us, which brought her masters much gain by soothsaying:

The same followed Paul and us, and cried, saying, These men are the servants of the most high God, which shew unto us the way of salvation.

And this did she many days. But Paul, being grieved, turned and said to the spirit, I command thee in the name of Jesus Christ to come out of her. And he came out the same hour.

Acts 16:16-18

Here Paul wanted *to do the works that Jesus did* – To cast out a spirit of divination in a damsel. Note what he did here. He just said in verse 18, *"I command thee in the Name of Jesus Christ to come out of her"* – and the spirit came out of her that same hour. Note that what Paul did here was to issue a command in the Name of Jesus. We have said that when you are face to face with the works that Jesus did what you should do is to command that it be done in the Name of Jesus and God manifesting in His capacity as Jesus Christ Himself would do the work. From what Peter did with the lame man at the Beautiful Gate and what Paul did here we can conclude that the method of asking in this case is to command what we want to be done in the Name of Jesus Christ. *Therefore what you do is not mere asking but commanding in His Name.* For such situations what we should do is to issue a command for what we want done and the command must be issued in the Name of Jesus. You can command a spirit to come out of someone. You can command somebody that is lame to stand up and walk. You can command somebody that is blind to see. You can command somebody that is sick to be healed etc.

4. IMPRISONED AND REQUIRING FREEDOM (ACTS 16:19-36)

And when her masters saw that the hope of their gains was gone, they caught Paul and Silas, and drew them into the marketplace unto the rulers,

And brought them to the magistrates, saying, These men, being Jews, do exceedingly trouble our city,

And teach customs, which are not lawful for us to receive, neither to observe, being Romans.

And the multitude rose up together against them: and the magistrates rent off their clothes, and commanded to beat them.

And when they had laid many stripes upon them, they cast them into prison, charging the jailor to keep them safely:

Who, having received such a charge, thrust them into the inner prison, and made their feet fast in the stocks.

And at midnight Paul and Silas prayed, and sang praises unto God: and the prisoners heard them.

And suddenly there was a great earthquake, so that the foundations of the prison were shaken: and immediately all the doors were opened, and every one's bands were loosed.

And the keeper of the prison awaking out of his sleep, and seeing the prison doors open, he drew out his sword, and would have killed himself, supposing that the prisoners had been fled.

But Paul cried with a loud voice, saying, Do thyself no harm: for we are all here.

How to use the Name Jesus

Then he called for a light, and sprang in, and came trembling, and fell down before Paul and Silas,

And brought them out, and said, Sirs, what must I do to be saved?

And they said, Believe on the Lord Jesus Christ, and thou shalt be saved, and thy house.

And they spake unto him the word of the Lord, and to all that were in his house.

And he took them the same hour of the night, and washed their stripes; and was baptized, he and all his, straightway.

And when he had brought them into his house, he set meat before them, and rejoiced, believing in God with all his house.

And when it was day, the magistrates sent the serjeants, saying, Let those men go.

And the keeper of the prison told this saying to Paul, The magistrates have sent to let you go: now therefore depart, and go in peace.
Acts 16:19-36

Paul and Silas were imprisoned and what they required here was their freedom so that they can be free to go and do the works. Freedom was a resource that they required in order to be able to do the works that Jesus did. So they prayed to God.

Living a Supernatural Life (Volume 2)

You can also see this as deliverance of the captives, which is one of the works that Jesus did. But note what they also did here. They were imprisoned and probably awaiting trial, which could lead to a death sentence. But instead of being cast down they started singing praises unto God and also praying. What they did has taken us away from the realm of the two instructions that Jesus gave into a higher realm, the realm of praising God. That is another dimension to prayer. What we can see here is the power that is in praise. Had they decided to command in the Name of Jesus that their bounds be loosed, they could no doubt have gotten their freedom. However it is obvious to us that they were not just looking for their freedom alone because if that was all that they were looking for they would not have waited in the prison after their bounds were loosed. But they stayed on even in the dark without moving away despite the fact that they had the freedom to escape.

Another major thing that we should note here is the power that is in praise. When they praised God, as a result of the praise there was a great earthquake, so that the foundations of the prison were shaken and all the doors were opened and every prisoner's bound loosed. Whatever prayer can do praise can do. That is much more than they would have asked for. Their praise brought God into their situation and Jesus Christ, the miracle worker, took over the entire situation and did miracles that they would not even have thought of. It not only gave them their freedom, it also gave the other prisoners their freedom. It also led to the salvation of the keeper of the prison and his family. It even led to the change of heart of the magistrates.

I say this because when it was morning the magistrates sent to the keeper of the prison and told him to release Paul and Silas. All these came about as a result of their praising God.

5. HEALING A MAN OF PALSY
(ACTS 9:32-34)

And it came to pass, as Peter passed throughout all quarters, he came down also to the saints which dwelt at Lydda.

And there he found a certain man named Aeneas, which had kept his bed eight years, and was sick of the palsy.

And Peter said unto him, Aeneas, Jesus Christ maketh thee whole: arise, and make thy bed. And he arose immediately.

Acts 9:32-34

Here Peter was at a point where he was faced with a man sick of the palsy **where he had to do the works that Jesus did** to heal Aneas of eight years of palsy. All he said was, **"Aneas, Jesus Christ maketh thee whole, arise and make thy bed"** and he arose immediately. You will see this in verse 34 above. Note this statement of Peter here. He did not have to pray to God the Father. He just commanded Aneas to arise and make his bed telling him that Christ has made him whole. There are some other things that we have to note here. The first and most important one is to find out when Jesus actually made the man whole.

Living a Supernatural Life (Volume 2)

Peter himself answered that question in 1 Peter 2:24. He said that we have been healed by the stripes that Jesus took.

Who his own self bare our sins in his own body on the tree, that we, being dead to sins, should live unto righteousness: by whose stripes ye were healed.
1 Peter 2:24

When did He take the stripe? Jesus took the stripes on the way to the Cross. Therefore the man did not receive his healing at the time that Peter spoke to him. He had been healed before Peter got to him. That was why Peter said Christ **has made thee whole. (Past-tense)** Healing is one of the redemption works that Jesus did. He redeemed our soul and spirit from sin and He redeemed our body from sickness. He did all these over two thousand years ago. But today most Christians only appreciate the redemption of their soul and spirit from sin. They don't seem to know that their body was also redeemed from sickness. You can see therefore that Peter did not call for the healing of this sick person. He said that he was already healed and therefore he should get up. We must have this understanding if we are to live in the miraculous. Christ has healed us of any disease that we can ever have.

This was done over two thousand years ago when He took the stripes on His body on the way to the Cross. That is what we are made to see from what Peter said above. Our mentality should therefore be that we have been healed. *If we agree that we have been healed why then are we still praying to be healed?*

How to use the Name Jesus

Praying for healing should no longer be necessary for us. If we are still praying for healing then we are making God a liar because what that amounts to is that we are saying that we have not been healed. What we have to do is command whatever is causing us to have the symptoms of sickness, despite the truth that we have been healed, to come out in the Name of Jesus. Whatever it is, it is making the Word of God ineffective in our lives, it is mocking our Christianity and we have shown in **Chapter 6** of **Volume 1** of this **"Living a supernatural life"** book series that we have every right to curse it in the Name of Jesus. The problem with most Christians is that we look at the symptoms of diseases and conclude that we are not healed.

But our healing has nothing to do with symptoms. As a Christian you don't have to come to your conclusion based on the symptoms that you can see, feel, hear, taste or smell. Even God gave us this advice through Paul in 2 Corinthians 4:18.

> *While we look not at the things which are seen, but at the things which are not seen: for the things which are seen are temporal; but the things which are not seen are eternal.*
> **2 Corinthians 4:18**

He said that we are not supposed to look at things which are seen by our senses and base our judgments on them, because they are temporary. Since symptoms are seen it follows that they are temporary and we are not supposed to look at them or base our judgments on them. Instead we should look at things which are not seen.

Perfect health which you cannot currently see, hear, taste, smell or feel is what you should look at and base your judgment on. Even though you cannot see the healing at the moment you should remember that as we are told by God through Paul in Romans 4:17 the way God works is that He calls those things which be not as though they were and if you believe Him then those things that He has called will appear or manifest.

> *As it is written, I have made thee a father of many nations, before him whom he believed, even God, who quickeneth the dead, and calleth those things which be not as though they were.*
>
> **Romans 4:17**

Therefore even though perfect health may not exist for you at the moment God has called it as though it had existed for you since two thousand years ago and if you believe God then the perfect health will manifest in your life.

He has said that you have been healed and if you believe Him you can make the healing to manifest. Your healing is already done but it is your stand in faith in God's Word that will make it to manifest.

6. RAISING OF THE DEAD (ACTS 9:36-41)

> *Now there was at Joppa a certain disciple named Tabitha, which by interpretation is called Dorcas: this woman was full of good works and almsdeeds which she did.*

How to use the Name Jesus

And it came to pass in those days, that she was sick, and died: whom when they had washed, they laid her in an upper chamber.

And forasmuch as Lydda was nigh to Joppa, and the disciples had heard that Peter was there, they sent unto him two men, desiring him that he would not delay to come to them.

Then Peter arose and went with them. When he was come, they brought him into the upper chamber: and all the widows stood by him weeping, and shewing the coats and garments which Dorcas made, while she was with them.

But Peter put them all forth, and kneeled down, and prayed; and turning him to the body said, Tabitha, arise. And she opened her eyes: and when she saw Peter, she sat up.

And he gave her his hand, and lifted her up, and when he had called the saints and widows, presented her alive.
Acts 9:36-41

Here again **Peter wanted to do the works that Jesus did, that is raising the dead.** Peter actually found it necessary to pray before doing the work. He prayed first then he faced the work. We are not told to whom Peter directed his prayer. It could have been to God as the Father in which case it will not be surprising because Jesus also did the same thing. What we can say is that Peter probably did not ask the Father to raise the dead. But he remembered that Jesus prayed.

Living a Supernatural Life (Volume 2)

Jesus prayed to God the Father when He was in a similar situation. Therefore if it is to God as the Father that Peter prayed, he probably would be asking for boldness or thanking God in advance like Jesus did when He raised Lazarus from the dead in John 11:39-44 as written below.

> *Then they took away the stone from the place where the dead was laid. And Jesus lifted up his eyes, and said, Father, I thank thee that thou hast heard me.*
>
> *And I knew that thou hearest me always: but because of the people which stand by I said it, that they may believe that thou hast sent me.*
>
> *And when he thus had spoken, he cried with a loud voice, Lazarus, come forth.*
>
> *And he that was dead came forth, bound hand and foot with graveclothes: and his face was bound about with a napkin. Jesus saith unto them, Loose him, and let him go.*
>
> **John 11:39-44**

But we can infer that he did not ask God as the Father to raise the dead. To do the work of Jesus you only need to command it to be done in Jesus Name. Peter could not have prayed that the Father should come and raise the dead. We say this because as written in the Scripture, when he was praying, he did not even face the dead body. It was after the prayer that he turned to the body and commanded her to arise.

How to use the Name Jesus

Peter was one of the three disciples that Jesus took along with Him when He raised Jarius's daughter from the dead. He was also there when Jesus raised Lazarus from the dead. He saw and heard Jesus prayed to the Father thanking the Father for hearing Him always after which He commanded Lazarus to rise up from the dead. It is therefore not surprising that Peter also prayed before issuing the command for the dead person to rise up here.

Therefore if Peter's prayer was to the Father we can assume that he must have prayed the type of prayer that Jesus prayed to the Father not that the Father should come and raise the dead. Something that we should also note here is that in verse 40 we are told that Peter asked all the people to leave the room before kneeling down to pray. Note that this is done to make sure that the unbelief of such people does not become an impediment to the fulfillment of the order given. It was after the prayer that he then turned to the body and commanded her to arise. Note that Peter did this by following the footsteps of Jesus, doing it as Jesus did when He raised the daughter of Jairus from the dead as written in Mark 5:35-42.

> *While he yet spake, there came from the ruler of the synagogue's house certain which said, Thy daughter is dead: why troublest thou the Master any further?*
>
> *As soon as Jesus heard the word that was spoken, he saith unto the ruler of the synagogue, Be not afraid, only believe.*

And he suffered no man to follow him, save Peter, and James, and John the brother of James.

And he cometh to the house of the ruler of the synagogue, and seeth the tumult, and them that wept and wailed greatly.

And when he was come in, he saith unto them, Why make ye this ado, and weep? the damsel is not dead, but sleepeth.

And they laughed him to scorn. But when he had put them all out, he taketh the father and the mother of the damsel, and them that were with him, and entereth in where the damsel was lying.

And he took the damsel by the hand, and said unto her, Talitha cumi; which is, being interpreted, Damsel, I say unto thee, arise.

And straightway the damsel arose, and walked; for she was of the age of twelve years. And they were astonished with a great astonishment.
Mark 5:35-42

You can see in verse 40 above that Jesus also got all the people to leave except the girl's father and mother and His three disciples. Only these five people went with Him into the girl's room where she was lying. There is one significant thing that happened here that we must take note of.

How to use the Name Jesus

The significance of this is that whenever you are at a point where you want miracles, signs and wonders to be done and you perceive that the majority of the people around have already fixed their minds on the fact that what you want done cannot be possible then it is advisable to ask the people to leave. You need to have with you where possible only the people who can believe that what you want to do can be done and will be done. You don't need to have around you people who will exhibit doubt or give contrary comments when you command the miraculous act to be done in the Name of Jesus. Peter actually followed Jesus' example here. Therefore there can be no reason why we should suppose that his prayer would be any different from that of Jesus.

There is nowhere in the Book of Acts of the Apostles where you will find that the disciples prayed to the Father asking the Father to come and do the works that Jesus did such as healing, raising the dead, opening the eyes of the blind or casting out devils etc. No! What they normally did was to command that such works be done in the Name of Jesus Christ and our Lord Jesus Christ always responded by confirming their words, establishing their commands and doing what they have commanded.

That is what He had promised before He left this world. In fact in the case of healing the sick or cripple they sometimes commanded the victims to stand up telling them that Jesus Christ had already healed them. Why then must we do it in a different way today? Why are we now praying asking God as the Father to come and heal the sick in the Name of Jesus?

We ought to follow the footsteps of the disciples to whom Jesus Christ spoke and gave these promises. They heard the instructions of Jesus Christ directly from His mouth and we can presume that they followed them to the letter. We must have the understanding that we have already been healed because that is what the Scriptures say.

7. HEALING OF A CRIPPLE (ACTS 14:8-10)

And there sat a certain man at Lystra, impotent in his feet, being a cripple from his mother's womb, who never had walked:

The same heard Paul speak: who stedfastly beholding him, and perceiving that he had faith to be healed,

Said with a loud voice, Stand upright on thy feet. And he leaped and walked.

Acts 14:8-10

Here is a case of the healing of a man who was a cripple from his mother's womb. This then was a case where Paul wanted to do the works that Jesus Christ did. All Paul did here was to command the crippled man to stand up since he perceived that the man had the faith to be healed.

The man heard the Word of God spoken by Paul and his faith increased Paul said with a loud voice, "Stand upright on thy feet" and the man leaped and walked. We had discussed earlier the healing of a lame man at the Beautiful Gate of the Temple by Peter.

What Paul did here was similar to what Peter did at the Beautiful Gate even though he did not mention the Name of Jesus. However his command was still based on the authority given to us by Jesus Christ. One major thing to note in this case however is what the Scripture said that Paul perceived. He perceived that the man had the faith to be healed. The faith must have come as a result of the man listening to the Word of God that Paul spoke or preached.

In the case of the man at the Beautiful Gate we were not told that the man had the faith to be healed. His faith was not necessary for him to be healed. However Peter had faith in the power that is in the Name of Jesus Christ because he knew that the power that is in the Name of Jesus could heal him. That was why Peter commanded him to stand up. He said that it was the Name of Jesus and faith in the Name of Jesus that healed the man. Therefore if you have faith in that Name it does not matter if the sick man has no faith in the Name, when you command he will still be made whole. God cannot be put in a strait jacket. The Name of Jesus has the power to heal the sick but either the sick person or the one giving the command or both of them must have faith in the Name.

8. RAISING OF THE DEAD (ACTS 20:9-12)

And there sat in a window a certain young man named Eutychus, being fallen into a deep sleep: and as Paul was long preaching, he sunk down with sleep, and fell down from the third loft, and was taken up dead.

Living a Supernatural Life (Volume 2)

> *And Paul went down, and fell on him, and embracing him said, Trouble not yourselves; for his life is in him.*
>
> *When he therefore was come up again, and had broken bread, and eaten, and talked a long while, even till break of day, so he departed.*
>
> *And they brought the young man alive, and were not a little comforted.*
>
> **Acts 20:9-12**

Eutychus who was listening to Paul's preaching fell asleep and fell from the third floor window. He fell down from the third loft and we are told that he was taken up dead. Therefore this was a case of Paul wanting to do the works that Jesus did, that of raising the dead.

Paul just fell on the boy and embraced him and then told the people not to be troubled and that the boy's life was in him. Even though Paul was not there when Jesus raised the dead he followed the footsteps of Jesus. If you want to raise somebody from the dead you must believe that such a person is not dead but asleep. When Jesus wanted to raise the dead daughter of a woman as written in Luke 8:49-54 and when He wanted to raise Lazarus from the dead as written by John the Apostle in John 11:11-23 He did not acknowledge that they were dead. He said that they were sleeping

> *While he yet spake, there cometh one from the ruler of the synagogue's house, saying to him, Thy daughter is dead; trouble not the Master.*

How to use the Name Jesus

But when Jesus heard it, he answered him, saying, Fear not: believe only, and she shall be made whole.

And when he came into the house, he suffered no man to go in, save Peter, and James, and John, and the father and the mother of the maiden.

And all wept, and bewailed her: but he said, Weep not; she is not dead, but sleepeth.

And they laughed him to scorn, knowing that she was dead.

And he put them all out, and took her by the hand, and called, saying, Maid, arise.
Luke 8:49-54

These things said he: and after that he saith unto them, Our friend Lazarus sleepeth; but I go, that I may awake him out of sleep.

Then said his disciples, Lord, if he sleep, he shall do well.

Howbeit Jesus spake of his death: but they thought that he had spoken of taking of rest in sleep.

Then said Jesus unto them plainly, Lazarus is dead.

> *And I am glad for your sakes that I was not there, to the intent ye may believe; nevertheless let us go unto him.*
>
> *Then said Thomas, which is called Didymus, unto his fellowdisciples, Let us also go, that we may die with him.*
>
> *Then when Jesus came, he found that he had lain in the grave four days already.*
>
> *Now Bethany was nigh unto Jerusalem, about fifteen furlongs off:*
>
> *And many of the Jews came to Martha and Mary, to comfort them concerning their brother.*
>
> *Then Martha, as soon as she heard that Jesus was coming, went and met him: but Mary sat still in the house.*
>
> *Then said Martha unto Jesus, Lord, if thou hadst been here, my brother had not died.*
> *But I know, that even now, whatsoever thou wilt ask of God, God will give it thee.*
>
> *Jesus saith unto her, Thy brother shall rise again.*
>
> **John 11:11-23**

If you look at the two passages above you will see that Jesus did not acknowledge that the daughter of the woman was dead.

How to use the Name Jesus

Neither did He acknowledge that Lazarus was dead except that His disciples did not understand Him so He had to tell them that Lazarus was dead. In Luke 8:52, He told the woman that she should not weep and that her daughter was merely sleeping. In the case of Lazarus, in John 11:11, He also said that Lazarus was asleep and he was going to wake him up.

It was when the disciples could not understand or comprehend what He was telling them that He told them that Lazarus was dead. Paul also did not agree that the boy was dead. He told the people there not to worry and that the boy's life was still in him. We are told that he fell on the boy and he probably prayed when he fell on the boy but we are not told what he said.

You must know that when you are face to face with the works that Jesus did and you have to take immediate action wanting miracles signs and wonders to be done then even though prayers to the Father may be offered at that point, the most imperative thing for you to do after that is to take control of the situation by giving the command for the necessary miracle to be done in the Name of Jesus.

That is what God expects you to do. As we had seen earlier in Exodus 14:15-16, that was what God told Moses when Moses cried to Him when the children of Israel got to the Red Sea. Moses cried to God but God told him to act. This is discussed further in detail in *Chapter 5* of this same book titled *"Your mouth is the vehicle"* in the section of that chapter titled, *"Speak to your mountains"*.

> *And the LORD said unto Moses, Wherefore criest thou unto me? speak unto the children of Israel, that they go forward:*
>
> *But lift thou up thy rod, and stretch out thine hand over the sea, and divide it: and the children of Israel shall go on dry ground through the midst of the sea.*
>
> **Exodus 14:15-16**

When you are face to face with a situation that requires that you do the works that Jesus did then it is time to take control of the situation and give the necessary command to cause miracles, signs and wonders to be done in the Name of Jesus. In such a situation you may not have time for prayer.

9. DEALING WITH A SERPENT BITE
(ACTS 28:3-6)

> *And when Paul had gathered a bundle of sticks, and laid them on the fire, there came a viper out of the heat, and fastened on his hand.*
>
> *And when the barbarians saw the venomous beast hang on his hand, they said among themselves, No doubt this man is a murderer, whom, though he hath escaped the sea, yet vengeance suffereth not to live.*
>
> *And he shook off the beast into the fire, and felt no harm.*

How to use the Name Jesus

Howbeit they looked when he should have swollen, or fallen down dead suddenly: but after they had looked a great while, and saw no harm come to him, they changed their minds, and said that he was a god.
Acts 28:3-6

This is a case that fulfills what Jesus said as written in Mark 16:17-18. He said that in His Name we shall take up serpents and we shall not be hurt. This means that if we are bitten by serpents, we shall not be hurt. He did not even say that we have to pray. Paul believed what Jesus said therefore when he was bitten by the snake he just shook the snake off into the fire and continued to do what he was doing. He was not in any way disturbed and he was not hurt.

And these signs shall follow them that believe; In my name shall they cast out devils; they shall speak with new tongues;

They shall take up serpents; and if they drink any deadly thing, it shall not hurt them; they shall lay hands on the sick, and they shall recover.
Mark 16:17-18

We are not told that he prayed to the Father here to save him from the venom of the snake. Neither did he give any command concerning the snake bite. He just believed what Jesus said and acted on it. He did not show any sign of doubt, unbelief or fear. That is the way to take these promises of Jesus. You must believe that they are true and if you do so you will not exhibit any doubt, fear or anxiety.

You will be calm and confident when you are faced with any dangerous and precarious situation even if it is life threatening. Jesus did not say above that they shall take up serpents and when they pray unto the Father it shall not hurt them. He said that they shall take up serpents and it shall not hurt them.

10. HEALING THE SICK OF FEVER (ACTS 28:7-10)

In the same quarters were possessions of the chief man of the island, whose name was Publius; who received us, and lodged us three days courteously.

And it came to pass, that the father of Publius lay sick of a fever and of a bloody flux: to whom Paul entered in, and prayed, and laid his hands on him, and healed him.

So when this was done, others also, which had diseases in the island, came, and were healed:

Who also honoured us with many honours; and when we departed, they laded us with such things as were necessary.
Acts 28:7-10

This is a case of healing, the healing of the father of Publius who was sick of a fever. We are told that **Paul prayed and laid his hands on him and healed him**. Paul was following the instruction that Jesus gave in Mark 16:17-18 concerning the laying on of hands on the sick which we have previously discussed.

How to use the Name Jesus

Jesus had said that one of the signs that will follow them that believe is that they will lay hands on the sick and they shall recover. We have discussed this previously. **What we should note here however was that Paul prayed first and then laid his hands on the sick man.** What most Christians do today is lay hands on the sick and then pray while their hands are on the sick. We are not told to whom Paul prayed. Even if he had directed his prayer to God the Father, he could not have asked the Father to come and heal the man because it was after the prayer that he then laid his hands on him *and healed him*. He could have asked for faith, for boldness, for revelation knowledge, for Jesus Christ to fulfill His promise of signs and wonders to be done, etc. We now know what we should ask God as the Father in the Name of Jesus and what we should command to be done in the Name of Jesus. When you lay hands on the sick, you then command the sickness to come out in the Name of Jesus. We now know that we have been healed by the stripes that Jesus took on the Cross because what God said through Apostle Peter in 1 Peter 2:24 is not a promise of healing.

> *Who his own self bare our sins in his own body on the tree, that we, being dead to sins, should live unto righteousness: by whose stripes ye were healed.*
> **1 Peter 2:24**

God did not say, *"Ye will be healed by the stripes that Jesus took"*. **NO!** God said, *"Ye were healed by the stripes that Jesus took"*. This is a statement of an accomplished fact not a promise of something to be done.

The statement is that you have been healed by the stripes that Jesus took on the Cross at Calvary and this is true for all people. All you need to do is to now ask yourself the following questions. Is the Word of God true? If you are convinced that it is true, then ask yourself this question. Did Jesus take the stripes?

If you are convinced that He did, then you know that you have been healed. This may sound strange but you don't need to pray for your healing, just believe it, and claim it. Then start living in the reality of it by making sure that you do those things that the sickness or disease has attempted to stop you from doing. As you do these, you will find that your freedom from the disease or sickness will manifest and become apparent not only to you but to everyone else.

You will not only gain your freedom from diseases but you will also have the faith and the courage to tackle diseases in any other person and get him his freedom. You have seen what the Apostles of old did after Jesus left whenever they wanted to do the works that Jesus did. Why then do we Christian of today completely neglect this instruction of Jesus to command in His Name when we want to do the works that He did?

WHY DO WE NOT FOLLOW THESE INSTRUCTIONS?

Why do we turn to God the Father instead and ask the Father in the Name of Jesus to come and do for us the works that Jesus did such as healing the sick?

How to use the Name Jesus

I guess this is because of the instruction of God through the Apostle James in James 5:14-16 where he told us that if anyone is sick he should call for the elders and the elders should pray over him. Definitely you will ask the question therefore, "What about the prayer of faith that James said should be prayed over the sick, which is written below? Doesn't that contradict my saying that you do not need to pray the type of prayer that most Christians now pray for the healing of the sick?"

> *Is any sick among you? let him call for the elders of the church; and let them pray over him, anointing him with oil in the name of the Lord:*
>
> *And the prayer of faith shall save the sick, and the Lord shall raise him up; and if he have committed sins, they shall be forgiven him.*
>
> *Confess your faults one to another, and pray one for another, that ye may be healed. The effectual fervent prayer of a righteous man availeth much.*
>
> **James 5:14-16**

Let us look at that Scriptures very closely. If you study the context of that Scripture very carefully, you will see that in truth it does not contradict what I am saying. Let me prove this to you.

There are three things in particular that I want you to note in that Scripture from these instructions of God through James. The three things that I will like you to note and consider are the following:

Living a Supernatural Life (Volume 2)

1. The question asked, *"Is any sick among you?"*
2. The directive *"Let him call the elders"*
3. The statement, *"The prayer of faith shall save the sick."*

IS ANY SICK AMONG YOU?

Firstly, I want you to note this question, which God asked through James here. *Is any sick among you?* That was an unusual question. The fact that God asked that question must mean that being sick was an unusual thing among them; otherwise there will be no need to ask that kind of question. It must mean that it was not common among them to be sick. We can conclude that they mostly knew their rights to the healing part of their redemption. If it were common to be sick among them, God would have said, "If anyone is sick among you," or "When anyone is sick among you", or "For those that are sick among you". He wouldn't have asked the question *"Is any sick among you?"*

LET HIM CALL THE ELDERS

Secondly, I want you to note that He said, *"Let him call the Elders"*. By this you can conclude from what God was telling them through James that whoever was sick among them must have missed the point somewhere. He must have either not known yet that he had been healed, or on the other hand, he has not believed the truth that Christ's redemption work had healed him. The reason therefore, why he was to call the Elders was because the Elders, who were supposed to be the leaders in the Church, were at least expected to know and believe these.

How to use the Name Jesus

They were supposed to know and believe in the truth that our salvation and redemption covers not only the healing and redemption of our souls from sin and its consequences but also the healing and redemption of our bodies from diseases as well as sicknesses and their consequences. This means that our healing is already done. It was assumed that the Elders should know that we had already been healed by the stripes that Jesus took. God is making us to know here that those who are sick are those who do not know or believe that healing is one of the benefits available in the atonement for them. That is, those who do not know that healing is a part of the benefits that they should derive from their redemption; which Isaiah referred to in Isaiah 12:3 as water, which they are supposed to draw out of the wells of salvation.

> ***Therefore with joy shall ye draw water out of the wells of salvation.***
> **Isaiah 12:3**

Most often the people who are troubled by sickness are people who have not seen or received this revelation that their sicknesses and diseases had been laid on Jesus Christ's body through the stripes that He took when He died for us. A Christian who cannot discern properly this truth that Jesus Christ had carried his diseases and sicknesses by the stripes that He took on His Body, will continue to be sick from time to time. That is what God said through Paul in 1 Corinthians 11:29-30 about our eating the Body of Christ not knowing what the Body represents and what it did for us. The Blood of Christ cleansed and washed away our sins but it was His Body that healed our body of its diseases.

Living a Supernatural Life (Volume 2)

For he that eateth and drinketh unworthily, eateth and drinketh damnation to himself, not discerning the Lord's body.

For this cause many are weak and sickly among you, and many sleep.
                    1 Corinthians 11:29-30

Both our sins and our sicknesses had been laid on Jesus on the Cross and He has taken away our sicknesses and diseases by the stripes that He took on His body on that Cross. Therefore as Christians, we do not have to be sick anymore just as we do not have to sin anymore. However just as many Christians still sin even though they now have power over sin, so also many Christians still live under the bondage of diseases and sicknesses even though they have been healed of these and they no longer have to bear diseases and sicknesses. As Christians, we need to know and live our daily life in the reality of this truth that all our sicknesses and diseases had been carried by Jesus on His body, and we don't have to carry these anymore.

If any Christian is carrying diseases or sicknesses on his body, it means that such a Christian is not living his life with that consciousness. Either he doesn't know that he has been healed or he knows but is not willing to believe this. **Get the right Scriptural perspective of yourself.** From what God is saying through James here, the Elders should at least, have enough faith in the truth that healing was already theirs, and that the healing of that sick person was already done. To buttress this point, you can see that He said that the Elders are to pray ***the prayer of faith*** for the sick person.

He did not say that they should pray a *prayer of healing* for the healing of the sick person. Since what the Scriptures say is that the sick person is already healed, they don't have to pray a prayer for his healing. *This Prayer of faith is to save and not to heal the sick* because the sick is already healed.

WHAT THEN IS THIS PRAYER OF FAITH?

Thirdly let us look at this *Prayer of faith*. Faith in what was He talking about? To my understanding, the prayer of faith is a prayer in which the Elders should affirm in this case their faith in the Covenant statements and promises of God regarding our having been healed. These include the statements that God had made to us believers concerning the benefits accruing to us through our salvation. This must be a prayer in which the Elders will affirm their faith in the truth that the sick person had been healed by the stripes that Jesus took. The Elders are then to use their authority, based on these statements of truth, to command the sick person to rise up in the Name of Jesus. They should command that whatever is causing the sickness should depart from the sick person in the Name of Jesus and to command the devil to keep his hands off that sick person in the Name of Jesus. The Elders are supposed to know that they have been given authority over the devil and his hosts to command them to hands off that individual. They also must have the faith to know that when they give their commands in the Name of Jesus, they will be obeyed. They should also know that they are now taken as righteous before God because they have been given the righteousness of Christ as a gift from God and now Christ has been made righteousness unto them.

Living a Supernatural Life (Volume 2)

They should also know and believe that they have not only been given righteousness as a gift but they are also sanctified and their sanctification has empowered them to be able to live a righteous life. That is the essence of what we are told by God through Paul written down in Romans 5:17-18 as well as in 1 Corinthians 1:30 by the same Paul. Therefore they should be able to give the command for the manifestation of the healing. Knowing and believing that they are righteous they will have no sin-complex. Therefore their prayers are bound to avail much before God.

> *For if by one man's offence death reigned by one; much more they which receive abundance of grace and of the gift of righteousness shall reign in life by one, Jesus Christ.*
>
> *Therefore as by the offence of one judgment came upon all men to condemnation; even so by the righteousness of one the free gift came upon all men unto justification of life.*
> **Romans 5:17-18**

> *But of him are ye in Christ Jesus, who of God is made unto us wisdom, and righteousness, and sanctification, and redemption:*
> **1 Corinthians 1:30**

We can see therefore that when the Elders, Pastors, and Church leaders of today now go to a sick person and start praying for such a sick person saying, "Lord heal him, Lord heal him", as is done these days, that is not the *prayer of faith* that God was talking about through James.

No doubt, they pray with a lot of zeal, but it is zeal that is not according to knowledge just as Paul said concerning the Roman Christians in Romans 10:2 that they had a zeal of God but not according to knowledge.

For I bear them record that they have a zeal of God, but not according to knowledge.
Romans 10:2

That is the reason why the healing does not come these days, as they ought to, because it is obvious that the Elders are not exercising their faith in God's Word. They may not even have the full knowledge of what God's Word says about our healing. They themselves may still have the belief that the healing is yet to come. This means that they have not discerned properly the role of the Body of Christ in the plan of our redemption. If what they want to pray for is the healing of the sick man then they are not really different from the sick man or from those that are not elders in their understanding of salvation. The sick man can also pray for his healing.

Whoever prays a prayer of healing for the sick man shows that he or she has not really gotten the complete understanding of the redemption work that Christ came to this earth to do. His redemptive work covers both the healing of our souls from sin and its effects and the healing of our bodies from diseases and sicknesses and their effects. James did not say the prayer of faith will heal the sick. No! He said the prayer of faith shall save the sick. Paul said that many of the Christians in the Church of Corinth were weak and sick because they did not discern properly the role of the body of Christ in the Redemption plan.

Living a Supernatural Life (Volume 2)

If the prayer of healing was what God intended that the Elders should pray, then He could just have said that the sick man should pray for his healing. God's Word says we have been healed by the stripes that Jesus Christ took on the Cross. Therefore we don't need to pray for healing. What we need to do is to command the sickness out of the sick person.

If we go and pray for healing for such a sick man therefore, we are either acting in ignorance, which means that we are not aware that the man had been healed or we are acting in unbelief, not believing what God has said concerning the healing that He has already given to man. In that case we are making God a liar. In Romans 10:17 we are told that faith comes by hearing, and hearing by the Word of God.

> *So then faith cometh by hearing, and hearing by the word of God.*
> **Romans 10:17**

Therefore if what you are hearing is "God please come and heal in Jesus Name", then your faith will be in the fact that the healing is yet to come.

That is what you will have faith for. But if what you are hearing is "God has healed you, therefore rise up and walk", then you will have faith in the truth that the healing is already done. If the Elders or leaders of the Church in the New Testament times were no different from the sick man in the level of their belief, and their understanding of the healing rights that we now have in the New Covenant, God would not have given them that instruction.

How to use the Name Jesus

The Elders in the Church are therefore supposed to have an understanding of the healing, which is already done, that Jesus Christ has purchased for us in the redemption plan. The prayer of faith is a prayer with authority demanding of the devil to keep his hands off that sick person, and claiming his healing, which was already accomplished over two thousand years ago when Jesus Christ died for us on the Cross at Calvary. It is not supposed to be a beggarly prayer begging God to come and heal the sick person. This is so because once you pray asking God to come and heal the sick person, it means that you do not have faith in the Word, which says that the sick man is already healed or you are making God a liar. You must also realize that the healing of the sick is one of the works that Jesus said that believers are supposed to do therefore when healing the sick you just command the sickness to come out in the Name of Jesus as commanded to do. That you may realize that with the work of salvation and redemption, which Jesus Christ did, you have already been healed, look at what God said through Paul in Galatians 3:13 and Ephesians 1:3, and through Peter in 2 Peter 1:2-3.

> *Christ hath redeemed us from the curse of the law, being made a curse for us: for it is written, Cursed is every one that hangeth on a tree:*
> **Galatians 3:13**

> *Blessed be the God and Father of our Lord Jesus Christ, who hath blessed us with all spiritual blessings in heavenly places in Christ:*
> **Ephesians 1:3**

Living a Supernatural Life (Volume 2)

> *Grace and peace be multiplied unto you through the knowledge of God, and of Jesus our Lord,*
>
> *According as his divine power hath given unto us all things that pertain unto life and godliness, through the knowledge of him that hath called us to glory and virtue:*
>
> 2 Peter 1:2-3

God is saying in these verses that:
You **have been healed** by the stripes that Jesus took.
You **have been redeemed** from the curse of the law.
You **have been blessed** with all spiritual blessings.
You **have been given** all things that pertain unto life.

God did not say that:
You **will be healed** by the stripes that Jesus took.
You **will be redeemed** from the curse of the law.
You **will be blessed** with all spiritual blessings.
You **will be given** all things that pertain unto life.

If you have been healed from your diseases by the stripes that Jesus took why are you still praying to God asking Him to heal you? It means that you do not believe what God said or you are making Him a liar..

If you have been redeemed from the curse of the law, why are you still praying to God to redeem you from such a curse? Why do I say this? I say this because we know that every disease and sickness is a part of the Curse of the Law and since you have been redeemed from the Curse of the Law it means that you have been redeemed from every disease and sickness.

How to use the Name Jesus

When you pray to be healed you are saying in effect that you have not been redeemed from the curse of the Law and what you are asking for is to be redeemed from it all over again.

If you have been blessed with all spiritual blessings, why are you still praying to God to bless you, knowing that all blessings are first spiritual before they manifest physically?

If you have been given all things that pertain unto life through the knowledge of Christ, why are you still praying to God to give you those things that pertain unto life? Since you get these through the knowledge of Christ you would do well to have a good knowledge of Christ, which is equivalent to having a good knowledge of the Word of God so that you can lay hold on the *"all things"* that God has already given you. This is because it is through the knowledge of the Word of God that you will lay hold on these things.

We can see therefore that many of us Christians are struggling to have what they already have? They are struggling to be what they are already? You don't have to pray to God for something that God said that He has already given you. If you are doing that then you are making God a liar.

What most Christians don't know however, is that even though God has given them all these things they will still have to contend with the enemy for them before they can get them even though they are already theirs. You can see this from what God told the children of Israel in Deuteronomy 2:24.

Living a Supernatural Life (Volume 2)

> *Rise ye up, take your journey, and pass over the river Arnon: behold, I have given into thine hand Sihon the Amorite, king of Heshbon, and his land: begin to possess it, and contend with him in battle.*
>
> **Deuteronomy 2:24**

He said that He has given them Sihon the Amorite, the king of Heshbon and his land. But He said that they will still have to rise up and begin to possess it by contending in battle for it with that king. God has also healed you. He has blessed you with all things. But you still have to contend with Satan and his forces for your health and for all that God has given you in order to possess them.

You should not be praying to God asking Him to heal you. He has already healed you but you can only possess your health by contending with Satan and his forces for it. You should not be praying to God to bless you. He has already blessed you. If you pray to God asking Him to do something, which He said that He has already done it means that you either do not know or you do not believe that He has done it. You are then making God a liar.

God has said through Prophet Hosea in Hosea 4:6 that the lack of knowledge is what leads His people to destruction. He also said through Isaiah in Isaiah 5:13 that the lack of knowledge is what leads His people into captivity. It is the lack of knowledge that has put many Christians in the bondage of sickness and diseases. Look at what He said below.

How to use the Name Jesus

My people are destroyed for lack of knowledge: because thou hast rejected knowledge, I will also reject thee, that thou shalt be no priest to me: seeing thou hast forgotten the law of thy God, I will also forget thy children.

Hosea 4:6

Therefore my people are gone into captivity, because they have no knowledge: and their honourable men are famished, and their multitude dried up with thirst.

Isaiah 5:13

We have discussed in *Volume 1* of the *"Living a supernatural life"* book series the role of God's angels as ministering to the heirs of salvation of which you are now one if you are born again. We have noted that they hearken not just to the Word of God but **to the voice of the Word of God.**

Therefore when the enemy comes with problems for which you know that God has already given you a solution, you know that it is the enemy who is not allowing you to take a hold of the solution that God has already provided for you.

That is a good situation in which you can command God's angels, by giving voice to the appropriate Word of God that will give you a solution to the problem. You can then command the angels of God in the Name of Jesus to go and take the hands of the enemy away from the situation and therefore make sure that the Word of God is fulfilled.

Living a Supernatural Life (Volume 2)

You may be wondering why I said earlier that we know that every disease and every sickness is a part of the Curse of the Law. I said this because we can see from Deuteronomy 28:61 that God grouped all diseases and sicknesses not already mentioned under the Curse of the Law and added them also to the Curse thereby making every disease a part of the Curse of the Law.

> *Also every sickness, and every plague, which is not written in the book of this law, them will the LORD bring upon thee, until thou be destroyed.*
> **Deuteronomy 28:61**

But note that God said, *"You have been"* NOT *"You will be"* redeemed from the curse of the law. This confirms the truth that you are already healed. If you have been healed, then you are healed. It is not something that you are expecting. It is something that is already done. Some people will say that it is a matter of semantics, but no, you must follow what God really said. It is really like what you have in a legal argument concerning a legal Agreement in a court of law. You have to examine all the phrases and clauses in the legal Agreement. It may mean the difference between your winning and losing the case and in this case, sometimes even between life and death.

Satan and his demons know those who have authority.

They know those who know that they have authority.

They know those who know how to enforce their authority.

How to use the Name Jesus

They also know those who are determined to enforce their authority and it is such people that they respect.

You can see these from what the evil spirits said when they met the seven sons of Sceva in Acts 19:13-15, who despite the fact that they were not sure of their authority over the evil spirits still attempted to command them.

Then certain of the vagabond Jews, exorcists, took upon them to call over them which had evil spirits the name of the Lord Jesus, saying, We adjure you by Jesus whom Paul preacheth.

And there were seven sons of one Sceva, a Jew, and chief of the priests, which did so.

And the evil spirit answered and said, Jesus I know, and Paul I know; but who are ye?
Acts 19:13-15

Those spirits recognized the people that were talking to them. There are also spirits behind most diseases and such spirits do recognize whoever is trying to command them. You have to make sure that you are recognized by the forces of darkness and that wherever you are the forces of darkness operating in that vicinity will start to tremble and react because you are there.

They know that you have authority over them. Therefore, from today, when sickness comes knocking, if you are born again, use the authority that you have to tell it where to go. When you speak to it you are actually speaking to the spirit behind it.

Living a Supernatural Life (Volume 2)

You have the authority to tell Satan to hands off, and he must leave, unless you are not exercising that authority with a conviction of faith. Exercising that authority requires that you have boldness, an unflinching and resolute conviction of faith and be in full submission to God. ***Those who know how to exercise their authority with conviction are the ones that Satan and his agents respect and obey.*** The evil forces of darkness operating in your vicinity must acknowledge your presence and respect the authority that you have over them to command them. Don't give any evil spirit the opportunity or the freedom to exercise any power over you.

THERE IS POWER IN THAT NAME

Jesus said miracles, signs and wonders will be following you. He said that you would do these miracles and wonders in His Name. This means that at the call of His Name, you will be able to do all these things. A few days after Jesus left this earth, Peter used that Name to raise a lame man at the Beautiful Gate as described in Acts 3:6. He said to the lame man,

> *"Silver and gold have I none; but such as I have give I thee: In the name of Jesus Christ of Nazareth rise up and walk."*
>
> **Acts 3:6**

Peter said, ***"But such as I have give I thee."*** We had shown earlier that the Name of Jesus now belongs to you also to be used by you to perform supernatural acts. Paul also used the Name in Acts 16:18 to cast out demons from a demon-possessed woman.

How to use the Name Jesus

> *I command thee in the name of Jesus Christ to come out of her. And he came out the same hour.*
>
> **Acts 16:18**

He said to the demons in the demon-possessed woman, *"I command thee in the Name of Jesus to come out of her"* and the demon came out of her. You have been shown that you now also have the rights to use that Name therefore use the Name with boldness to deal with the devil.

With the authority that you have to use the powerful Name of Jesus nothing should be daunting to you any longer. The Name of Jesus is your instrument for achieving the supernatural. This is so because God has given great powers to that Name. All powers in heaven and in earth are now vested in that Name. He gave us an insight into the powers that He has given that Name through Apostle Paul in Philippians 2:9-11.

> *Wherefore God also hath highly exalted him, and given him a name which is above every name:*
>
> *That at the name of Jesus every knee should bow, of things in heaven, and things in earth, and things under the earth;*
>
> *And that every tongue should confess that Jesus Christ is Lord, to the glory of God the Father.*
>
> **Philippians 2:9-11**

Living a Supernatural Life (Volume 2)

This means that when the Name is invoked against anything, whether the thing is in heaven, in earth or under the earth, it must bow its knee. This means that it must acknowledge the authority that is in that Name. It must obey and do whatever it is commanded to do in that Name. The Name of Jesus in your mouth is so powerful that, if you only know how powerful it is, you can with it bring under cheap control any contrary situation that you come across. You must always be conscious of the truth that Satan and his demons tremble and bow at the call of that Name of Jesus. They may pretend not to but in actual fact they tremble when they hear that Name. God gave us an insight into the power and the attributes that are in that Name through Prophet Isaiah in Isaiah 9:6, even before Jesus Christ came into this world. Look at what he said below. He said,

> *"For unto us a child is born, unto us a son is given: and the government shall be upon his shoulder: and his name shall be called Wonderful, Counsellor, The mighty God, The everlasting Father, The Prince of Peace."*
> **Isaiah 9:6**

From the above insight that God gave us concerning the Name we can see that the following attributes are embedded in it:

His Name is *Wonderful* therefore at the call of that Name **"Jesus"** into any situation; wonderful things, amazing things and breathtaking things are bound to happen.

How to use the Name Jesus

His Name is *Counsellor* therefore at the call of that Name **"Jesus"** into any situation; guidance and direction is received; the insight of the Wisdom of God is brought into that situation.

His Name is *The Mighty God* therefore at the call of that Name **"Jesus"** into any situation; a compelling, mighty, powerful and potent force is forcefully brought to bear upon that situation.

His Name is *Everlasting Father* therefore at the call of that Name **"Jesus"** into any situation; a fatherly, loving and caring assurance of a lasting and permanent solution is brought into that situation.

His Name is *The Prince of Peace* therefore at the call of that Name **"Jesus"** into any turbulent, unstable, confused, chaotic or violent situation; calm, stability, order and peace are immediately brought into the situation.

Anything that is dead if you call the Name of Jesus into it, life must instantly come into it because *there is life in that Name.* That is what God told us through John in John 20:31. Therefore you can bring life into anything through that Name. All you need to do is believe that there is life in the Name. Believe that there is power in that Name. Have faith in the Name and the Name will perform miracles in your life.

> *But these are written, that ye might believe that Jesus is the Christ, the Son of God; and that believing ye might have life through his name.*
> **John 20:31**

Living a Supernatural Life (Volume 2)

All afflictions, sufferings, miseries or burdens that may come on any man have come mainly as consequences of the sin of man that brought the wrath of God upon man. But the Name of Jesus was given to us so as to deliver us from our sins and therefore from the consequences of the sins. That is what God told us through Matthew in Matthew 1:21.

> *And she shall bring forth a son, and thou shalt call his name JESUS: for he shall save his people from their sins.*
> **Matthew 1:21**

Therefore no matter what affliction, suffering or burden you may be going through as a consequence of any sin, if you will only repent of the sin, at the call of the Name of Jesus it must bow. The affliction, suffering or burden must bow and obey whatever command it is given in that Name. That shows how powerful and potent the Name of Jesus is.

You can therefore see that if you are going to live a supernatural life above all afflictions, sufferings, miseries and burdens, commanding in the Name of Jesus will be your main access route to it. The Name is the major key that you will need. Faith in the Name is a must for miracles, signs and wonders to happen.

The Name and faith in the Name of Jesus is your access route to the supernatural. The Name and faith in the Name is the route alright but the major vehicle that you will need to carry you through that access route is your mouth.

Therefore you must be bold in using your mouth to give the command in faith for whatever you want in the Name of Jesus. Whatever you hoped for, ask for it in faith in that Name and you will get it, for it is that Name and faith in the Name that gives substance to your hope and turns it into reality.

That Name of Jesus is a supernatural weapon given to every believer with which he can fight evil forces and also demand and draw whatever he wants from the bank of heaven where all resources are stored.

Use the Name **Jesus** with boldness and understanding. However, the amount of power that you will be able to demonstrate with that Name as a believer will depend on how great a revelation you have of the power that is vested in the Name, your faith in the Name and how prepared you are to use your mouth to command in the Name because your mouth is the vehicle that you will use for the delivery of the power that is now vested in that Name of Jesus.

HOW DO YOU DEVELOP FAITH IN THE NAME?

We are told by God through Paul in Romans 10:17 that faith comes by hearing and hearing by the Word of God.

So then faith cometh by hearing, and hearing by the word of God.
Romans 10:17

Therefore what you need to do is to study the Word of God to see the power that is in that Name and as you study and practice the use of the Name your faith in the Name will start to rise. Once you have faith in the Name if you use the Name to ask for anything from God you will get it. If faith in the Name is in place I can assure you that while you are still thinking even before you ask for anything God will answer you. Is it not written in Ephesians 3:20 that He can do exceeding abundantly above all that we can ask or think? Yet God Himself said in Isaiah 65:24 that before you call He will answer and while you are yet speaking He will hear. All you need to do therefore is just have faith in the Name of Jesus and ask in that Name.

> *Now unto him that is able to do exceeding abundantly above all that we ask or think, according to the power that worketh in us,*
> **Ephesians. 3:20**

> *And it shall come to pass, that before they call, I will answer; and while they are yet speaking, I will hear.*
> **Isaiah 65:24**

IGNORE PEOPLE'S OPINION OF YOU

If you want your faith in that Name to grow you must only focus your mind on what God thinks or say of you and not on what any man says or thinks of you.

Don't listen to the devil just believe only what the Word says. Keep practicing the use of your faith. Remember that evil things were said of Jesus too.

How to use the Name Jesus

Don't allow other people's opinion of you to intimidate you. Jesus must have been mocked and ridiculed as a child because of His background. Remember that He was born by a mother whose pregnancy was not normal but questionable in the sight of people. You can imagine the type of subtle ridicule He must have gone through from His relatives and from the people in the community where He grew up. He did not allow this to distract Him. People will also mock you. They will hate you. If your commands in faith are not being obeyed they will ridicule you. On the other hand if they are being obeyed they will accuse you of using devilish powers. He said in Luke 6:22-23 that you are blessed when such things are done to you. You should rejoice because your reward is great in heaven.

> *Blessed are ye, when men shall hate you, and when they shall separate you from their company, and shall reproach you, and cast out your name as evil, for the Son of man's sake.*
>
> *Rejoice ye in that day, and leap for joy: for, behold, your reward is great in heaven: for in the like manner did their fathers unto the prophets.*
>
> **Luke 6:22-23**

When such a thing happens to you see it as part of the devil's tricks to discourage and frighten you from exercising your faith on a continuous basis. The devil knows that if you do not exercise and practice the use of your faith on a continuous basis to tackle problems it will not develop. Therefore do not seek to be loved by the world because the world will never love you.

Living a Supernatural Life (Volume 2)

They will never love you because you are no longer with them. You are no longer of this world. They are from beneath; you are from above. You are light but they are in darkness. That is basically what Jesus was saying about Himself in John 8:23 and also about us in John 15:18-19.

> *And he said unto them, Ye are from beneath; I am from above: ye are of this world; I am not of this world.*
> **John 8:23**

> *If the world hate you, ye know that it hated me before it hated you.*

> *If ye were of the world, the world would love his own: but because ye are not of the world, but I have chosen you out of the world, therefore the world hateth you.*
> **John 15:18-19**

Do not seek to be understood by the world. The world cannot understand you because everything you do will be foolishness to the world. The world cannot understand what you do neither can the world know them because what you do can only be discerned spiritually. That is what God made us to see through Apostle Paul in 1 Corinthians 2:14.

> *But the natural man receiveth not the things of the Spirit of God: for they are foolishness unto him: neither can he know them, because they are spiritually discerned.*
> **1 Corinthians 2:14**

PAST FAILURES SHOULD NOT BOTHER YOU

If you think of your past failures in the use of your faith in Jesus and the Name of Jesus you will not be able to develop your faith. This is because the devil will use such thoughts of past failures to bring doubt into your mind. But James has made us to know in James 1:6-7 that doubt will not allow us to get anything from God. Therefore do not allow any thoughts of doubt to linger in your mind. Whenever Satan brings the thoughts of doubt into your mind expunge that thought by using the Word of God to fight it.

But let him ask in faith, nothing wavering. For he that wavereth is like a wave of the sea driven with the wind and tossed.

For let not that man think that he shall receive any thing of the Lord.
James 1:6-7

If you concern yourself too much with your past you will not be able to move forward. The past has nothing to do with what you can do through God today. Free your present from your past. The past cannot determine your future unless you choose to remain in the past. Jesus warned against this in Luke 9:62.

And Jesus said unto him, No man, having put his hand to the plough, and looking back, is fit for the kingdom of God.
Luke 9:62

Living a Supernatural Life (Volume 2)

Do not have a looser mentality. Be positive and believe that even if you have tried your faith and failed many times you will win with it. Don't allow your past failures to become strong holds of Satan in your life. Take a cue from Abraham Lincoln, one of America's greatest Presidents, who was elected President of United States of America in 1860. He failed in business in 1831. From 1832 to 1858 he was defeated in more than nine different elections for the legislature, Congress, Senate and even as a Vice President. He even suffered a nervous breakdown in-between. Even though he had tried for all the possible political offices and failed he still decided in 1860 to contest for the biggest of all post, that of the President of the United States of America and this time he succeeded. If he had allowed his past failures to bother him he would never have become the President of the United States of America.

If you want your faith especially your faith in the Name of Jesus to develop you must not allow the past failures that you have had in the use of your faith in that Name to weigh you down. Keep exercising your faith and it will develop. May the Lord God Himself give you a revelation of the power that is in the Name **JESUS,** Amen.

CHAPTER 5

YOUR MOUTH IS THE VEHICLE

The vehicle for releasing the supernatural is your mouth. This is because when you speak right words they are enforceable. That is what God told us through Job in Job 6:25. Therefore speak only right words because right words are forcible.

> *"How forcible are right words! but what doth your arguing reprove?"*
> **Job 6:25**

This shows that you should be very careful about the words that come out of your mouth. Do not be a lousy talker. Do not be a negative talker who is always speaking negative words concerning the circumstances and situations around him or that he is going through. Speak positively all the time. Your mouth is the vehicle that you will use to release the supernatural. **Therefore speak right words because right words are forcible and the supernatural is in your mouth.** What you say will determine what you get in life. Therefore speak right words all the time.

Living a Supernatural Life (Volume 2)

God's Words are right words because they are pure. That is what Psalm 19:8 says. No Word of God is void of power. That is what God tells us through Prophet Isaiah in Isaiah 55:11. Therefore God's Words are the right words to speak. When you speak God's Words they will be enforced because right words are forcible as written in Job 6:25 above.

> *The statutes of the LORD are right, rejoicing the heart: the commandment of the LORD is pure, enlightening the eyes.*
> **Psalm 19:8**

> *So shall my word be that goeth forth out of my mouth: it shall not return unto me void, but it shall accomplish that which I please, and it shall prosper in the thing whereto I sent it.*
> **Isaiah 55:11**

In the original Greek language that was used for the New Testament whenever the Word of God is mentioned in most cases, they either use the Greek word **LOGOS** or the Greek word **RHEMA** to represent the Word of God. Basically we can see that there is the written Word of God called **LOGOS** and there is the spoken Word of God, which is spoken directly to our spirit or in the form of a revelation called **RHEMA**. The two are different from one another but of the two the **RHEMA** Word is the more powerful.

As we have explained in *Volume 1* of this *"Living a Supernatural life"* book series, the **RHEMA** Word of God is usually directed to someone at a particular point in time and for a specific purpose.

Such **RHEMA** can come either through a revelation received from reading, hearing or meditating on the written Word of God **LOGOS** or it can be spoken directly into one's spirit by God. As one reads, hears or meditates on the written Word of God, a specific word, sentence or verse of the Scriptures can be released and spoken to one's spirit, which gives him a revelation concerning the use of such words, sentence or verse for a specific purpose.

Once this happens the Word thus given becomes a **RHEMA** word from God to that individual for that specific purpose. When the Word of God is revealed to an individual for a specific purpose, such revealed Word of God is a **RHEMA** Word of God. In Luke 3:2, we are told that the Word of God came to John. You will see that in the original Greek that Word of God that came to John was called **RHEMA**. Therefore what John heard must have come to him in the form of a revelation or Words spoken to his spirit.

> *Annas and Caiaphas being the high priests, the word of God came unto John the son of Zacharias in the wilderness.*
> **Luke 3:2**

It is such hearing in the form of revelation from the Word of God that builds up faith not the mere hearing of the written Word of God **LOGOS** So no matter how much you read and hear the Scriptures if you do not read or hear to receive a revelation Word **RHEMA** from what you are reading or hearing little faith will develop from it because the **RHEMA** has a deeper foundation in you than the **LOGOS**.

Living a Supernatural Life (Volume 2)

In Romans 10:17 we are told that faith comes by hearing and hearing by the Word of God. In the original Greek the Word of God referred to here is the **RHEMA** Word of God.

> *So then faith cometh by hearing, and hearing by the word of God.*
> **Romans 10:17**

It is the hearing of the **RHEMA** Word of God that brings faith not the reading or the hearing of **LOGOS** because faith normally comes as a result of revelation received from hearing the spoken Word. You should also note that it is the revelation Word **RHEMA** from the Word of God that was referred to when Jesus said in Luke 4:4 that man shall not live by bread alone but by every Word of God.

> *And Jesus answered him, saying, It is written, That man shall not live by bread alone, but by every word of God.*
> **Luke 4:4**

When Peter was told by Jesus in Luke 5:4-5 to launch out into the deep and let down his nets for a draught Peter replied to say, *"Master, we have toiled all the night and have taken nothing: nevertheless at thy Word I will let down the net."* The Word that Peter mentioned here was called **RHEMA** not **LOGOS** in the original Greek since it was a revealed Word to him. Therefore the Word of God that Peter referred to when he said at thy Word was the **RHEMA** Word of God because the Word was spoken to him directly for a specific purpose and for a specific situation.

Your Mouth is the Vehicle

Now when he had left speaking, he said unto Simon, Launch out into the deep, and let down your nets for a draught.

And Simon answering said unto him, Master, we have toiled all the night, and have taken nothing: nevertheless at thy word I will let down the net.
Luke 5:4-5

Therefore once you receive a **RHEMA** Word from God specifically directed to you concerning any situation, just like Peter did here when he was told to launch into the deep for a draught, no matter what your doubts may be, no matter how daunting or impossible the situation may be, you can always say like Peter said, *"Nevertheless at thy Word,"* and face the situation with that **RHEMA** Word from God and victory will surely come your way.

This is so because if you look at the original Greek version of the Scripture, you will see that the Word of God referred to as the Sword of the Spirit written in Ephesians 6:17 with which we are supposed to fight the enemy is *the revealed spoken Word of God* **RHEMA** not the **LOGOS**. Even though we know that **LOGOS** can give birth to **RHEMA**, it is the **RHEMA** Word of God that we are supposed to use as the *Sword of the Spirit*. It is therefore futile to brandish the book as the *Sword of the Sprit*.

And take the helmet of salvation, and the sword of the Spirit, which is the word of God:
Ephesians 6:17

Living a Supernatural Life (Volume 2)

In Luke 1:37 in the King James Version (KJV) we are told that nothing is impossible with God. The translation of the same verse in the World English Bible Version (WEB) says, *"For everything spoken by God (RHEMA) is possible."* The translation of the same verse in the American Standard Version (ASV) says, *"No Word of God (RHEMA) shall be void of power"*. So it is the **RHEMA** Word of God that has the power, which makes impossibilities possible.

> *For with God nothing shall be impossible. (KJV)*
> *For everything spoken by God is possible. (WEB)*
> *For no word from God shall be void of power. (ASV)*
> **Luke 1:37**

This is so because the **RHEMA** Word of God not only has power it actually has creative power because we are told in Hebrews 11:3 that God framed the worlds by His Word. If you look at the original Greek translation of the New Testament you will see that the Word of God referred to with which He framed or created the world was the **RHEMA** Word of God.

> *By faith we understand that the worlds have been framed by the word of God, so that what is seen hath not been made out of things which appear.*
> **Hebrews 11:3**

Therefore talk by what God can do not what you can do. Talk the **RHEMA** Word of God as received by you. Give your commands using the **RHEMA** Word of God spoken directly to you, which you have received.

Your Mouth is the Vehicle

Even if your commands are not based on direct revelation spoken to you by God, at least they should be based on revelation that you have received through the reading of, hearing of or meditating on the Word of God. Remember what Jesus said in John 6:63 that the Words that He spoke out were spirit and life? It is the **RHEMA** Word of God that Jesus was referring to here not the **LOGOS**. This means that such **RHEMA** words from God are spiritual substances. That is to say that they have spiritual attributes among which is power and life. You need to understand this.

> *It is the spirit that quickeneth; the flesh profiteth nothing: the words that I speak unto you, they are spirit, and they are life.*
> **John 6:63**

You are now a partaker of the divine nature of God. That is what God said through Peter concerning you in 2 Peter 1:3-4.

> *According as his divine power hath given unto us all things that pertain unto life and godliness, through the knowledge of him that hath called us to glory and virtue:*
>
> *Whereby are given unto us exceeding great and precious promises: that by these ye might be partakers of the divine nature, having escaped the corruption that is in the world through lust.*
> **2 Peter 1:3-4**

Living a Supernatural Life (Volume 2)

This means that you now have the divine nature of God. The divine nature of God operates insides of you. If that is the case, since the **RHEMA** Word of God is spirit and life it means therefore that the revealed words of God that you speak out are also spirit and life and they are enforceable. Therefore you should never confess defeat, failure, lack, poverty, sickness and diseases or anything contrary to God's destiny for your life because your words are spirit and life.

Whatever you say would materialize because your words have life in them. They have the power to manifest especially if they are based on the **RHEMA** Words of God that have been spoken to you concerning a particular situation. That is why you are told through Job in Job 22:29 that when men are cast down, then you should say, *"There is lifting up"*. Get a revelation of this and speak it out.

> *When men are cast down, then thou shalt say, There is lifting up; and he shall save the humble person.*
> **Job 22:29**

If you can meditate on this long enough to turn it into a revealed **RHEMA** Word spoken directly to you from God then you will get the lifting up instead of the casting down that everyone else is going through. God also said through Prophet Joel in Joel 3:10, that when you are weak you should say that you are strong. So also when tou are poor say that you are rich.

> *Beat your plowshares into swords, and your pruninghooks into spears: let the weak say, I am strong.*
> **Joel 3:10**

Your Mouth is the Vehicle

You must meditate daily on this Scripture and other supporting Scriptures related to it to receive a revelation of the Words as **RHEMA** Words that is spoken directly to you by God. If you are having difficulty in getting this revealed to you personally and you are having doubts as your mind ponders this then you will not be able to get this picture of you being strong revealed to you. Get the image of you being strong in your mind and start to focus your mind on this image.

So that you can get the picture of you being strong revealed to you, add to your meditation and receive the revelation of the Words written in Philippians 4:13, which say that Christ is the One who strengthens you to do all things. Therefore it is His strength that you will use. Since God can do anything it follows that through that His strength you can do all things. You therefore should no longer see yourself as weak.

> *I can do all things through Christ which strengtheneth me.*
> **Philippians 4:13**

But after you have meditated on these two Scriptures if you still have not got that revelation and Satan is still questioning your stand that you are strong and making you feel or pointing to you telling you that you are weak then you can also add to your meditation and receive a revelation of the Words written by Apostle Paul in 2 Corinthians 12:9-10, which says that the strength of Jesus Christ, which you are using is made perfect in weakness. Therefore it is when you are weak that you are actually strong.

Living a Supernatural Life (Volume 2)

> *And he said unto me, My grace is sufficient for thee: for my strength is made perfect in weakness. Most gladly therefore will I rather glory in my infirmities, that the power of Christ may rest upon me.*
>
> *Therefore I take pleasure in infirmities, in reproaches, in necessities, in persecutions, in distresses for Christ's sake: for when I am weak, then am I strong.*
>
> **2 Corinthians 12:9-10**

By the time you have meditated on these three Scriptures for sometimes you are bound to start seeing yourself in the position of strength that God has put you. That revelation is bound to come. You are bound to start talking tough to your problems and nothing will make you afraid anymore. You must practice this over and over again from time to time.

If Satan still puts doubt in your mind however and is telling you or putting it in your mind that you are weak suggesting to you that a weak man cannot be strong at the same time then add to your meditation and receive the revelation of the Words spoken by God through Paul in Philippians 2:13, which says that it is God who actually works in you both to do and to will of His good pleasure. If god is the One working in you how can you be weak?

> *For it is God which worketh in you both to will and to do of his good pleasure.*
>
> **Philippians 2:13**

Therefore you should see that you are not really the one doing anything anyway. It is the God who now lives in you that does them. Definitely there is nothing that God cannot do. Therefore if God is the One working in you then you cannot be weak for there is nothing impossible for God to do. Before you knew that it was Christ's strength that you were using it was possible for the devil to be telling you that you are weak. But you now know that you not only have Christ's strength at your disposal, you are not even the one going to make use of that Christ's strength. It is God Himself who is the owner of the strength who will use it to do the work through you. Can Satan say that God will not know how to use His own strength? No! But if per adventure Satan is still putting doubts in your mind by telling you that you cannot claim God's strength for your weakness then you can add to your meditation and receive a revelation of the Words of Hebrews 11:34, which states that it is out of weakness that God will make you strong. Therefore it is out of your weakness that you are made strong. If you can have a revelation of these Words of God and receive them as **RHEMA** words of God specifically spoken to you for the situation that you are going through then you can rest assured that the words of 2 Corinthians 12:10 written by Paul, which we had earlier mentioned, *"When I am weak then I am strong"* will be revealed to you and at that stage Satan must leave with his thought of your being weak.

Quenched the violence of fire, escaped the edge of the sword, out of weakness were made strong, waxed valiant in fight, turned to flight the armies of the aliens.
                              Hebrews 11:34

Living a Supernatural Life (Volume 2)

Therefore I take pleasure in infirmities, in reproaches, in necessities, in persecutions, in distresses for Christ's sake: for when I am weak, then am I strong.
                                2 Corinthians 12:10

Being conscious of this and using it to fight your battles will help you to live a supernatural life above your natural senses or abilities and above the symptoms that you can see, hear, taste, smell or feel. If you must be strong you must reject all negative words such as defeats, failure, lack, poverty, sickness and diseases that attempt to hang on to you. Stand firm on what the Word of God says. You must do so boldly even in the face of overwhelming evidences of facts against your stand on the Word of God. You must remember that those evidences are mere *facts* not the **truth**. The **truth** is whatever the Word of God says. Never confess these facts with your mouth.

If you are weak, you should say that you are strong. If you are sick, you should say that you are healed and healthy. If you are barren, you should say that you are fruitful. If you are poor, you should say that you are rich. You should not only say these but you should also continue to imagine yourself to be whatever you are saying. That is you should imagine yourself strong, in health, fruitful and rich. Once you can visualize these and create their images or pictures in your mind by ruminating over them continuously, focusing your mind or inner sight on them you will get to the point where they will become real to you and materialize physically and you will see that quite soon it is what you say that you will get in the end.

Your Mouth is the Vehicle

When you get the revelation knowledge of God's Words, such God's Words in your mouth are enforceable because they are spirit and they are life. With your new divine nature of God, the revealed Words of God that you speak out are also spirit and they are life. They are also enforceable. ***The word that you speak out is a major key that will decide whether you will live a supernatural life or not.*** Until you begin to make bold declarative statements based on the **RHEMA** Word of God that you have received your creative ability will not manifest. Remember the story of David and Goliath? If you study that story very well, you will note that the difference between Saul and David was not just God. It was obvious that God was going to be the One to fight the battle so they could rest assured that Goliath was finished and they had already won based on the promises that God had made concerning Israel's enemies. You can see this in the various promises of God to the children of Israel. In Deuteronomy 20:1-4 and also in Deuteronomy 33:27, God promised them that He would be fighting their wars for them. He told them not to fear and that they should not tremble because of any enemy.

> *When thou goest out to battle against thine enemies, and seest horses, and chariots, and a people more than thou, be not afraid of them: for the LORD thy God is with thee, which brought thee up out of the land of Egypt.*
>
> *And it shall be, when ye are come nigh unto the battle, that the priest shall approach and speak unto the people,*

> *And shall say unto them, Hear, O Israel, ye approach this day unto battle against your enemies: let not your hearts faint, fear not, and do not tremble, neither be ye terrified because of them;*
>
> *For the LORD your God is he that goeth with you, to fight for you against your enemies, to save you.*
> **Deuteronomy 20:1-4**
>
> *The eternal God is thy refuge, and underneath are the everlasting arms: and he shall thrust out the enemy from before thee; and shall say, Destroy them.*
> **Deuteronomy 33:27**

God had already spoken His Words written down in **LOGOS** against their enemies. Both Saul and David had access to the God of Israel that made these promises and to the written Word of God **LOGOS** where the promises were recorded. But it was David who, knowing the power in the Word of God had processed these written promises of God **LOGOS** in his mind sufficiently in the past to have received the revelation knowledge **RHEMA** of those Words as specifically meant for him even though the promises were meant for the whole of Israel.

He knew the promises that God had made to Israel concerning her enemies but he received the revelation of these promises as the Word of God spoken directly to him for that particular situation. He knew his God, and he knew what his God was capable of doing.

Your Mouth is the Vehicle

David has meditated long enough as a child on these promises of God to Israel and had made these promises personal to himself. He was therefore able to speak out boldly against Goliath based on this revealed Word of God. He said,

"This day will the Lord deliver thee into my hand and I will smite thee and take thine head from thee; and I will give the carcases of the host of the Philistines this day unto the fowls of the air and to the wild beasts of the earth; that all earth may know that there is a God in Israel."

No doubt about it, David was so sure of the Covenant that God had with Israel. Not only that, he knew his God and he was so sure of his God. A small boy sure of defeating the entire host of the Philistines. David knew that God is a Covenant-keeping God and God honoured His Word as we can see from 1 Samuel 17:45-47.

Then said David to the Philistine, Thou comest to me with a sword, and with a spear, and with a shield: but I come to thee in the name of the LORD of hosts, the God of the armies of Israel, whom thou hast defied.

This day will the LORD deliver thee into mine hand; and I will smite thee, and take thine head from thee; and I will give the carcases of the host of the Philistines this day unto the fowls of the air, and to the wild beasts of the earth; that all the earth may know that there is a God in Israel.

Living a Supernatural Life (Volume 2)

> *And all this assembly shall know that the LORD saveth not with sword and spear: for the battle is the LORD'S, and he will give you into our hands.*
>
> **1 Samuel 17:45-47**

Saul probably also knew of the promises. He must have heard of these promises of God concerning the enemies of Israel and also the stories of the miracles that God had wrought in the past. But he probably never processed these Words in his mind so that he can go beyond having just information knowledge of these Words or promises meant generally for everybody to receiving the revelation knowledge specifically meant for him from the Words and promises. Definitely he did not receive these as **RHEMA** Words of God meant specifically for him.

As far as Saul was concerned they are just promises of God written down as **LOGOS** in the Scriptures. He did not receive them as spoken Words of God meant specifically for him. But David received God's Words as spoken directly to him for the specific purpose of dealing with Israel's enemies who at that particular moment were the Philistines army led by Goliath.

Because David had received this **RHEMA** from God and he knew what his God was capable of, he spoke out Goliath's death. He proclaimed it loud so that the people could hear it. David spoke out the right words, and they were enforced because right words are enforceable. When you have received a **RHEMA** Word from God you must shout it out.

You need to proclaim it. So you too can also speak out what you want. Speak the right words. Speak to God and let God speak to you then speak God's Words to things. Meditate on the Words of God that you have received in your mind, which are applicable to the mountains of your life until you receive the revelation knowledge from such Words. Once that is done you should speak the revealed Words, which are God's **RHEMA** Words or promises spoken directly to you concerning those mountains of your life. Speak them out loudly and the mountains will move.

The case of most Christians is similar to that of David and the other children of Israel. God is the God for all of Israel and His Words are meant for all Israelites, but when Goliath came only David knew that he had this Covenant keeping God who had spoken concerning their enemies and he David had received the revelation of the Words and promises of God as spoken directly to him for the specific situation that they were facing at that time. It is the same with you today. Once you are born-again, you have God living inside you just like He lives inside any other born-again Christian and you have His many promises and even Covenant promises to you concerning the problems facing you. If you are willing to read and meditate on these promises you can hear His **RHEMA** words to you concerning any problem facing you.

Just like David did you too can process the various promises that God has made until you get a revelation of the promises in the form of **RHEMA** words spoken directly to you concerning your situation.

Living a Supernatural Life (Volume 2)

As a born-again Christian, you have become a carrier of the power of God and the wisdom of God because Jesus Christ who is the power of God and the wisdom of God is now living in you. But it is only those Christians who are aware of the God that is living inside them, what their God is capable of doing and who set themselves up to receive the **RHEMA** Word from God through their prayers, reading and meditating on the Word of God who will reap the benefits of the God that lives in them.

The level of the revelation that you have of the Word of the God that is living inside of you that you receive as **RHEMA** Word from God will determine the level of the manifestation of His power and exploits that God can demonstrate through you. That is also what will determine the level of supernatural living that you can attain in life. That is why it is so written in Daniel 11:32 that those who do know their God shall be strong and they shall do exploits. This is true because there is no way you can know the power that your God has and not trust Him.

> *And such as do wickedly against the covenant shall he corrupt by flatteries: but the people that do know their God shall be strong, and do exploits.*
> **Daniel 11:32**

So, it is the man who knows this truth, who has received a revelation of this truth, who is conscious of it, who can proclaim it out boldly and make use of it, that will reap the benefits of the power and the wisdom that now reside in him.

Your Mouth is the Vehicle

God is living inside of every born-again Christian. Signs and wonders are supposed to be following every believer. But it is only those who know Him and who are aware that He is living inside them and have received the **RHEMA** Words from the promises of God, which states that they will do miracles, signs and wonders that God will be able to use to do the miracles, signs and wonders. If you can always wait to get the **RHEMA** Word from God concerning every situation that you come across in life you can live a perpetual supernatural life here on earth. You will be able to sail over every wave of problem.

To help you do this you need the Holy Spirit because when the Holy Spirit gives you a direction concerning any problem you can consider that problem solved. You can consider that direction as a **RHEMA** Word from God. You can then release the supernatural, which is in your mouth to end the problem.

SPEAK OUT THE WORD OF GOD

We have said before that the Words of God are right Words. They are not only right Words, but we also said that the spoken Words of God are the means by which you can send the angels of God to work on your declarations.

This is so because angels are supposed to run errands for you through the **RHEMA** Words of God that you have received with which you can send them. Therefore make bold declarations from the Word of God, which you have received as **RHEMA** and send them.

SEND GOD'S ANGELS

The angels of God are ministering angels, ministering to the needs of those people who are heirs of salvation, one of which you are, if you are born-again. That is what God made us to understand through Paul in Hebrews 1:14

> *Are they not all ministering spirits, sent forth to minister for them who shall be heirs of salvation?*
> **Hebrews 1:14**

If you are born-again then you are one of the heirs of salvation referred to in that Scripture, therefore angels are supposed to be ministering to you. They are ministering angels all right! They will minister to you. But there is a proviso that you must note. It is this. They hearken to the **voice** of the Word of God. So it is the spoken Words of God **RHEMA** that you speak out that activates them. It is not every word that you speak that activates them. You activate them by giving voice to the **RHEMA** Word of God that you have received, which is applicable to your situation. The easiest way to get the angels of God to hearken unto you and minister to you is to send them by speaking to them the spoken Word of God **RHEMA**, which you have received. Therefore give voice to the Word of God. You will get faster results when you send them with such spoken Words of God than when you send them using your own words. The voice of the Word of God is the Operating Language that they have been programmed to function by. That is what God made us to understand through David in Psalm 103:20.

Your Mouth is the Vehicle

> ***Bless the LORD, ye his angels that excel in strength, that do his commandments, hearkening unto the voice of his word.***
> **Psalm 103:20**

In fact, angels can be likened to the modern day electronic computers. The computer hardware, without any Operating Systems software loaded into it is just a like junk-box. But when the Operating Systems is loaded into it, then application software packages can be loaded into it to make the computer to perform whatever functions we want it to perform. The Operating Systems that the computer is running on is what helps the computer to be able to interpret, analyze and effect the instructions written in the applications software package.

Similarly it is unto the voice of Word of God that angels hearken. That is their own Operating Systems that they run on. If you speak anything contrary to the Word of God to them, you incapacitate them. So when you receive a revelation of the Word of God **RHEMA** that is appropriate to your case, shout it out. That releases the angels of God to go and work on your behalf to make sure that God's Words, which you have received and spoken out are brought to fulfillment. But please note that when you do release them, you do not pray to them. ***You don't pray to angels. You don't worship angels. You only send them or release them on assignments in the Name of Jesus Christ.*** They are supposed to minister to you. They are your messengers. They are ministering angels. You must also note that you are to do all things in the Name of Jesus Christ, as instructed in Colossians 3:17.

Living a Supernatural Life (Volume 2)

> *And whatsoever ye do in word or deed, do all in the name of the Lord Jesus, giving thanks to God and the Father by him.*
> **Colossians 3:17**

The ministry of angels is an awesome power made available to you for your use by God because angels are supposed to be extremely strong. To show you just how strong angels are, let us look at a few situations where they were used in the Scriptures.

Firstly Let us consider the destruction of Sodom and Gomorrah as described for us in Chapter nineteen of Genesis. God used only two angels to effect the complete destruction of these great cities. If just two angels can destroy two cities that are supposed to be big cities during the period of this story you can imagine what twelve legions of angels can do if they are set against your adversaries no matter how many they may be. Yet if the need arises you can call upon God to send as many as twelve legions of angels to your aid. That is seventy-two thousand angels. Why do I say that you too can call upon that many angels? This is because Jesus said in John 20:21 that it is as the Father hath sent Him that He is now also sending you.

> *Then said Jesus to them again, Peace be unto you: as my Father hath sent me, even so send I you.*
> **John 20:21**

What that means is that whatever facilities was made available to Jesus when He was around on earth are now available for you to use also.

Your Mouth is the Vehicle

Now He said in Matthew 26:53 that He could call on His Father in Heaven to send twelve legions of angels to come and help Him if the need arose. You now have God for your Father also, and you have been sent as Jesus was sent with the resources available to Him now available to you also. You can now do whatever Jesus could do when He was here on earth. The inference from this is that you too can call on the Father to send you twelve legions of angels if the need arises.

> *Thinkest thou that I cannot now pray to my Father, and he shall presently give me more than twelve legions of angels?*
> **Matthew 26:53**

Secondly when an angel came to lead Peter out of prison, as soon as the angel came, the chains binding Peter just fell off his hands. He did not even have to loosen them. They just fell off. When they got to the gate, the gate just opened before them. The angel did not even have to touch the prison gate. Look at the story below as written down in Acts 12:7-10.

> *And, behold, the angel of the Lord came upon him, and a light shined in the prison: and he smote Peter on the side, and raised him up, saying, Arise up quickly. And his chains fell off from his hands.*
>
> *And the angel said unto him, Gird thyself, and bind on thy sandals. And so he did. And he saith unto him, Cast thy garment about thee, and follow me.*

> *And he went out, and followed him; and wist not that it was true which was done by the angel; but thought he saw a vision.*
>
> *When they were past the first and the second ward, they came unto the iron gate that leadeth unto the city; which opened to them of his own accord: and they went out, and passed on through one street; and forthwith the angel departed from him.*
>
> **Acts 12:7-10**

Even the gate of the city just opened before them. He did not have to touch it either. If a gate can just open before them without their having to touch it then you can imagine what they can do if they have to touch or even force the gate open. Angels have such awesome power that the human mind cannot even comprehend. That should show you the extent of the strength of the angels of God. You can now be aided by as much as twelve legions of angels. **Waoh!**

Thirdly, In Isaiah 37:21-36 when Sennacherib and his armies came against King Hezekiah. We are told that an angel of the Lord destroyed the armies of Sennacherib. Just one angel destroyed one hundred and eighty five thousand of them. Please read the story below.

> *Then Isaiah the son of Amoz sent unto Hezekiah, saying, Thus saith the LORD God of Israel, Whereas thou hast prayed to me against Sennacherib king of Assyria:*

Your Mouth is the Vehicle

This is the word which the LORD hath spoken concerning him; The virgin, the daughter of Zion, hath despised thee, and laughed thee to scorn; the daughter of Jerusalem hath shaken her head at thee.

Whom hast thou reproached and blasphemed? and against whom hast thou exalted thy voice, and lifted up thine eyes on high? even against the Holy One of Israel.

By thy servants hast thou reproached the Lord, and hast said, By the multitude of my chariots am I come up to the height of the mountains, to the sides of Lebanon; and I will cut down the tall cedars thereof, and the choice fir trees thereof: and I will enter into the height of his border, and the forest of his Carmel.

I have digged, and drunk water; and with the sole of my feet have I dried up all the rivers of the besieged places.

Hast thou not heard long ago, how I have done it; and of ancient times, that I have formed it? now have I brought it to pass, that thou shouldest be to lay waste defenced cities into ruinous heaps.

Therefore their inhabitants were of small power, they were dismayed and confounded: they were as the grass of the field, and as the green herb, as the grass on the housetops, and as corn blasted before it be grown up.

But I know thy abode, and thy going out, and thy coming in, and thy rage against me.

Because thy rage against me, and thy tumult, is come up into mine ears, therefore will I put my hook in thy nose, and my bridle in thy lips, and I will turn thee back by the way by which thou camest.

And this shall be a sign unto thee, Ye shall eat this year such as groweth of itself; and the second year that which springeth of the same: and in the third year sow ye, and reap, and plant vineyards, and eat the fruit thereof.

And the remnant that is escaped of the house of Judah shall again take root downward, and bear fruit upward:

For out of Jerusalem shall go forth a remnant, and they that escape out of mount Zion: the zeal of the LORD of hosts shall do this.

Therefore thus saith the LORD concerning the king of Assyria, He shall not come into this city, nor shoot an arrow there, nor come before it with shields, nor cast a bank against it.

By the way that he came, by the same shall he return, and shall not come into this city, saith the LORD.

For I will defend this city to save it for mine own sake, and for my servant David's sake.

Your Mouth is the Vehicle

> *Then the angel of the LORD went forth, and smote in the camp of the Assyrians a hundred and fourscore and five thousand: and when they arose early in the morning, behold, they were all dead corpses.*
>
> **Isaiah 37:21-36**

This is to the sort of help that you too can get when the angel of the Lord is with you ministering to your needs. When that happens, every obstacle in your way will just give way. That is an awesome power that is available to you. David wrote in the Psalms of this kind of happening when the angel of the Lord was leading the Israelites away from Pharaoh. He said and I quote, ***"The Sea saw it and fled"***. What did the sea see? The sea saw the angel of the Lord leading them. The angel of the Lord was with them therefore they did not have to do anything. The sea just saw the angel with them and fled before them. The sea trembled at the presence of the angel who was with them.

Even the mountains skipped like rams and the little hills like lambs before them. Look at David's vivid description of the incidence in Psalm 114:1-8 as written below.

> *When Israel went out of Egypt, the house of Jacob from a people of strange language;*
>
> *Judah was his sanctuary, and Israel his dominion.*
>
> *The sea saw it, and fled: Jordan was driven back.*

> *The mountains skipped like rams, and the little hills like lambs.*
>
> *What ailed thee, O thou sea, that thou fleddest? thou Jordan, that thou wast driven back?*
>
> *Ye mountains, that ye skipped like rams; and ye little hills, like lambs?*
>
> *Tremble, thou earth, at the presence of the Lord, at the presence of the God of Jacob;*
>
> *Which turned the rock into a standing water, the flint into a fountain of waters.*
>
> **Psalm 114:1-8**

If you can catch the awesomeness of the situation that David was describing here, you will know what great power angels have. Before an angel of the Lord (probably our Lord Jesus Christ Himself) mountains skipped like rams, hills ran like lambs and the sea even fled. If you can only catch the awesomeness of the situation described here you will know the awesome power that is now available to you through the ministry of God's angels and you will realize that you need not fear the enemy anymore. Look at what our Lord Jesus said in Matthew 26:53 again written below, when some people came to arrest Him and one of His own people lifted a sword to defend Him. He said that He could pray to His Father, and He would send down more than twelve legions of angels to His aid. (That is, more than seventy-two thousands angels as explained earlier.)

Your Mouth is the Vehicle

Thinkest thou that I cannot now pray to my Father, and he shall presently give me more than twelve legions of angels?
Matthew 26:53

Now let us look more closely at John 20:21 to see what Jesus said about how He is now sending you as His Father had sent Him.

Then said Jesus to them again, Peace be unto you: as my Father hath sent me, even so send I you.
John 20:21

This statement of Jesus is very important because He is telling us there that we are supposed to have the same level of backing, support and assistance that He had.

This means that the facilities that were made available to Jesus when He was sent are now available to you too and such facilities include the availability of as many as twelve legions of angels that can come to your aid if the need arises. It also means that you are tapping your power from the same source that Jesus tapped His power from when He was here on earth What this means is that you also now have the power and authority to call on the Father to give you more than twelve legions of angels to come to your aid when such a need arises.

But you must remember that angels hearken mainly to the voice of the Word of God that is the Word of God, which you have received that you have given voice to.

Therefore as you pray to God, whenever the need arises you can call down as many as twelve legions of angels to come to your aid at any time. God will send them down to you. This is one source of power and help that is available to Christians, which many have not or do not even know how to take advantage of. Some who do know this are also misguided because rather than see angels as messengers they pray to them and virtually worship them. But since the angels of God will not receive worship from anybody it is the angels of Satan that their worship attracts. *The supernatural is in your mouth. Release it by sending the angels of God.* If the sea can run because of one angel of the Lord, what will it do if it sees twelve legions of angels? It will probably dry up completely.

SPEAK TO YOUR MOUNTAINS

Jesus said in Matthew 17:20, *"Ye shall say to this mountain remove hence to yonder place and it shall remove".* He did not say, "Ye shall pray about this mountain asking that it be removed." What He is saying here is that we have to speak directly to our mountains not pray about our mountains. But most of us will rather pray about our mountains than speak to them.

> *And Jesus said unto them, Because of your unbelief: for verily I say unto you, If ye have faith as a grain of mustard seed, ye shall say unto this mountain, Remove hence to yonder place; and it shall remove; and nothing shall be impossible unto you.*
> **Matthew 17:20**

Your Mouth is the Vehicle

The reason why we do this today is that most of us Christians do not have the confidence to speak to our mountains. Instead they pray about our mountains. We pray and pray about our mountains and of course the mountains don't move. They don't move because we are supposed to speak directly to them and command them to move. Prayer is good but you are not told to pray about the mountain asking God to come and remove it. No! You are told to speak to it yourself. God has given you the authority to use His power to move them. Use it! Do you want to see the supernatural? If you do, then speak directly to your mountains. The Christians of today will rather pray about their mountains because they do not have the faith to believe that if they speak and command the mountains, their command will be obeyed. The main reason why many Christians do not have any power in the words they speak out to their mountains is because they just speak their own words to such mountains without waiting to hear what to say from God. If they will only wait to hear God's Words specifically spoken to them meant for the mountain, they will see that the mountain will move when they command it using such **RHEMA** Word, which they have received from God. Let's look again at exactly what Jesus told us in Matthew 17:20.

> *And Jesus said unto them, Because of your unbelief: for verily I say unto you, If ye have faith as a grain of mustard seed, ye shall say unto this mountain, Remove hence to yonder place; and it shall remove; and nothing shall be impossible unto you.*
> **Matthew 17:20**

He said, *"If ye shall say unto this mountain..."* You may not know it, but I put it to you that it is mainly because of your unbelief or lack of knowledge that you *pray about* your mountains instead of waiting on God to receive the **RHEMA** from the Word of God to you, which you can speak directly and boldly to command the mountains. Another reason why many so called Christians of today pray about their mountains rather than speak directly to them is because they are not really of God nor are they abiding in Him therefore they cannot hear and receive God's **RHEMA** as stated in John 8:47.

> *He that is of God heareth the words of God: for this cause ye hear them not, because ye are not of God.*
> **John 8:47**

Many also do not believe in the truth that they have the authority to command their mountains and that God can work miracles, signs and wonders through them. Yet that is exactly what Jesus said you would do if you have the necessary faith. He said, *"If ye shall say unto this mountain."* Anything that stands between you and your God-given destiny or your objective in God is a mountain that should be removed. Speak directly to it. Whatever problem you come across constitutes a type of mountain. Therefore speak directly to it. The mountains that you come across in your journey through life can come in any form, but no matter the form that they come in, you are supposed to speak directly to them. Whatever is not allowing you to function as God has ordained for you is a mountain and must be removed. Speak directly to it and it will move.

Your Mouth is the Vehicle

The power and the authority to move anything is in your mouth. If you are sick, that sickness is a mountain that you must move. Speak directly to it. If you are poor, then poverty is a mountain that you must move. Speak directly to it. If you find yourself failing in your endeavours, then the failure syndrome is a mountain that you must move. Speak directly to it. If you owe a debt that debt is a mountain in your life that you must move. Put the bills of that debt before you

If you have been attacked by unfruitfulness or barrenness, then that barrenness is a mountain to you, and you must remove it. Speak directly to it.

You are supposed to speak boldly and directly to the mountains and problems of your life and command them to move. You don't need to pray about them to move them. God said that you should speak to them. Command them to move. The supernatural is in your mouth. Release the supernatural by speaking to your problems. Declare what you want. Even where you find that someone or some forces are behind the problem that should not stop you from declaring what you want. Declare what you want regardless of what the current situation is. What you want the situation to become is what you should declare. Don't waste your time giving the current situation your thoughts and mind. What you want is what you should focus your thoughts and mind upon and it is what you should declare with your mouth. When you command what you want into existence the current situation will move away whether you command it to do so or not because light and darkness can never be together.

When God wanted light darkness was there but God did not bother about the darkness. He just commanded the light that He wanted to come and darkness moved to the side. To bring this home to you and show you exactly how you look to God when you pray to Him about your mountains instead of commanding them as He has instructed you to do, take a look at the following parable which will better explain this to you..

A PARABLE OF THE RICH MAN AND HIS SON

Now the kingdom of heaven can be likened to a conglomerate owned by a very and powerful man. The conglomerate included very large estates of industries, banks, firms and all kinds of businesses all over the world. The rich man even had great influence with the governments in most of the countries of the world. He had great powers. He had working for him a great number of employees, workers and servants. On his retirement, this rich and powerful man had a son to whom he transferred the authority to run his entire conglomerate by making him the Chief Executive Officer (CEO) of his entire organization. In effect, he gave his son all authority and power to take all the necessary decisions required for the smooth running of the organization. But after the son became the CEO and took over the running of the organization, whenever any of the employees, workers or even servants within the organization does anything wrong, the son, who is now the CEO will go to his father and beg him to instruct or discipline them.

Your Mouth is the Vehicle

What will you think of that son? Won't you see him as incompetent or irresponsible? What do you think the rich man will think of his son? Yet as a born-again Christian that is exactly what you look like to God, who is now your Father, whenever you find that any sickness or disease is worrying you or you find yourself with one major challenge of affliction and you pray to Him to come and deal with them.

It is the same thing when you have anything acting as an obstacle to your success in life or to the destiny that God has ordained for you and you pray to Him to help you deal with it. God, your Father, has already given you the authority and dominion over demons, evil spirits and over all the powers of your enemies. He has said that you have been healed of all diseases. He has said that whatever you decree will be established for you. He has said that nothing shall by any means hurt you. He has told you to speak to your mountains and tell them to move. What more do you want Him to do?

Look at the prayer of the disciples after Peter and John were arrested, beaten and then released by the council of the High Priest, Rulers and Elders and told not to preach in the Name of Jesus anymore. They prayed to God all right, but they did not pray that God should deal with these their enemies. No! Instead they prayed that God would give them boldness to speak the Word and that when they speak the Word the Lord should stretch forth His hand to heal and that signs and wonders may be done by the Name of Jesus His Holy child. Note that they said that the Name of Jesus should do the signs and wonders. Therefore it is the Name of Jesus that will do the work.

Living a Supernatural Life (Volume 2)

This means that whenever they have any mountains before them what they expected was that if they called on the Name of Jesus the necessary signs and wonders required to solve their problems and move the mountains will be done by Jesus.

Suppose that in this earthly realm you are a prince and your father is a king, surely everybody will respect you as the prince. Even though you are not the king, you are the son of a king. For this reason you will be highly respected. No one will just come to you and harass you or insult you. That is the way it is also in the spiritual realm. You are a son of God so all the forces of darkness must show you respect. The reason why most Christians do not receive the respect of the enemy forces is because those enemy forces know that these Christians do not know that they are the sons of the King of kings, God Himself.

As a son of God all enemy forces should be afraid and shiver when they come across you but they know that you are not aware of your status. If you are not aware that you are the prince nobody will respect you. God has assured you that if you have even a small faith, and you command the mountains that you come across to move in the Name of Jesus, they will move. Even Satan can no longer overcome you. He knows that. He knows that he has been defeated by Jesus. He no longer has power over you. But if you do not know it yourself Satan will pretend that he can overcome and subdue you and he will start to manifest some form of power, which is actually fake power, before you.

Your Mouth is the Vehicle

You will then think that he has power not knowing that he is actually very afraid that you may find out the truth that he has no power. When you know this truth it gives you freedom. God has given you authority and power through Jesus Christ, but it is your duty to enforce that authority using the power. God will not come down and enforce it for you.

Whatever power Satan is exhibiting over you is what you have conceded to him either through ignorance or laziness. You are now far above all the forces of darkness and they know it. You are above sickness, you are above diseases, and you are above all forms of oppression and affliction. They are of the kingdom of darkness but you now belong to the kingdom of light and light must always overcome darkness. I am not saying that problems and afflictions will not come your way. What I am saying is that you now have the power to overcome them. You must have that superiority complex over the enemy forces and enforce your authority over them. You are supposed to reign over them in this life *now*. That is what God has told us in Revelation 5:10 and Romans 5:17.

> *And hast made us unto our God kings and priests: and we shall reign on the earth.*
> **Revelation 5:10**

> *For if by one man's offence death reigned by one; much more they which receive abundance of grace and of the gift of righteousness shall reign in life by one, Jesus Christ.*
> **Romans 5:17**

Living a Supernatural Life (Volume 2)

Your reigning is not only for the future life. You are supposed to be reigning in this life right here on earth now. I am not saying that you should not pray to God. You have to pray to God all the time. That is the instruction that God gave us through Paul the Apostle in 1 Thessalonians 5:17. He said,

> *"Pray without ceasing."*
> **1 Thessalonians 5:17**

Yes, you are supposed to pray without ceasing. But you must learn and know how to pray to God. You must know the sort of things that you are supposed to pray to God for. You must learn not to ask amiss because it is possible to ask amiss. There is no point asking God to do what He said that He has already done or asking the Father to do what Christ says He will do or what He has given you the authority to do yourself. I want you to look again at the model prayer, which Jesus gave us in Matthew 6:9-13 as written down below.

> *After this manner therefore pray ye: Our Father which art in heaven, Hallowed be thy name.*
>
> *Thy kingdom come. Thy will be done in earth, as it is in heaven.*
>
> *Give us this day our daily bread.*
>
> *And forgive us our debts, as we forgive our debtors.*

Your Mouth is the Vehicle

And lead us not into temptation, but deliver us from evil: For thine is the kingdom, and the power, and the glory, for ever. Amen.
Matthew 6:9-13

You will see from this model prayer that Jesus gave us above that, in the case of our problems or needs, we are supposed to use our prayers in advance of such problems or needs asking God to avert, ward off or prevent such problems and meet such needs before they actually arise in our lives.

This means that we are to use our prayers to the Father as a kind of inoculation or vaccination to immunize us well in advance against such problems or needs. But when a problem or need actually arises and is starring you in the face, then it is time for you to act by facing the problem or need squarely and giving the commands that will give you a solution and your freedom.

This is so because the problem or need will most of the time come so suddenly and require immediate solution and as such there may not even be enough time for prayers. Problems will always come for you as a Christian but you must be prepared for them and see them as mere challenges.

When you are face to face with such a challenge, then you must use the authority that God has given you and command in the Name of Jesus what you want to happen to it. Praying may then not be the most imperative thing to do. Prayer prepares you for the day of confrontation but when it comes it is time for your commands.

Living a Supernatural Life (Volume 2)

The best way to tackle the problem is to receive the **RHEMA** Word of God spoken to you concerning to the problem or need and then use such **RHEMA** Word to command the problem to go. A Christian that knows this and practices it is the Christian that can walk in the miraculous and live a supernatural life here on earth. Jesus Christ gave us this authority through what He said to us in Luke 10:19 as well as Mark 16:15-18.

> *Behold, I give unto you power to tread on serpents and scorpions, and over all the power of the enemy: and nothing shall by any means hurt you.*
> **Luke 10:19**

> *And he said unto them, Go ye into all the world, and preach the gospel to every creature.*
>
> *He that believeth and is baptized shall be saved; but he that believeth not shall be damned.*
>
> *And these signs shall follow them that believe; In my name shall they cast out devils; they shall speak with new tongues;*
>
> *They shall take up serpents; and if they drink any deadly thing, it shall not hurt them; they shall lay hands on the sick, and they shall recover.*
> **Mark 16:15-18**

Before you face the problem you can go into prayer not necessarily asking God to come and solve the problem but that God should give you boldness to face it.

Your Mouth is the Vehicle

You can also pray that He should perform the necessary miracle through the Name of Jesus Christ when you give the command using the Name of Jesus Christ. You can also ask God to give you the **RHEMA** Word to be used against the problem so that you can face the problem squarely after your prayer.

After you have prayed to God, you must come out of that prayer believing that God has heard you and that during the prayer you should wait to receive the **RHEMA** Word from God to be used specifically for the problem. Therefore when you now come face to face with a challenge for which you require the supernatural hands of God, you should be able to thank God. You should be able to tell God that you know that He has heard you like Jesus did at the grave of Lazarus. But concerning the challenge all you need to do at that time is to boldly give the appropriate commands in the Name of Jesus based on the **RHEMA** Word of God that you have received from God to draw out the supernatural. That was how Jesus did it at the grave of Lazarus. That is how you are supposed to do it. Let us consider two or three examples to show you exactly how you are supposed to tackle challenges when they come.

Firstly, in the model prayer that Jesus gave us, He said that we should say, "And lead us not into temptation but deliver us from evil." It is obvious therefore that He must have prayed this prayer several times. But we should note what He did when temptation came against Him face to face as recorded in Luke 4:1-13. When that happened there was no time for this prayer. It was then time for action, facing the devil and giving commands based on the Word of God.

And Jesus being full of the Holy Ghost returned from Jordan, and was led by the Spirit into the wilderness,

Being forty days tempted of the devil. And in those days he did eat nothing: and when they were ended, he afterward hungered.

And the devil said unto him, If thou be the Son of God, command this stone that it be made bread.

And Jesus answered him, saying, It is written, That man shall not live by bread alone, but by every word of God.

And the devil, taking him up into an high mountain, shewed unto him all the kingdoms of the world in a moment of time.

And the devil said unto him, All this power will I give thee, and the glory of them: for that is delivered unto me; and to whomsoever I will I give it.

If thou therefore wilt worship me, all shall be thine.

And Jesus answered and said unto him, Get thee behind me, Satan: for it is written, Thou shalt worship the Lord thy God, and him only shalt thou serve.

Your Mouth is the Vehicle

And he brought him to Jerusalem, and set him on a pinnacle of the temple, and said unto him, If thou be the Son of God, cast thyself down from hence:

For it is written, He shall give his angels charge over thee, to keep thee:

And in their hands they shall bear thee up, lest at any time thou dash thy foot against a stone.

And Jesus answering said unto him, It is said, Thou shalt not tempt the Lord thy God.

And when the devil had ended all the temptation, he departed from him for a season.
Luke 4:1-13

What He did then was to face the tempter squarely, to counter whatever he did or said with the appropriate Word of God and to command the tempter to get behind Him. Look at the story below. You can use prayer as a spiritual inoculation taken in advance against temptation or spiritual warfare. But when temptation or spiritual warfare really comes it is time for you to act and give commands in the Name of Jesus.

You will note that after Jesus replied the devil with the **LOGOS** Word of God saying, *"It is written......."* **twice,** the devil himself started to quote **LOGOS** from the Scriptures to support his own argument in the temptation. Jesus therefore realized at that point that the devil will not easily give in and will not leave Him alone.

Living a Supernatural Life (Volume 2)

At that point He realized that He needed more than the **LOGOS** Word of God to tackle the devil and He must have paused to receive the **RHEMA** Word from God with which to tackle the devil. This is so because as you can see, His next answer to the devil, was received by Him as a **RHEMA** Word of God to Him to be used specifically for that situation, even though it was taken from the **LOGOS** Word of God. You can see this from the answer that He gave the devil in verse twelve. He did not say *"It is written….."* but this time He said, *"It is said….."* So He replied the devil with the **RHEMA** Word spoken to Him by God. The devil had no answer to that because he only has access to the **LOGOS**. The devil knows what is written in the **LOGOS** and can always seek to counter the **LOGOS** Word of God with another **LOGOS** Word of God to support his arguments. So he can always say, **"It is also written"**. But once you take him to the **RHEMA** arena as Jesus did here and tell him the **RHEMA** Word that God has spoken to you saying, *"It is said……"* he will have no answer to that. This is so because he cannot say *"It is also said….."* since God has not told him anything. Therefore he must see himself as defeated at that point and he will leave you alone. If you have not gotten the point yet, then perhaps this second case will show it to you more clearly.

Secondly, let us look at the case of Moses and the children of Israel when they came face to face with the Red Sea obstacle as recorded for us in Exodus 14:9-16. Here was a case begging for an immediate and if possible an instant solution.

Your Mouth is the Vehicle

It was a critical case. Praying to God at this point was not the most urgent thing to do in this critical case. That is what God told Moses in verse 15. God told him to take action.

> *But the Egyptians pursued after them, all the horses and chariots of Pharaoh, and his horsemen, and his army, and overtook them encamping by the sea, beside Pihahiroth, before Baalzephon.*
>
> *And when Pharaoh drew nigh, the children of Israel lifted up their eyes, and, behold, the Egyptians marched after them; and they were sore afraid: and the children of Israel cried out unto the LORD.*
>
> *And they said unto Moses, Because there were no graves in Egypt, hast thou taken us away to die in the wilderness? wherefore hast thou dealt thus with us, to carry us forth out of Egypt?*
>
> *Is not this the word that we did tell thee in Egypt, saying, Let us alone, that we may serve the Egyptians? For it had been better for us to serve the Egyptians, than that we should die in the wilderness.*
>
> *And Moses said unto the people, Fear ye not, stand still, and see the salvation of the LORD, which he will shew to you to day: for the Egyptians whom ye have seen to day, ye shall see them again no more for ever.*

> *The LORD shall fight for you, and ye shall hold your peace.*
>
> *And the LORD said unto Moses, Wherefore criest thou unto me? speak unto the children of Israel, that they go forward:*
>
> *But lift thou up thy rod, and stretch out thine hand over the sea, and divide it: and the children of Israel shall go on dry ground through the midst of the sea.*
>
> **Exodus 14:9-16**

This is a good example of the way God expects you to act when you come face to face with a critical challenge that requires an urgent solution. When you come to the point where immediate and urgent action is required from you, how do you tackle such situations? Look at what happened to Moses here.

Looking at this story we can see that Moses and the Israelites had come face to face with a problem that required an immediate solution. Pharaoh and the Egyptian army were pursuing them from behind and drawing near to them. The Red Sea was before them staying there as an obstacle that would not allow them to pass. If they attempt to go either to their left side or their right side Pharaoh's army will catch up with them. At that moment, the Red Sea was a mountain to them that must be removed immediately. Moses started crying to God. That is the same thing that we do today when we come face to face with problems. But note what God asked Moses.

Your Mouth is the Vehicle

God asked, *"Wherefore criest thou unto me? Speak unto the children of Israel that they go forward: But lift up thy rod, and stretch out thine hand over the sea, and divide it:"*

This should be a major eye-opener to us today because what God is saying there is this, *"This is not the time for praying to Me, it is the time for you to act by facing the challenge squarely, commanding it and taking the necessary action against it using your rod."* God has already given him a rod with which he was supposed to do miracles, signs and wonders. That is what God said to Moses in Exodus 4:17. The rod was in his hand but instead of using it he faced God crying to Him. The time for crying was over. It was time for using his rod.

> *And thou shalt take this rod in thine hand, wherewith thou shalt do signs.*
> **Exodus 4:17**

He started calming the children of Israel telling them what God can do and what will happen but he did not use the rod in his hand and he did not give any command. God told Moses to command the children of Israel to move forward even though the sea was before them. He also told him to take the necessary action by stretching forth his hand and using his rod against the Red Sea. It was time to give commands to the situation. We also behave today like Moses did then. Whenever we come face to face with daunting challenges, we start praying to God crying, saying what God can do, how powerful He is and how the challenge will disappear.

However that does not make the challenge to disappear. Instead of giving commands and taking control of the situation we ask God to come and help us to fight the situation whereas God has already put in our hands what we need to fight with and win.

Just like He gave to Moses He has also given us a Rod to use for this dispensation. As you can see from what is written in Isaiah 11:1 Jesus Christ is the Rod out of the stem of Jesse.

> *And there shall come forth a rod out of the stem of Jesse, and a Branch shall grow out of his roots:*
> **Isaiah 11:1**

Therefore Jesus Christ is the Rod given to us for this dispensation. But we have also emphasized all along in this book series that Jesus Christ is an embodiment of God's Word. You will see this from what God told us through Apostle John by combining what is written in John 1:1-3 and John 1:14. Therefore Jesus Christ is the Word of God and is God.

> *In the beginning was the Word, and the Word was with God, and the Word was God.*
>
> *The same was in the beginning with God.*
>
> *All things were made by him; and without him was not any thing made that was made.*
> **John 1:1-3**

Your Mouth is the Vehicle

And the Word was made flesh, and dwelt among us, and we beheld his glory, the glory as of the only begotten of the Father, full of grace and truth.
John 1:14

From what Prophet Isaiah said we can see therefore that Jesus Christ who is the Word of God is our Rod for this dispensation. Therefore we can say that our Rod for this dispensation is the Word of God. The Word of God is the Rod that we have been given with which to do signs and wonders in this dispensation. To confirm this further look at what God said in Micah 6:9.

The LORD'S voice crieth unto the city, and the man of wisdom shall see thy name: hear ye the rod, and who hath appointed it.
Micah 6:9

This says that the Rod is to be heard therefore we can see that the Rod is the Word of God. The **ROD** given to you for this dispensation is supposed to be heard. ***"Hear ye the Rod"***

Therefore it follows that you are supposed to speak out the Word of God as the Rod given to you for the working of miracles, signs and wonders for this dispensation.

If you want to know how to use this Rod then look at what Jesus Himself said in John 14:13-14 and also in John 16:23-24. He said that whatever you ask in His Name will be given to you.

And whatsoever ye shall ask in my name, that will I do, that the Father may be glorified in the Son.

If ye shall ask any thing in my name, I will do it.
John 14:13-14

And in that day ye shall ask me nothing. Verily, verily, I say unto you, Whatsoever ye shall ask the Father in my name, he will give it you.

Hitherto have ye asked nothing in my name: ask, and ye shall receive, that your joy may be full.
John 16:23-24

Therefore commanding in His Name using the Word of God as the Rod is what will give you victory in every situation in this dispensation.

Not only that, Jesus Himself said that it is in His Name that you would do miracles, signs and wonders. He said this just before He departed in Mark 16:17-18. You now know the role that His Name plays from what Peter said about His Name and the healing of the lame man at the Beautiful gate in Acts 3:16.

And these signs shall follow them that believe; In my name shall they cast out devils; they shall speak with new tongues;

Your Mouth is the Vehicle

They shall take up serpents; and if they drink any deadly thing, it shall not hurt them; they shall lay hands on the sick, and they shall recover.
Mark 16:17-18

And his name through faith in his name hath made this man strong, whom ye see and know: yea, the faith which is by him hath given him this perfect soundness in the presence of you all.
Acts 3:16

Therefore as you can see from what Peter said above it is the Name of Jesus Christ through faith in His Name that does the miracles, signs and wonders. So the Word of God is our Rod and the Name of Jesus when called will cause Jesus Christ to do miracles, signs and wonders. His Name, through faith in His Name gets the miracle done. The way to use this Rod that you have been given is to use the Word of God to command whatever you want done in His Name and He will do it as written in John 14:14 below.

If ye shall ask any thing in my name, I will do it.
John 14:14

Therefore whenever you come face to face with a challenge, praying asking God to come and solve the problem is not necessarily the most urgent thing for you to do, rather it is more critical then for you to seek the **RHEMA** Word that you can use to command the situation to move in the Name of Jesus.

Living a Supernatural Life (Volume 2)

This is so because Jesus and the Name Jesus is the Rod that you have been given in this dispensation for the working of miracles, signs and wonders. You are to speak the Word of God to your mountains and command them to move in the Name of Jesus Christ. God expects you to do so whenever you come face-to-face with problems. Note that when you come face-to-face with a problem it may be so urgent that there may be no time for prayer. You just have time to give your command in the Name of Jesus.

For every mountain that you come across in life there is the Word of God that will move it. If you search for such words and use them to command it to move in the Name of Jesus it must move. Speak the **RHEMA** Word of God that you have received concerning the mountain to the mountain and command it using the Name of Jesus because everything must bow at the call of that Name of Jesus Christ according to what we are told by Paul the Apostle in Philippians 2:9-11.

> *Wherefore God also hath highly exalted him, and given him a name which is above every name:*
>
> *That at the name of Jesus every knee should bow, of things in heaven, and things in earth, and things under the earth;*
>
> *And that every tongue should confess that Jesus Christ is Lord, to the glory of God the Father.*
>   **Philippians 2:9-11**

Your Mouth is the Vehicle

Thirdly, let us look once again at the case of Peter and John when they came face to face with a lame man at the Beautiful gate of the Temple that they wanted to heal as recorded for us by Luke in Acts 3:1-8. At that point Peter did not bother to pray for healing for this man. He just commanded the healing in the Name of Jesus. This was the first open miracle that the disciples did shortly after Jesus left them so we can assume that the instructions that Jesus gave them must still be fresh in their minds and that it is His instructions that they are following.

Now Peter and John went up together into the temple at the hour of prayer, being the ninth hour.

Now Peter and John went up together into the temple at the hour of prayer, being the ninth hour.

And a certain man lame from his mother's womb was carried, whom they laid daily at the gate of the temple which is called Beautiful, to ask alms of them that entered into the temple;

Who seeing Peter and John about to go into the temple asked an alms.

And Peter, fastening his eyes upon him with John, said, Look on us.

And he gave heed unto them, expecting to receive something of them.

Living a Supernatural Life (Volume 2)

> *Then Peter said, Silver and gold have I none; but such as I have give I thee: In the name of Jesus Christ of Nazareth rise up and walk.*
>
> *And he took him by the right hand, and lifted him up: and immediately his feet and ankle bones received strength.*
>
> *And he leaping up stood, and walked, and entered with them into the temple, walking, and leaping, and praising God.*
>
> **Acts 3:1-8**

Here is a case in which Peter and John had come face to face with a lame man that they wanted to heal. This happened not so long after Jesus left them. You will note here that they did not border to pray to God about this. They did not ask God to come and heal the man. Instead Peter in verse six talked directly to the lame man by commanding him to rise up and walk in the Name of Jesus. He also took the necessary action in verse seven by taking the man by the right hand and lifting him up.

Therefore when you are face to face with a mountain that you want to move, rather than start praying to God asking Him to remove the mountain, it will be more expedient for you to command the mountain to move in the Name of Jesus Christ using the Word of God. Remember that Jesus said, *"If ye shall say unto this mountain......"* He did not say, *"If ye shall pray about this mountain......"* Therefore the better thing to do is to speak to the mountain and command it to move in the Name of Jesus Christ

Your Mouth is the Vehicle

Command it using the Word of God instead of praying to God asking Him to move the mountain. You must then take the necessary action in faith to move it. You know that the Word of God is God as we are told in John 1:1. The Word of God is God. Therefore when you use the Word of God to command a situation, you are actually calling God into that situation.

> ***In the beginning was the Word, and the Word was with God, and the Word was God.***
> **John 1:1**

The supernatural is in your mouth therefore release it. Your mouth can speak death to failure or life to success. It can speak death to fear and doubt or life to faith. It can speak death to poverty or life to prosperity. It can speak death to barrenness or life to fruitfulness.

Therefore speak life not death. Command with your mouth. What most believers of today do is pray to God asking Him to come and deal with the devil for them. But God has already given us the power to do this ourselves.

God has told us that the responsibility for dealing with the devil and getting him to leave us alone is ours. That is basically the essence of what God is telling us through Apostle Peter in 1 Peter 5:8-9 and also through Apostle James in James 4:7.

> ***Be sober, be vigilant; because your adversary the devil, as a roaring lion, walketh about, seeking whom he may devour:***

Living a Supernatural Life (Volume 2)

> *Whom resist stedfast in the faith, knowing that the same afflictions are accomplished in your brethren that are in the world.*
> **1 Peter 5:8-9**

> *Submit yourselves therefore to God. Resist the devil, and he will flee from you.*
> **James 4:7**

Note that in this passage, God warned us to beware of the devil who is going about as a roaring lion looking for whom to devour. I want you to note the following points about what God is telling us in that passage.

The devil is going about *as a roaring lion. He is not a roaring lion* but he goes about like one. So he is just pretending to have power, he doesn't really have any power over you. The real lion is the Lion of the tribe of Juda who is Jesus Christ as written in Revelation 5:5.

> *And one of the elders saith unto me, Weep not: behold, the Lion of the tribe of Juda, the Root of David, hath prevailed to open the book, and to loose the seven seals thereof.*
> **Revelation 5:5**

1. It is you who should resist the devil in faith. It is not God that has to resist him for you. Often what most Christians believe is that God will resist him for them.

2. It is when you resist the devil that he will flee from you. If you do not resist him he will not leave you alone. That is what God made us to understand through James in James 4:7 above.

But note that if he is to flee from you when you resist him, then according to that James 4:7 above you must be in submission to God yourself.

What many believers in Christ do today however is that they pray to God asking Him to come and resist Satan for them. They expect God to be the One that will make Satan to flee from them. But what God said here is quite clear and explicit. He said that we are to do the resisting of Satan ourselves. We are to resist him steadfast in faith and order him to move. When we do this, Satan will flee from us.

But most Christians are not willing to do this. Instead the tradition in most Christian Churches is that they list all that Satan and his agents are doing to them. They then pray that God should fight Satan on their behalf. In some cases they even ask God to kill all such satanic agents that they believe are the ones responsible for whatever predicament they may find themselves.

God has already given you the power to overcome Satan. God has given you the Rod with which to do exploits and show your enemies the power of God that is working in you. You must be willing to demonstrate this power to your enemies. In fact God expects you to do so because if you do not do so your enemies will not submit to you. God made this clear to Moses from what is written in Exodus 4:21 when He reminded Moses that he must not forget to demonstrate the miracles, signs and wonders that He has put in his hand before Pharaoh.

Living a Supernatural Life (Volume 2)

And the LORD said unto Moses, When thou goest to return into Egypt, see that thou do all those wonders before Pharaoh, which I have put in thine hand: but I will harden his heart, that he shall not let the people go.
Exodus 4:21

God knew that it was possible for Moses to get to Pharaoh and not demonstrate the power that has been given to him through the rod that he had. This could happen as a result of fear or even forgetfulness. He might also not have seen the importance of demonstrating the power given to him.

That was why God reminded him and instructed him to make sure that he showed to Pharaoh the power that He had put in his hand.

It is the same thing with many Christians today. As a Christian, God has given you power to be able to demonstrate to your enemies all the abilities of God that God has now vested in you through the Word and the Name of Jesus. God expects you to demonstrate before all people the power that is in the Name of Jesus Christ who is the Rod that you have been given in this dispensation. It was the demonstration of the power of God that was in Moses' hand that made Pharaoh to submit to Moses. If you do not demonstrate the power that is in the Name of Jesus Christ that you now have to your enemies they will not submit themselves to you. Even for God we are made to understand in Psalm 66:3 that it is through the greatness of His power that His enemies submit to Him.

Your Mouth is the Vehicle

Say unto God, How terrible art thou in thy works! through the greatness of thy power shall thine enemies submit themselves unto thee.

Psalm 66:3

If it takes the demonstration of the power of God for His enemies to submit to Him then it is obvious that you will have to demonstrate the power of God that now resides in you if your enemies are to submit to you also. You will definitely have to demonstrate power to get your enemies to submit to you.

As we have shown earlier the Name of Jesus and your faith in that Name plays a very prominent role in your ability to demonstrate this power and consequently live a supernatural life here on earth. We have shown you how important a role the Name plays in your being able to demonstrate the power of God as well as your right to the use of that Name and how to use that Name with your mouth as the vehicle. If you are not willing to demonstrate the power of God that you now have to your enemies they will not submit themselves to you. Instead those enemies will seek to flex their muscles against you to demonstrate their own fake power to you and get you to submit to them. It is this demonstration of fake power in the form of symptoms that some people see or feel and immediately submit to the enemy's antics virtually admitting defeat.

That is why you find them making such statements as, **"I am sick, I am finished"** etc. There is great power in the Name of the Lord Jesus Christ that you have been given.

Living a Supernatural Life (Volume 2)

That is what we are made to see from what God said through Jeremiah in Jeremiah 10:6. Use the Name to demonstrate the power of God to your enemies.

> *Forasmuch as there is none like unto thee, O LORD; thou art great, and thy name is great in might.*
> **Jeremiah 10:6**

Jesus Christ and in particular His Name is your Rod for doing miracles, signs and wonders in this dispensation. That is why He is called a ***Rod*** out of the stem of Jesse in Isaiah 11:1.

> *And there shall come forth a rod out of the stem of Jesse, and a Branch shall grow out of his roots:*
> **Isaiah 11:1**

You have Jesus Christ, the Word as your ***Rod*** for doing the supernatural. Your mouth is the vehicle. Use your mouth because you are the prophet of your own destiny. Speak out and command because from what is written in Proverbs 18:21 your words have the power of death and life and they give you what you see in your life.

> *Death and life are in the power of the tongue: and they that love it shall eat the fruit thereof.*
> **Proverbs 18:21**

The pitfall for many of the Christians of today however is that when they command in the Name of Jesus they expect to see the physical manifestation of their command immediately.

Your Mouth is the Vehicle

If they do not see this, they then conclude that their command has not been obeyed and they start entertaining doubts in their minds. What they ought to know is that when they give such commands in the Name of Jesus it is the fulfillment of their commands that is immediate; the physical manifestation of their commands may take some time. It is this that we want to look at in the next Chapter.

If we can only remember that we are not the one doing the work but Jesus Christ is the miracle worker. We are just the conduit through which He does the miracles. That is what we can infer from what God wrote through Paul in Philippians 2:13.

> *For it is God which worketh in you both to will and to do of his good pleasure.*
> **Philippians 2:13**

Therefore it is not you who decides what to do. It is not you who decides how to do it. God is the One that decides what to do as well as how it will be done. It is God who works in you according to His will not according to your will. Therefore why worry yourself when you command and you do not see any sign that your command have been obeyed.

After you have commanded just wait because if you can wait in faith you are bound to see your command have been effected and you see that your command has been obeyed. Remember also that there can be stiff opposition to your commands because what you are involved in is really a spiritual battle and there will be forces that will contend your authority to command.

Living a Supernatural Life (Volume 2)

They will therefore resist your command. But if you stand firm in your faith in Jesus and in His Name with which you pronounce your command you will have what you say in the end.

CHAPTER 6

THE FULFILLMENT OF YOUR COMMAND IS IMMEDIATE

The day of your declaration is the day they are spiritually fulfilled. As soon as you declare or decree anything, it is fulfilled. ***But the physical manifestation may take some time.*** Remember when Jesus Christ went to the synagogue and He was given the Scripture to read. On that occasion He seized the opportunity to proclaim His mission not as something yet to be fulfilled but as something that was fulfilled on that very day. He read from the Scriptures as written down in Luke 4:16-21. After reading, we are told that He began to say unto them ***"This day is this Scripture fulfilled in your ears."*** Read the text below.

> *And he came to Nazareth, where he had been brought up: and, as his custom was, he went into the synagogue on the Sabbath day, and stood up for to read.*

> *And there was delivered unto him the book of the prophet Essays. And when he had opened the book, he found the place where it was written,*
>
> *The Spirit of the Lord is upon me, because he hath anointed me to preach the gospel to the poor; he hath sent me to heal the brokenhearted, to preach deliverance to the captives, and recovering of sight to the blind, to set at liberty them that are bruised,*
>
> *To preach the acceptable year of the Lord.*
>
> *And he closed the book, and he gave it again to the minister, and sat down. And the eyes of all them that were in the synagogue were fastened on him.*
>
> *And he began to say unto them, This day is this scripture fulfilled in your ears.*
>
> **Luke 4:16-21**

Note that Jesus Christ did not wait for the manifestation of His destiny. Even though it had not manifested physically yet, He said ***"THIS DAY"*** (i.e. before the physical manifestation). You must note that **the day of your declaration is the day that it is fulfilled.** It may take time to manifest, but the fulfillment is immediate. As soon as you declare anything, it is equivalent to planting a seed, which will germinate if nurtured by you. The process of germination starts as soon as you plant it. But you have to nurture it so that the germination will manifest.

The fulfillment of your Command is immediate

You have to continue nurturing it as it grows so that it reaches maturity in order to produce the fruits that you will reap. It is when it starts to produce fruits that it becomes clear and it is then that your profiting will appear for all to see. Your declaration is equivalent to your seed planting. The fulfillment is equivalent to the seed germination while the manifestation is equivalent to the fruiting stage when all can see it and enjoy the benefits with you. The Word of God and the other words spoken from your mouth are spiritual seeds that have life, which as soon as you speak out begin to germinate and will eventually yield the fruits that you will harvest.

That is what Jesus Himself said in Luke 8:11. You know every seed has life in it to reproduce itself a million fold. No matter how small the seed may be the power of life, a great force that will push the earth to come out is resident inside it, ready to act as soon as it is planted. So are the words that you plant as spiritual seeds. When you plant seeds, you will eventually reap the harvest provided you nurture your seeds to grow and mature to the point of bearing fruits. God said in Genesis 8:22 that seed time and harvest time will never end as long as the earth remains.

> *"Now the parable is this: The seed is the word of God."*
> **Luke 8:11**

> *While the earth remaineth, seedtime and harvest, and cold and heat, and summer and winter, and day and night shall not cease.*
> **Genesis 8:22**

Living a Supernatural Life (Volume 2)

Therefore if you sow seeds and you water the seeds you are bound to harvest the fruits. Because the words that you speak out with your mouth are spiritual seeds, you should always make sure that you speak right words into your life. In particular, speak the Word of God into your life. When you speak right words, you are planting the right spiritual seeds into your life, and you will eventually reap the harvest of the words that you have spoken. Never speak any words contrary to what the Word of God says regarding any situation that you may find yourself. For every bondage or affliction that you may find yourself in, there is a Word of God that can get you out of it. All you have to do is find it, believe it, meditate on it until it is rooted in your spirit and becomes a **RHEMA** Word to you then speak it out boldly and forcefully into your situation. We have said in *Volume 1* of this *"Living a supernatural life"* book series that the Word of God is not only a **seed** but also the **water** that your seed needs to be watered with in order to grow and eventually yield the right fruits for you. Once your seed is planted you should water it on a continuous basis. You do this by the speaking of the appropriate supporting Word of God to the seed. Without watering you will not be able to reap the fruit. We have also explained that if the word that you plant as seed is the Word of God, and you also water it with the spoken Word of God by confessing the positive Word of God to it on a continuous basis, then without any doubt you are bound to get the right fruits. Whatever you say will eventually manifest as fruits. Note also that it is not only what you say about yourself, but also what you say about others and what others say about you that will eventually manifest.

The fulfillment of your Command is immediate

That is why it is not good for you to say bad things about other people because whatever you say will eventually manifest physically. It is also not good for you to allow other people to speak negative words into your life unchallenged because whatever they say can also be effected in your life if it is not rejected by you. Note what Jesus said, which is written down for us in Mark 11:23. He said, *"He shall have whatsoever he saith"*

> *For verily I say unto you, That whosoever shall say unto this mountain, Be thou removed, and be thou cast into the sea; and shall not doubt in his heart, but shall believe that those things which he saith shall come to pass; he shall have whatsoever he saith.*
>
> **Mark 11:23**

Jesus did not say, *"He shall have whatsoever good things he saith"* Jesus did not say, *"He shall have whatsoever he saith about himself"* It does not matter what you say whether it is good or it is bad; it is what you say that you will have. So, say good things always.

This is also true of any other person, not just you alone. When somebody speaks anything negative or bad into your life, he can also have whatsoever he said. Therefore when someone says any negative thing against you, it is a bad seed planted into your life and you must condemn it immediately to uproot it from your life. That is what God said that you should do in Isaiah 54:17. God will not condemn it for you. It must be done by you.

> *No weapon that is formed against thee shall prosper; and every tongue that shall rise against thee in judgment thou shalt condemn. This is the heritage of the servants of the Lord, and their righteousness is of me, saith the Lord.*
>
> **Isaiah 54:17**

It is actually like a curse planted into your life. However, as a born-again Christian living in the will of God you need not worry yourself about this because you have the power to reject it. This is so because Jesus said in Matthew 16:19 that He will give you the keys to the kingdom of Heaven and anything that you bind here on earth will be bound in heaven and anything that you lose here on earth will be loosed in heaven. This now gives you the power to choose what you want in order to be able to effect the right choice as God directed in Deuteronomy 30:19. So it is your choice. You have the choice and you have been given the power to make the right choice.

> *And I will give unto thee the keys of the kingdom of heaven: and whastsoever thou shalt bind on earth shall be bound in heaven: and whatsoever thou shalt loose on earth shall be loosed in heaven.*
>
> **Matthew 16:19**

> *I call heaven and earth to record this day against you, that I have set before you life and death, blessing and cursing: therefore choose life, that both thou and thy seed may live:*
>
> **Deuteronomy 30:19**

The fulfillment of your Command is immediate

Therefore you must reject any negative thing spoken into your life immediately and command it to be bound in the Name of Jesus. Once you reject it, your rejection here on earth is sealed in heaven and the curse will be terminated immediately. Your rejection is equivalent to your binding it. That is why you must reject any bad thing said into your life, because when you reject it, your rejection is sealed in heaven. But when you do not reject it, that is equivalent to your accepting it and your acceptance will also be sealed in heaven.

You have been given the authority to either accept or reject it. You must note this promise of Jesus very well because many Christians go to God in their prayers asking Him to come and bind or loose things for them, to come and open or close doors for them. God has already given you the keys with which to do these. It is what you accept that God will confirm. It is therefore your responsibility to first bind before God does so, to first loose before God does so, to first open before God opens and to first close before God closes. God has given you the right to do these. Whatever you want God to bind or loose for you in heaven you first bind or loose it here on earth. Remember that Christ has promised you in Luke 10:19 a mouth and wisdom, which none of your adversaries can resist. Therefore when you command anything it must obey you. It cannot resist you. You can bind and loose anything. That is the essence of the promise that Jesus made to us in Matthew 16:19, which we considered in the previous page. To help you in the binding and loosing process, you can also use the Word of God, which says that Christ has redeemed you from the curse of the law. That is what God said in Galatians 3:13-14.

Living a Supernatural Life (Volume 2)

> *Behold, I give unto you power to tread on serpents and scorpions, and over all the power of the enemy: and nothing shall by any means hurt you.*
> **Luke 10:19**

> *Christ hath redeemed us from the curse of the law, being made a curse for us: for it is written, Cursed is every one that hangeth on a tree:*
>
> *That the blessing of Abraham might come on the Gentiles through Jesus Christ; that we might receive the promise of the Spirit through faith.*
> **Galatians 3:13-14**

If you have been redeemed from the curses, why should you allow any curse to be put on you again? Whatever you say or you allow to be said into your life unchallenged will eventually manifest in your life.

But you have been given the right and the authority to reject any negative word or curse spoken into your life and to accept every positive word or blessing spoken into your life. Whatever you accept is what God will accept for you.

Do you remember the story of the fig tree that Jesus Christ cursed? If you look at what is written by Mark in Mark 11:13-14, 20 and 21 you will note that the manifestation of that proclamation of Jesus Christ against the fig tree did not occur until the following day on their return journey.

The fulfillment of your Command is immediate

And seeing a fig tree afar off having leaves, he came, if haply he might find any thing thereon: and when he came to it, he found nothing but leaves; for the time of figs was not yet.

And Jesus answered and said unto it, No man eat fruit of thee hereafter for ever. And his disciples heard it.

Mark 11:13-14

And in the morning, as they passed by, they saw the fig tree dried up from the roots.

And Peter calling to remembrance saith unto him, Master, behold, the fig tree which thou cursedst is withered away.

Mark 11:20-21

When you make a pronouncement it is equivalent to planting a seed. In the natural when you plant a seed there is life in the seed and that life will make it to start to germinate under the ground. But the germination may not manifest immediately above the ground. As soon as Jesus spoke to the fig tree and commanded that it should die it immediately started to dry from its roots, which is the source of its life.

But it was not apparent yet above the ground that anything was happening to the tree. It is the same thing that happens when you command a disease to leave. The fulfillment of your command is set in motion immediately and the disease starts to die from its roots where its source of life is located.

Living a Supernatural Life (Volume 2)

But you may not see any sign of it yet on the outside. However if you stand firm and do not go back to doubt that your command has been obeyed, which is equivalent to uprooting the seed that you have planted, then the germination will eventually manifest for all to see. If the Lord God can command and needed time for it to manifest it is obvious that you will also need time for your commands to manifest. Therefore when you declare anything, even though it is fulfilled as soon as you declare it, the manifestation may not occur immediately. But you should not let this worry you. If you have the faith and you hold on to the confession without any wavering or doubt in your mind, the manifestation will eventually come. You must keep assuring yourself that you are in total control of whatever is happening in your life or around you. Once you command, take it that it is fulfilled and get on with any other thing that you are doing. Don't think about it anymore for it is in the process of such thinking that doubts can come into your mind as to whether what you have declared will be fulfilled or not. Rather than think about this it will be better for you to meditate on what the Word says concerning it. Just look for the supporting Word of God and keep confessing it.

To bring this home to you, let us look at another example in the Scriptures. Remember the story of Elijah written in 1 Kings 18:41-45 when he said that it would rain? That story is recorded below to help you to visualize what really happened.

> *And Elijah said unto Ahab, Get thee up, eat and drink; for there is a sound of abundance of rain.*

The fulfillment of your Command is immediate

So Ahab went up to eat and to drink. And Elijah went up to the top of Carmel; and he cast himself down upon the earth, and put his face between his knees,

And said to his servant, Go up now, look toward the sea. And he went up, and looked, and said, There is nothing. And he said, Go again seven times.

And it came to pass at the seventh time, that he said, Behold, there ariseth a little cloud out of the sea, like a man's hand. And he said, Go up, say unto Ahab, Prepare thy chariot, and get thee down, that the rain stop thee not.

And it came to pass in the mean while, that the heaven was black with clouds and wind, and there was a great rain. And Ahab rode, and went to Jezreel.
                                      1 Kings 18:41-45

As you can see from this story Elijah spoke out what he wanted proclaiming that there is a sound of an abundance of rain even though there was no sign of it. Immediately he declared what he wanted in the physical realm, it was already fulfilled in the spiritual realm. But the manifestation in the physical realm did not come immediately. Six times he had to ask his servant to go and look out to check if the rain is coming and six times the servant came back with a negative answer. Despite this Elijah never gave up. He kept praying and kept saying; *"There will be rain, go back and check."* And as a result of his stand in faith the rain eventually came because he stuck to his confessions.

Living a Supernatural Life (Volume 2)

The rain came because our God is a God that confirms the words of His servants, and performs the counsel of His messengers. That is what God told us through Isaiah in Isaiah 44:26. Elijah knew that he had the authority to command even non flesh-and-blood or inanimate objects and have his command obeyed. You also have the power to do so. If you were in Elijah's position and you said that it will rain and there was no sign of the rain, as soon as they check the first time and there was no sign of rain, you will start to fear what the people around especially the king would do to you.

> *That confirmeth the word of his servant, and performeth the counsel of his messengers; that saith to Jerusalem, Thou shalt be inhabited; and to the cities of Judah, Ye shall be built, and I will raise up the decayed places thereof:*
> **Isaiah 44:26**

You will start to fear that they may mock you. You will also probably not continue boldly with your proclamation. You may even start to give excuses. You will not have the boldness to tell your servant to keep going back to look. You will be afraid that even your servant will mock you.

It is doubt that normally stops the fulfillment of our commands from the germinating to the manifestation stage. You must not give up on your declarations. If you hold on to them they will eventually manifest physically for all to see. Many believers are waiting for God to give the commands for the miraculous to happen in their lives but they will have to wait long if they are expecting God to do so.

The fulfillment of your Command is immediate

God has already given you the power to give the commands and He has told you that what He does is to confirm whatever His servants say. As a New Covenant saint you are much more than His servant, you are now His son. If He will confirm what His servants say, it is much more certain that He will confirm what His sons say? Elijah who was His servant knew that he had such an authority. That was why he was able to give his command with boldness. He knew that his authority to command extended to all of God's creation and was not limited to just commanding flesh and blood beings. He also knew that whatever commands he gave must be obeyed. If Elijah can command the elements and they obeyed him you can also do so. Don't you know that ***you even have the potential for a higher level of authority and anointing than that of Elijah*** or any old Covenant saint? That is the essence of what Jesus said in Matthew 11:11. Look at what He said. He said,

> *"Verily I say unto you, Among them that are born of women there hath not risen a greater than John the Baptist: notwithstanding he that is least in the kingdom of heaven is greater than he."*
>
> **Matthew 11:11**

This means that you are greater than any old-Covenant saint. Whatever any old Covenant saint can do you can do more. You can give the command to bring about whatever you want to happen because whatever you command God will confirm. Many believers do not think that when they give a command for the miraculous to happen it will manifest. They do not see themselves as pious enough to be used by God for this purpose.

Living a Supernatural Life (Volume 2)

They believe that only some people who the Holy Spirit have endowed with the gift of the working of miracles can do so and get what they command effected immediately. But that was not what Jesus Christ our Lord said. Take a look again at Mark 16:17-18 written below to see what Jesus said. He said,

> *"And these signs shall follow them that believe; in my name shall they cast out devils; they shall speak with new tongues;*
>
> *They shall take up serpents; and if they drink any deadly thing, it shall not hurt them; they shall lay hands on the sick, and they shall recover."*
>
> Mark 16:17-18

Jesus did not say, *"And these signs shall follow them that have the gift of the working of miracles."* He did not say, *"And these signs shall follow them that have the gift of faith."* He did not say, *"And these signs shall follow them that have the gift of healing."* No! He said, *"And these signs shall follow them that believe."* True! Some people have been endowed with the gift of faith, the gift of healing or the gift of the working of miracles but the Scripture above refers to **all that believe**.

Therefore if you are a believer the signs and wonders that Jesus referred to in the above Scripture are supposed to be following you. If the signs are not following you it must means that you are not a believer. You are just one of those who think that they are believers whereas they are not. If you are a believer when you command any situation your command must be obeyed.

The fulfillment of your Command is immediate

This is so because, as we had seen earlier from what is written in Matthew 16:19, Jesus promised that He would give you the keys of the kingdom of Heaven such that whatever you bind here on earth would be bound in Heaven and whatever you lose here on earth would be loosed in Heaven. He said,

> *"And I will give unto thee the keys of the kingdom of heaven: and whatsoever thou shalt bind on earth shall be bound in heaven: and whatsoever thou shalt loose on earth shall be loosed in heaven."*
> **Matthew 16:19**

This means therefore that whatever you command to happen here on earth is also sealed as such in Heaven. Jesus also said in Luke 21:15 and I repeat it here again, that He would give you a mouth and wisdom, which none of your adversaries shall be able to gainsay or resist. Look at what He said below.

> *For I will give you a mouth and wisdom, which all your adversaries shall not be able to gainsay nor resist.*
> **Luke 21:15**

Therefore whatever you command cannot resist the command that you give it. It must obey whatever you say. No enemy, no adversary can resist your commands if you know your rights. Keep these two verses before you all the time. They will help you to remember always that whatever you command must obey you when you command it. You can command any situation and it will obey you.

Living a Supernatural Life (Volume 2)

In particular you can command diseases and they must obey you. We have discussed and shown that you can command diseases in *Chapter 5* of the *Volume 1* of this *"Living a supernatural life"* book series written by the same author.

Now, we have shown that you can live a supernatural life here on earth and we have given you some of the major keys that you will need as well as the vehicle that you will use to get you there. Let us now turn our attention to the practice of actually living the supernatural life. In this next Chapter we shall discuss what you need to do and what you need to be in order that you can live a supernatural life. These will help you in the practice of supernatural living.

CHAPTER 7

PRACTICING SUPERNATURAL LIVING

In this Chapter we shall look at those things that you must do or be if you want to live a supernatural life here on earth through the words that come out of your mouth. Some of these may look obvious to you; some of them may not look so obvious. Some may even look too simplistic. But they are all necessary if you want to live a supernatural life here on earth. Let us now look at each of them.

1. PREACH THE GOSPEL OF CHRIST

The major reason why you are given supernatural powers as a believer in Christ is so that you can preach the Gospel of Christ. The miracles, signs and wonders are meant to confirm the Word of God that you speak out. When Jesus was sending His disciples to go and preach on what looked like a practical test to try out what they have learned from Him, He gave them power and authority to go and preach the Gospel. The same thing is true of us today. When you take up the mission of preaching the Gospel he equips you with power and continues to confirm whatsoever you say.

Living a Supernatural Life (Volume 2)

With His disciples He equipped them with the power to heal the sick, cleanse the lepers, raise the dead and cast out devils. Then He sent them out to go and preach. You will see this story recorded in Matthew 10:1-8.

> *And when he had called unto him his twelve disciples, he gave them power against unclean spirits, to cast them out, and to heal all manner of sickness and all manner of disease.*
>
> *Now the names of the twelve apostles are these; The first, Simon, who is called Peter, and Andrew his brother; James the son of Zebedee, and John his brother;*
>
> *Philip, and Bartholomew; Thomas, and Matthew the publican; James the son of Alphaeus, and Lebbaeus, whose surname was Thaddaeus;*
>
> *Simon the Canaanite, and Judas Iscariot, who also betrayed him.*
>
> *These twelve Jesus sent forth, and commanded them, saying, Go not into the way of the Gentiles, and into any city of the Samaritans enter ye not:*
>
> *But go rather to the lost sheep of the house of Israel.*
>
> *And as ye go, preach, saying, The kingdom of heaven is at hand.*

Practicing Supernatural Living

Heal the sick, cleanse the lepers, raise the dead, cast out devils: freely ye have received, freely give.
Matthew 10:1-8

So, you can see that He gave them this power to support them in the work of preaching the Gospel because He knew that people would not believe unless they see such supernatural acts. He had said in John 4:48 that people will not believe unless they see miracles, signs and wonders. Therefore the miracles are necessary for the propagation of the gospel.

Then said Jesus unto him, Except ye see signs and wonders, ye will not believe.
John 4:48

So, it is obvious that the power to do supernatural acts is given to the believer so that he can preach to unbelievers and when they see the supernatural acts, they would believe. Therefore if you are not willing to preach the Gospel of Christ, who is the owner of the power then do not expect to do much of such supernatural acts. Jesus said as written in John 14:12-14 that if you ask for anything in His Name He would do it. But He started that discourse by saying that you would do the works that He did and even greater works. Then He followed by saying that whatever you ask for in His Name He would do it. What He expects you to do therefore is to command that the works you want to do be done in His Name. You must realize that Christ is the owner of the power that you want to use. Therefore you must do everything according to His prescription.

> *Verily, verily, I say unto you, He that believeth on me, the works that I do shall he do also; and greater works than these shall he do; because I go unto my Father.*
>
> *And whatsoever ye shall ask in my name, that will I do, that the Father may be glorified in the Son.*
>
> *If ye shall ask any thing in my name, I will do it.*
>
> **John 14:12-14**

Now, the works that He did are listed in Matthew 4:23 and these include preaching the Gospel, healing all manner of sickness and healing all manner of disease among the people.

> *And Jesus went about all Galilee, teaching in their synagogues, and preaching the gospel of the kingdom, and healing all manner of sickness and all manner of disease among the people.*
>
> **Matthew 4:23**

You cannot leave out the work of preaching the Gospel of Christ and expect to do the other works of healing all manner of sickness and all manner of disease among the people.

Jesus Himself is the One that works these miracles, signs and wonders and He does them to confirm His Words when you preach His Gospel.

Finally, look also at where He promised that this power would be following you as a believer in Mark 16:15-17. He preceded the promise with this same assignment, which He gave you as a believer by saying that you should go into the entire world and preach the Gospel to every creature. After He had departed this world, as His disciples obeyed Him and went out to preach the Gospel everywhere, we are told in verse twenty of that Mark Chapter sixteen, Mark 16:20 that the Lord, that is Jesus, was working with them confirming the Word with signs following. If you are not preaching the Word don't expect the signs to be following you.

And he said unto them, Go ye into all the world, and preach the gospel to every creature.

He that believeth and is baptized shall be saved; but he that believeth not shall be damned.

And these signs shall follow them that believe; In my name shall they cast out devils; they shall speak with new tongues;

And they went forth, and preached every where, the Lord working with them, and confirming the word with signs following. Amen.

Mark 16:15-17, 20

So, when you preach the Gospel of Christ, Jesus Christ Himself will be working with you and it is He who will do the miracles, signs and wonders to confirm His Word that you speak.

Therefore, basically you are given this power so that when you preach you will demonstrate the power of God and when others see it they will believe also. It is the Word of God that the miracles confirm. It is therefore a basic necessity that you must be doing the works that Christ did if you are to have this power fully and practically demonstrated in your life. This means that you must be preaching the Gospel of Christ for it is the Word of God that you speak that the miracles will confirm.

2. PROCLAIM WHAT YOU WANT

Proclaim what you want because that's the way God does it. Often times what most Christians do is fight a defensive fight against the enemy. The enemy comes with a problem and they start binding and cursing the problem. Why not be on the offensive and proclaim what you want, rather than wait for the enemy to bring what he has and you start fighting back. Ignore the antics of the enemy and proclaim what you want. In Genesis 1:3 God said, ***"Let there be light"***-- and darkness left. That is exactly how you are supposed to function, because you are created in God's image, a carbon copy. You are also a partaker of His divine nature. Therefore you are supposed to act in His likeness, which means like He does. This means that you must proclaim what you want. Pronounce what you want into existence. Follow the example of God. It was true that darkness was there but God did not bind darkness. He did not bother to bind darkness. He did not bother Himself taking action against darkness. God pronounced the light that He wanted into existence and darkness moved to the side and gave way for light.

That is exactly how you are supposed to function. If God had bound darkness then perhaps we would probably have no darkness today and there would have been no nights. What a world it would have been with no rest!

So if sickness comes, there is no need for you to bind sickness, even though you have the power to bind it. That is a long route to your destination. Just say, *"Let there be perfect health"*, and take your stand in faith and sickness will pack and run away.

If failure comes just proclaim, *"Let there be success"*, and take your stand in faith and failure will pack and leave you alone. After all, failure is not supposed to hang around you. Don't seat waiting for what the devil brings to you. Be on the offensive.

If poverty comes just proclaim, *"Let there be prosperity"*, and poverty will pack its baggage and leave you alone. Wherever you have deficiency just proclaim surplus and that is what you will get.

If barrenness comes just proclaim, *"Let there be fruitfulness"*, and barrenness will find its way out of your life. That is the way God does it. You too must learn to do it that way. Also remember that death and life are in the power of your tongue. That is what God told us through Solomon in Proverbs 18:21.

Death and life are in the power of the tongue: and they that love it shall eat the fruit thereof.
Proverbs 18:21

Instead of using His mouth to proclaim death to darkness, God proclaimed life to light. And darkness gave way. Had God proclaimed darkness to be bound we would not have darkness today. It would have been difficult for man to rest as he does today in the night for there would have been no night. Therefore you can speak life instead of death. So, proclaim life. Some of the things that are working against you and you are currently praying to destroy today may end up being the catalyst for your growth tomorrow. What you say can produce life or death. It can produce death to diseases, death to lack, death to failure, death to barrenness and death to all types of afflictions and even to good things. But preferably speak words that will produce life to health, life to success, life to victory. When you proclaim life to health, you are automatically proclaiming that sickness leaves. When you proclaim life to success, you are automatically proclaiming that failure leaves. When you proclaim life to prosperity, you are automatically proclaiming that poverty and lack leave. It is what you say that you will get. Therefore why not proclaim life instead of death?

WHATEVER YOU CANNOT PROCLAIM YOU CANNOT POSSESS

Whatever you cannot proclaim with your mouth you should not expect to possess. Even God had to proclaim things into existence, so why not you? Follow the footstep of the Father. You are created to act and function like Him. You are created to create things by pronouncing them into existence.

Practicing Supernatural Living

I know that there are some traditions that do oppose people speaking out what they want boldly, but as a Christian you must speak out what you want. You must speak it out boldly. For whatever you say is what you will get. Therefore beware of traditions.

3. BEWARE OF THE TRADITION OF MEN

I know that traditionally some people have been brought up not to open their mouths to proclaim what they want. This is because there are situations where such acts are considered as a rude or proud behaviour traditionally. You now know that it is by opening your mouth wide that you will achieve your full potential in Christ. By following after such traditions therefore you will not be able to achieve your full potential in Christ. Therefore don't let traditions inhibit you from opening your mouth. They will tell you that what you are saying cannot be true. Open your mouth wide. God has warned us to beware and not allow any man to tie us down with the tradition of men. That is the essence of the warning that He gave through Apostle Paul in Colossians 2:8.

> *Beware lest any man spoil you through philosophy and vain deceit, after the tradition of men, after the rudiments of the world, and not after Christ.*
> **Colossians 2:8**

So do not let traditions inhibit you from opening your mouth wide and proclaiming what you want. You must beware and not let people push you into saying or doing things that inhibits the outflow of God's power through your mouth by following the traditions of men.

Living a Supernatural Life (Volume 2)

For example, when you start to proclaim things and they get established, tradition will start to say that you are using some form of magical powers. This is because people tend to believe that God is no longer in the business of doing miracles. To them the devil is now the miracle worker.

They will start to say all kinds of evil things about you. But never mind; they are actually secretly envious of you. There are traditional prejudices against the supernatural use of God's power. This is because Satan the enemy knows that he is under threat whenever such powers are exhibited. Therefore he will do anything to stop it by maligning you. But remember that they did the same thing to Christ. Jesus Himself even told us that we would suffer such persecutions as He suffered but such will turn to a testimony for us. Jesus Himself said so in Luke 21:12-13.

> ***But before all these, they shall lay their hands on you, and persecute you, delivering you up to the synagogues, and into prisons, being brought before kings and rulers for my name's sake.***
>
> ***And it shall turn to you for a testimony.***
> ***Luke 21:12-13***

As you attempt to live a supernatural life and practice to live your new nature in Christ, oppositions will rise up against you and persecutions may even come. But as you can see above, you need not worry about such persecutions because Jesus said that it would turn to you for a testimony.

This means that such things will lead to your authentication or confirmation as a Christian and a genuine follower of Christ. It will bring you glory instead of the shame that the opposition planned for you. Such oppositions will help to bring about the manifestations of God's power. You don't have to follow the habits or customs of the people where they do not agree with what the Word says. In truth, there are times when the following of tradition makes the Word of God of no effect in our lives. (i.e. ineffective).

So if you follow what traditions say, you can end up making the Word of God ineffective in your life. That is what Jesus said as written down in Matthew 15:5-6. He said,

"But ye say, Whosoever shall say to his father or his mother, It is a gift, by whatsoever thou mightest be profited by me;

And honour not his father or his mother, he shall be free. Thus have ye made the commandment of God of none effect by your tradition."
Matthew 15:5-6

Therefore beware of traditions. Traditionally when you talk boldly they may say that you are forward or boasting, but don't worry, you can boast in the Lord. Therefore boast in the Lord because boasting in the Lord is permitted. What is not permitted is boasting your own power. But when you know that it is not you who actually does the work you will stop boasting in your own power.

4. BOAST IN THE LORD

Boasting in the Lord is permitted for you. Don't be afraid of what people will say. You can boast in the Lord. In Psalm 34:2 God made us to know through David that we can do so.

> *My soul shall make her boast in the LORD: the humble shall hear thereof, and be glad.*
> **Psalm 34:2**

Boast in what the God in you can do, not what you can do. Without Him, you can do nothing. But with Him and through Him, you can do all things. Also from what is written in 1 Corinthians 1:31 God made us to understand through Apostle Paul that we can glory in the Lord. Glory in what God can do through you and not in what you can do on your own. As you do this you are exhibiting testimonies, which can be the key to your victory.

> *That, according as it is written, He that glorieth, let him glory in the Lord.*
> **1 Corinthians 1:31**

So, don't let anybody tell you that you are proud when you proclaim what you want or when you proclaim what the Word of God says that you are in Christ and what you can do in Christ. That is not pride. You are only living and doing it like God created you to do things. So, be bold in your loud talking. That was the way Jesus did it when He came physically to this earth. If you want Jesus' type of results then you must do it in His way.

Practicing Supernatural Living

You can boast in the Lord your God all day long. That is not considered pride by God. That is acceptable to God. That is what David made us to understand in Psalm 44:8.

> *In God we boast all the day long, and praise thy name for ever. Selah.*
> **Psalm 44:8**

What God does not want is for you to be comparing or measuring yourself against others and commending yourself. That is the essence of what God is telling us through Apostle Paul in 2 Corinthians 10:12-15. This is because it is not he that commended himself that is approved of God. It is God Himself who commends those that are approved of Him. That is what we are told in 2 Corinthians 10:18. Therefore study the Word to get yourself approved of Him.

> *For we dare not make ourselves of the number, or compare ourselves with some that commend themselves: but they measuring themselves by themselves, and comparing themselves among themselves, are not wise.*
>
> *But we will not boast of things without our measure, but according to the measure of the rule which God hath distributed to us, a measure to reach even unto you.*
>
> *For we stretch not ourselves beyond our measure, as though we reached not unto you: for we are come as far as to you also in preaching the gospel of Christ:*

Living a Supernatural Life (Volume 2)

> *Not boasting of things without our measure, that is, of other men's labours; but having hope, when your faith is increased, that we shall be enlarged by you according to our rule abundantly,*
>
> **2 Corinthians 10:12-15**

> *For not he that commendeth himself is approved, but whom the Lord commendeth.*
>
> **2 Corinthians 10:18**

You can boast but only boast in the Lord not in yourself or any other person; not in what you or any other person can do but in what God can do. Let the people around you know what your God is capable of doing. God wants to be advertised in your life. He wants to be advertised in your business.

Our God is a God that wants to be advertised. He is not a God that shies away from being advertised. He does not shy away from telling people what He is capable of. Remember His many *"I am"* statements of power, ability and confidence stating what He is capable of?

In Exodus 3:6 He said, *"I am the God of Abraham, the God of Isaac and the God of Jacob."* Proclaim Him as God.

> *Moreover he said, I am the God of thy father, the God of Abraham, the God of Isaac, and the God of Jacob. And Moses hid his face; for he was afraid to look upon God.*
>
> **Exodus 3:6**

Practicing Supernatural Living

In Exodus 3:14 He told Moses, *"I AM that I AM". "I AM hath sent me unto you."* Proclaim Him as the "I AM"

> *And God said unto Moses, I AM THAT I AM: and he said, Thus shalt thou say unto the children of Israel, I AM hath sent me unto you.*
>
> **Exodus 3:14**

In Psalm 81:10 He said, *"I am the Lord thy God, which brought thee out of the land of Egypt."* Proclaim Him as the Deliverer.

> *I am the LORD thy God, which brought thee out of the land of Egypt: open thy mouth wide, and I will fill it.*
>
> **Psalm 81:10**

In Isaiah 41:4 He said, *"I the Lord the first and with the last; I am He"*. Proclaim Him as the Everlasting God.

> *Who hath wrought and done it, calling the generations from the beginning? I the LORD, the first, and with the last; I am he.*
>
> **Isaiah 41:4**

In Isaiah 42:8 He said, *"I am the Lord: that is my Name: and my glory will I not give to another."* Proclaim His Glory.

> *I am the LORD: that is my name: and my glory will I not give to another, neither my praise to graven images.*
>
> **Isaiah 42:8**

Living a Supernatural Life (Volume 2)

In Isaiah 43:11 He said, *"I even I am the Lord; and beside me there is no saviour."* Proclaim Him as the Only Saviour

> *I, even I, am the LORD; and beside me there is no saviour.*
>
> **Isaiah 43:11**

In Isaiah 44:6 He said, *"I am the first and I am the last and beside me there is no God."* Proclaim Him as the Only God.

> *Thus saith the LORD the King of Israel, and his redeemer the LORD of hosts; I am the first, and I am the last; and beside me there is no God.*
>
> **Isaiah 44:6**

In Isaiah 46:5 He said, *"To whom will ye liken me and make me equal and compare me that we may be like?"* Proclaim Him as a God greater than all gods.

> *To whom will ye liken me, and make me equal, and compare me, that we may be like?*
>
> **Isaiah 46:5**

In Isaiah 46:9 He said, *"I am God and there is none else, I am God and there is none like me."* Proclaim Him as the Only God.

> *Remember the former things of old: for I am God, and there is none else; I am God, and there is none like me,*
>
> **Isaiah 46:9**

In Isaiah 46:10 He said, *"My counsel shall stand and I will do all my pleasure."* Proclaim Him as the All-Powerful God.

> *Declaring the end from the beginning, and from ancient times the things that are not yet done, saying, My counsel shall stand, and I will do all my pleasure:*
> **Isaiah 46:10**

When you give words of testimony about what God has done or is doing in your life or in someone else's life you are actually unleashing a great weapon that will give you victory over your enemies. That is the essence of what God is telling us through John in Revelation 12:11. The word of your testimony is a major weapon that you can use to defeat the enemy.

> *And they overcame him by the blood of the Lamb, and by the word of their testimony; and they loved not their lives unto the death.*
> **Revelation 12:11**

You can boast of the God who is in you. You can boast of what you are in God. In fact, when you merely state what God is in you or what you are in God people around you will become uncomfortable with you and they will say that you are boasting because what you will be saying will look intimidating to them. They may even say that you are mad like they said of Jesus when He stated who He was. When you boast in the Lord God stating what He can do and what He is doing in you it will unleash a great weapon for living a supernatural life.

Living a Supernatural Life (Volume 2)

That was one of the weapons that David used against Goliath. He boasted of His God saying that God will work and all will know that there is a God in Israel because of the mighty work that He will do. Look at what he said in 1 Samuel 17:45-46.

> *Then said David to the Philistine, Thou comest to me with a sword, and with a spear, and with a shield: but I come to thee in the name of the LORD of hosts, the God of the armies of Israel, whom thou hast defied.*
>
> *This day will the LORD deliver thee into mine hand; and I will smite thee, and take thine head from thee; and I will give the carcases of the host of the Philistines this day unto the fowls of the air, and to the wild beasts of the earth; that all the earth may know that there is a God in Israel.*
> **1 Samuel 17:45-46**

Paul also boasted in the Lord when he said that he can do all things through Christ who strengthened him. He said this in his Epistle to the Philippians in Philippians 4:13. He said,

> *"I can do all things through Christ which strengtheneth me."*
> **Philippians 4:13**

You too should be able to boast in the Lord and say with confidence that you can also do all things through Christ who strengthens you. You should learn to boast in the Lord at all times and in every situation.

Practicing Supernatural Living

As you can see therefore boasting in the Lord is acceptable. It is not only acceptable it is actually desirable. God likes to proclaim who He is and show that He is the only true God. He likes it when His people boast in showing who their God is and what He is capable of.

We should learn to boast in the Lord our God and not in our own power or achievements. We must be able to differentiate the two. Boasting in the Lord is not pride. However it is possible to boast in the Lord and have pride in our hearts. In that case we are taking the credit for what God is doing in our lives and what God is doing through us.

When we do this we are crossing the line into the realm of pride. God hates pride and He made this known to us in several places in the Scriptures. We can see this in Proverbs 16:18 and Proverbs 29:23. God actually hates the proud, we can see in Proverbs 6:16-17 and also in Proverbs 16:5. We can boast in the Lord but we must not allow that to lead us to pride because as we are told by Apostle John in 1 John 2:16 pride is not of God.

> *Pride goeth before destruction, and an haughty spirit before a fall.*
> **Proverbs 16:18**

> *A man's pride shall bring him low: but honour shall uphold the humble in spirit.*
> **Proverbs 29:23**

> *These six things doth the LORD hate: yea, seven are an abomination unto him:*

A proud look, a lying tongue, and hands that shed innocent blood,
           Proverbs 6:16-17

Every one that is proud in heart is an abomination to the LORD: though hand join in hand, he shall not be unpunished.
             Proverbs 16:5

For all that is in the world, the lust of the flesh, and the lust of the eyes, and the pride of life, is not of the Father, but is of the world.
             1 John 2:16

Apart from all the things discussed in this Chapter, there are some other important things that you must do or be if you are to practice supernatural living. These are discussed in detail in the remaining Chapters of this book. The first of these is that you must learn to see beyond the natural realm.

CHAPTER 8

SEE BEYOND THE NATURAL

To live a supernatural life, you must be conscious of the supernatural life power that you have resident in you. You must be conscious of your heavenly nature. You must see the invisible with your spiritual eyes and call it into becoming visible for the physical eyes to see. You must see beyond the natural. You must see beyond the symptoms. That was what God did in the creation of the worlds. He called the invisible to become visible. The light was not visible when God called it into being. It was darkness that was visible but God saw the light that was invisible and called it forth. The light that He called forth became visible. God created you to act like Him and do what He does. God created all things through the Word. Without the Word was not anything created that was created.

Now as a believer in Christ you have the same Word that God spoke out to create all things living inside you. Therefore do it as God did it, see beyond the natural and speak the Word out. How do you see beyond the natural? ***Through the eyes of faith in the Word.*** That is God's advice to us through Paul in 1 Corinthians 4:18.

Living a Supernatural Life (Volume 2)

> *While we look not at the things which are seen, but at the things which are not seen: for the things which are seen are temporal; but the things which are not seen are eternal.*
> **2 Corinthians 4:18**

What this means is that you should stop looking at things from the natural point of view. For every bad situation that you can see, there is a good one that God has given you that can replace it, which you may not see physically yet. Look at the good one with your spiritual eye and speak the good one out.

Beyond every sickness is the provision for health, which God has given you. Therefore see beyond the sickness, which may be currently visible and be conscious of the health, which may not yet be visible. See the health and call it forth. It will manifest and become visible.

Beyond every lack is the provision for abundance, which God has given you. Therefore see beyond the lack, which may be currently visible and be conscious of the abundance, which may not yet be visible. See the abundance and call it forth. It will manifest and become visible.

Beyond every failure is the provision for success, which God has given you. Therefore see beyond the failure, which may currently be visible and haunting you, and be conscious of the success, which may not yet be visible. See the success and call it forth. It will manifest and become visible.

See Beyond the Natural

Beyond every defeat is the provision for victory, which God has given you. Therefore see beyond the defeat, which may currently be visible and be conscious of the victory, which may not yet be visible. See the victory and call it forth. It will manifest and become visible.

Beyond every temptation and affliction of life is the provision for an escape route and deliverance that God has given you. Therefore see beyond the temptation and affliction, which you may be currently going through and be conscious of the escape route and deliverance, which may not yet be apparent or visible to you. See the escape route and the deliverance and call them forth. They will become visible and manifest and you will be freed from the affliction and temptation.

For example when a disease or sickness threatens, don't be too mindful of that sickness. Instead be conscious of what God said through Peter in 1 Peter 2:24, where He said that you have been healed by the stripes that Jesus Christ took on the Cross, and then call your healing into manifestation by speaking it into existence. Speak the Word of God into your situations.

> *Who his own self bare our sins in his own body on the tree, that we, being dead to sins, should live unto righteousness: by whose stripes ye were healed.*
> **1 Peter 2:24**

When you feel lonely, see beyond the loneliness and only be conscious of what Jesus said in Matthew 28:20 that He is with you always even unto the end of the world. God is always with you.

Living a Supernatural Life (Volume 2)

> *Teaching them to observe all things whatsoever I have commanded you: and, lo, I am with you alway, even unto the end of the world. Amen.*
> **Matthew 28:20**

If you know and believe that He is with you always, how can you feel alone or lonely? How can you sing "Pass me not, Oh gentle Saviour?" Jesus Christ said that He will be with you all the time therefore He cannot pass you by. Remember that the Holy Spirit is living right inside of you. So how can you feel lonely?

Since I became conscious of the truth that the Holy Spirit was living right inside of me, I have been having a fantastic time fellowshipping with Him. There has not been a dull moment for me since then. I converse with Him freely and we discuss practically every issue that comes my way.

This brings me to the type of prayer that many Christians pray today. Many times what we pray asking God to give us are things, which He has told us in His Word that He has already given us. All we now need do is thank Him for them. If we are still praying that He should give us such things, then it means that we do not believe that He has already given them to us or we are making Him a liar.

For example, many Christians pray asking God to come down and join them in their worship service. But He said that He is with you always. Therefore praying for Him to come down and join you in your worship service means that you don't have the belief that He is already with you.

They also pray that He should come and fill whoever is going to speak or preach the Word to them. This shows that many Christians do not believe in the truth that God is living inside whoever is going to speak or preach the Word to them since he is a born-again Christian. But God says that He is with you always, and that the Holy Spirit is living in you. That includes whoever is going to speak or preach to you if he is a born-again Christian. Remember that faith comes by hearing and hearing by the Word of God. That is what God said in Romans 10:17.

So then faith cometh by hearing, and hearing by the word of God.
Romans 10:17

So if what you are hearing all the time is that God should come down and join you, then it means that your faith will be in the fact that God is not with you all the time, but will only come down and join you when you call Him to do so. As for me, I know the truth that He is with me all the time.

He actually lives inside me and I live in Him. So I will not pray that He should come down and join me. I will thank Him for His presence with me always. You are to speak out what you believe; that is the spirit of faith as we are made to see by Paul in 2 Corinthians 4:13.

We having the same spirit of faith, according as it is written, I believed, and therefore have I spoken; we also believe, and therefore speak;
2 Corinthians 4:13

Living a Supernatural Life (Volume 2)

If you want to believe that God is not yet with you then you can continue to pray the prayer that He should come down and join you. You may pray with zeal but that kind of prayer is not according to knowledge.

To show you just how much of a mistake you are making when you pray asking God to come down and join you let us look at what the Word of God has to say about this. What we can see from the Word of God is that God is not only with you, He is in front of you, He is behind you, He is underneath you, He is above you, He is around you, He is living inside you and you are inside Him. That is what He made us to see from what He told us in the Scriptures. Let us look at each of these statements. By the time we look at all these you should be convinced that God is with you at all times.

GOD IS IN FRONT OF YOU

This is true because we are told in Isaiah 52:12, in Isaiah 45:2 and in Deuteronomy 31:8 that the Lord will go before you.

> *For ye shall not go out with haste, nor go by flight: for the LORD will go before you; and the God of Israel will be your rereward.*
> **Isaiah 52:12**

> *I will go before thee, and make the crooked places straight: I will break in pieces the gates of brass, and cut in sunder the bars of iron:*
> **Isaiah 45:2**

See Beyond the Natural

And the LORD, he it is that doth go before thee; he will be with thee, he will not fail thee, neither forsake thee: fear not, neither be dismayed.
Deuteronomy 31:8

David referred to something that the sea saw in front of the Israelites and fled in Psalm 114:3-7. He said it was the presence of the God of Jacob that the sea saw that made the sea to flee, the mountains to skip like rams and the hills like lambs. It was God going before them that the sea saw and fled. Even though they could not see God He was there in front of them just as He is in front of you too today. You may not be able to see Him before you but He is there and He is there like a mighty warrior that your enemies will see and run.

The sea saw it, and fled: Jordan was driven back.

The mountains skipped like rams, and the little hills like lambs.

What ailed thee, O thou sea, that thou fleddest? thou Jordan, that thou wast driven back?

Ye mountains, that ye skipped like rams; and ye little hills, like lambs?

Tremble, thou earth, at the presence of the Lord, at the presence of the God of Jacob;
Psalm 114:3-7

GOD IS BEHIND YOU

This is true because we are told in Isaiah 58:8 that the glory of the Lord shall be your rereward, which actually means that the glory of the Lord shall be your rear guard. As stated through Prophet Isaiah in Isaiah 30:21 the God that is behind you is the One that will talk into your ears from behind you when you need instruction or direction.

> *Then shall thy light break forth as the morning, and thine health shall spring forth speedily: and thy righteousness shall go before thee; the glory of the LORD shall be thy rereward.*
> **Isaiah 58:8**

> *And thine ears shall hear a word behind thee, saying, This is the way, walk ye in it, when ye turn to the right hand, and when ye turn to the left.*
> **Isaiah 30:21**

You should realize therefore that even though you cannot see your back God is there. That should give you an assurance that whatever may come at you from the back even though you cannot see it God who can see it is there to protect you.

The back is the most difficult part of the body to protect and defend against an attacker. But God has made adequate provision for your protection on the back side so that you should be able to rest assured under all circumstances and in any situation.

See Beyond the Natural

GOD IS UNDERNEATH YOU

This is true because as we can see from what we are told in Deuteronomy 33:27 the everlasting arm of the Lord is underneath you. With His hand underneath you it is sure that you are safe because He will thrust out every enemy from before you. He will give the command to destroy your enemies.

> *The eternal God is thy refuge, and underneath are the everlasting arms: and he shall thrust out the enemy from before thee; and shall say, Destroy them.*
> **Deuteronomy 33:27**

GOD IS ABOVE YOU

This is also true because from Songs of Solomon 2:4 you can see that God's love is the banner over His saints among which you are one. Therefore God's banner is above you.

> *He brought me to the banqueting house, and his banner over me was love.*
> **Songs of Solomon 2:4**

God is the God in heaven above. He is also the God in the earth beneath. That is what we are made to understand from what is written in Deuteronomy 4:39. Therefore God is above you and God is beneath you. This is the easiest for most Christians to accept because they believe that God is somewhere up there. Therefore they have no problem believing that He is above them.

Living a Supernatural Life (Volume 2)

> *Know therefore this day, and consider it in thine heart, that the LORD he is God in heaven above, and upon the earth beneath: there is none else.*
>
> **Deuteronomy 4:39**

The fact that you cannot see Him with your physical eyes does not mean that He is not there above you or beneath you. The truth is that He has stretched His banner over you. Therefore be confident and know that you are very well secured.

GOD IS AROUND YOU

God is not only before you in front of you or behind you; He is not only above you or underneath you, God is actually around you. This means that God surrounds you. That is what we are made to understand by what David said in Psalm 125:2.

> *As the mountains are round about Jerusalem, so the LORD is round about his people from henceforth even for ever.*
>
> **Psalm 125:2**

What this means is that God surrounds you completely. The Lord is actually a wall of fire around you. That is what we are made to see in Zechariah 2:5.

> *For I, saith the LORD, will be unto her a wall of fire round about, and will be the glory in the midst of her.*
>
> **Zechariah 2:5**

GOD IS IN YOU

Now God not only surrounds you God is actually in you. He is in you through His Spirit. He lives in you. This means that you have become His tabernacle. This is a mystery that the human mind cannot comprehend. You have become God's temple. That is what we are told in 1 John 3:24 and 1 Corinthians 3:16.

> *And he that keepeth his commandments dwelleth in him, and he in him. And hereby we know that he abideth in us, by the Spirit which he hath given us.*
> **1 John 3:24**

> *Know ye not that ye are the temple of God, and that the Spirit of God dwelleth in you?*
> **1 Corinthians 3:16**

Since you are now His temple where He lives He will take care of you and not let anything defile you. That is what we are told by God through Paul in the next verse 1 Corinthians 3:17.

> *If any man defile the temple of God, him shall God destroy; for the temple of God is holy, which temple ye are.*
> **1 Corinthians 3:17**

You should therefore rest assured that God Himself is the One looking out for whatever attempts to pollute or defile you. God further confirmed that He is in you by what He said in 1 Corinthians 6:19 through Paul the Apostle.

> *What? know ye not that your body is the temple of the Holy Ghost which is in you, which ye have of God, and ye are not your own?*
>
> **1 Corinthians 6:19**

We are told here that it is not only that God is living in you but that you actually belong to Him. You can therefore see that your apprehensions about what may be happening to you are baseless because God who owns you and sees you as his house will obviously protect what belongs to Him. Get a revelation of this truth that your body is a temple of God, where God lives and that it belongs to God and your worries will be over.

YOU ARE IN GOD

To make absolutely sure that you are well protected God now puts you in Himself. Everything that we have said so far showed that you are actually enclosed in God. This is a mystery that cannot be comprehended with the ordinary human mind but it is the truth for that is what the Bible made us to understand from what Paul said in Colossians 3:3.

> *For ye are dead, and your life is hid with Christ in God.*
>
> **Colossians 3:3**

How can you be hidden in God, have God in front of you, behind you, underneath you, above you, around you, in you, and with all these still be praying that God should come and join you? Get this revelation of God's presence with you.

GOD IS WITH YOU

Obviously God is with you and you do not know it. God is not only with you He is actually with you like a mighty terrible one as written in Jeremiah 20:11. It is obvious therefore that *God is always with you.* Just like God did for Job as stated by Satan in Job 1:10 and Job did not know it, God has built a hedge around you to protect you and all that belongs to you.

> *But the LORD is with me as a mighty terrible one: therefore my persecutors shall stumble, and they shall not prevail: they shall be greatly ashamed; for they shall not prosper: their everlasting confusion shall never be forgotten.*
> **Jeremiah 20:11**

> *Hast not thou made an hedge about him, and about his house, and about all that he hath on every side? thou hast blessed the work of his hands, and his substance is increased in the land.*
> **Job 1:10**

It is obvious therefore that God is always with you. He is not only with you, He surrounds you with Himself, He is above you, He is underneath you, He is in front of you and He is behind you.

Wherever you turn God is there. How can you therefore still be praying begging that He should come and join you? God is for you but you don't know it and if God be for you who can be against you and win? Nobody! Romans 8:31.

What shall we then say to these things? If God be for us, who can be against us?
Romans 8:31

It is this realization that God is always with us and that there is nowhere that we are that God is not there that made David to write about God's omnipresence with us in Psalm 139:1-14 to say that we cannot hide ourselves from God. He knows all our movements and He is always with us whether we go under the earth or under the sea. God is with us everywhere we go. Look at what David said below:

O LORD, thou hast searched me, and known me.

Thou knowest my downsitting and mine uprising, thou understandest my thought afar off.

Thou compassest my path and my lying down, and art acquainted with all my ways.

For there is not a word in my tongue, but, lo, O LORD, thou knowest it altogether.

Thou hast beset me behind and before, and laid thine hand upon me.

Such knowledge is too wonderful for me; it is high, I cannot attain unto it.

Whither shall I go from thy spirit? or whither shall I flee from thy presence?

See Beyond the Natural

If I ascend up into heaven, thou art there: if I make my bed in hell, behold, thou art there.

If I take the wings of the morning, and dwell in the uttermost parts of the sea;

Even there shall thy hand lead me, and thy right hand shall hold me.

If I say, Surely the darkness shall cover me; even the night shall be light about me.

Yea, the darkness hideth not from thee; but the night shineth as the day: the darkness and the light are both alike to thee.

For thou hast possessed my reins: thou hast covered me in my mother's womb.

I will praise thee; for I am fearfully and wonderfully made: marvellous are thy works; and that my soul knoweth right well.
Psalm 139:1-14

You must always see beyond the natural. If you can only see and know that God is with you everywhere you go all the time nothing will be daunting to you anymore. In Proverbs 15:3 the Bible says that the eyes of the Lord are in every place. Be conscious of this truth that His eyes are everywhere.

The eyes of the LORD are in every place, beholding the evil and the good.
Proverbs 15:3

Living a Supernatural Life (Volume 2)

God is not only in every place but we actually live and move in Him. That is what we are told in Acts 17:28.

> *For in him we live, and move, and have our being; as certain also of your own poets have said, For we are also his offspring.*
>
> **Acts 17:28**

As written in Isaiah 43:2 therefore whatever trouble you may be going through God is there with you to protect you. He has promised that He will be everywhere with you whether in the river, in the water, in the fire He has said that He will be there to protect you.

> *When thou passest through the waters, I will be with thee; and through the rivers, they shall not overflow thee: when thou walkest through the fire, thou shalt not be burned; neither shall the flame kindle upon thee.*
>
> **Isaiah 43:2**

When you have enemies all around you, see beyond the enemies, be conscious of what God said to us in Romans 8:31, in Romans 8:37 and in 2 Kings 6:16, and know that those that are with you are much more than those that are with your enemies. Know that you are more than a conqueror through Christ. You should be conscious of the truth that the One in you is greater than your enemies as stated in 1 John 4:4.

> *What shall we then say to these things? If God be for us, who can be against us?*
>
> **Romans 8:31**

See Beyond the Natural

Nay, in all these things we are more than conquerors through him that loved us.
Romans 8:37

And he answered, Fear not: for they that be with us are more than they that be with them.
2 Kings 6:16

Ye are of God, little children, and have overcome them: because greater is he that is in you, than he that is in the world.
1 John 4:4

The One in you is greater than the one in the world. If that is the case then you know that no power can overcome you unless of course you have agreed to be defeated. The words that you speak should show that you know this truth and if you do then you should exhibit absolute confidence and no fear. If God be for you, how can you fear any enemy? Do you think that any of your enemies can face God, fight with God and win against God? If you know that they cannot, then there is no need to exhibit fear in any way about anything or any situation that you may find yourself. If you exhibit any fear at all, it means that you do not believe this truth or you really do not know the God that is in you because Daniel 11:32 says that those who do know their God shall be strong and they shall do exploits.

And such as do wickedly against the covenant shall he corrupt by flatteries: but the people that do know their God shall be strong, and do exploits.
Daniel 11:32

Living a Supernatural Life (Volume 2)

If you know the God who is with you and that your enemies cannot win against Him, then relax and feel confident that with God on your side and you on the inside of God, you will overcome any enemy that comes against you. You must see beyond the enemies that are against you. See your victory, which God has already pronounced. Always see beyond the natural. ***Don't just read the Word or hear the Word; see what the Word of God says.*** Like Prophet Habakkuk said in Habakkuk 2:1 go beyond the hearing of the Word to seeing what the Word says. That is a major key to your living a supernatural life.

> *I will stand upon my watch, and set me upon the tower, and will watch to see what he will say unto me, and what I shall answer when I am reproved.*
> **Habakkuk 2:1**

Use your power of imagination to see whatever you want and then use your mouth to speak it out thereby calling it into manifestation. If you can fix your mind on it you will see it eventually. Don't let your mind wonder about. Fix your mind on what the Word of God says about what you want. You are created to see into the invisible, to speak and bring into existence anything that your mind can imagine or that you can see with your spiritual eyes using the Word of God. You can speak the invisible into becoming visible just like God did. As a born-again Christian, you are supposed to be living a life above the natural realm. You are supposed to live above your senses. That in essence is what God told us in 2 Corinthians 5:7 through Apostle Paul.

See Beyond the Natural

For we walk by faith, not by sight:
2 Corinthians 5:7

You are supposed to walk by faith in what the Word says concerning any situation that you may find yourself, not by your senses. Are you sure that you are walking by faith?

You should be living a life beyond natural explanation. That is, you should be breathing and living a Supernatural Life. *You can actually start to live your own heaven right now here on earth.* If you can walk by faith rather than by sight you will see great miracles signs and wonders following you.

YOU CAN START TO LIVE YOUR OWN HEAVEN HERE ON EARTH

It is possible for you to begin to live your heaven right now here on earth. If it is not possible Jesus Christ will not ask us to pray to the Father in Matthew 6:9-10 and Luke 11:2 saying, *"Thy will be done on earth as it is in Heaven."*

After this manner therefore pray ye: Our Father which art in heaven, Hallowed be thy name.

Thy kingdom come. Thy will be done in earth, as it is in heaven.
Matthew 6:9-10

> *And he said unto them, When ye pray, say, Our Father which art in heaven, Hallowed be thy name. Thy kingdom come. Thy will be done, as in heaven, so in earth.*
> **Luke 11:2**

By deduction, from what Jesus said in these Scriptures, we can say that it is possible to have God's will in Heaven here on earth right now. When you have God's will in heaven here on earth, it is equivalent to your living a heavenly life here on earth. How then can you create your heaven here on earth now? Let us look at what God did to create His own heaven and earth. We are told in Genesis 1:1 that,

> *"In the beginning God created the heaven and the earth."*
> **Genesis 1:1**

God created His own Heaven and earth with His Word. Jesus Christ who is the Word with which God created the Heaven and the earth is now living inside you. By supernatural living, using the same Word of God that God used, who now lives in you, it is possible for you too to create and live your own heaven here on earth. This means that you can live your heaven here on earth even before you get to the real Heaven.

This is because there is a relationship between the supernatural and the natural. That is what God told us in Hebrews 11:3 through Apostle Paul where He made us to understand that the things which, are seen originates from things, which are not seen.

See Beyond the Natural

Through faith we understand that the worlds were framed by the word of God, so that things which are seen were not made of things which do appear.
Hebrews 11:3

God framed His worlds by His Words. You better start framing your own world by your own words in particular by the Word of God spoken through your mouth, thereby making things to be seen from things, which are not currently seen. The Word of God is supernatural. Speak the supernatural into your natural situations. Whatever things you are seeing in your life today are the result of the words that you have been speaking into your life. Those things that you speak forth today, which you have not yet seen are what will give birth to the things that you will see tomorrow.

The words that you speak out today are like eggs and it is your faith that incubates the eggs until they are hatched to become the birds or the snakes that you see tomorrow. That is because as stated in the verse above, natural things, which are seen are made from supernatural things, which are not seen. God further confirmed this in His Word in Romans 1:20 through Paul. He said,

"For the invisible things of him from the creation of the world are clearly seen, being understood by the things that are made, even his eternal power and Godhead; so that they are without excuse:"
Romans 1:20

Living a Supernatural Life (Volume 2)

We know that the visible (clearly seen) things are made from things that are invisible. You are supposed to call the invisible to become visible by speaking it into existence. Whatever you want you can call it to manifest. You have the power to do so. When any affliction comes into your life, see your freedom from the affliction. This is because even though you are currently going through and experiencing the affliction, your freedom from it, which you cannot currently see because it is invisible to you, is more real than the visible affliction that you are going through. That is the essence of what God is telling you through Apostle Paul in 2 Corinthians 4:18.

While we look not at the things which are seen, but at the things which are not seen: for the things which are seen are temporal; but the things which are not seen are eternal.
                                                2 Corinthians 4:18

What God is saying here is that whatever affliction you may be going through, which you can see right now is temporary and it is not what you are supposed to fix your mind and thoughts upon. Instead fix your sight, thoughts and mind on whatever the Word of God says positively about your victory over that affliction even though you cannot currently see it. If you can do so that is what will eventually manifest in your life.

When failure comes and is starring you in the face, see success because the success, which is currently invisible to you, is more real than the failure that you can now see.

See Beyond the Natural

That is what the Word of God says and that is the truth. But many Christians even see the failure before it actually comes. They fix their sight on the temporary things and not the eternal things. You are advised by God to fix your eyes on the permanent or eternal things not on the temporary things.

When poverty comes threatening and is starring you in the face, see prosperity because the prosperity, which is currently invisible to you, is more real than the poverty that you can now see. That is what the Word says and that is the truth.

When lack comes threatening and is starring you in the face, see abundance because the abundance, which is currently invisible to you, is more real than the lack that you can now see. That is what the Word says and that is the truth.

When sickness comes furiously threatening and the symptoms are starring you in the face and knocking you around, see health because the health, which is currently invisible to you, is more real than the sickness and its symptoms that you can now see. That is what the Word of God says and that is the truth.

When barrenness comes threatening and the symptoms are starring you in the face and everything that you can see point to it, see fruitfulness because the fruitfulness, which is currently invisible to you, is more real than the barrenness that you can now see. That is what the Word of God says and that is the truth.

Living a Supernatural Life (Volume 2)

When defeat comes threatening and is starring you in the face and even knocking you around, see victory because the victory, which is currently invisible to you, is more real than the defeat that you can now see. That is what the Word of God says and that is the truth. He said in Romans 8:37 that we are more than conquerors through Him that loved us.

> *Nay, in all these things we are more than conquerors through him that loved us.*
> **Romans 8:37**

However, most Christians today only look at the visible and temporary things. They allow their natural senses to rule them. They look at symptoms and situations rather than the provision for perfect health and victory that God has provided for them.

Rather than see the provision for health, prosperity, success, abundance, fruitfulness and the victory that they have in-Christ and call these into existence, they instead see sickness, poverty, lack; barrenness, defeat, failure and these are the things that they use their own mouths to call into existence.

Many Christians call afflictions, sickness, poverty, lack, barrenness, defeat and failure into their lives even before they actually see them. Before these are actually visible, once they can just see or feel a semblance of a symptom of any of these they use their mouths to call them into existence. Note they have not really seen the symptom they have merely seen what looks like the symptom. That is why you hear Christians making such statements as the following:

"I think I am going to have a fever."
"I think I am having a cold."
"I think I am going to be sick."
"I am as poor as a church rat."
"Oh what a fool I am."

Even worse still, you find them saying, *"I have a fever." "I have a cold." "I am sick."* When they go to the hospital and doctors tell them that they have cancer, they just accept it and start saying it about. *"Oh I have cancer."* And of course, when they start going about confessing it then they have bought it from Satan and it will make a home in their body.

But if they reject it and start to confess that they cannot have it using their confession to confront it and war against it, then it will eventually leave them. You can consider any such negative diagnosis from doctors as similar to a negative prophetic statement made into your life and just as you are advised by God through Paul in 1 Timothy 1:18 to do a warfare with the positive prophecies spoken into your life to make sure that they come to pass, so likewise must you do a warfare against the negative prophetic statements spoken into your life to make sure that they do not come to pass. This is an issue that most Christians do not take cognizance of. They just sit down on prophecies expecting them to be fulfilled automatically in their lives.

> *This charge I commit unto thee, son Timothy, according to the prophecies which went before on thee, that thou by them mightest war a good warfare;*
> **1 Timothy 1:18**

Living a Supernatural Life (Volume 2)

We showed in **Chapter 4** of **Volume 1** of this **"Living a supernatural life"** book series that your words are the spiritual currencies with which you purchase spiritually what you get physically. Jesus said, **"For he shall have whatsoever he saith!"** Therefore you shall have whatsoever you say.

God said, **"Let the weak say I am strong."** Therefore by deduction, **"Let the poor say I am rich." "Let he that failed say I am a success." "Let the sick say I am healed, I am well."** etc.

What Christians should do when given negative diagnosis or report of their condition based on the symptoms and situations that doctors can see or observe is to note it and not give their assent to it or make any statements with their mouths in support of the negative report that they have been given from the symptoms and circumstances. Instead they should reject it and call what they want such as perfect health, prosperity, success, or victory into existence with their mouth.

What they have called, even though not currently seen, will eventually manifest and become visible if they do not relent in their confession. This is because whatever you keep confessing will eventually manifest in your life. Not only that, you must also be aware of the truth that the Kingdom of God is within you. That is what Jesus said in Luke 17:20-21.

> *And when he was demanded of the Pharisees, when the kingdom of God should come, he answered them and said, The kingdom of God cometh not with observation:*

See Beyond the Natural

Neither shall they say, Lo here! or, lo there! for, behold, the kingdom of God is within you.
Luke 17:20-21

This means that the Kingdom of God is already resident inside you. Since Jesus Christ is the power of God. We know that the power and authority that controls the Kingdom is the Spirit of God. That Spirit is now resident inside you and it is from Him that the instructions as to what you do and what you become should come, not from any doctor or anybody else. You should not worry about the forces around you. The authority and control, which is in this world system, should not worry you because you know that the government that is controlling your life as well as what happens to you is within you. You are not under the world system anymore. You live in the world but you are no longer of the world. So whatever may be happening to them in the world, you should have the assurance in your mind that it doesn't have to affect you anymore. You are under a different government now. You are supposed to be enjoying the Kingdom of God here on earth right now.

A LIVING PROOF

What you say is what you get. I know and I have experienced this many times before. I have a friend who is a highly qualified Consultant Pathologist specializing in neuro-Pathology. He is an extremely experienced doctor and a great expert, who many, including other Consultant doctors, come to consult concerning all types and forms of ailments, sicknesses and diseases. Through my association with him, I was able to know some of the symptoms for many types of diseases.

Since knowing these, I find that as soon as I believe that I can see or feel anything that looks like or feels like the symptoms of a particular disease, I just find myself saying, *"I think I am going to have the disease"*. The law of the spirit that says what you say is what you get immediately goes into operation. Before you know it, the symptoms will be becoming real to me and I soon start to feel like the disease is already with me. Another law of the spirit that says whatever you greatly fear will eventually come upon you and whatever you are afraid of will come unto you also goes into operation. Before you know it therefore, I start using the drugs for the disease, to stop a disease, which I used my own mouth to call into my body.

Now I know better! It is the confession of most people coupled with the fear that they have of certain diseases that has brought such diseases to their doorstep because whatever you fear will soon come upon you.

SPEAK GOD'S WORD TO YOUR SITUATIONS

When doctors tell you that you have a disease take the report but do not give your consent by saying with your own mouth that you have the disease. Instead look into the invisible and see good health and call it out into existence. In particular, use the Word of God to bring the invisible into becoming visible so that all can see it. For the Word of God is God and carries the abilities of God. That is what God tells us through Apostle John in John 1:1-4.

See Beyond the Natural

In the beginning was the Word, and the Word was with God, and the Word was God.

The same was in the beginning with God.

All things were made by him; and without him was not any thing made that was made.

In him was life; and the life was the light of men.

John 1:1-4

Note the following four points about the Scripture written above in John 1:1-4.

1. The Word of God is God

2. Everything was made by the Word, and without the Word was not anything made that was made.

3. There is life in the Word. So, when you speak the Word of God; there is creative life in it.

4. The Word of God when spoken appropriately to a dying or dead thing can bring life into it.

If you are to enjoy the fulfillment of the many great promises to you in the Scriptures then you must see beyond your natural situations and see in line with what the Scripture says with your spiritual eyes of faith. The Word when spoken can bring into existence what does not presently exist because the Word of God has creative abilities and potential. This is so because as soon as you speak the Word of God into a situation, you bring God into that situation.

Living a Supernatural Life (Volume 2)

Since the Word of God is God and it is the Word of God that created all things therefore the Word of God spoken from your mouth can create things. You should also note what God said through John in 1 John 5:4. He said,

> *"For whatsoever is born of God overcometh the world: and this is the victory that overcometh the world, even our faith."*
> **1 John 5:4**

Whatever is born of God overcomes the world. Obviously the Word of God is born of God; therefore the Word must always overcome the world.

So whatever you may be experiencing in the world, if you speak the appropriate Word of God into it, the Word is bound to overcome it. That is why knowing the Word of God is very important to us as Christians.

For we know that we get whatever we say and if what we say comes from the Word of God, then we know that we will get those things, which God Himself wants for us.

You should also note what God said through Paul the Apostle in 1 Corinthians 2:16. He said that as a born-again Christian one major attribute that you have now is that you have the mind of Christ.

> *For who hath known the mind of the Lord, that he may instruct him? But we have the mind of Christ.*
> **1 Corinthians 2:16**

That is part of your heavenly nature and you can live that heavenly nature here on earth. It is part of your new-birth benefits and heritage. So you should think like Christ. You now have the ability to reason like Christ. Therefore anything that comes to your mind, you should check first that it agrees with the Word before accepting it. That was what Christ did when He was here on earth. He spoke only the correct words because He sieved or filtered out those that did not come from God. That's what He told us in John 5:30. He said,

> *"I can of mine own self do nothing: as I hear, I judge: and my judgment is just; because I seek not mine own will, but the will of the Father which hath sent me."*
> **John 5:30**

If you saturate your mind with the Word of God, then it will be like the mind of Christ. You will be able to sieve out that which does not agree with the Word of God whenever it comes into your mind. You will be able to take into captivity thoughts that come to you which are contrary to the Word. You have the weapons to do this according to 2 Corinthians 10:4-6.

> *For the weapons of our warfare are not carnal, but mighty through God to the pulling down of strong holds;*
>
> *Casting down imaginations, and every high thing that exalteth itself against the knowledge of God, and bringing into captivity every thought to the obedience of Christ;*

Living a Supernatural Life (Volume 2)

And having in a readiness to revenge all disobedience, when your obedience is fulfilled.
2 Corinthians 10:4-6

You are supposed to cast down imaginations and every high thing that exalts itself against what the Word of God says and bring every thought that comes into your mind into captivity. You are supposed to bring them captive to obey and fall in line with what the Word says by subjecting them to the Word.

Anything that comes into your mind, which is contrary to what the Word says you should cast it out of your mind so that you can only think and see in line with what the Word of God says. When you can see the invisible in line with the Word of God that you have spoken into any situation, then you will start to live a supernatural life here on earth. You will then start to dominate your circumstances.

So stop being carried away by symptoms and what you can see, hear, taste, smell or feel physically. Stop making confessions based on what you see, smell, taste, hear, feel or what you are going through. See what the Word of God says and base your confessions on that.

Walk by the Word! Live by the Word! Not by what you see, hear, taste, smell or feel by your senses physically.

Put your natural senses under your control; don't allow them to dictate your reaction to any situation. Live by faith based on what the Word of God says and not by faith based on what your senses are telling you. That is what walking in faith is all about.

When you do these, you will not only overcome the world but your victory over all the circumstances of life will then be sure because your victory is already guaranteed. You have already overcome the world. See this! See beyond the natural realm.

YOUR VICTORY IS ALREADY GUARANTEED

When it concerns Satan and his demons, "Fear not", for if you can only see into the invisible, you will know that as confirmed in 2 Kings 6:16, which we have discussed earlier those that be with you are more than those that be with them that are against you. Therefore there is no need for you to fear in any situation.

And he answered, Fear not: for they that be with us are more than they that be with them.
2 Kings 6:16

Your victory is already guaranteed if you will only open your mouth to proclaim it. You have won if you will only believe it.

Regardless of what the situation may be speaking to you it is your victory that you should see. Look at what God said through John in 1 John 4:1-4. From what God said you should understand that you are fighting a war in which you have already been declared the winner. Your opponents in this war are the evil spirits that are not of God. And you have already won the battle against them. That is the essence of what God is saying in that Scripture.

Living a Supernatural Life (Volume 2)

Remember that we have said that most of the afflictions and problems that you are going through have spirits behind them. But regardless of whatever spirits may be behind any affliction that you are going through what God is telling you here in 1 John 4:1-4 is that you have already overcome them.

> *Beloved, believe not every spirit, but try the spirits whether they are of God: because many false prophets are gone out into the world.*
>
> *Hereby know ye the Spirit of God: Every spirit that confesseth that Jesus Christ is come in the flesh is of God:*
>
> *And every spirit that confesseth not that Jesus Christ is come in the flesh is not of God: and this is that spirit of antichrist, whereof ye have heard that it should come; and even now already is it in the world.*
>
> *Ye are of God, little children, and have overcome them: because greater is he that is in you, than he that is in the world.*
> **1 John 4:1-4**

Because you are now born of God you have overcome the world and it is your faith that will give you the victory. That is what God is also telling us gain through John in 1 John 5:4-5. He said,

> *"For whatsoever is born of God overcometh the world: and this is the victory that overcometh the world, even our faith.*

See Beyond the Natural

> *Who is he that overcometh the world, but he that believeth that Jesus is the Son of God?"*
> **1 John 5:4-5**

Therefore see beyond the circumstances that you may be facing and through faith see into the supernatural realm. See the Christ in you who is the hope of your glory. If you can see the Christ in you, shame and reproach will no longer be your portion. If you can see the Christ in you, you will see yourself prosperous, rich and wealthy. You will see yourself healed, strong and healthy. If you can see the Christ in you, you will see yourself successful, victorious and triumphant. You will see yourself blessed, sanctified, consecrated and holy. If you can see the Christ in you, you will see yourself vigorous, robust, resilient, full of life and energetic. You will see yourself forgiven, cleansed, restored, justified and made righteous. You will be transformed into a daring, fearless, brave, bold and courageous person. The Word of God says in Revelation 5:10 that you are a king and a priest unto God and you are supposed to be reigning here on earth.

> *And hast made us unto our God kings and priests: and we shall reign on the earth.*
> **Revelation 5:10**

Kings are supposed to reign and if they are to reign then they must have a dominion or territory that they are supposed to reign over. It does not matter what the condition that you are going through right now says, if you can see the Christ that lives in you, you will see yourself as a king and reigning right now here on earth.

Living a Supernatural Life (Volume 2)

Remember that you are a spirit-being living in a body and having a soul. A major function of the spirit that you are is perception. It is with your spirit that you perceive things. With the spirit you can perceive yourself as a king reigning over all the circumstances and situations of life that you come across. Imagine yourself as reigning and you will surely reign because whatever you can imagine you can achieve. That is what God said in Genesis 11:6.

> *And the Lord said, Behold, the people is one, and they have all one language; and this they begin to do: and now nothing will be restrained from them, which they have imagined to do.*
> **Genesis 11:6**

Fear not, if you are a believer in Christ and walking according to God's will, you have all that it takes to be a winner. When you know the truth about the realities of your New Birth's invisible nature, which is discussed in great detail in **Volume 3** of this **"Living a Supernatural life"** book series written by the same author you will know that you have all that it takes to live a triumphant and supernatural life right here on earth. To do so however threesome other things that you must do or be and these are discussed in the remaining chapters of this book. One of such major conditions is that *you must abide in Christ.* That is the subject that we shall look into in the next Chapter.

CHAPTER 9

ABIDE IN CHRIST

We know that we now have power and authority over all the powers of the forces of darkness. But often the problem is that the majority of Christians have not been able to demonstrate this power that they now have. Instead the forces of darkness are the ones demonstrating their fake powers over them.

A major reason why they are not able to do so is that they are not abiding in Christ, as they ought to. Jesus Christ said in John 15:7 that it is when you abide in Him and His Word abides in you that you will ask whatever you want and it would be done for you.

> *If ye abide in me, and my words abide in you, ye shall ask what ye will, and it shall be done unto you.*
> **John 15:7**

Therefore as you can see, a major condition for getting what you want from God is abiding in Christ. Most Christians know the other condition that the Word should abide in them. It is this condition that they should abide in Christ that they are not so sure of.

Living a Supernatural Life (Volume 2)

To understand this, you must note that it is when people see you demonstrating the power of God, doing the works of miracles, signs and wonders that they will believe in the God that you serve. It is when you can get people convinced to also become believers in Christ that you are really yielding fruits. But you cannot yield much fruits unless you are abiding in Christ. That is what Jesus said in John 15:5.

> *I am the vine, ye are the branches: He that abideth in me, and I in him, the same bringeth forth much fruit: for without me ye can do nothing.*
>
> **John 15:5**

What then did Jesus mean by saying that we should abide in Him? Basically what Jesus meant by abiding in Him is to walk as He walked. We are made to know this from what He told us through John in 1 John 2:6, which is written below. Therefore if you want to abide in Christ it means that you must walk as He walked. One of the things that you require if you are to walk as Jesus walked is that you must love your brothers. This is because He told us through John in 1 John 2:10 that if we love our brother then we are abiding in the light. We know from what He also told us through John the Apostle in 1 John 1:5 that God is light and we also know that Jesus Christ is the light of the world. Therefore what He is telling us here is that if we love our brother then we are abiding in Him.

> *He that saith he abideth in him ought himself also so to walk, even as he walked.*
>
> **1 John 2:6**

> *He that loveth his brother abideth in the light, and there is none occasion of stumbling in him.*
> **1 John 2:10**

> *This then is the message which we have heard of him, and declare unto you, that God is light, and in him is no darkness at all.*
> **1 John 1:5**

To abide in Him it is not only that you must love your brother but also you must not even give room to sin in your life. That is what He also made us to know through John in 1 John 3:6.

> *Whosoever abideth in him sinneth not: whosoever sinneth hath not seen him, neither known him.*
> **1 John 3:6**

Therefore if you want the power of God to show and be fully demonstrated in your life so that you can live a supernatural life then you must abide in Christ and if you are to abide in Christ you must run from sin. *You must not only run from sin, you must not keep any malice against anybody. You must forgive all that sin against you. You must love all people and have compassion for them.*

These are major keys to your living a supernatural life here on earth. Jesus did most of His miracles out of compassion for the people. You will also be able to do supernatural acts if they are done out of compassion for others and not for your own self-glorification and pride.

Living a Supernatural Life (Volume 2)

If you love your brother you will have compassion for him. If you have compassion for your brother you will be moved when you see him hurting and that will cause you to want to do something about his hurt. It is that kind of feeling that will move God and will lead to His working supernaturally through you to change the situation of such a person. Finally, if you allow the Holy Spirit who is living in you to teach you all things then that will guarantee your abiding in Christ. That is what God said through John in 1 John 2:27.

> *But the anointing which ye have received of him abideth in you, and ye need not that any man teach you: but as the same anointing teacheth you of all things, and is truth, and is no lie, and even as it hath taught you, ye shall abide in him.*
>
> **1 John 2:27**

You can see from what we have said so far concerning abiding in Christ that it is not possible for you to live a godly-based supernatural life unless you are abiding in Christ.

This is because it is only when you are abiding in Christ and His Word is abiding in you that you can get whatever you ask of the Lord. Some people do live a devilish type of supernatural life doing counterfeit miracles, signs and wonders that are based on devilish wisdom and not based on the power from God. That is not the type of supernatural life that we are talking about in this book. It is such people that Jesus referred to as workers of iniquity in Matthew 7:22-23.

Abide in Christ

> *Many will say to me in that day, Lord, Lord, have we not prophesied in thy name? and in thy name have cast out devils? and in thy name done many wonderful works?*
>
> *And then will I profess unto them, I never knew you: depart from me, ye that work iniquity.*
> **Matthew 7:22-23**

If you abide in Christ, His feet will become your feet and you will be able to walk as He walked. His eyes will become your eyes and you will be able to see the invisible. His hands will become your hands and you will be able to do what He did. His mind will become your mind. You have been told by God through Apostle Paul in 1 Corinthians 2:16 that you now have the mind of Christ. With that mind you will be able to think as He thought and His thoughts will become your thoughts. Therefore your actions, which will be supernatural in nature will be His actions because He will be the One working through you.

> *For who hath known the mind of the Lord, that he may instruct him? But we have the mind of Christ.*
> **1 Corinthians 2:16**

If you abide in Christ the Scripture says that there can be no more condemnation for you. That is what we are made to see from what God said through Apostle Paul in Romans 8:1. This means that you can approach God with absolutely no guilt-conscience.

> *There is therefore now no condemnation to them which are in Christ Jesus, who walk not after the flesh, but after the Spirit.*
> **Romans 8:1**

If you abide in Him even though there will be storms in the world you will have peace of mind because there will be peace in your mind. That is what Jesus Himself told us in John 16:33.

> *These things I have spoken unto you, that in me ye might have peace. In the world ye shall have tribulation: but be of good cheer; I have overcome the world.*
> **John 16:33**

If you abide in Christ then you are joined with Him and you are one spirit with Him. That is what we can see from what Apostle Paul wrote in 1 Corinthians 6:17.

> *But he that is joined unto the Lord is one spirit.*
> **1 Corinthians 6:17**

HOW DO YOU MAINTAIN THIS UNION WITH CHRIST?

It is very important that you keep your union with Christ intact. There are three things that you must take cognizance of if you are to maintain your union with Christ. The first one is that you must have faith in Christ because just like all the other benefits that you derive from your salvation; you get this union with Christ by faith. That is what we are told in Ephesians 3:17.

Abide in Christ

That Christ may dwell in your hearts by faith; that ye, being rooted and grounded in love,
Ephesians 3:17

Another necessary condition required for you to be able to maintain your union with Christ is that you must have His word in you and you must be feeding on that Word continuously. That is what we can see in 1 John 2:24 and John 6:56. This is extremely important. You must be Word-loaded if you want to be recognized high flyer in the Kingdom

Let that therefore abide in you, which ye have heard from the beginning. If that which ye have heard from the beginning shall remain in you, ye also shall continue in the Son, and in the Father.
1 John 2:24

He that eateth my flesh, and drinketh my blood, dwelleth in me, and I in him.
John 6:56

It is not only that you must be feeding on the Word a third condition according to 1 John 3:24 is that you must be obeying the Word if you want to maintain your union with Christ. God honours those who obey His Word. If you want to be honoured by God then obey His Word.

And he that keepeth his commandments dwelleth in him, and he in him. And hereby we know that he abideth in us, by the Spirit which he hath given us.
1 John 3:24

Living a Supernatural Life (Volume 2)

NO OPPRESSION CAN SUBDUE YOU

When you abide in Christ then you will enjoy God's presence all the time. Then it can be said of you that the Lord is with you. Let us take the story of Joseph in Genesis 39:20-21 to see what happens when God is with you.

> *And Joseph's master took him, and put him into the prison, a place where the king's prisoners were bound: and he was there in the prison.*
>
> *But the Lord was with Joseph, and shewed him mercy, and gave him favour in the sight of the keeper of the prison.*
>
> **Genesis 39:20-21**

Joseph's brothers hated him. The wife of his master planned evil against him. The king was incensed against him and he was put in prison where the king's prisoners were bound. Joseph was shown favour in the prison because the Lord was with him and the Lord showed him mercy and favour.in the sight of the keeper of the prison. When you abide in Christ you will have the Lord with you and when the Lord is with you according to what He said in Romans 8:31 it really does not matter who is against you. No matter what evil is planned against you it cannot succeed against you. It will only work for your good as we are told in Romans 8:28. This should be your mindset at all times and in every situation/

> *What shall we then say to these things? If God be for us, who can be against us?*
>
> **Romans 8:31**

And we know that all things work together for good to them that love God, to them who are the called according to his purpose.
Romans 8:28

That is why it is so important that we must abide in Christ. Abiding in Christ is imperative for any Christian that will be used by God in this end time.

YOU CAN PASS THROUGH ANY SITUATION

When Shedrack, Meshack and Abednigo were thrown into a fire as recorded in Daniel 3:24,30 we are told that the Lord was in the fire with them so the fire could not burn them. Therefore if the Lord is with you He will be with you in every situation. You will not be left alone in any situation that you may find yourself. It does not matter what you may be going through as long as God is there with you your victory is sure. Even if you are in a furnace so long as God is there with you it will be well with you.

Then Nebuchadnezzar the king was astonied, and rose up in haste, and spake, and said unto his counsellors, Did not we cast three men bound into the midst of the fire? They answered and said unto the king, True, O king.

Then the king promoted Shadrach, Meshach, and Abed-nego, in the province of Babylon.
Daniel 3:24, 30

Living a Supernatural Life (Volume 2)

YOU WILL BE GOD-CONSCIOUS

When you abide in Christ and you become one with Him you will not be self-conscious anymore. You will become God-conscious.

When you are no longer self-conscious you will not be self-seeking. God is love and when you are one with God you will not seek your own. That is what we are told by God through Paul in 1 Corinthians 13:4-5.

> *Charity suffereth long, and is kind; charity envieth not; charity vaunteth not itself, is not puffed up,*
>
> *Doth not behave itself unseemly, seeketh not her own, is not easily provoked, thinketh no evil;*
> **1 Corinthians 13:4-5**

When you are God-conscious whatever you may be going through in your life, no matter how tortuous you may find it you will see it as God working in your life and you will expect the end result to be good. Take a look once again at Joseph's case. Despite all the schemes and plans against him and all the victimization that he went through he still believed that it was God that was working in his life. Take a look at what he said in Genesis 45:5-7.

> *Now therefore be not grieved, nor angry with yourselves, that ye sold me hither: for God did send me before you to preserve life.*

Abide in Christ

For these two years hath the famine been in the land: and yet there are five years, in the which there shall neither be earing nor harvest.

And God sent me before you to preserve you a posterity in the earth, and to save your lives by a great deliverance.
Genesis 45:5-7

Despite what his brothers did to him he did not weigh himself down with the bad in what they did instead he was able to see their actions as God's plan to help them believing that was why God sent him to Egypt ahead of them so that when the need arose he was already positioned in Egypt in readiness to bail them out of their troubles. When you abide in God you will always see God working in every situation of your life and once you can do this you can always turn everything that is not working for you to your advantage as a result of how you accept them. When problems or challenges come your way the attitude with which you receive them matters for it is your attitude to them that will determine what will happen to you. Let us look at two characters in the Scripture and compare the way they received the challenges of their lives. We shall look at Jacob Joseph's father and compare his reaction to the challenges that came his way with Paul's reaction to his own challenges when he was faced with a similar situation.

In the case of Jacob some of the challenges that he had to face in his old age included losing one of his sons Joseph that he believed had died. Another one of his sons Simeon was imprisoned in Egypt.

Living a Supernatural Life (Volume 2)

His youngest son Benjamin was to be taken away from him. Not only that, even the famine in the land became worse. Now look at his reaction and attitude to all these in Genesis 42:36. He said, *"All these things are against me."* He was only able to see the negative side of his challenges.

> *And Jacob their father said unto them, Me have ye bereaved of my children: Joseph is not, and Simeon is not, and ye will take Benjamin away: all these things are against me.*
> **Genesis 42:36**

Now let us look at the case of Paul the Apostle. He said that he was in trouble on every side, yet he was not depressed. He was perplexed, but not in despair. He was persecuted but not forsaken. He was cast down but not destroyed. You will see all this in 2 Corinthian 4:8-10.

> *We are troubled on every side, yet not distressed; we are perplexed, but not in despair;*
>
> *Persecuted, but not forsaken; cast down, but not destroyed;*
>
> *Always bearing about in the body the dying of the Lord Jesus, that the life also of Jesus might be made manifest in our body.*
> **2 Corinthians 4:8-10**

You will think that should weigh Paul down. But look at his reaction as written in 2 Corinthians 4:17. He saw all as, *"Our light afflictions, which is but for a moment."*

For our light affliction, which is but for a moment, worketh for us a far more exceeding and eternal weight of glory;
2 Corinthians 4:17

He also saw these as working towards his glory and that *all these things are working together for his good* as he said in Romans 8:28. Jacob saw all his challenges as things that were against him. But as you can see in Romans 8:28 written below Paul saw his own challenges as working together for his good.

And we know that all things work together for good to them that love God, to them who are the called according to his purpose.
Romans 8:28

Let us look in a greater detail at what happened to Paul so that you can see the gravity of his challenges. Look at what he said in 2 Corinthians 12:7 as well as what he said in 2 Corinthians 11:23-27. He said that a messenger of Satan was sent to buffet him. He was shipwrecked. He was stoned. He was beaten. He went through all sorts of perils of robbers. He was imprisoned and suffered from weariness, hunger, thirst, cold and nakedness. He went through all these yet he was audacious enough to call these *light afflictions.*

And lest I should be exalted above measure through the abundance of the revelations, there was given to me a thorn in the flesh, the messenger of Satan to buffet me, lest I should be exalted above measure.
2 Corinthians 12:7

> *Are they ministers of Christ? (I speak as a fool) I am more; in labours more abundant, in stripes above measure, in prisons more frequent, in deaths oft.*
>
> *Of the Jews five times received I forty stripes save one.*
>
> *Thrice was I beaten with rods, once was I stoned, thrice I suffered shipwreck, a night and a day I have been in the deep;*
>
> *In journeyings often, in perils of waters, in perils of robbers, in perils by mine own countrymen, in perils by the heathen, in perils in the city, in perils in the wilderness, in perils in the sea, in perils among false brethren;*
>
> *In weariness and painfulness, in watchings often, in hunger and thirst, in fastings often, in cold and nakedness.*
> **2 Corinthians 11:23-27**

Satan had buffeted Paul with all sorts of afflictions and must have thought that he has driven Paul into a corner where Paul will have to acknowledge the heavy oppression that he was going through and give up his ministry.

But Paul must have shocked Satan when he took all that Satan had to throw at him and called them all ***"Our light afflictions."*** This must have been very disappointing to Satan. It must have deflated Satan's ego. That is the way to deal with Satan and reduce him to a toothless bulldog.

Satan threw everything he had at Paul but that would not stop Paul from going ahead with his ministry. Paul deflated Satan's ego by showing that even the best shots that Satan had to throw at him were really nothing to him. That must have made Satan feel very weak. Satan fired his best shots at Paul and turned everything he had at him but Paul just shrugged them off and saw them as *light afflictions.* There is a great lesson in this for us Christians. We should never give Satan the opportunity to rejoice over us. Instead whatever Satan may be throwing at us we should decide to ignore it and keep rejoicing. That will get Satan confused because he doesn't know how to handle that kind of situation. When you are God-conscious nothing the enemy throws at you will matter to you. Abiding in Christ will make you God-conscious. Another case to look at is that of Joseph against whom his brothers schemed all kinds of evil and whom they eventually sold. He was not bitter. He was so God-conscious that he did not see the ordeal that he went through as an affliction. Instead he saw it as God working through it to preserve his people. Look at Genesis 45:5-8 to see what he said.

> *Now therefore be not grieved, nor angry with yourselves, that ye sold me hither: for God did send me before you to preserve life.*
>
> *For these two years hath the famine been in the land: and yet there are five years, in the which there shall neither be earing nor harvest.*
>
> *And God sent me before you to preserve you a posterity in the earth, and to save your lives by a great deliverance.*

So now it was not you that sent me hither, but God: and he hath made me a father to Pharaoh, and lord of all his house, and a ruler throughout all the land of Egypt.
Genesis 45:5-8

THE GOD-CONSCIOUS ATTITUDE

To illustrate further what a God-conscious attitude means let us look at this story of two friends who travelled in the same vehicle to a city about a hundred miles away from their home.

On their way back midway to their destination their vehicle was involved in a terrible accident that left both of them unconscious and virtually dead. They were both rushed to the hospital and after several months and several operations in the hospital they both regained their consciousness and a major part of their health.

Two years later one of the friends was travelling on that same route in a vehicle with some friends. When they got to the place where the accident occurred he pointed the place to his friends and told them, *"This is the terrible place where I had the accident that almost ended my life."*

The other friend also travelled on that route with most of virtually the same friends some two weeks later. But when he got to the accident spot he told his friends, *"This is the glorious place where God wrought a great miracle in my life by saving me from death."*

Abide in Christ

The same thing happened to both of them but each one saw the situation differently. One was God conscious, the other was not. The way you see a situation will determine your attitude to the situation. Your attitude to an affliction will determine whether you will have victory over the affliction or whether the affliction will overwhelm you. If you can try to see the positive side of the affliction you can turn it into a blessing. When you praise God even when an affliction seem to be overwhelming you on all sides you are tapping into one of the most potent spiritual weapons available to the Christian with which to fight the devil and his forces. This is so because when you praise God in the midst of an affliction you are bringing God into the situation and you are using a spiritual weapon that always confuses Satan and his forces. It wins against them in every situation.

This weapon of praise has been used by God's people in the past and it won them great victories. One great example of this is written in 2 Chronicles 20:15-25. It describes Jehoshaphat's victory over the Moabites and the Ammonites using the weapon. The Scriptures said that while the children of Israel were singing praises to God the Lord set ambushments against the children of Ammon, Moab and mount Seir that came against them and they were smitten.

> *And he said, Hearken ye, all Judah, and ye inhabitants of Jerusalem, and thou king Jehoshaphat, Thus saith the Lord unto you, Be not afraid nor dismayed by reason of this great multitude; for the battle is not yours, but God's.*

Living a Supernatural Life (Volume 2)

To morrow go ye down against them: behold, they come up by the cliff of Ziz; and ye shall find them at the end of the brook, before the wilderness of Jeruel.

Ye shall not need to fight in this battle: set yourselves, stand ye still, and see the salvation of the Lord with you, O Judah and Jerusalem: fear not, nor be dismayed; to morrow go out against them: for the Lord will be with you.

And Jehoshaphat bowed his head with his face to the ground: and all Judah and the inhabitants of Jerusalem fell before the Lord, worshipping the Lord.

And the Levites, of the children of the Kohathites, and of the children of the Korhites, stood up to praise the Lord God of Israel with a loud voice on high.

And they rose early in the morning, and went forth into the wilderness of Tekoa: and as they went forth, Jehoshaphat stood and said, Hear me, O Judah, and ye inhabitants of Jerusalem; Believe in the Lord your God, so shall ye be established; believe his prophets, so shall ye prosper.

And when he had consulted with the people, he appointed singers unto the Lord, and that should praise the beauty of holiness, as they went out before the army, and to say, Praise the Lord; for his mercy endureth for ever.

Abide in Christ

And when they began to sing and to praise, the Lord set ambushments against the children of Ammon, Moab, and mount Seir, which were come against Judah; and they were smitten.

For the children of Ammon and Moab stood up against the inhabitants of mount Seir, utterly to slay and destroy them: and when they had made an end of the inhabitants of Seir, every one helped to destroy another.

And when Judah came toward the watch tower in the wilderness, they looked unto the multitude, and, behold, they were dead bodies fallen to the earth, and none escaped.

And when Jehoshaphat and his people came to take away the spoil of them, they found among them in abundance both riches with the dead bodies, and precious jewels, which they stripped off for themselves, more than they could carry away: and they were three days in gathering of the spoil, it was so much.
                                  2 Chronicles 20:15-25

When you abide in Christ you will have God with you all the time and when God is with you it no longer matters who is against you. This is because when God is with you your becoming great is a forgone conclusion. That was what happened to David as written down for us in 2 Samuel 5:10. You will also be strengthened and magnified exceedingly by God. That happened to Solomon as we are told in 2 Chronicles 1:1.

Living a Supernatural Life (Volume 2)

> *And David went on, and grew great, and the Lord God of hosts was with him.*
>
> **2 Samuel 5:10**

> *And Solomon the son of David was strengthened in his kingdom, and the Lord his God was with him, and magnified him exceedingly.*
>
> **2 Chronicles 1:1**

When your enemies see that the Lord is with you they will be forced to fall in line with you because their hands will be weakened against you. That was what happened to king Asa as we can see from what is written down for us in 2 Chronicles 15:9. When God is with you no matter whom your enemy may be, no matter what afflictions may come your way, God will deliver you from all of them. He will not only deliver you He will also give you favour and wisdom. That was what He did for Joseph as we are told in Acts 7:9-10. If you can be fully God-conscious and totally void of self-consciousness then God will anoint you with a full measure of the Holy Ghost and with power as He did for Jesus as we are told in Acts 10:38.

> *And he gathered all Judah and Benjamin, and the strangers with them out of Ephraim and Manasseh, and out of Simeon: for they fell to him out of Israel in abundance, when they saw that the Lord his God was with him.*
>
> **2 Chronicles 15:9**

> *And the patriarchs, moved with envy, sold Joseph into Egypt: but God was with him,*

And delivered him out of all his afflictions, and gave him favour and wisdom in the sight of Pharaoh king of Egypt; and he made him governor over Egypt and all his house.
Acts 7:9-10

How God anointed Jesus of Nazareth with the Holy Ghost and with power: who went about doing good, and healing all that were oppressed of the devil; for God was with him.
Acts 10:38

THERE WILL BE WILDERNESS EXPERIENCE

That God is with you or that you abide in Him does not mean that you will be totally free from all afflictions. There will be periods when you will still have to go through the wilderness experience. Look at what Jesus said in Matthew 13:21 below.

Yet hath he not root in himself, but dureth for a while: for when tribulation or persecution ariseth because of the word, by and by he is offended.
Matthew 13:21

He said **when** tribulation or persecution arises not *if* tribulation or persecution arises. Therefore that these will arise is a forgone conclusion. It is not *if* it arises but **when** it arises. So it is bound to come and the time of its coming you will probably not know in advance.

Living a Supernatural Life (Volume 2)

In fact whenever there is a new door of opportunity opening to you there will be adversaries wanting to close that door and stop you from entering into the fullness of that opportunity. That was what Paul the apostle made us to see concerning his own situation by what he wrote in 1 Corinthians 16:9. There is bound to be opposition to your destiny. The enemy will not want you to achieve the destiny that God has planned for you. That in essence is what Jesus is telling us in Matthew 11:12. He is telling you that the Kingdom of Heaven will not be handed over to you on a platter of gold. You will have to contend for it with the enemy. Only those who are willing to contend with the enemy for it will be able to take it by force because you require force to take it.

> *For a great door and effectual is opened unto me, and there are many adversaries.*
> **1 Corinthians 16:9**

> *And from the days of John the Baptist until now the kingdom of heaven suffereth violence, and the violent take it by force.*
> **Matthew 11:12**

Every affliction that comes your way you should see it as an opportunity to prove to God that you really believe His promises and what He has said about you. Some afflictions will stretch your faith so much that you will almost be questioning in your heart as to whether those statements of God concerning you are really true. God will be watching you to see how such afflictions will affect your trust in His word. God uses such afflictions to see how much trust you have in His Word. We should see afflictions as trials of our faith.

An example of this is the case of Abraham. God has promised him that he would be the father of a great nation in Genesis 12:2 yet even up to his old age he still had no child. God must have been studying him to see whether despite all contrary signs that he was seeing Abraham will still trust in His Word.

> *And I will make of thee a great nation, and I will bless thee, and make thy name great; and thou shalt be a blessing:*
> **Genesis 12:2**

No matter what affliction you may be going through at any time of your life you must see it as a preparation for a higher calling, which is bound to come once you can scale through the affliction. That was the case with Abraham. God tested him and God is still doing the same thing that He did to Abraham to us today.

For every tunnel of affliction that you go through there is glory waiting for you at the end of the tunnel. But you have to go through this wilderness experience from time to time. It is going through such experiences that develops the fruit of the Spirit such as patience in you. That is what we can see in Romans 5:3-4.

> *And not only so, but we glory in tribulations also: knowing that tribulation worketh patience;*
>
> *And patience, experience; and experience, hope:*
> **Romans 5:3-4**

Living a Supernatural Life (Volume 2)

Once you become a born again Christian you are no longer flowing along in the same direction with the world but against the world. So you are bound to have opposition. Therefore adversaries must come. You cannot pray them away. You have to face them and fight them. That is the only way for you to get over them. Many Christians try to pray their adversaries away. But they won't go away. The earlier you get to know that you have to face them and fight them, the better because they will not go away. They may hide for some time but they are bound to come back.

Adversaries are there to scare you but you are created to scare them and to have dominion over them. You no longer have the spirit of fear so they should not scare you. You now have the Spirit of power and of love and of a sound mind. That is what we are made to know from what Paul wrote in 2 Timothy 1:7. God has also promised you in 1 Corinthians 10:13 that He will not allow any affliction or trial that you cannot cope with to come your way.

> *For God hath not given us the spirit of fear; but of power, and of love, and of a sound mind.*
> **2 Timothy 1:7**

> *There hath no temptation taken you but such as is common to man: but God is faithful, who will not suffer you to be tempted above that ye are able; but will with the temptation also make a way to escape, that ye may be able to bear it.*
> **1 Corinthians 10:13**

Abide in Christ

You should be confident when you face any trial or adversary knowing that God allowed it to come your way because He knows that you can overcome it. Therefore no matter how terrible or difficult the affliction or trial may be you should rest assured and know that you can and will overcome it. God even went further to say that should in case the situation seems to be too much for you and your faith seems not to be able to stand the trial, He has provided a way of escape from it for you. Considering this promise of God I don't see why any Christian should not be confident to face any affliction that comes his way. In fact we should approach all afflictions and trials with the type of confidence that will make the devil feel miserable.

Never cast away your confidence in times of afflictions or trials because your confidence is one of the major assets that you will require to get over the trial or affliction. That is what Hebrews 10:35 is telling us in essence. You must always see yourself as the victor in any situation.

Cast not away therefore your confidence, which hath great recompence of reward.
Hebrews 10:35

No matter how terrible or extreme the affliction can be keep encouraging yourself in the Lord and stay put in the Lord. Look at David's case. After he was anointed to be king he still had to go through all types of afflictions to the point that he had to run for his dear life. But we are told in 1 Samuel 30:6 that despite all these David encouraged himself in the Lord his God.

Living a Supernatural Life (Volume 2)

> *And David was greatly distressed; for the people spake of stoning him, because the soul of all the people was grieved, every man for his sons and for his daughters: but David encouraged himself in the LORD his God.*
> **1 Samuel 30:6**

David encouraged himself in the Lord. That was his staying power and as we can see he eventually got over all his troubles. Encourage yourself in the Lord because when the Lord is with you and holding you by the right hand nothing can overcome you. No affliction or trial can oppress you for God will subdue even nations before you. He will loose the loins of kings to open before you all gates of opportunities and nothing shall shut the gates. God will go before you and make the places that have been made crooked by the afflictions straight. He will break in pieces the Gates of brass and cut asunder the bars of iron that has been built in your life to restrain your progress. Everything blocking your part of progress will be shattered by God. And the thing to note about this is that you may not even need to fight the battle. God will fight for you.

God will give you the treasures of darkness and the hidden riches of secret places so that you may know that He is the Lord who has called you by your name and surnamed you by giving you His Name though you have not really known Him. The God that you have who is girding you is the God of Israel and the only God. There is no other God besides Him. These are what He made us to know through Prophet Isaiah from what He said through Isaiah in Isaiah 45:1-6.

Thus saith the LORD to his anointed, to Cyrus, whose right hand I have holden, to subdue nations before him; and I will loose the loins of kings, to open before him the two leaved gates; and the gates shall not be shut;

I will go before thee, and make the crooked places straight: I will break in pieces the gates of brass, and cut in sunder the bars of iron:

And I will give thee the treasures of darkness, and hidden riches of secret places, that thou mayest know that I, the LORD, which call thee by thy name, am the God of Israel.

For Jacob my servant's sake, and Israel mine elect, I have even called thee by thy name: I have surnamed thee, though thou hast not known me.

I am the LORD, and there is none else, there is no God beside me: I girded thee, though thou hast not known me:

That they may know from the rising of the sun, and from the west, that there is none beside me. I am the LORD, and there is none else.
Isaiah 45:1-6

How can you have this kind of assurance from God and not be confident in the face of any affliction. It is therefore absolutely imperative that you should abide in Christ so that you will have God's presence with you in all situations and all these will be true of you.

Living a Supernatural Life (Volume 2)

Wherever you are and whatever may be happening to you if God's presence is not with you then you are not safe. God's presence with us is very important in our daily journey through life. That was why when God told Moses that he would be taking the children of Israel to Canaan Moses said to God in Exodus 33:15 that if His presence will not go with them he should not let them go.

> *And he said unto him, If thy presence go not with me, carry us not up hence.*
> **Exodus 33:15**

As you can see, when you abide in Christ and you become one with Him, you will be clothed with His righteousness and His righteousness will become your righteousness. That is what we are made to see in Philippians 3:9.

> *And be found in him, not having mine own righteousness, which is of the law, but that which is through the faith of Christ, the righteousness which is of God by faith:*
> **Philippians 3:9**

Being clothed with the righteousness of Christ will help you approach God for anything without any inhibition. This relates to one of the other things that you need to do if you are to be able to live a supernatural life here on earth. This is that you must live your life without a sin-complex, which is only possible if you abide in Christ. ***You must have no sin-complex.*** That is what we shall discuss in the next Chapter.

CHAPTER 10

HAVE NO SIN-COMPLEX

The Psalmist in Psalm 66:18 says if you regard iniquity in your heart the Lord will not hear you.

> *If I regard iniquity in my heart, the Lord will not hear me:*
> **Psalm 66:18**

Therefore if you have any sin-complex in your heart, you will not have the courage to approach God and feel confident that you will receive what you ask from Him. When you have any sin-complex Satan will give you the guilt conscience and put doubt in you to make you feel unworthy before God to receive anything from Him. But even if you have committed sins, that should not deter you from opening your mouth wide to give your command. Confess your sins to God then ask for His forgiveness and repent of the sins. Once you repent of your sins and change, your guilt-conscience should go. There is no condemnation for you anymore. That is what God told us through Apostle Paul. For it is written in Romans 8:1 that:

Living a Supernatural Life (Volume 2)

> *There is therefore now no condemnation to them which are in Christ Jesus, who walk not after the flesh, but after the Spirit.*
> **Romans 8:1**

God also confirmed this through James in James 5:15 as written below.

> *And the prayer of faith shall save the sick, and the Lord shall raise him up; and if he have committed sins, they shall be forgiven him.*
> **James 5:15**

This means that if you are suffering any affliction as a result of sins that you have committed, you can still be forgiven. Therefore there is no reason for you to have any sin-complex. Finally the Word of God that He gave us through Apostle John in 1 John 1:9 also establishes the faithfulness of God to forgive us our sins if we will only confess our sins and repent of them.

> *If we confess our sins, he is faithful and just to forgive us our sins, and to cleanse us from all unrighteousness.*
> **1 John 1:9**

Therefore God is not holding anything against you now. Jesus has used His blood to clean up your way to God and remove all the obstacles between you and God. If you will only confess your sins and repent of them, God is willing to forgive you. Don't let any sin or inferiority complex deny you of your victory over your enemies. Be bold. If you are born-again, it is Jesus that has the final say in your affairs not the devil.

Have no Sin-complex

The devil has been defeated. If you keep yourself properly aligned with Christ by consecrating yourself, the devil has no more say in your affairs, unless you allow him. Remember that it is the effectual fervent prayer of him that has no sin-complex but who has a righteousness-complex that availeth much with God. That is what God is telling us in James 5:16.

> *Confess your faults one to another, and pray one for another, that ye may be healed. The effectual fervent prayer of a righteous man availeth much.*
> **James 5:16**

For your prayer to avail much, righteousness-complex is a must. This is because if you have the sin-complex Satan will use this against you to bombard your mind with guilt-consciousness thereby making you feel unworthy to receive anything from God. But I want you to note that Jesus is in charge today. He has the final say on your affairs now. The devil doesn't have to permit you anything. The promises that God made to you do not depend on the devil to be fulfilled. The devil has no say concerning them. It is over with the devil in your life if you want it so. You are supposed to be in Christ now. Therefore if you stay where you are supposed to be, that is in Christ then it is Jesus Christ that God sees and not you when He looks at you. You have now been clothed with the righteousness nature of Jesus Christ as a free gift. He has now been made righteousness unto you. It is His righteousness that God sees when He looks at you. He doesn't see your sinful nature provided that you stay in Christ. That is the main reason why Jesus died for you.

Living a Supernatural Life (Volume 2)

It is so that His righteousness can cover your sins that He is made righteousness unto you. That is what we are told by Paul in 1 Corinthians 1:30. If you are born-again and living a consecrated life unto God then you are now unto God a sweet savour of Jesus Christ. That is the essence of what God is also telling us through Apostle Paul in 2 Corinthians 2:15.

> *But of him are ye in Christ Jesus, who of God is made unto us wisdom, and righteousness, and sanctification, and redemption:*
> **1 Corinthians 1:30**

> *For we are unto God a sweet savour of Christ, in them that are saved, and in them that perish:*
> **2 Corinthians 2:15**

This means that when God looks at you now it is not your own righteousness or sin that He sees but the righteousness of Jesus Christ with which you are now clothed. This is the reason why most Christians fail to get their prayers answered by God. It is because they just cannot see themselves in right-standing with God. They still have the sin-complex. In Numbers 23:23 we are also told concerning the Israelites of the flesh that there is no more enchantment or divination against them.

> *Surely there is no enchantment against Jacob, neither is there any divination against Israel: according to this time it shall be said of Jacob and of Israel, What hath God wrought!*
> **Numbers 23:23**

Have no Sin-complex

Now you are the spiritual Israelite. God is saying the same thing to you. So be conscious of the truth that there is no enchantment or divination against you anymore.

Therefore you should not fear anything. God is not holding anything against you. Therefore do not be restrained to open your mouth. Jesus Christ has already destroyed the works of the devil. That is what God has told us through Apostle John in 1 John 3:8 as written below.

> *He that committeth sin is of the devil; for the devil sinneth from the beginning. For this purpose the Son of God was manifested, that he might destroy the works of the devil.*
> **1 John 3:8**

Jesus came to destroy the works of the devil and He has actually destroyed them. That is an accomplished truth. So you do not need to fear whatever the devil may do to you. As a born-again Christian you are now kept by the power of God through faith. That is what God has also told us through Peter in 1 Peter 1:3-5. Therefore your sustenance has nothing to do with the devil anymore. Therefore free yourself from this ***devil-this devil-that syndrome***. By this syndrome you are merely making the devil more important than he really is.

> *Blessed be the God and Father of our Lord Jesus Christ, which according to his abundant mercy hath begotten us again unto a lively hope by the resurrection of Jesus Christ from the dead,*

Living a Supernatural Life (Volume 2)

> *To an inheritance incorruptible, and undefiled, and that fadeth not away, reserved in heaven for you,*
>
> *Who are kept by the power of God through faith unto salvation ready to be revealed in the last time.*
>
> 1 Peter 1:3-5

Satan can no longer touch you and get away with it unless you agree with him and allow him to do so either consciously or subconsciously. You are completely free from him. But you have the responsibility to keep yourself from him. That is confirmed by what God said through John in 1 John 5:18.

> *We know that whosoever is born of God sinneth not; but he that is begotten of God keepeth himself, and that wicked one toucheth him not.*
>
> 1 John 5:18

He says that he that is begotten of God keepeth himself and the devil cannot touch him. If you are born-again you are now begotten of God and you are the one that He is talking about, because that is what God told us through Peter in 1 Peter 1:3.

> *Blessed be the God and Father of our Lord Jesus Christ, which according to his abundant mercy hath begotten us again unto a lively hope by the resurrection of Jesus Christ from the dead,*
>
> 1 Peter 1:3

Have no Sin-complex

God is talking about you in 1 John 5:18 above. The wicked one is not supposed to touch you anymore. He can no longer touch you unless you allow him. He is not permitted to do so but you must keep yourself clear of him, therefore do not invite him to touch you. If he does, without God's permission he is going beyond his bounds, and you are supposed to tell him so. You are supposed to command him to keep off and he will obey. You have the authority to command whatever is touching you, which is not of God. Use the authority that you now have. The devil and his forces have no power over you. We showed this in *Volume 1* of this *"Living a supernatural life"* book series.

You can always tell Satan where to go just like Jesus did when he came to tempt Him and when he came into Simon Peter. We have mentioned this earlier, and it was Jesus Himself that gave you this authority over Satan and his demons. He confirmed this by what He said as written down in Luke 10:19. He said,

> *"Behold, I give unto you power to tread on serpents and scorpions, and over all the power of the enemy: and nothing shall by any means hurt you."*
>
> **Luke 10:19**

So what are you afraid of? The devil has no power over you or your affairs anymore. Christ has destroyed the works of the devil. But you have to know this to dominate in life. If you do not know this, Satan and his forces will dominate you instead. It is your lack of knowledge that Satan preys upon most of the time. Resist him with Word and he will flee from you.

Living a Supernatural Life (Volume 2)

It is when you know the power that you now have and you are convinced in your mind that it is over and above the power of the enemy that you can have dominion over your enemy. This is the crux of the problem for most Christians. They believe that the devil has some power, which is far above what they have or what they can demonstrate. But the works of the devil has been destroyed. What are these works of the devil that has been destroyed by Christ? The works of the devil include all forms of wickedness and Christ came to destroy these.

They include sicknesses, diseases, barrenness, failure, lack, poverty, spiritual arrows, evil marks, and yokes of afflictions, curses and all types of bondages. But Christ came to destroy all these. The works of the devil is the cause of everything that is not working in your life. Christ came to destroy all of them. If Christ came to destroy the works of the devil, you may be wondering whether He did really destroy them. God clearly stated this through Apostle Paul in Colossians 2:15.

And having spoiled principalities and powers, he made a shew of them openly, triumphing over them in it.
Colossians 2:15

This is a vivid description of what Christ did with the devil and all his forces of darkness after He defeated them. Therefore we not only know that Christ came to destroy the works of the devil, we now also know for sure that He did destroy them. It is an accomplished truth. He even made a public show of their defeat in the spiritual realm.

Have no Sin-complex

Christ not only defeated the devil and his forces, but He conquered them, took them captive, paraded them the way a conqueror parades his captives and made an open show of them. Therefore the works of the devil should not give you much concern if you live your life in Christ as God prescribed. Christ has also blotted out the handwriting of ordinances that was against you, which was contrary to you. He took it out of the way and nailed it to the Cross. That is what God also said through Apostle Paul in Colossians 2:14.

Blotting out the handwriting of ordinances that was against us, which was contrary to us, and took it out of the way, nailing it to his cross;
Colossians 2:14

There is nothing against you anymore or contrary to you, which Christ had not taken care of. Therefore you need to fear nothing now except God. The devil is not in control of your life. You can have a perfect control of your life if you have no sin or inferiority complex. The devil has no more power over you unless you give it to him through your actions, inactions or your thoughts. Therefore be bold in your commands. Have a positive Scriptural image of yourself. If you really know who you are, what you are, what you have, what you can do and where you are now in Christ you will be very bold in standing against the devil. This is so because you are in such a position of strength and authority now in Christ that even the devil is afraid of you any time he comes near where you are. But you must know these if you are to have dominion over him.

Living a Supernatural Life (Volume 2)

Because you don't know this he still pretends and demonstrate his fake power to you. Now that you are born-again you need to purge yourself from the belief that you are a sinner; otherwise you will not be bold enough to approach God for your needs. You were a sinner but you are no longer a sinner.

If you do not purge yourself of that believe, you will always have a reason why you do not believe that you will get what you asked from God. And that reason will stand like an obstacle or barrier blocking your way to your blessings. It will make your faith very weak.

You will not be able to stand in faith to ask for your needs from God. Even where you cannot pinpoint a particular sin in your life, you will still not be able to stand boldly with all authority and confidence to ask for what you want from God.

You will still be saying to yourself, "Perhaps there is one sin of commission or omission, which I don't know still in my life." Of course, the devil will be happy to help you bring doubts into your mind, with the resultant effect that you will not be totally sure that you will get what you asked for. And it is sure that you will not get it because that is what God told us through James in James 1:6-8.

> *But let him ask in faith, nothing wavering. For he that wavereth is like a wave of the sea driven with the wind and tossed.*
>
> *For let not that man think that he shall receive any thing of the Lord.*

Have no Sin-complex

A double minded man is unstable in all his ways.
James 1:6-8

You are now a partaker of the divine nature. Therefore you have to know that you are now righteous by nature and that the righteousness of Christ now belongs to you because you are in Christ. You must not allow the devil to plant any guilt conscience or complex in you. You are supposed to stand before God covered with the righteousness of Christ with all boldness and confidence. Your position before God now is not like that of a man accused in a law court, who was found guilty, but pardoned. No!

Your position before God now is like that of a man accused in a law court but was found not guilty and acquitted because someone else was found with the guilt. By so doing your own guilt was totally erased and removed. Obviously, you know that there is a difference between the two. While one man can walk about boldly and say that he has done nothing wrong, the other man will always have that constraint in his mind, knowing that he was actually found guilty, only that he was pardoned. Your position with God is this; you actually committed a crime, but while the court proceeding and cross-examination was going on, someone called Jesus Christ came out to say that the account for that crime should be debited to Him and He took the guilt and carried the penalty for the crime as if He committed the crime. As a result of this, you were acquitted, the court found Jesus Christ guilty, and He then went on to serve the punishment that you should have served.

Living a Supernatural Life (Volume 2)

After the court judgment, how do you think that judge will see you? Do you believe that he will still see you as being guilty? No, the judge will not see you as guilty, because he has already sent the guilty one to jail. The judge will see you as a free citizen who is entitled in law to all his rights as a citizen of the country. That is your situation now with God. Before God, you are totally acquitted of any sin.

There is no longer any condemnation for you. The handwriting of ordinances against you has been taken out of the way. You have been cleansed from all your sins. Therefore you must get out of your sin-complex, and you must put on a righteousness-complex. Take a look at what God said concerning you in Romans 8:1, in 1 John 1:7, in Colossians 2:14, in Hebrews 10:16-17 and also in Romans 5:9 as written below.

> *There is therefore now no condemnation to them which are in Christ Jesus, who walk not after the flesh, but after the Spirit.*
> **Romans 8:1**

> *But if we walk in the light, as he is in the light, we have fellowship one with another, and the blood of Jesus Christ his Son cleanseth us from all sin.*
> **1 John 1:7**

> *Blotting out the handwriting of ordinances that was against us, which was contrary to us, and took it out of the way, nailing it to his cross.*
> **Colossians 2:14**

Have no Sin-complex

This is the covenant that I will make with them after those days, saith the Lord, I will put my laws into their hearts, and in their minds will I write them;

And their sins and iniquities will I remember no more.
Hebrews 10:16-17

Much more then, being now justified by his blood, we shall be saved from wrath through him.
Romans 5:9

Because you are now in Christ and God now sees you through Christ. He no longer sees you as a sinner. This is something that is most difficult for many Christians to accept. They just find it so difficult to rid themselves of their sin-complex. But without getting rid of the sin-complex they cannot approach God with confidence. But you are supposed to approach God in confidence and with boldness when you want anything from Him. That is what God made us to understand by what He said through Apostle Paul in Ephesians 3:12. You should also note that it is only when you approach Him without a sin-complex, but with a righteousness-complex that your prayers to Him can become very effective, and result-oriented. That is what He made us to know by what He said through Apostle James in James 5:16.

In whom we have boldness and access with confidence by the faith of him.
Ephesians 3:12

Living a Supernatural Life (Volume 2)

> *Confess your faults one to another, and pray one for another, that ye may be healed. The effectual fervent prayer of a righteous man availeth much.*
>
> **James 5:16**

You need to know your rights and privileges now before God, if you want to enjoy all the benefits of your being born again. You should allow the blood of Christ, which was used, for the atonement of your sins, to purge your conscience from all sin complexes, for that is one of the functions of the blood of Christ. That is what we are told by God in Hebrews 9:14.

> *How much more shall the blood of Christ, who through the eternal Spirit offered himself without spot to God, purge your conscience from dead works to serve the living God?*
>
> **Hebrews 9:14**

As you can see from the passage above, it is when your conscience is purged of its sin complex that you can really serve God with all your heart. When you remove the sin-complex that you have and put on the righteousness-complex, you will no longer have any doubts in your mind that you will receive anything that you ask from God.

Instead you will have a very strong faith that you will be given anything that you asked of God. With the strong faith now in place, you will definitely get whatever you asked for according to what He told us in Hebrews 11:6 through Apostle Paul, which is written below.

Have no Sin-complex

> *But without faith it is impossible to please him: for he that cometh to God must believe that he is, and that he is a rewarder of them that diligently seek him.*
> **Hebrews 11:6**

You must have the sin-complex purged from your mind completely, because whether you do so or not is what will make or break your Christian adventure, or your Christian life. It is only when you get to the point of realizing and effecting this in your life that you can boldly speak out the words of authority to control the circumstances around you.

You should feel free and be at liberty now to ask what you want of God. You are free to ask without any complex. You now have an absolute and glorious liberty. That is what God tells us in 2 Corinthians 3:17 and also in Romans 8:21 through Paul the Apostle.

> *Now the Lord is that Spirit: and where the Spirit of the Lord is, there is liberty.*
> **2 Corinthians 3:17**

> *Because the creature itself also shall be delivered from the bondage of corruption into the glorious liberty of the children of God.*
> **Romans 8:21**

The characteristics that you now have in Christ are all discussed in *Volume 3* of this *"Living a supernatural life"* book series by the same author. You will do well to read that volume. If you can read it and imbibe what is written in it Satan will no longer be your problem.

Living a Supernatural Life (Volume 2)

Satan will no longer be able to hang his works around you. You will have the confidence and boldness to stand against Satan and his forces. You will no longer be afraid to proclaim what you want because you will know that the Spirit that is now living in you is not the spirit of fear but that of power, and of love and of a sound mind, which is also the Spirit of adoption as a child of God. That is what we are told in 2 Timothy 1:7 as well as in Romans 8:15. So you need not be afraid of the devil and his forces anymore. They should no longer frighten you because they no longer have any power or authority over you.

> *For God hath not given us the spirit of fear; but of power, and of love, and of a sound mind.*
> **2 Timothy 1:7**

> *For ye have not received the spirit of bondage again to fear; but ye have received the Spirit of adoption, whereby we cry, Abba, Father.*
> **Romans 8:15**

You should also know as we are told in 1 John 4:4 that the Spirit that is now living in you is far greater than Satan or any of his hosts that is in this world. The Word of God says that the One living in you is greater than the one living in the world. Therefore you must have the greater-One mentality. It should be your mindset at all times that the greater One is in you.

> *Ye are of God, little children, and have overcome them: because greater is he that is in you, than he that is in the world.*
> **1 John 4:4**

HAVE A RIGHTEOUSNESS-COMPLEX

When you look at the life of Jesus Christ when He was here on earth, the thing that will strike you most is that He had a very strong righteousness-complex. That was why He was so bold whenever He addresses the situations around Him. He spoke to diseases and demons with confidence and they obeyed Him. He spoke to a tree, the wind, and they all obeyed Him. That was because He had no sin-complex that could cause any doubt in His mind. He knew that He had a right-standing with God, without any guilt complex, and He confessed this all the time. For an example, look at what He said in John 14:30.

Hereafter I will not talk much with you: for the prince of this world cometh, and hath nothing in me.
John 14:30

He was so sure of the truth that there was nothing that Satan can use to have any foothold in His life. You are also in the same position now.

You should have no sin-complex in your mind. You may say, "Well Jesus is God Himself, so He can have no sin-complex, but I am only a man". But I want to remind you that you are not just any man any longer, you are also now a god, for that is what you are called by God through David in Psalm 82:6. Jesus also confirmed this when He made reference to it as written down in John 10:34-35. You are not just any god; you are a son of the Most High God. The Almighty God is your Father, you are His son and like begets like.

Living a Supernatural Life (Volume 2)

> *I have said, Ye are gods; and all of you are children of the most High.*
> **Psalm 82:6**

> *Jesus answered them, Is it not written in your law, I said, Ye are gods?*
>
> *If he called them gods, unto whom the word of God came, and the scripture cannot be broken;*
> **John 10:34-35**

You see yourself as powerless. You think that you have no power over the circumstances and situations that you come across in life because you are a man. What about Peter? What about Paul? What about Elijah and Elisha? They were men just like you are, but during their time here on earth, they commanded diseases, demons, fire, rain and prayed prayers that were effected immediately. Definitely such things as barrenness or unfruitfulness could not stand before them. Even death had no power before them. Yet according to Jesus in Matthew 11:11 as a New Covenant saint you have the potential for a more powerful anointing than any of them.

> *Verily I say unto you, Among them that are born of women there hath not risen a greater than John the Baptist: notwithstanding he that is least in the kingdom of heaven is greater than he.*
> **Matthew 11:11**

This statement was made by Jesus Himself who we know is the creator of man according to John 1:1-5,14.

Have no Sin-complex

In the beginning was the Word, and the Word was with God, and the Word was God.

The same was in the beginning with God.

All things were made by him; and without him was not any thing made that was made.

In him was life; and the life was the light of men.

And the light shineth in darkness; and the darkness comprehended it not.

And the Word was made flesh, and dwelt among us, (and we beheld his glory, the glory as of the only begotten of the Father,) full of grace and truth.
John 1:1-5,14

We must know that Jesus is quite aware of what He has loaded into man when He made that statement and He who knows everything about us can express that kind of confidence in us then it is obvious that we should have the confidence to face any battle that the devil may bring our way. We should stand firm against the devil and not be afraid of him.

It is only people who are afraid of the devil that are timid while standing against him. A Christian that knows the truth about the devil cannot be afraid of him. Get a true Scriptural picture of the devil and who you are in Christ and your fear of the devil will vanish forever.

Living a Supernatural Life (Volume 2)

To get a true Scriptural picture of the devil I will suggest that you read *Chapter 1* of *Volume 1* of this *"Living a Supernatural Life"* book series where the author explained this in detail. After reading this your fear of the devil will vanish forever. Also read the *Volume 3* of this *"Living a Supernatural Life"* book series to discover the Scriptural picture that God really has of you and it will change you forever.

If you are not afraid of the devil, you have to be firm in standing against him. In fact, I will say that you should be violent and assertive against the devil in your commands. But if this is to be the case then *you must be very sensitive to the Holy Spirit,* which brings me to the next thing that you must do if you want to walk in the miraculous and live a supernatural life. That is what we shall discuss in the next Chapter. It is only when you are sensitive to the Holy Spirit that you can have the correct Scriptural pictures of the devil and yourself.

CHAPTER 11

BE SENSITIVE TO THE HOLY SPIRIT

I will give you an example here to show you how the Holy Spirit can lead one. I had been told several times that I had been given the gift of faith, the gift of healing and gift of the working of miracles. God had told me personally, and God had also sent several other Prophets and men of God to tell me this.

At one time the calling was so strongly felt by me that I decided to take it up and virtually rushed into it. My faith was very strong in the truth that I had the gift of healing, the gift of faith and the gift of the working of miracles. I believed then that anytime I command a disease to come out of someone it must obey me.

So, I started doing so, but to my surprise the diseases in most cases did not obey me. I was terribly disappointed about this. So, I went back to the Holy Spirit, very subdued and shocked, and I asked the Spirit why the diseases are not obeying my commands.

Living a Supernatural Life (Volume 2)

I asked, *"After all, You have told me that I have been given the gift of healing, the gift of faith and the gift of the working of miracles. You said that all I have to do is just command and it will be so. Why then are they not obeying my commands?"*

I am giving you here what the Holy Spirit gave me as the answer to my questions so that you too can gain from it. It actually enlightened me. I wrote down the answer that the Holy Spirit gave me and I will just put it down verbatim for you. I want you to note in particular what the Holy Spirit said concerning who it is that is doing the healing. If you know that it is not your show then of course there will be no need for you to try to take any glory for yourself. The Holy Spirit said to me:

*"Well it is because you are not doing it the way that you ought to do it. Remember that Jesus Christ who is the example to you said that He did nothing on His own, but as He hears from **Me**, so He did. That is the way that you are to operate if you want to be sure that you are operating in **My** will. You should not just decide on your own that you want to heal this man or that man. Wait to be instructed by **Me** to do so. Then I will give you the instruction as to how, or which method of approach to use and when you follow it, the healing will come instantly.*

*If you are moved to heal somebody, you must first ask **Me** whether to do so and if permitted, you will then ask **Me** what approach to use. If you can remember, when I instructed you to go and heal your friend's child, I told you what to say.*

Be Sensitive to the Holy Spirit

*When you went there, and did exactly as I instructed you, the child was healed instantly. So it is important that you get the direction from **Me** before attempting to heal anybody. I will not leave you in the dark at any point, so if you ask **Me**, I will tell you whether to go ahead or not, and what to do. If you do not ask **Me** first, and you just go ahead and give a healing command, then you are on your own. Remember that I am doing the healing, yours is just to command as I order you. So if you command without **Me** involved, then how can you get the healing to manifest? It will be easy for you when you give commands if you know that the commands are not really yours. There will be no need therefore for you to worry yourself about the fulfillment of the commands that you speak out. You don't have to worry that you will be mocked if your commands are not obeyed because they are not even your commands anyway. In any case once you wait to hear the **RHEMA** Word from **Me** before you give the commands you know and you are sure that the commands will be obeyed."*

That statement of Jesus that the Holy Spirit referred me to was spoken by Jesus in John 5:30, as written below. As you can see from that answer, which the Holy Spirit gave me, it is obvious that the reason why I could not do the healing and the work of miracles was because I was not following the leading of the Spirit.

I can of mine own self do nothing: as I hear, I judge: and my judgment is just; because I seek not mine own will, but the will of the Father which hath sent me.

John 5:30

Not only that, I confused the situation regarding who was actually doing the healing. I knew all along that it was God that does the healing, but I thought that I had to command and then God will do the healing. Now I know that it is God that also starts the command process. *My role therefore is just that of a loudspeaker that speaks out loudly what God has said quietly into my heart, so that God can effect what He wills, not what I will.*

A typical example of how to wait for the leading of the Holy Spirit is shown in the story of Paul when he visited Philippi in Acts 16:16-18 where Paul met a damsel who was possessed with an evil spirit and who was following Paul and his group around saying, *"These men are the servants of the most high God which showed unto us the way of salvation."*

> *And it came to pass, as we went to prayer, a certain damsel possessed with a spirit of divination met us, which brought her masters much gain by soothsaying:*
>
> *The same followed Paul and us, and cried, saying, These men are the servants of the most high God, which shew unto us the way of salvation.*
>
> *And this did she many days. But Paul, being grieved, turned and said to the spirit, I command thee in the name of Jesus Christ to come out of her. And he came out the same hour.*
>
> **Acts 16:16-18**

Be Sensitive to the Holy Spirit

She followed Paul and his group around for many days but Paul did not say a word to her. This was because Paul knew that he was dealing with an evil spirit. He therefore did not want to go into any combat with this spirit until such a time that he has received the Words with which to do the battle from the Holy Spirit.

As soon as he received the necessary Words with which to do the battle he attacked the spirit in the damsel and commanded it to come out of the damsel in the Name of Jesus and it did so immediately. He waited to be directed by the Holy Spirit. If it were you, because you are irritated, you would have attacked and command the spirit instantly.

But had he not waited until such a time that he had received the **RHEMA** Words to use as well as the go-ahead signal from the Holy Spirit, his command would have ended in not being obeyed and he could have ended up being challenged or even attacked by the evil spirit like it was done to the seven sons of Sceva as we are told in Acts 19:13-16, which is written below.

> *Then certain of the vagabond Jews, exorcists, took upon them to call over them which had evil spirits the name of the Lord Jesus, saying, We adjure you by Jesus whom Paul preacheth.*
>
> *And there were seven sons of one Sceva, a Jew, and chief of the priests, which did so.*
>
> *And the evil spirit answered and said, Jesus I know, and Paul I know; but who are ye?*

Living a Supernatural Life (Volume 2)

> *And the man in whom the evil spirit was leaped on them, and overcame them, and prevailed against them, so that they fled out of that house naked and wounded.*
>
> **Acts 19:13-16**

You must be sensitive to the Holy Spirit because Christ who is the One that does the miracles uses the Power of the Holy Spirit. You can see this from what He said when He cast out the devil from a man that was blind and dumb so that the man could see and speak. The Pharisees believed that He was using a prince of the devil Beelzebub to cast out devils. But Jesus told them that He cast out the devil through the power of the Holy Spirit. You can see the story in Matthew 12:22-30.

> *Then was brought unto him one possessed with a devil, blind, and dumb: and he healed him, insomuch that the blind and dumb both spake and saw.*
>
> *And all the people were amazed, and said, Is not this the son of David?*
>
> *But when the Pharisees heard it, they said, This fellow doth not cast out devils, but by Beelzebub the prince of the devils.*
>
> *And Jesus knew their thoughts, and said unto them, Every kingdom divided against itself is brought to desolation; and every city or house divided against itself shall not stand:*

Be Sensitive to the Holy Spirit

> *And if Satan cast out Satan, he is divided against himself; how shall then his kingdom stand?*
>
> *And if I by Beelzebub cast out devils, by whom do your children cast them out? therefore they shall be your judges.*
>
> *But if I cast out devils by the Spirit of God, then the kingdom of God is come unto you.*
>
> *Or else how can one enter into a strong man's house, and spoil his goods, except he first bind the strong man? and then he will spoil his house.*
>
> *He that is not with me is against me; and he that gathereth not with me scattereth abroad.*
> **Matthew 12:22-30**

That same Spirit of God that Jesus said was the One in Him that He was using to do the miracles is the Holy Spirit that is now living in you also. Therefore that same Spirit is the One that Jesus who is the miracle worker will also use to do the miracles through you. That was why Jesus said in Acts 1:8 that if you truly have this Holy Spirit of God you will receive power. With this power God will be able to perform miracles, signs and wonders through you.

> *But ye shall receive power, after that the Holy Ghost is come upon you: and ye shall be witnesses unto me both in Jerusalem, and in all Judaea, and in Samaria, and unto the uttermost part of the earth.*
> **Acts 1:8**

Living a Supernatural Life (Volume 2)

The role of the Holy Spirit in the life of a Christian that wants to live a supernatural life on earth is discussed in much detail in *Volume 4* of this *"Living a supernatural life"* book series written by the same author. Once the Holy Spirit gives you a directive your stand on that issue must no longer be in doubt. *You must command the devil and be violent against him.* That is what we shall discuss in the next Chapter.

CHAPTER 12

BE VIOLENT AGAINST THE DEVIL

If everything that is evil in your life is the work of the devil, then you need to be very angry at the devil. You need to be, especially now that you know that his works had been destroyed; yet he is still trying to hang those works on you, and torment you with them. That his works has been destroyed can be seen from what is written in 1 John 3:8 and Hebrews 2:14.

He that committeth sin is of the devil; for the devil sinneth from the beginning. For this purpose the Son of God was manifested, that he might destroy the works of the devil.
                                        1 John 3:8

Forasmuch then as the children are partakers of flesh and blood, he also himself likewise took part of the same; that through death he might destroy him that had the power of death, that is, the devil;
                                        Hebrews 2:14

Living a Supernatural Life (Volume 2)

From what you can see in these Scriptures, the devil's works have been destroyed. We are also told in Hebrews 2:14 above that he used to have the power of death. I said that he used to have the power of death because you will notice that the Scriptures say he *had*, which is past tense. But we now know that he no longer has the power of death because as Christ Himself confirmed in Revelation 1:18, the power of death is now with Christ who now *has* the keys of hell and death.

> *I am he that liveth, and was dead; and, behold, I am alive for evermore, Amen; and have the keys of hell and of death.*
> **Revelation 1:18**

Satan can only threaten you with death he no longer has the power over you to actually effect it unless you surrender that power over to him. Therefore even though the devil can bring or offer death to you, he no longer has the power to force it upon you. You have the power to reject it when he brings it to you. He can bring death-threatening situations to you to cause you to fear and thereby accept death but he no longer has the power to actually ask death to take you. Most of those who die resign to death and accept death when they see or suffer death-threatening situations thrown at them by Satan. They do so because they believe that death has the right to take them away. That is why death takes them. Let us look at the stories of Stephen and Paul who both went through similar situations and experiences in the hands of Satan. Satan got the people to stone Stephen as recorded in Acts 7:57-60 thereby threatening death by making him to see the beckoning hands of death.

Be Violent Against the Devil

Then they cried out with a loud voice, and stopped their ears, and ran upon him with one accord,

And cast him out of the city, and stoned him: and the witnesses laid down their clothes at a young man's feet, whose name was Saul.

And they stoned Stephen, calling upon God, and saying, Lord Jesus, receive my spirit.

And he kneeled down, and cried with a loud voice, Lord, lay not this sin to their charge. And when he had said this, he fell asleep.
Acts 7:57-60

What did Stephen do? Stephen accepted the offer of death. He even called upon God to receive his spirit. Satan offered him death and he accepted it probably believing it was God's will, so death took him. Since his mind was fixed on death and had accepted it, there was nothing that God could do about it.

Before death can take you away you must have agreed in your mind to have death either as a result of the thought that you are just too weak to continue or for some other reasons. But no matter what the reason may be the important thing is that you must agree with it or resign to it in your mind. According to Proverbs 23:7, it is as you think in your mind that you would be. Therefore if your mind accepts death so shall it be for you. If you mind does not accept death it cannot force you and take you away by force. Please note this very important point.

Living a Supernatural Life (Volume 2)

> *For as he thinketh in his heart, so is he: Eat and drink, saith he to thee; but his heart is not with thee.*
>
> **Proverbs 23:7**

Now to show you just what I mean by saying that death cannot forcibly take you and that it is you who will decide to accept death, look at what happened to Paul in Acts 14:19-20 when he faced a similar situation to Stephen. He was stoned and cast out of the city just like Stephen was. He was even taken to be dead. But unlike Stephen, Paul did not accept death. Instead what we are told was that he rose up and came into the city.

> *And there came thither certain Jews from Antioch and Iconium, who persuaded the people, and, having stoned Paul, drew him out of the city, supposing he had been dead.*
>
> *Howbeit, as the disciples stood round about him, he rose up, and came into the city: and the next day he departed with Barnabas to Derbe.*
>
> **Acts 14:19-20**

So as you can see if you refuse to accept death when it calls it cannot forcibly take you away. This means that you have the choice. You can always reply death that you will not die but you will live to declare the glory of the Lord like David did in Psalm 118:17. Let this be your stand when death comes.

> *I shall not die, but live, and declare the works of the LORD.*
>
> **Psalm 118:17**

Be Violent Against the Devil

Death has no power over you. It can call at any time but you have the power to refuse it. If you exercise that power with confidence and authority it must obey you.

You should not accept death unless it is time for you to go. Therefore be violent against the devil whenever he brings death and offers it to you. React angrily against him. If you are not angry at the devil, he will not leave you alone. He will seek to dominate you. You must react angrily against the devil and all his agents. No matter what affliction the devil may be tormenting you with, you need to wrest your freedom from the devil by force. He will not give it to you without a fight.

Instead of being angry with the devil and his agents however, what most people do is get angry at other people, thinking or alluding that these other people are the cause of their suffering. I want you to know that the devil and his demons are behind everything that is not working in your life. You must see diseases, sicknesses, failure, lack, poverty, barrenness and all afflictions as agents of the devil.

The devil may sometimes use people as agents to perpetuate his schemes against you. He may even use you against yourself. Don't allow that to take you out of your focus. The real person behind the mask is the devil. He is the one that you must face squarely. Don't waste your time fighting with other people; it is the devil that you need to face and fight with and your fight with him must be a fight of faith. You need to be violent against the devil and his forces because you will not wrest your freedom from them in a casual, easy or peaceful way.

Living a Supernatural Life (Volume 2)

Walking in the miraculous with signs and wonders and living a supernatural life is not for the spiritual weaklings. If you want to walk in the miraculous, you must be bold and strong spiritually. You must be daring spiritually. Remember that from the days of John the Baptist, the Kingdom of Heaven suffereth violence and it is the violent that takes it by force. That is what Jesus said in Matthew 11:12. He said,

> *"And from the days of John the Baptist until now the kingdom of heaven suffereth violence, and the violent take it by force."*
>
> **Matthew 11:12**

Therefore be bold, be courageous and be angry with the wicked. That is holy anger. You cannot possess your possessions from the devil by smiling at him. In your anger possess your possessions by force. Even God is angry with the wicked. He is angry with the wicked every day. That is what God made us to know through King David in Psalm 7:11..

> *God judgeth the righteous, and God is angry with the wicked every day.*
>
> **Psalms 7:11**

But in your anger do not sin. Do not pray that God should come and kill your enemies. Pray for your enemies.

Know this: All the things that the devil throws at you are just mere **FACTS**. They are not necessarily the **TRUTH** so don't accept them unless they agree with the Word of God.

They are just symptoms or photographs that he throws at you so that he can get you to fear. He knows that when you fear you would build negative thoughts inside your mind and these thoughts will make you to speak the wrong words out with your mouth, thereby making the wrong confessions. But whenever he throws such **FACTS** or symptoms at you, use the **TRUTH** of the appropriate Word of God to stop them. Most of your afflictions are first thrown into your mind as thoughts and symptoms through your senses.

Sickness, poverty, failure, lack, barrenness and all those other afflictions that you see or feel on your body or around you start just as mere symptoms or photographs that Satan throws into your mind through your body senses to give your mind a negative picture and wrong perspective of the situation of things. He wants your mind to accept them as the true picture of your situation. But they are just mere **FACTS**, which he wants you to accept as **TRUTHS**. We know however that they are just facts, not truths. You are supposed to use the **TRUTH** of the Word of God to fight his **FACTS** and the way to do this is to speak the **TRUTH** of the appropriate Word of God into such situations. For the Word of God is **TRUTH**. That is what Jesus Himself said in John 17:17. He said,

> *"Sanctify them through thy truth: thy word is truth."*
> **John 17:17**

Rationalizing the absolute truth by the natural mind is what science has sought to do but which science has now found impossible.

Living a Supernatural Life (Volume 2)

It is impossible for the natural mind to comprehend the **TRUTH**. What the natural mind calls the **TRUTH** are **FACTS** and not necessarily the absolute **TRUTH**. Only the Word of God is the absolute **TRUTH**. So, let us join Paul and say as he stated in Romans 3:4 *"Let God be true and everyone else liars"*.

> *God forbid: yea, let God be true, but every man a liar; as it is written, That thou mightest be justified in thy sayings, and mightest overcome when thou art judged.*
> **Romans 3:4**

Accept God as God and deal with him as God. Believe His Word, and use His Word to resist all the assaults from the devil. Satan fears the Word of God therefore resist him with the Word of God and he will have to run away from you. God admonished us through James in James 4:7 to submit ourselves to Him and resist the devil and the devil will flee from us.

> *Submit yourselves therefore to God. Resist the devil, and he will flee from you.*
> **James 4:7**

Your fight with the devil and his forces and your resistance to them should be one of faith and nothing else. You are asked to fight the good fight of faith as written in 1 Timothy 6:12. That is the only fight that you are permitted to fight as a Christian, *the good fight of faith,* and you do this by resisting the devil in faith with the Word as you are asked to do in 1 Peter 5:9.

Be Violent Against the Devil

Fight the good fight of faith, lay hold on eternal life, whereunto thou art also called, and hast professed a good profession before many witnesses.
1 Timothy 6:12

Whom resist stedfast in the faith, knowing that the same afflictions are accomplished in your brethren that are in the world.
1 Peter 5:9

He said in James 4:7 above that when we resist him he will flee from us. It is by resisting the devil that you will get him off your back. If you are not willing to resist him, your struggling will continue and you should not expect to live a life above the natural realm. Satan only respects those who resist him in faith. Until you resist the devil in faith, he will not flee from you. Until you stand up against him in faith, which God referred to as the good fight of faith, he will not leave you alone.

Until you react angrily against sickness or barrenness and confess the Word of God violently to resist them, you will not have health or fruitfulness. The day you react against them in faith with knowledge and commitment is the day that they will leave you alone. They will not only leave you alone but that day you will gain your freedom from them absolutely.

Until you react angrily against failure and confess the Word of God violently to resist it, you will not have success. The day you react against it in faith with knowledge and commitment, that day, failure will leave you alone and you will gain your freedom from failure.

Living a Supernatural Life (Volume 2)

Until you react angrily against poverty and confess the Word of God violently to resist it, you will not have riches or prosperity. The day you react against it in faith with knowledge and commitment, that day, poverty will say goodbye to you.

You have to be angry with any satanic agent that tampers with your destiny. Be angry with the witches, occult forces and everybody that tamper with your destiny. You should proclaim the Word of God against their schemes to fight their schemes against you. Proclaim what you want from what the Word of God says and resist in faith what Satan has brought by being steadfast in your believe that what the Word of God says must come to pass and it shall be so. Satan and his forces will not leave you alone unless you resist them. They can only threaten you; they cannot win against you if you stand steadfast in faith. But you must note the following.:

Where they threaten sickness, you use the Word of God to proclaim health.

Where they threaten death, you use the Word of God to proclaim life.

Where they threaten failure, you use the Word of God to proclaim success.

Where they threaten lack, you use the Word of God to proclaim abundance.

Where they threaten barrenness, you use the Word of God to proclaim fruitfulness.

Whatever they may threaten you with, see it as *facts* and instead proclaim what the Word of God says, which is the **TRUTH**. What you proclaim will determine what you get.

CONTEND FOR YOUR POSSESSIONS

Satan will contend all your new birth inheritances in Christ and promises with you. You have to contend with the devil and his agents to possess your possessions. Even where God has given you your possessions, they will not just fall on your lap. God still expects you to contend for them because Satan will not allow you to have them without giving you a fight for them.

It is very important that you know this therefore I will explain it again. God said this to the children of Israel as we can see written in Deuteronomy 2:24. He is saying the same thing to us Christians today. Look at what He said below. He said,

> *"Rise ye up, take your journey, and pass over the river Arnon: behold, I have given into thine hand Sihon the Amorite, king of Heshbon, and his land: begin to possess it, and contend with him in battle."*
> **Deuteronomy 2:24**

Note that even though God has already given them the land of the Amorites and their king of Heshbon, He told them that they would still have to contend with that king in battle for the land.

Living a Supernatural Life (Volume 2)

The land and the king had already been given to them by God, yet they still had to fight a battle with that king before they could possess the land. What God promised them therefore was that when they go and fight for the land, they would win the battle. But if they had just sat down and said that God had already given them the land and do not fight to possess it, the land would never become theirs. If you follow their story you will note that wherever they did contend they got the land. So it is with you today. Many of the things that God has promised you that you are, that you have, or that you can do are there alright for you but you will still have to contend with the enemy for them.

If you do not contend with the enemy for your possessions, you would never possess them. You should arise and contend with the mountains of your life. God told us in Micah 6:1 *"Let the hills of your life hear your voice".*

> *Hear ye now what the LORD saith; Arise, contend thou before the mountains, and let the hills hear thy voice.*
> **Micah 6:1**

If you don't contend with the mountains and hills of your life you will not be able to command them to move for you and you will not be able to reign over them in life. Yet God's intention for you is that you reign over all the circumstances and situations that you come across in life. How do you contend with the mountains and hills of your life? You do so by speaking to them and commanding them because you have authority over them.

YOU ARE MEANT TO REIGN IN LIFE SPEAK TO YOUR MOUNTAINS

What are the mountains of your life? Those daunting problems that you have that are making you to run helter skater; they are your mountains. They are the mountains of your life. Contend with them. Speak directly to them and command them. You are supposed to reign over them.

What are the hills of your life? Those little problems that are nagging you; they are your hills. They are the hills of your life. Speak directly to them and command them. Let them hear your voice. You are supposed to reign over them. You are supposed to reign in this life. That is what God told us through Apostle John in Revelation 5:10.

> *And hast made us unto our God kings and priests: and we shall reign on the earth.*
> **Revelation 5:10**

Your mind must be fixed on the truth that you are supposed to reign in life because as far as God is concerned He has made you a king and given you the power and authority to reign in life. As a king you must have subjects that you reign over. But if what you have in your mind is that you are a slave or that you cannot reign in life then there is nothing that God can do about it *for it is as you think in your mind that you will be.* God cannot change the picture that you have of yourself in your heart. You will have to do this yourself.

Living a Supernatural Life (Volume 2)

It is written in Philemon 14 that without your mind nothing will be done. So also it is with God. God will do nothing without your mind agreeing with Him.

> *But without thy mind would I do nothing; that thy benefit should not be as it were of necessity, but willingly.*
> **Philemon 14**

If you believe in your mind that you are to reign in life you will proclaim it so and you will contend with all the mountains and hills of your life that will not allow you to reign in life. Then God will effect your reign in life. However, if you are not willing to contend with the mountains and hills of your life you will not reign over them as you have been destined to do in life. Remember that you have been given the power to speak to and command the mountains of your life. In Luke 21:15, Jesus said that He has given you a mouth and wisdom which those mountains and hills of your life cannot resist.

> *For I will give you a mouth and wisdom, which all your adversaries shall not be able to gainsay nor resist.*
> **Luke 21:15**

With that mouth and wisdom that you have been given you are supposed to contend with and speak directly to the mountains and hills of your life and command them to move. If you give your command in faith they will move. That is what Jesus made us to understand by what He said in Matthew 17:20.

Be Violent Against the Devil

And Jesus said unto them, Because of your unbelief: for verily I say unto you, If ye have faith as a grain of mustard seed, ye shall say unto this mountain, Remove hence to yonder place; and it shall remove; and nothing shall be impossible unto you.
                                    Matthew 17:20

Praying about the mountains and hills of your life is good but that is not what Jesus said that you should do here. If you want them to move you must speak directly to them and command them to move. That is the way that you can reign in life over all your adversaries. *Speak directly to them.*

HAVE HOLY ANGER

It is what you proclaim that you will get therefore speak what you want into reality. Do you know what God said to the children of Israel in Exodus 22:18? He said that they should not even allow a witch to live. That is God's instruction to you today also. I am not saying that you should go about killing witches. But even if a witch must live, he must not live at your expense. You can always stop his antics against you. There is no need to be frightened of any blood-sucking witch or workers of evil as many Christians do today. Instead of being frightened of them what you should do is resist them with the Word of God. After all you drink the more potent Blood of Christ when you have the Lord's Supper in Communion.

Thou shalt not suffer a witch to live.
                                    Exodus 22:18

Living a Supernatural Life (Volume 2)

God is very angry with the wicked that contends your possessions with you. He says that He will feed them with their own flesh and their own blood. He said so through the Prophet Isaiah in Isaiah 49:24-26. You can also see from that Scripture that whoever contends your possessions with you is actually contending it with God. How can such a person ever win?

> *Shall the prey be taken from the mighty, or the lawful captive delivered?*
>
> *But thus saith the LORD, Even the captives of the mighty shall be taken away, and the prey of the terrible shall be delivered: for I will contend with him that contendeth with thee, and I will save thy children.*
>
> *And I will feed them that oppress thee with their own flesh; and they shall be drunken with their own blood, as with sweet wine: and all flesh shall know that I the LORD am thy Saviour and thy Redeemer, the mighty One of Jacob.*
>
> **Isaiah 49:24-26**

God is telling you here that He will contend with the enemy that contends your possessions with you. You must have the right Scriptural perspective of yourself and the facilities that are now available to you. It is then that you can have confidence when you face the enemy. Many Christians are so afraid of the enemy that they allow fear to dictate their actions. How can you be afraid of any enemy when God says that He will contend with any enemy that contends your possessions with you? If you it means you don't believe in God.

It is the enemy that brings sickness and diseases, lack, failure, barrenness and all types of afflictions and oppressions into your life. Confess and proclaim the Word of God against him. Stand in faith against the enemy and no enemy will be able to overcome you. It is the enemy that should fear you now. Any disease, sickness, evil spirit or even man that attempts your life for evil, you should proclaim and confess the Word of God against it. No evil force should win against you. Evil forces cannot win against you if you are willing to stand in faith against them.

You must have God's type of anger against the forces of darkness. It is holy anger. It is when you have this type of anger against all things that are evil that you can be said to truly fear God and live a life that is above the natural realm. When you live a consecrated life for God you will abhor evil because like it is said in Job 1:1 of Job when you fear the Lord your God you will eschew evil. It is then that you can live a perfect life before God. It is then that the supernatural will become your natural way of life.

> *There was a man in the land of Uz, whose name was Job; and that man was perfect and upright, and one that feared God, and eschewed evil.*
> **Job 1:1**

When you fear the Lord you will hate evil. That is why we are told in Proverbs 8:13 that the fear of the Lord is to hate evil. You cannot fear the Lord and not hate evil.

The fear of the LORD is to hate evil: pride, and arrogancy, and the evil way, and the froward mouth, do I hate.

Proverbs 8:13

You are permitted to hate evil. It is not a sin to hate evil. You are not only to hate it you must fight it with the Word of God.

FIGHT EVIL DON'T SYMPATHIZE WITH IT

Many people sympathize with the afflictions that come their way by their behaviour. But they don't really know that they are doing so. Stop sympathizing with disease, sickness and illness. Stop sympathizing with failure. Stop sympathizing with lack. They are not of God. Stop sympathizing with barrenness. Stop sympathizing with any affliction that comes from Satan. You don't have to do so. When you are entertaining them you are actually sympathizing with them. You have entertained them long enough. You have sympathized long enough with them. Instead of sympathizing with them fight them and you will overcome them. You have sympathized long enough with sicknesses and diseases. Instead of sympathizing with sicknesses and diseases fight them and you will overcome them. You have sympathized long enough with failure. Instead of sympathizing with failure fight it and you will overcome it. You have sympathized long enough with poverty. Instead of sympathizing with poverty fight it and you will overcome it. You have sympathized long enough with lack. Instead of sympathizing with lack fight it and you will overcome it.

Be Violent Against the Devil

You have sympathized long enough with barrenness. Instead of sympathizing with barrenness fight it and you will overcome it. You have sympathized long enough with afflictions. Instead of sympathizing with afflictions fight them and you will overcome them.

Don't even allow anybody to sympathize with you. You don't need anybody's sympathy concerning any affliction. What you need to do is fight against the affliction head-on. When people come to sympathize with you, what that really means is this. They are saying to you that you are weak and seeing the problem confronting you as stronger than you are. Let them know that you are far above the problem and therefore you don't need their sympathy. You are far above the problem because as stated by Paul the Apostle in Ephesians 2:6 you are now sitting where Jesus Christ is sitting, which according to Ephesians 1:19-23 is far above all principality and power and might and dominion and everything that is named not only in this world but also in the world to come. Get a revelation of this.

> *And hath raised us up together, and made us sit together in heavenly places in Christ Jesus:*
> **Ephesians 2:6**

> *And what is the exceeding greatness of his power to us-ward who believe, according to the working of his mighty power,*

> *Which he wrought in Christ, when he raised him from the dead, and set him at his own right hand in the heavenly places,*

Living a Supernatural Life (Volume 2)

> *Far above all principality, and power, and might, and dominion, and every name that is named, not only in this world, but also in that which is to come:*
>
> *And hath put all things under his feet, and gave him to be the head over all things to the church,*
>
> *Which is his body, the fulness of him that filleth all in all.*
> **Ephesians 1:19-23**

Seating where you are therefore, it is obvious that you don't need anybody's sympathy because you are far above the affliction that is threatening or harassing you for which they are sympathizing with you. Let the people trying to sympathize with you know this truth that you are far above all afflictions. You don't need anybody's sympathy. Instead what you should do is to exercise your authority over the offending affliction.

People don't normally sympathize with somebody that they think is above and in control of the situation that he is in. They only sympathize with those that they think are under pressures and forces or situations that seem to be above them, or with people that are carrying weights or burdens that they believe are too heavy for them to carry or deal with.

Do not entertain anybody's sympathy. You don't really need it because the truth is that you are far above whatever is attacking you. When you accept such sympathy, you are indirectly accepting weakness.

You have to react angrily against sickness and disease, against failure, against barrenness, against lack and poverty, against the sympathy of people, against any affliction and all other forces of darkness that seek to attack and subdue you. Let them know that you are far above them and they cannot threaten you. Let the people know that you are far above such forces of darkness and that you don't need anybody's sympathy. Contend with the enemy for your possessions. You cannot possess your possessions by mere wishing for them. You have to contend with the enemy for them through your confessions and you must be violent with your confessions.

BE VIOLENT WITH YOUR CONFESSIONS

As we have noted earlier, the Kingdom of heaven suffereth violence and it is the violent that take it by force. You are of that Kingdom now and to establish yourself in the Kingdom you have to do it by force. The devil will contend your membership of the Kingdom with you all the way. He will also contest every one of your possessions with you. He will test you to see whether you really know your rights. Therefore you have to be violent with the devil to assert your rights. I repeat here again what Jesus said in Matthew 11:12. He said,

> *"And from the days of John the Baptist until now the kingdom of heaven suffereth violence, and the violent take it by force."*
> **Matthew 11:12**

Living a Supernatural Life (Volume 2)

Be steadfast in your faith in the Word of God. Be violent with your confession of the Word of God. Proclaim loud into existence what you want. ***Don't be a closed-mouth Christian.*** Open your mouth wide and proclaim what you want. You can't close your mouth and win as a Christian. Your victory will come through your mouth because Christianity is a spoken confession. Christians who close their mouths thinking wrongly that by so doing they are showing humility only give Satan a field-day to subject them to all sorts of unnecessary afflictions and misery. Some even do this thinking wrongly that they are suffering for God or that God must have approved of their suffering. God is not the One behind your suffering. He knows about it, Yes! But He is not the One inflicting suffering upon you.

There is power in your mouth if you will only use it and you must love to use it if you are to reap its benefits. Remember that the supernatural life power, that is the power of life and death, is in your mouth. That is what God said through Solomon in Proverbs 18:21 as we have noted earlier. He said,

> *"Death and life are in the power of the tongue: and they that love it shall eat the fruit thereof."*
> **Proverbs 18:21**

That is, you can speak death or you can speak life. So when death calls and is threatening, speak life. You can speak barrenness or you can speak fruitfulness, so when barrenness calls and is threatening, speak fruitfulness. You can speak defeat or you can speak victory, therefore when defeat comes and is starring you in the face, speak victory.

Be Violent Against the Devil

You can speak sickness or you can speak health, so when sickness comes and is starring you in the face, speak health. You can speak failure or you can speak success, so when failure comes knocking at your door, speak success. You can speak poverty or you can speak prosperity, so when poverty starts to knock at your door, speak prosperity. It all depends on how you use your mouth. It is with your mouth that you will make the confession unto your salvation from any of these. That is the essence of what God is telling us through Apostle Paul in Romans 10:10.

> *For with the heart man believeth unto righteousness; and with the mouth confession is made unto salvation.*
> **Romans 10:10**

God even gave us the lead through Joel in Joel 3:10 by telling us how to use our mouths to talk. He said that when we are weak, we should say we are strong. *"Let the weak say, I am strong."*

> *Beat your plowshares into swords, and your pruninghooks into spears: let the weak say, I am strong.*
> **Joel 3:10**

You should never say that you are weak because Jesus Christ is now your strength. That is the essence of what is written in Philippians 4:13.

> *I can do all things through Christ which strengtheneth me.*
> **Philippians 4:13**

Living a Supernatural Life (Volume 2)

If Christ's strength is now your strength then you ought to know that this strength of Christ, which you now have is made perfect in weakness as we are told by Paul in 2 Corinthians 12:9.

> *And he said unto me, My grace is sufficient for thee: for my strength is made perfect in weakness. Most gladly therefore will I rather glory in my infirmities, that the power of Christ may rest upon me.*
> **2 Corinthians 12:9**

If the strength of Jesus that you now have is made perfect in weakness then the weaker you are the stronger you really are. That is what Apostle Paul was making us to understand from what God said through him in 2 Corinthians 12:10

> *Therefore I take pleasure in infirmities, in reproaches, in necessities, in persecutions, in distresses for Christ's sake: for when I am weak, then am I strong.*
> **2 Corinthians 12:10**

Paul said, "When I am weak then am I strong." Hence you can see that the weaker you are the stronger you actually are. As a truly born-again redeemed Christian there is strength in your weakness. Therefore don't let the devil frighten you with weakness. If he brings the thought of weakness to you then let him know that the weaker you are the stronger you are. The same philosophy is indicated by what God said through Isaiah in Isaiah 33:24.

Be Violent Against the Devil

And the inhabitant shall not say, I am sick: the people that dwell therein shall be forgiven their iniquity.
Isaiah 33:24

God is saying here that you should not say that you are sick. Instead you should say that you are healthy. Speak out what you want with your mouth not what you are going through. If what you are going through does not please you speak out what you really want because it is the fruit of what you say with your mouth that you will reap. But remember that it is only if you love to use your mouth that you will eat that fruit of victory as stated in Proverbs 18:21.

Death and life are in the power of the tongue: and they that love it shall eat the fruit thereof.
Proverbs 18:21

This means that you will only enjoy the fruit of the Words that you speak out with your mouth and your tongue if you love to use it. Look at the various promises of God appropriate to your situation and confess them with your mouth. Don't let what God said concerning the children of Israel in Isaiah 42:22 be your own portion or true of you. They were closed-mouth. Just look at what God said concerning them below. He said,

> "*But this is a people robbed and spoiled; they are all of them snared in holes, and they are hid in prison houses: they are for a prey, and none delivereth; for a spoil, and none saith, Restore.*"
> **Isaiah 42:22**

Living a Supernatural Life (Volume 2)

All kinds of evil things happened to them but they could not speak out against what they were going through. They were closed-mouth. None could say restore.

If you do not love to use your tongue or your mouth, or you are afraid or timid to open your mouth and use it then don't expect to eat the fruit of life when death calls. We have explained this thoroughly in the *Volume 1* of this *"Living a supernatural life"* book series.

Don't be a closed-mouth Christian. Speak out what you want. When you do this, you should expect to eat the fruit of victory when defeat calls. If you are a closed-mouth Christian then it will not be possible for you to eat the fruit of health when sickness calls, or the fruit of fruitfulness when barrenness calls, or the fruit of prosperity when poverty calls.

There is power in the Word of God. In truth, God's Word is God's power. Therefore speak out God's Word all the time to all the situations of your life.

GOD'S WORD IS GOD'S POWER

To show you that God's Word is God' power, take a look at what we are told by John in John 1:1, 14. This shows us as we already know that Jesus Christ is the Word of God.

> *In the beginning was the Word, and the Word was with God, and the Word was God.*

Be Violent Against the Devil

> *And the Word was made flesh, and dwelt among us, and we beheld his glory, the glory as of the only begotten of the Father, full of grace and truth.*
> **John 1:1, 14**

However if we also look at 1 Corinthians 1:24 we will see as God made us to see through Apostle Paul that Jesus Christ is also the power of God.

> *But unto them which are called, both Jews and Greeks, Christ the power of God, and the wisdom of God.*
> **1 Corinthians 1:24**

Combining the two Scriptures above therefore we can conclude that the Word of God is the power of God. Therefore use the Word of God freely to fight with the devil. It is by so doing that you fight the good fight of faith. There is power in the Word of God that you speak. Use the Word as **LOGOS** and also use the **RHEMA** Word of God that is revealed to you which you have received to fight the devil.

USE BOTH LOGOS AND RHEMA TO FIGHT

When God's Word begins to flow freely from your mouth power will come forth. Proclaim the **LOGOS** Word of God by saying *"It is written… It is written… It is written…"*, like Jesus did, as written in the Gospel in Luke 4:1-14 when Satan came to tempt Him. In every situation the Word of God is your defense.

Living a Supernatural Life (Volume 2)

You can see this as written in Luke 4:1-14 below. Also meditate on God's Words and open your spirit to receive the **RHEMA** Words from God for any situation that you may find yourself and proclaim the Word by saying, *"It is said..." "It is said…" "It is said...."* Then you will have the stunning type of victories that Jesus had over Satan and his forces as explained in *Chapter 8* of the *Volume 1* of this *"Living a supernatural life"* book series written by the same author.

And Jesus being full of the Holy Ghost returned from Jordan, and was led by the Spirit into the wilderness,

Being forty days tempted of the devil. And in those days he did eat nothing: and when they were ended, he afterward hungered.

And the devil said unto him, If thou be the Son of God, command this stone that it be made bread.

And Jesus answered him, saying, It is written, That man shall not live by bread alone, but by every word of God.

And the devil, taking him up into an high mountain, shewed unto him all the kingdoms of the world in a moment of time.

And the devil said unto him, All this power will I give thee, and the glory of them: for that is delivered unto me; and to whomsoever I will I give it.

Be Violent Against the Devil

If thou therefore wilt worship me, all shall be thine.

And Jesus answered and said unto him, Get thee behind me, Satan: for it is written, Thou shalt worship the Lord thy God, and him only shalt thou serve.

And he brought him to Jerusalem, and set him on a pinnacle of the temple, and said unto him, If thou be the Son of God, cast thyself down from hence:

For it is written, He shall give his angels charge over thee, to keep thee:

And in their hands they shall bear thee up, lest at any time thou dash thy foot against a stone.

And Jesus answering said unto him, It is said, Thou shalt not tempt the Lord thy God.

And when the devil had ended all the temptation, he departed from him for a season.

And Jesus returned in the power of the Spirit into Galilee: and there went out a fame of him through all the region round about.
                                    Luke 4:1-14

Let us do it as Jesus did it using the Word, both **LOGOS** and **RHEMA**, to reply the enemy then we shall have the Jesus' type of results. Satan knows the power that is in the Word.

Living a Supernatural Life (Volume 2)

When you use the Word against him, he has no answer to the Word especially if it is the revealed Word of God **RHEMA**. Your best tactics against Satan is to use the Word of God to fight him. If you look at the story of the temptation of Jesus Christ in Luke 4:1-14 above you will see how Jesus dealt with Satan by using **LOGOS** the written Word of God and giving the knock-out punch by using **RHEMA** the spoken Word from God. Look carefully at the Scripture above and see exactly how Jesus tackled Satan with the Word of God. That passage was put in the Scriptures to show us exactly how to deal with Satan.

The way to resist Satan therefore is with the Word of God. Fire the Word of God all the time to every situation of your life. The Word is your spiritual atomic bomb against the forces of the kingdom of darkness. *"It is written", "It is written"* and even preferably *"It is said", "It is said"* must become your natural way of speaking. If you don't fire the Word against the forces of the kingdom of darkness, you will just be minced meat for them. You will not be on top of your circumstances. You must believe that there is power in the Word of God spoken through your mouth. You must therefore speak the Word out. It is by the words that you speak to them that you will either take your freedom from them or be enslaved by them. Jesus Himself told us so in Matthew 12:37. He said,

> *"For by thy words thou shalt be justified, and by thy words thou shalt be condemned."*
> **Matthew 12:37**

CONFESS YOUR WAY TO YOUR SALVATION

From the last Scripture you can see that it is the words that you speak that decide what happens to you. When diseases and sicknesses come at you, rebuke them with your mouth. It is your mouth that will get you out of their snare and give you deliverance from them. You know that the words from your mouth can snare you if you speak out the wrong words. That is what we are made to see from what is written in Proverbs 6:2.

> *Thou art snared with the words of thy mouth, thou art taken with the words of thy mouth.*
> **Proverbs 6:2**

Even though you may believe in your heart, you must declare your salvation with your mouth. It is with your mouth that you will declare your salvation from any affliction. That is what God made us to know by what He said through Apostle Paul in Romans 10:10.

> *For with the heart man believeth unto righteousness; and with the mouth confession is made unto salvation.*
> **Romans 10:10**

If you believe speak it out because as we have explained in *Chapter 3* of *Volume 1* of this *"Living a supernatural life"* book series, faith speaks out what it believes. It is when your enemies and adversaries hear you that they will be afraid and come out of wherever they are hiding. Therefore speak out and let them hear you.

Living a Supernatural Life (Volume 2)

If the enemy forces don't hear your voice they will not come out of their hiding places. It is when they hear your commands that they will obey you. If they don't hear you command them then don't expect them to move. It is as soon as they hear you that they will submit themselves to you. That is what God made us to understand in 2 Samuel 22:45-46 through King David.

> *Strangers shall submit themselves unto me: as soon as they hear, they shall be obedient unto me.*
>
> *Strangers shall fade away, and they shall be afraid out of their close places.*
> **2 Samuel 22:45-46**

The forces of Satan are now strangers to you because you no longer belong to their kingdom of darkness. You now belong to the Kingdom of Light. Therefore as you can see, you cannot be silent and get them to obey you. It is when they hear you that they will come out of their hiding places and obey you. As a born-again Christian, you can no longer condescend to the situations that Satan and his forces bring to you.

You must declare your inheritance in Christ boldly and openly so that people can hear you and in particular so that Satan and his forces can hear you. It is only when you do these that you can free yourself from the forces of evil. God wants you to live a supernatural life here on earth but you must be willing to venture into the supernatural realm and not be contented with staying in the natural realm. Now that you know your potential in Christ, venture into the supernatural realm.

JESUS WANTS YOU TO LIVE IN THE SUPERNATURAL REALM

As long as you are a believer what Jesus wants for you is a supernatural life. He said those who believe in Him shall do the works that He did. He said that they would even do greater works than He did. That is what He said in John 14:12.

> *Verily, verily, I say unto you, He that believeth on me, the works that I do shall he do also; and greater works than these shall he do; because I go unto my Father.*
> **John 14:12**

He said those that believe in Him the supernatural signs shall follow them about. The signs come as a result of the power that would be operating through such believers. The signs are meant for the believers so once you are a believer the signs should follow you. That is what He said in Mark 16:17-18. If you want the signs to follow you then you must believe. That is the only prerequisite for the sign to follow you.

> *And these signs shall follow them that believe; In my name shall they cast out devils; they shall speak with new tongues;*
>
> *They shall take up serpents; and if they drink any deadly thing, it shall not hurt them; they shall lay hands on the sick, and they shall recover.*
> **Mark 16:17-18**

Living a Supernatural Life (Volume 2)

The problem with most Christians however is that the signs are not following them. The signs are meant to follow only the believers. Many profess to be Christians but they are not believers therefore the signs are not following them. The only qualification that you need for the signs to be following you is to be a believer. Are you a believer? Search yourself and ask yourself whether you are truly a believer because if you are, the signs should be following you. God is not a respecter of persons. Once you believe the signs must follow you. That was why He said to us through the Apostle Paul in 1 Corinthians 12:7 that the manifestation of the Spirit is given to every man to profit. God does not discriminate. He wants to use every man.

> *But the manifestation of the Spirit is given to every man to profit withal.*
> **1 Corinthians 12:7**

You don't have to be a Prophet, an Evangelist, a Pastor, a Bishop, an Apostle, an Elder or a Deacon for the signs to follow you. No! All you need is to be a believer in Jesus Christ. If you can dare to believe God and not be afraid, He will use you to work the miracles, signs and wonders that will lead others to Christ. The miracles and signs only follow them that believe.

Remember when Jesus walked on the sea as written in Matthew 14:25-31. All the disciples saw Jesus walking on the sea. But it was only Peter who decided that He was also going to walk on the sea. He was able to walk on the sea because he believed in Jesus Christ and was willing to trust His Word.

And in the fourth watch of the night Jesus went unto them, walking on the sea.

And when the disciples saw him walking on the sea, they were troubled, saying, It is a spirit; and they cried out for fear.

But straightway Jesus spake unto them, saying, Be of good cheer; it is I; be not afraid.

And Peter answered him and said, Lord, if it be thou, bid me come unto thee on the water.

And he said, Come. And when Peter was come down out of the ship, he walked on the water, to go to Jesus.

But when he saw the wind boisterous, he was afraid; and beginning to sink, he cried, saying, Lord, save me.

And immediately Jesus stretched forth his hand, and caught him, and said unto him, O thou of little faith, wherefore didst thou doubt?
Matthew 14:25-31

As long as Peter believed in Jesus Christ, he was able to do what Jesus did which was to walk on the sea but when he feared and doubt entered into him like the others he started to sink. You can see the immediate difference that resulted from his unbelief that led to doubt and led to fear. ***The signs are only for the believers. Supernatural living is only for believers.*** If you truly believe, the signs will be following you.

Living a Supernatural Life (Volume 2)

We have shown on the previous page that by what Jesus said in John 14:12 it is His wish that you do what He did and even do greater works than He did. That was why Jesus was not against Peter walking on the sea. When Peter expressed the desire to walk on the sea, Jesus said, "come" to him because He wanted Peter to do what He did. Jesus is also saying, "come" to you. He wants you to do miracles, signs and wonders like He did but you must know that these signs don't follow doubters; they only follow believers.

Therefore if the signs are not following you then you are a doubter not a believer. Jesus said the signs shall follow them that believe. Therefore you can know if you are a believer by the signs following you. God is not the One holding you back from doing miracles. God wants you to do miracles. But you must be a believer if miracles, signs and wonders are to be following you. The problem with most Christians is that many do not believe God enough to be able to dare to venture into that realm of supernatural living. They tie themselves down by their unbelief and the traditions of this world.

Don't tie down yourself by the traditions of men or by the knowledge and thinking of this world. The world does not believe that Jesus is alive and still doing miracles. Even many so-called Christian denominations do not believe anymore in miracles. The funniest thing to me is that when some Christians these days try to do the miracles that Jesus said believers will do other Christians turn round to say that such miracles have been done using the power of the devil. To them the devil has the power to do miracles and is doing miracles but God is no longer in the business of doing miracles.

Be Violent Against the Devil

But I want you to know that God is looking for the people that He can use to touch the world. It is only those who believe in Him explicitly and who are bold to face the adversary head-on that He can use. He has given you all the tools that you require to answer His call. But you have to believe that you have such capabilities through Him because He has loaded you with such tremendous power..

You must believe that He has loaded you with immense power that cannot be reproached by any enemy. To see how potentially powerful you are now take a look at His various promises to you as found in the following verses of the Scriptures. John 14:12, Mark 16:15-18, Luke 10:19 and Luke 9:1 and Matthew 16:19 just to mention a few.

> *Verily, verily, I say unto you, He that believeth on me, the works that I do shall he do also; and greater works than these shall he do; because I go unto my Father.*
> **John 14:12**

> *And he said unto them, Go ye into all the world, and preach the gospel to every creature.*
>
> *He that believeth and is baptized shall be saved; but he that believeth not shall be damned.*
>
> *And these signs shall follow them that believe; In my name shall they cast out devils; they shall speak with new tongues;*

> *They shall take up serpents; and if they drink any deadly thing, it shall not hurt them; they shall lay hands on the sick, and they shall recover.*
>
> **Mark 16:15-18**

> *Behold, I give unto you power to tread on serpents and scorpions, and over all the power of the enemy: and nothing shall by any means hurt you.*
>
> **Luke 10:19**

> *Then he called his twelve disciples together, and gave them power and authority over all devils, and to cure diseases.*
>
> **Luke 9:1**

> *And I will give unto thee the keys of the kingdom of heaven: and whatsoever thou shalt bind on earth shall be bound in heaven: and whatsoever thou shalt loose on earth shall be loosed in heaven.*
>
> **Matthew 16:19**

Meditate on these verses until you accept them as true of you but note that even after you believe these you will still have to be bold because Satan will try to scare you and make you feel that you are powerless. He will try to contend with you everything that God has given you or promised you. You must exhibit boldness if you want to be able to stand firm against Satan and his forces. The requirements for boldness and how to achieve them are what we shall discuss in the next Chapter.

CHAPTER 13

BE BOLD

One thing that inhibits people from proclaiming what they want openly and making a strong confession of their faith and expectations is that they are afraid that they may be ridiculed if what they say does not manifest immediately. So, they feel shy and frightened to proclaim what they want openly. Yet unless they can proclaim what they want out boldly, loudly and openly, they may not be able to live the supernatural life that is rightfully theirs. This is because ***supernatural living is only for the bold and the confident in Christ.*** When it pertains to living a supernatural life here on earth, boldness is a very necessary attribute. You cannot be a successful Christian unless you are bold and confident.

You must be bold in your speaking, you must be bold in your action, you must not fear. You know you are supposed to be righteous now because you have been given God's righteousness as a gift. If you are conscious of your righteousness, you will be bold as a lion because God said so through King Solomon in Proverbs 28:1. He said,

> *"The wicked flee when no man pursue: but the righteous are bold as a lion."*
> **Proverbs 28:1**

I know this statement of God through King Solomon is true for me because whenever my mind is free of guilt-consciousness my boldness increases. *If you fear or worry you cannot live a supernatural life. You must live in divine boldness if you want to live a supernatural life.* Let me give here five steps for you to take that will help you to have divine boldness. In order to have divine boldness so that you can boldly speak out and proclaim the invisible into becoming visible, you must have no guilt consciousness. The Lord has seen you as righteous but your conscience may still be giving you that guilty feeling. *To shake off this guilt-feeling and have divine boldness, you must do the following five things.*

1. LIVE RIGHT

Live right, and expunge sin from your life. If you do this then the guilt or sin-consciousness will leave you and you will have a righteousness-consciousness. Once you have that, you will be as bold as a lion as is written in Proverbs 28:1, which we have noted earlier. Sin always brings fear. That was why when Adam sinned, he became afraid. Look at what happened to him and what he said in Genesis 3:8-11. But fear is the enemy of faith and always contending with faith. You cannot have fear and be in faith at the same time. When fear wins against faith then worry takes over.

> *And they heard the voice of the LORD God walking in the garden in the cool of the day: and Adam and his wife hid themselves from the presence of the LORD God amongst the trees of the garden.*

Be Bold

> *And the LORD God called unto Adam, and said unto him, Where art thou?*
>
> *And he said, I heard thy voice in the garden, and I was afraid, because I was naked; and I hid myself.*
>
> *And he said, Who told thee that thou wast naked? Hast thou eaten of the tree, whereof I commanded thee that thou shouldest not eat?*
> **Genesis 3:8-11**

Adam's sin made him to be afraid. So it is with you today. Sin inhibits your interactions with God. When a Christian sins, his confidence will be lacking when he approaches God for anything. There will be doubts in his mind as to whether God will answer him or not. Sin always creates a gulf between man and God because God hates sins.

If you live in sin you cannot live a supernatural life here on earth. It is our sins that make it impossible for God to answer our prayers and give us our requests. That is the essence of what God is telling us through Prophet Isaiah in Isaiah 59:1-2.

> *Behold, the LORD'S hand is not shortened, that it cannot save; neither his ear heavy, that it cannot hear:*
>
> *But your iniquities have separated between you and your God, and your sins have hid his face from you, that he will not hear.*
> **Isaiah 59:1-2**

Therefore if you have the sin-complex you will not have the confidence to approach God and believe that whatever you command will be effected. But if you have no sin-complex, you will have the confidence that God would give whatever you command and your confidence in the eventual fulfillment and manifestation of whatever you command will rise. That is the reason why God has given you the righteousness of Christ as a free gift so that you can come to Him with no sin or guilt complex. It is then that you can approach God with confidence and boldness. The sin-complex and the guilt-complex are great tools that Satan uses against Christians. He makes sure that Christians are saddled with these thereby eroding their confidence in their ability to receive anything from God.

2. HAVE A GOOD KNOWLEDGE OF GOD

The Bible says in Daniel 11:32 that you will be strong if you have a good knowledge of your God.

> *And such as do wickedly against the covenant shall he corrupt by flatteries: but the people that do know their God shall be strong, and do exploits.*
> **Daniel 11:32**

When you know God, you will know what God is capable of doing. You will know, in answer to the question that God put to you in Jeremiah 32:27, where He asked if there was anything too hard for Him, *you will know that there is nothing too hard for God.*

Be Bold

> *Behold, I am the LORD, the God of all flesh: is there any thing too hard for me?*
> **Jeremiah 32:27**

You will know that He is mighty in battle as David knew judging by what He was inspired by God to say in Psalm 24:8 after the many battles that he fought and won. David came to the conclusion that God is strong and mighty in battle.

> *Who is this King of glory? The LORD strong and mighty, the LORD mighty in battle.*
> **Psalm 24:8**

You will know that He is with you as a mighty terrible One as Jeremiah knew judging by what Jeremiah was inspired by God to say in Jeremiah 20:11.

> *But the LORD is with me as a mighty terrible one: therefore my persecutors shall stumble, and they shall not prevail: they shall be greatly ashamed; for they shall not prosper: their everlasting confusion shall never be forgotten.*
> **Jeremiah 20:11**

And *you will know that He is mighty in you* as He made us to understand through what Apostle Paul wrote in 2 Corinthians 13:3.

> *Since ye seek a proof of Christ speaking in me, which to you-ward is not weak, but is mighty in you.*
> **2 Corinthians 13:3**

Living a Supernatural Life (Volume 2)

How can you know that your God is mighty in battle, that nothing is too hard for Him and that He is mighty in you and not be bold? How can you know that with your God on your side those that are with you are more than those that are with your enemies and not be bold? How can you know that with your God on your side He would supply whatever you need according to His riches in glory and not be bold? Therefore if you know your God, you will be strong, you will be bold and you will say boldly what you want and it shall be so. You will not fear anything because you will know that with your God inside of you, every situation can be put under cheap control. If you want to know God, then you must be still and confident. You must not be fretful or anxious. He said through David in Psalm 46:10 that you should be still if you want to know that He is God. But you cannot be still unless you are confident.

> *Be still, and know that I am God: I will be exalted among the heathen, I will be exalted in the earth.*
> **Psalm 46:10**

In any case, it is when you are confident and quiet that you can exhibit God's strength. It is when you are still and totally put your trust in God that God will come in strongly to help you. It is only then that you will know how strong and mighty God is. When you are fretful and anxious, it shows that you have not totally put your trust in God. You cannot exhibit His strength when you are fretful, disturbed and anxious because your strength is in your quietness and confidence. That is what God made us to know through Isaiah in Isaiah 30:15.

Be Bold

For thus saith the Lord GOD, the Holy One of Israel; In returning and rest shall ye be saved; in quietness and in confidence shall be your strength: and ye would not.
Isaiah 30:15

It is important that you know God because if you do not know Him, then you cannot be said to be His follower. That is what Jesus Himself said in John 10:14.

I am the good shepherd, and know my sheep, and am known of mine.
John 10:14

Your faith can only be as strong as the knowledge that you have of the object of your faith. So, the more of God you know, the more the faith you will have in Him. You know that it is how much faith you have that will also determine how much manifestation of God's power He can exhibit through you in your life and in other people's lives. Therefore you must have a good knowledge of God. You must have a good knowledge of God because it is only when you know Him that you can be persuaded that He is able to keep that, which you have committed to Him. You will then be able to say with confidence what Paul said in 2 Timothy 1:12 that you know whom you believed and you are persuaded that He is able.

For the which cause I also suffer these things: nevertheless I am not ashamed: for I know whom I have believed, and am persuaded that he is able to keep that which I have committed unto him against that day.
2 Timothy 1:12

Living a Supernatural Life (Volume 2)

God's Word is the truth and we know from what Jesus said in John 8:32 that when one contacts this truth about any situation in life, he can gain his liberty from all the oppressive forces of darkness concerning that situation in his life.

> *And ye shall know the truth, and the truth shall make you free.*
> **John 8:32**

Finally, even though as a result of your new birth according to 2 Peter 1:3-4, you have been given all things that pertain unto life and godliness, which includes supernatural powers, you can only have access to these through your knowledge of Christ.

> *According as his divine power hath given unto us all things that pertain unto life and godliness, through the knowledge of him that hath called us to glory and virtue:*
>
> *Whereby are given unto us exceeding great and precious promises: that by these ye might be partakers of the divine nature, having escaped the corruption that is in the world through lust.*
> **2 Peter 1:3-4**

But Christ who is God is also the Word of God. Therefore what God is telling you through Peter is that it is your knowledge of the Word of God that will give you access to those things that you have been given by God. The more knowledge of the Word you have the more of your salvation benefits you can access.

3. BE FILLED WITH THE HOLY SPIRIT

If you are born-again, you have the Holy Spirit of power and you should not fear anything anymore. That, in essence, is what God is telling us through Apostle Paul in 2 Timothy 1:7.

> *For God hath not given us the spirit of fear; but of power, and of love, and of a sound mind.*
> **2 Timothy 1:7**

God is talking here through Paul of the Holy Spirit, which now lives in you. He says the Spirit that lives in you now is not a spirit of fear. This is also repeated in Romans 8:15, where God is saying that you are no longer under the bondage of fear. The Spirit that you received is not the spirit of bondage to fear but the Spirit of power, of love and of a sound mind. He is also the Spirit of adoption.

> *For ye have not received the spirit of bondage again to fear; but ye have received the Spirit of adoption, whereby we cry, Abba, Father.*
> **Romans 8:15**

That Spirit was given to you so that you can be adopted to become a son of God. How can a son of God fear anything, knowing that **"With God all things are possible"** and your Father is an all-powerful God that can do anything? Therefore if you are filled with the Holy Spirit, then you will be bold because you will remember what God told us through Prophet Isaiah in Isaiah 59:19 concerning the Spirit now living in you..

> *So shall they fear the name of the LORD from the west, and his glory from the rising of the sun. When the enemy shall come in like a flood, the Spirit of the LORD shall lift up a standard against him.*
>
> Isaiah 59:19

That was where God said that anytime the enemy comes flooding into your life with a situation that seems insurmountable; it is then that this Spirit of the Lord in you will lift up a standard against the enemy. The Holy Spirit inside you is a Spirit of power. So you can rest assured and be in perfect peace knowing that nothing the enemy does can overcome you. His presence should increase your boldness. You are free, therefore be bold. If you fear now, it is because you choose to fear, not because fear has any power over you. This is so because as we have said earlier you no longer have the spirit of fear but that of power, of love and of a sound mind. That is what God told us through Paul in 2 Timothy 1:7, (written on previous page). Therefore you do not have that spirit of fear anymore. If you fear, you either have not received, or don't know you have received the Holy Spirit. You probably also have not given Him the room to operate.

WHY FEAR WHEN YOU HAVE WON THE BATTLE EVEN BEFORE IT STARTED?

God has given you everything that you need to overcome fear. There is no need for you to fear then take a look at what is written in 1 John 4:4.

Be Bold

If we go by what God told us in that 1 John 4:4, you will see that you are actually fighting a *fixed-fight* in which the winner had already been fixed to be you even before the fight starts. Look at what God said below.

Ye are of God, little children, and have overcome them: because greater is he that is in you, than he that is in the world.
1 John 4:4

So the fight that you are in is already lost and won. It is already lost by your enemies. You have already won. You have already overcome your enemies, so there is no need to fear anymore. Your victory is your faith. That is what we are told by John in 1 John 5:4-5. If you are losing then check your faith because your faith gets you the victory. That is what the Scripture says. You have won the battle because as we have explained earlier, even when the battle is hottest it is then that the Holy Spirit that you now have in you will lift up a standard against your enemies. Therefore no matter how hot the fight is you are well covered and you will always come out the winner. You can only loose now if you choose to loose. It is your choice. You can no longer fear under any condition. The role of the Holy Spirit in the life of a believer and His contribution to the supernatural life of the believer is discussed in much detail in *Volume 4* of this *"Living a supernatural life"* book series.

For whatsoever is born of God overcometh the world: and this is the victory that overcometh the world, even our faith.

Living a Supernatural Life (Volume 2)

> *Who is he that overcometh the world, but he that believeth that Jesus is the Son of God?*
> **1 John 5:4-5**

4. HAVE LOVE IN YOUR HEART

Because there is no fear in love, if you have love in your heart, you will not fear. This is because perfect love cast out fear. That is what God told us through John in 1 John 4:18.

> *There is no fear in love; but perfect love cassette out fear: because fear hath torment. He that feareth is not made perfect in love.*
> **1 John 4:18**

So when you love, fear disappears, for you will have no cause to fear anything. Therefore you will have the boldness to speak out whatever you want. If love is in your heart you will have no fear and you will therefore be bold.

5. HAVE WISDOM

Wisdom is just applied-knowledge. It is the correct application of knowledge. That is the definition that Jesus Himself gave to wisdom in Matthew 7:24-26, where He said that the wise man is the one that heareth His teachings and obeys them. The foolish man is the one that heareth His teachings and refuses to obey them. ***Therefore if the wisdom of God is to answer to you then you must put into practice what you are reading and learning from this book and from the Word of God.***

Be Bold

> *Anyone who hears and obeys these teachings of mine is like a wise person who built a house on solid rock.*
>
> *Rain poured down, rivers flooded, and winds beat against that house. But it did not fall, because it was built on solid rock.*
>
> *Anyone who hears my teachings and doesn't obey them is like a foolish person who built a house on sand.*
>
> **Matthew 7:24-26**

Note that they both heard the Word, but the difference between the wise man and the foolish man is that the wise man applied it, but the foolish man did not. Therefore wisdom is the correct application of knowledge. Wisdom will embolden you. That is what God said through Solomon in Ecclesiastes 8:1.

> *Who is as the wise man? and who knoweth the interpretation of a thing? a man's wisdom maketh his face to shine, and the boldness of his face shall be changed.*
>
> **Ecclesiastes 8:1**

Therefore when you have the knowledge of God's Word about any situation apply it and you will become emboldened about the situation. When you have divine boldness you will not hesitate, or be ashamed, to open your mouth wide and proclaim the situations that you want into existence. This is so because having a knowledge of the Word gives you freedom to act without fear and stability.

Living a Supernatural Life (Volume 2)

When the wisdom of God answers to you, your life will be stable and you will be able to enjoy the strength that is in salvation. That is what God told us through Prophet Isaiah in Isaiah 33:6.

> *And wisdom and knowledge shall be the stability of thy times, and strength of salvation: the fear of the LORD is his treasure.*
> **Isaiah 33:6**

The stability will come because once this wisdom of God answers to you, it becomes quite easy and natural for you to be given proper direction in life. This is so because this divine wisdom is profitable to direct, which means that you will be properly directed to profiting if you have this wisdom. God said so through Solomon in Ecclesiastes 10:10. Therefore any knowledge of the Word that you have apply it. It will be to your profit.

> *If the iron be blunt, and he do not whet the edge, then must he put to more strength: but wisdom is profitable to direct.*
> **Ecclesiastes 10:10**

As explained earlier if you have a good knowledge of God you will be strong and you will do exploits, which is another way of saying that you will be bold and you will live a supernatural life. That is what we are made to understand in Daniel 11:32. You are now Righteous as we have shown earlier and the Scriptures say in Proverbs 28:1 that a righteous man is as bold as a lion. Therefore boldness should be one of your attributes now as a redeemed born-again Christian.

Be Bold

And such as do wickedly against the covenant shall he corrupt by flatteries: but the people that do know their God shall be strong, and do exploits.
Daniel 11:32

The wicked flee when no man pursueth: but the righteous are bold as a lion.
Proverbs 28:1

According to Proverbs 24:5 when a man has knowledge his strength increases. When he applies the knowledge he becomes strong. Therefore a wise man is strong.

A wise man is strong; yea, a man of knowledge increaseth strength.
Proverbs 24:5

From the combination of the above two Scripture verses we can see that **wisdom leads to strength** and **strength leads to exploits or supernatural living**. Therefore we can say that **wisdom leads to exploits or supernatural living.** You cannot have this wisdom of God and not be bold. Christ who is the wisdom of God, the power of God and the Word of God is now living in you and He will direct you appropriately in every situation that you come across. Be bold therefore because once your boldness is in place, and you proclaim what you want in faith, it will definitely come to pass.

To expatiate on the wisdom of God that is now in you I want to remind you that according to what Apostle Paul wrote in 1 Corinthians 2:16 you now have the mind of Christ.

Living a Supernatural Life (Volume 2)

> *For who hath known the mind of the Lord, that he may instruct him? But we have the mind of Christ.*
> **1 Corinthians 2:16**

But this Christ whose mind is now in you is also according to what Paul wrote in 1 Corinthians 1:24,30 is the wisdom of God and now unto us the wisdom of God. When you have and accept Jesus Christ you have the wisdom of God.

> *But unto them which are called, both Jews and Greeks, Christ the power of God, and the wisdom of God.*

> *But of him are ye in Christ Jesus, who of God is made unto us wisdom, and righteousness, and sanctification, and redemption:*
> **1 Corinthians 1:24,30**

You must give this wisdom of God the room to operate in your life if you want to live a supernatural life of power. This is because when this wisdom of God answers to you, you become possibilities unlimited. Once you can give this wisdom the room to operate in your life it only requires your patience to get the results that you want because you will need patience. That is what we shall discuss in the next Chapter.

CHAPTER 14

BE PATIENT

Even though the fulfillment of your declaration is immediate you need patience if you must see the physical manifestation. Patience is necessary for your loud talking. You must patiently wait for the physical manifestation of your declaration. Don't be afraid or ashamed if what you said is not manifesting immediately. It will do so eventually. Never loose heart because what you said did not manifest the first time you said it. You can rest assured that it will eventually manifest. Just keep confessing what you want and it will eventually manifest. You need patience. Remember Elijah when he proclaimed in 1 Kings 18:41-46 that it would rain? If you do let us take a close look at the story as written below.

> *And Elijah said unto Ahab, Get thee up, eat and drink; for there is a sound of abundance of rain.*
>
> *So Ahab went up to eat and to drink. And Elijah went up to the top of Carmel; and he cast himself down upon the earth, and put his face between his knees,*

Living a Supernatural Life (Volume 2)

> *And said to his servant, Go up now, look toward the sea. And he went up, and looked, and said, There is nothing. And he said, Go again seven times.*
>
> *And it came to pass at the seventh time, that he said, Behold, there ariseth a little cloud out of the sea, like a man's hand. And he said, Go up, say unto Ahab, Prepare thy chariot, and get thee down, that the rain stop thee not.*
>
> *And it came to pass in the mean while, that the heaven was black with clouds and wind, and there was a great rain. And Ahab rode, and went to Jezreel.*
>
> *And the hand of the LORD was on Elijah; and he girded up his loins, and ran before Ahab to the entrance of Jezreel.*
>
> **1 Kings 18:41-46**

After Elijah proclaimed that there would be rain, he asked his servant to go outside and look for the signs. The servant came back to say that there was no sign of rain. But Elijah did not give up. He kept telling him to go back and look. He did not border himself about anything that Ahab may say. The servant went to look seven times before he saw some clouds gathering, and the rain came eventually. This shows that if you command and it is not manifesting immediately, if you have the patience to wait in faith your command will manifest eventually. Had Elijah been discouraged before that seventh time, the rain would probably never have come.

Be Patient

The rain came because Elijah believed that the rain would eventually come. The rain came because God not only performs the words of His Prophets, He also watches over His words to perform. In truth He not only watches over them, He hastens them to perform. That is what God told us through Prophet Jeremiah in Jeremiah 1:12.

> *Then said the LORD unto me, Thou hast well seen: for I will hasten my word to perform it.*
> **Jeremiah 1:12**

If you were the one in Elijah's situation, immediately you declared that it will rain and they looked out the first time and there was no sign of rain, you will start to feel shy and afraid that you will be ridiculed. I doubt if you will even have the courage to tell them to go out and look once again not to talk of six times. But there was Elijah. He was not discouraged. He sent out his servant seven times before the manifestation came. We are told in James 5:17 that Elijah was a man subject to like passions as we are, so he is not different from you and me.

> *Elias was a man subject to like passions as we are, and he prayed earnestly that it might not rain: and it rained not on the earth by the space of three years and six months.*
> **James 5:17**

A proof of the fact that Elijah is not different from you and me can be seen from the way he ran for his life when he heard that Jezebel was looking for him to kill him.

Living a Supernatural Life (Volume 2)

This was a man that had just come down from Mount Carmel, where he called down the strange fire of God that consumed his burnt sacrifice, and the wood, and the stones, and the dust and licked up the water that was in the trench of the altar.

Definitely a man that God can use to work such a miracle and who defeated four hundred and fifty Baal priests and prophets should obviously know that God is capable of dealing with one woman. But because he was a man just like you and me, the fear of this woman called Jezebel gripped him.

Almost immediately after that great miracle work that God worked through him in 1 Kings 18:19-38, he started running from this woman who wanted to kill him because of his killing of the Baal prophets. This shows that he was just a human being like you who will run for his dear life when death threatens. Look at the story of his flight as narrated in 1 Kings 19:1-4 below.

> ***And Ahab told Jezebel all that Elijah had done, and withal how he had slain all the prophets with the sword.***
>
> ***Then Jezebel sent a messenger unto Elijah, saying, So let the gods do to me, and more also, if I make not thy life as the life of one of them by to morrow about this time.***
>
> ***And when he saw that, he arose, and went for his life, and came to Beersheba, which belongeth to Judah, and left his servant there.***

But he himself went a day's journey into the wilderness, and came and sat down under a juniper tree: and he requested for himself that he might die; and said, It is enough; now, O LORD, take away my life; for I am not better than my fathers.

1 Kings 19:1-4

If you had been the one, you would have probably said that your God that answered you on Mount Carmel would surely come to your aid especially against just one woman, especially a woman that is supposed to be fighting for Baal. You would probably not run for that woman. That shows you that Elijah was subject to like passions that you are subject to, even worse.

YOU ARE CAPABLE OF A HIGHER ANOINTING THAN ANY OLD COVENANT SAINT

In truth, today as a born-again Christian you are potentially greater than and therefore capable of operating with a much higher order of anointing than Elijah or any of the old Covenant saints including Moses, Joshua or Elisha. That is basically the meaning of what Jesus said in Matthew 12:41-42, John 20:21 as well as in Matthew 11:11 when combined.

The men of Nineveh shall rise in judgment with this generation, and shall condemn it: because they repented at the preaching of Jonas; and, behold, a greater than Jonas is here.

Living a Supernatural Life (Volume 2)

> *The queen of the south shall rise up in the judgment with this generation, and shall condemn it: for she came from the uttermost parts of the earth to hear the wisdom of Solomon; and, behold, a greater than Solomon is here.*
>
> **Matthew 12:41-42**

> *Then said Jesus to them again, Peace be unto you: as my Father hath sent me, even so send I you.*
>
> **John 20:21**

> *Verily I say unto you, Among them that are born of women there hath not risen a greater than John the Baptist: notwithstanding he that is least in the kingdom of heaven is greater than he.*
>
> **Matthew 11:11**

I want you to really get to know what Jesus is saying here. If you do, you will know just how powerful you are in Christ. Because what Jesus is saying in those verses is that the least of us born-again Christians operating under this New Covenant of God for man today is greater (or can operate with a higher anointing) than the greatest of all the people that operated under the Old Covenant. Because you are now operating under this New Covenant, you have the capability to do whatever Jesus did and even more than what He did. He said that He is sending you as He was sent. It follows therefore because you are sent as He was sent the same power that supported Him is now supporting you.

Be Patient

Therefore your mental attitude should be, *"whatever Jesus can do I can do."* That is what Jesus Himself said as written in John 14:12. I did not say it on my own. He said,

> *"Verily, verily, I say unto you, He that believeth on me, the works that I do shall he do also; and greater works than these shall he do; because I go unto my Father."*
> **John 14:12**

You now have at your disposal the power and abilities of God right inside of you. The power that is now resident in you has the ability and the force of heaven behind it. This is so because Jesus is now living in you. It was the same power that was operating inside Jesus when He was on earth.

You now have the Holy Spirit that raised Jesus up from death living in you. Not only these, you now also have His mind as well, that is the mind of Christ. That is what God told us through Apostle Paul respectively in Romans 8:11 and 1 Corinthians 2:16.

> *But if the Spirit of him that raised up Jesus from the dead dwell in you, he that raised up Christ from the dead shall also quicken your mortal bodies by his Spirit that dwelleth in you.*
> **Romans 8:11**

> *For who hath known the mind of the Lord, that he may instruct him? But we have the mind of Christ.*
> **1 Corinthians 2:16**

Therefore if someone under the Old Covenant can command the elements and he is obeyed, you are in a better position to do so under this New Covenant. However regardless of the higher anointing potential that you have, if you want to see the supernatural in your life you also require patience for you to see the physical manifestation of whatever commands you give. Once you have the faith, all you need is the patience to wait for the manifestation of the fulfillment of your commands. So when you speak and the manifestation does not come, if you stick to your confessions with faith the manifestation will eventually come. All you have to do is to just wait patiently for it in faith not doubting that what you have said will come to pass. If you wait for it you will surely see it because it will surely come. That was what God made Habakkuk to understand in Habakkuk 2:3. He is telling you the same thing today that there is an appointed time for it. Whatever you command will eventually manifest at the appointed time. It will surely manifest. Therefore wait patiently in faith for it.

> *For the vision is yet for an appointed time, but at the end it shall speak, and not lie: though it tarry, wait for it; because it will surely come, it will not tarry.*
> **Habakkuk 2:3**

You are to wait in faith for the physical manifestation of your confessions. That is what God said to Prophet Habakkuk in continuation of the discourse above in verse four, in Habakkuk 2:4. He said, *"But the just shall live by faith"*. So you need faith in your patience.

Be Patient

> *Behold, his soul which is lifted up is not upright in him: but the just shall live by his faith.*
>
> **Habakkuk 2:4**

Elijah exercised this type of patience when he proclaimed that there would be rain. He waited patiently in faith for it, and it eventually came. We should do the same thing. That is also the advice that God gave us in Hebrews 10:36 through Apostle Paul. Patience is therefore required for your loud talking if you are to see its manifestation.

> *For ye have need of patience, that, after ye have done the will of God, ye might receive the promise*
>
> **Hebrews 10:36**

You have need of patience as you go on talking and making bold declarations before the manifestation of what you are saying comes to light. Just keep saying it and believe every word you speak out. Suddenly the things you have been saying will come to pass. It is then that your profiting will become apparent to all.

Remember that your declarations are fulfilled as soon as you make the pronunciation but they may not manifest immediately. Manifestation may take time. Just make your pronunciation and believe that it will manifest. We have explained in *Volume 1* of this *"Living a supernatural life"* book series that the words that you speak out are seeds, which you sow into your life. When you sow them you will reap what you sow.

Living a Supernatural Life (Volume 2)

We also explained how it is necessary for you to water the seeds with continual confession of the appropriate Word of God in order for them to germinate, grow and yield the fruits that you will reap. If you sow and do not water your seed it will not germinate and you will not be able to reap any fruit.

Now take a close look at the Parable of the Sower, which Jesus narrated as written down in Luke 8:5-8 by Luke the Physician and the explanation that He gave to the parable as written down in Luke 8:11-15. There are some principles of sowing and reaping that Jesus discussed here that I will like you to take note of because they are very important and they determine the type of results that you get when you sow.

> *A sower went out to sow his seed: and as he sowed, some fell by the way side; and it was trodden down, and the fowls of the air devoured it.*
>
> *And some fell upon a rock; and as soon as it was sprung up, it withered away, because it lacked moisture.*
>
> *And some fell among thorns; and the thorns sprang up with it, and choked it.*
>
> *And other fell on good ground, and sprang up, and bare fruit an hundredfold. And when he had said these things, he cried, He that hath ears to hear, let him hear.*
>
> **Luke 8:5-8**

Be Patient

Now the parable is this: The seed is the word of God.

Those by the way side are they that hear; then cometh the devil, and taketh away the word out of their hearts, lest they should believe and be saved.

They on the rock are they, which, when they hear, receive the word with joy; and these have no root, which for a while believe, and in time of temptation fall away.

And that which fell among thorns are they, which, when they have heard, go forth, and are choked with cares and riches and pleasures of this life, and bring no fruit to perfection.

But that on the good ground are they, which in an honest and good heart, having heard the word, keep it, and bring forth fruit with patience.

Luke 8:11-15

You will notice in the parable that the seed in this case was the Word of God. The Sower was Jesus Christ Himself. For the seeds, which He sowed on good ground, He said in verse fifteen that they brought forth fruit **with patience**. So even though Jesus Christ was the One doing the sowing of the Word and they were sown on good ground, they still required patience to bring forth fruits. Definitely if Jesus's Word will require patience to produce results it is obvious that yours will even require more patience to produce results.

Living a Supernatural Life (Volume 2)

Remember that we are told in John 3:34 that He had not been given the Spirit by measure, yet He needed patience. If Jesus can need patience to get results you need it even the more.

> *For he whom God hath sent speaketh the words of God: for God giveth not the Spirit by measure unto him.*
> **John 3:34**

That is why Paul advised us in Hebrews 10:36, which we have written previously that we have need of patience after we might have done all the necessary things to get results. This means that after you have done all the talking, commanding and decreeing, and you have exhibited the necessary faith, you will still need to wait in patience in order to get the result that you are expecting. Always bear this in mind and wait patiently.

To receive the promises of God and get their physical manifestations in your life you need patience. Therefore we can say that if you must live a supernatural life here on earth then you need patience.

Remember that God said that His Word is a seed. When you speak it out you are sowing a seed. When you sow a seed you normally wait for it to germinate, grow and bear fruit. And during the period of waiting you will also be watering it. That was why Jesus said that the Word needed patience to bring forth fruit. Therefore you need patience before you can reap the benefits of the words that you are speaking out.

Be Patient

If after making your declaration concerning what you want based on the Word of God, you start to speak words that contradict your declaration then what you are doing is uprooting the seed that you planted. You will thereby stop the germination process. Remember that your word, which is the seed, has life in it and as soon as it is planted the life in it goes into action to start the germination process. When Jesus spoke to the fruitless fig tree in Mark 11:13-14 and commanded that no one would eat fruit from it from henceforth it started dying immediately but its death did not manifest immediately. However by the following morning as they were passing by as written in Mark 11:20-21 they saw that the fig tree had withered and died. The reply to Jesus' command though fulfilled did not manifest immediately.

You need patience! No matter the degree or quality of your faith patience is still necessary. Patience will help to stabilize your commitment and establish your eventual success. ***You don't sow and reap. You sow, wait and reap.***

> *And seeing a fig tree afar off having leaves, he came, if haply he might find any thing thereon: and when he came to it, he found nothing but leaves; for the time of figs was not yet.*
>
> *And Jesus answered and said unto it, No man eat fruit of thee hereafter for ever. And his disciples heard it.*
>
> **Mark 11:13-14**

And in the morning, as they passed by, they saw the fig tree dried up from the roots.

And Peter calling to remembrance saith unto him, Master, behold, the fig tree which thou cursedst is withered away.

Mark 11:20-21

SEE YOUR WORDS AS SEEDS

Jesus told us in the parable of the sower in Luke 8:5,11 that a sower went out to sow his seeds and in His explanation He said the seed is the Word of God.

A sower went out to sow his seed: and as he sowed, some fell by the way side; and it was trodden down, and the fowls of the air devoured it.

Now the parable is this: The seed is the word of God.

Luke 8:5,11

When you speak the Word of God out concerning a situation you are planting a seed. Three things that you must realize about the growth of seeds are:

1. Just as the natural seeds that a farmer plants obeys God's natural laws for the growth of seeds so does the Word of God that you speak out obeys the spiritual laws of God for the growth of seeds.

Be Patient

2. A seed has life in it. It has the miracle life to reproduce itself many fold and you release this power to reproduce itself when you sow it. When you sow a seed of maize you can get in return a harvest of thousands of maize seeds if not millions.

3. Seeds when sown will only bring forth their kind. When you sow an orange seed it can only bring forth an orange fruit. Similarly a mango seed will only bring forth a mango fruit. That means you will only reap what you sow. The same is true when you sow the Word of God.

You must sow a seed if you want to reap. You must sow in your heart the seed of what you want to reap because according to what the Scripture says in Galatians 6:7 it is whatsoever you sow that you will reap.

Be not deceived; God is not mocked: for whatsoever a man soweth, that shall he also reap.
Galatians 6:7

When many Christians are sick they will pray and fast to get healing but will not plant a single healing seed from the Word of God. Yet they are expecting God to answer them. Even though God works miracles He will not normally break His own law that says, *"What you sow is what you reap."* To reap healing from God you must sow healing seeds in your heart. To reap success fruits from God you must sow success seeds in your heart. You only reap what you sow.

When a farmer sows, even though he cannot see what is happening to the seed under the ground he knows that the power of life in the seed to reproduce itself has already been released and is at work under the ground. He commits what he has sown to the laws of God and goes about confident that he will eventually reap a harvest of what he has sown. He knows that it will take some time for the seeds to bring forth a harvest so he waits patiently for the harvest but while waiting he nourishes the soil, waters it and at the same time starts to plan for his harvest as though the harvest is already a reality.

We should do the same with the Word of God that we sow. After sowing it we should commit it to God and know in our hearts that the life power in that word-seed to reproduce has been released as soon as we planted it and even though we cannot see anything yet it is already working and we shall eventually reap our harvest. Therefore all our confessions and actions should point at the fact that we know that God will keep His promises and that the Word of God will bring forth the harvest in due time. The preparation for the harvest must be apparent from our actions. We must therefore start to talk as if we have already reaped the harvest. All our confessions and actions should be geared to nourishing and watering the Word of God in our heart knowing that we shall surely reap the harvest.

HAVE A STABLE MIND

An impatient man will end up being a man with an unstable mind and any man with an unstable mind cannot excel in life.

This is very true because whatever you will become starts from your inside. That is what we are made to see from what the Scriptures say in Proverbs 23:7. Look at what that Scripture says below and ponder it in your mind.

> *For as he thinketh in his heart, so is he: Eat and drink, saith he to thee; but his heart is not with thee.*
>
> **Proverbs 23:7**

Your life cannot be different from your thoughts. You cannot be thinking sickness and have health. You cannot be thinking poverty and have prosperity. You cannot be thinking failure and have success. It is your mind that determines your size. It is your mind that determines your health. You can see this from what God said through John in 3 John1:2.

> *Beloved, I wish above all things that thou mayest prosper and be in health, even as thy soul prospereth.*
>
> **3 John 1:2**

God wants prosperity for you but it depends on what you have in your mind. If your mind is already conditioned to poverty and lack you cannot be wealthy. Similarly if your mind is already conditioned to sickness you cannot lead a healthy life. Yes! God wants health for you. Yes! God said that you have been healed but it is as you see it in your mind that it will be. When you are always thinking sickness, disease and expecting sickness to come it will be difficult for you to see yourself living a disease-free life.

Living a Supernatural Life (Volume 2)

God said that He has given you power but it is as you see it in your mind that it will be with you. You cannot be double-minded and get anything from God. That is what God made us to see from what He said through James in James 1:6-8.

> *But let him ask in faith, nothing wavering. For he that wavereth is like a wave of the sea driven with the wind and tossed.*
>
> *For let not that man think that he shall receive any thing of the Lord.*
>
> *A double minded man is unstable in all his ways.*
> **James 1:6-8**

If you are unstable in your thoughts then you cannot excel in life. For example if you are unstable in your thoughts about diseases then you cannot excel against diseases. But when you have a stable mind anchored on very strong faith then nothing can be impossible to you. That is what Jesus made us to see in Mark 9:23.

> *Jesus said unto him, If thou canst believe, all things are possible to him that believeth.*
> **Mark 9:23**

To see the effect of an unstable mind look at what Jacob Reuben's Father said to his son Reuben in Genesis 49:3-4 when he was blessing his children just before he died. He said, **"Reuben unstable as water, thou shalt not excel"** As you can see therefore instability is virtually a curse.

Be Patient

> *Reuben, thou art my firstborn, my might, and the beginning of my strength, the excellency of dignity, and the excellency of power:*
>
> *Unstable as water, thou shalt not excel; because thou wentest up to thy father's bed; then defiledst thou it: he went up to my couch.*
> **Genesis 49:3-4**

One of the most pathetic cases in the Scriptures of how an unstable mind can affect ones destiny is that of John the Baptist. Let us look briefly at his case. You will remember that Jesus said concerning John the Baptist that of all men born of a woman in the Old Covenant none was greater than John the Baptist. That was what Jesus said in Matthew 11:11.

> *Verily I say unto you, Among them that are born of women there hath not risen a greater than John the Baptist: notwithstanding he that is least in the kingdom of heaven is greater than he.*
> **Matthew 11:11**

Jesus said that John was greater than all men born of a woman under the Old Covenant. But he died a lowly death. You may say that Jesus Christ also died a lowly death but that was His destiny as this has been prophesied concerning Him long before He came to the world. But that is not the case with John the Baptist. John the beloved said in John 10:41 that John the Baptist did no miracle. That is not a credit for John for there are more miracles inside John the Baptist than there are inside Elijah, Elisha, Moses or any of the other Old Covenant Saints.

And many resorted unto him, and said, John did no miracle: but all things that John spake of this man were true.

John 10:41

So why was John the Baptist unable to do any miracle? At the root of John's problem was doubt. He had an unstable mind. That was what murdered his potential. He had the Word, but he lacked the power because the faith to make the Word work was not there. If you look at what is written in the Scriptures in Matthew 11:1-11 the doubting nature of John will be clear to you. Read this below.

And it came to pass, when Jesus had made an end of commanding his twelve disciples, he departed thence to teach and to preach in their cities.

Now when John had heard in the prison the works of Christ, he sent two of his disciples,

And said unto him, Art thou he that should come, or do we look for another?

Jesus answered and said unto them, Go and shew John again those things which ye do hear and see:

The blind receive their sight, and the lame walk, the lepers are cleansed, and the deaf hear, the dead are raised up, and the poor have the gospel preached to them.

Be Patient

And blessed is he, whosoever shall not be offended in me.

And as they departed, Jesus began to say unto the multitudes concerning John, What went ye out into the wilderness to see? A reed shaken with the wind?

But what went ye out for to see? A man clothed in soft raiment? behold, they that wear soft clothing are in kings' houses.

But what went ye out for to see? A prophet? yea, I say unto you, and more than a prophet.

For this is he, of whom it is written, Behold, I send my messenger before thy face, which shall prepare thy way before thee.

Verily I say unto you, Among them that are born of women there hath not risen a greater than John the Baptist: notwithstanding he that is least in the kingdom of heaven is greater than he.

        Matthew 11:1-11

He sent his disciples to Jesus saying, *"Art thou He that should come or do we look for another?"* That was a strange question coming from him. This is so because if you remember, he was the one who revealed who Jesus was during His baptism. Look at what transpired between him and Jesus in Matthew 3:13-17. Then you can conclude that it was a strange question from him.

> *Then cometh Jesus from Galilee to Jordan unto John, to be baptized of him.*
>
> *But John forbad him, saying, I have need to be baptized of thee, and comest thou to me?*
>
> *And Jesus answering said unto him, Suffer it to be so now: for thus it becometh us to fulfil all righteousness. Then he suffered him.*
>
> *And Jesus, when he was baptized, went up straightway out of the water: and, lo, the heavens were opened unto him, and he saw the Spirit of God descending like a dove, and lighting upon him:*
>
> *And lo a voice from heaven, saying, This is my beloved Son, in whom I am well pleased.*
>
> **Matthew 3:13-17**

If you note the reply that Jesus gave to John's disciples in *Verse 4* of that Chapter 11 of Matthew, the doubting nature of John will become even more apparent to you and strike you even the more. Jesus said, **"Go and show John again those things which you do hear and see......."** He said, **"Go and show him AGAIN."** **"AGAIN"** This shows that it is not the first time that He would send to John explaining things to him. That was why Jesus asked the people the question in *Verse 7*. He said unto the multitude concerning John, **"What went ye out into the wilderness to see? A reed shaken with the wind?"** Jesus is describing here the unstable nature of John comparing him with a reed that the wind shakes about like a yo-yo.

Be Patient

If you look at **Verse 6** of that same Matthew Chapter 11 you will see one of the things that doubt and an unstable mind causes. Jesus said in that **Verse 6**, *"And blessed is he whosoever shall not be offended in Me."* What Jesus is saying there is also applicable in reverse. What He said is equivalent to, *"And cursed is he whosoever shall be offended in Me."* John was offended in Jesus because his reasoning was that if Jesus was the Messiah that they had expected then He should have saved him from the prison of Herod. But since Jesus did not come to save him then his reasoning was that He couldn't be the Messiah that they had been expecting. John was offended in Jesus and therefore he lost his blessing. John should not have died the type of lowly death that he died with his head given to one harlot's daughter as a gift.

Doubt and unstable mind always create offense and it will deny you of your blessing. Doubt is the greatest enemy you have to your potential for fulfilling the supernatural life destiny that God has for you. One of the attributes of a stable mind is patience. Do you know why doubt or an unstable mind is such a great opponent to your achieving the potential that God has destined for you? It is because what you don't believe, you cannot become. That is a law that stands whether you agree with it or not. Just as doubt is the greatest enemy to your achieving your potential so is faith the greatest booster to your achieving your potential.

You will notice that one of the greatest attributes that Paul exhibited in his ministry was faith. His ministry was based on faith. That is what he said in Romans 10:8 as written below.

Living a Supernatural Life (Volume 2)

> *But what saith it? The word is nigh thee, even in thy mouth, and in thy heart: that is, the word of faith, which we preach;*
> **Romans 10:8**

Without faith you cannot live a supernatural life. The school of faith is the school of exploit, fulfillment and victory. If you are to live a supernatural life your vision must be faith-driven.

If your vision is not faith-driven then it is dead because the fulfillment of every vision is based on faith. No matter what field you are and what you are planning to do your vision must be faith-driven. Look again at what God told Habakkuk in Habakkuk 2:3-4 concerning his vision as written below.

> *For the vision is yet for an appointed time, but at the end it shall speak, and not lie: though it tarry, wait for it; because it will surely come, it will not tarry.*
>
> *Behold, his soul which is lifted up is not upright in him: but the just shall live by his faith.*
> **Habakkuk 2:3-4**

So the fulfillment of every vision is based on faith. Your faith determines what happens to you in life. This means that regardless of what you want to do or be in life your vision is determined by the limit of your faith. Jesus Himself said in Matthew 9:29, "According to your faith be it unto you."

Be Patient

Then touched he their eyes, saying, According to your faith be it unto you.
Matthew 9:29

So, it is to you according to your faith. It is not to you according to the devil but according to your faith. Many Christians believe that it is the devil that determines their situations. No! It is not according to the devil it is according to your faith. It is not according to the economic situation of where you are either because many Christians believe that the economic situation where they are is what determines what happens to them. Have you not seen people whose life booms even during a period of economic downturn? Neither is it according to the people you know or according to the Government in power. No! No! It is according to your faith that it will be with you. You must get this straight. The future of your vision is faith-determined. Faith is the driver of your vision. No matter what vision God gave you and the strategy you may have, without faith the vision will never be achieved.

The main reason why doubt comes into the mind of most Christians is that they look at the circumstances and symptoms and it what they can see, hear, smell, taste, feel or even their experience that they base their judgments on. But we have been advised by God not to do this in 2 Corinthians 4:18.

While we look not at the things which are seen, but at the things which are not seen: for the things which are seen are temporal; but the things which are not seen are eternal.
2 Corinthians 4:18

Living a Supernatural Life (Volume 2)

How can you look at things not seen? Only with the eyes of faith! It is faith that will cause that victory, success or blessing which you cannot currently see to become visible so that you take hold of it. With faith you have to believe first before you see it and not the other way round.

What causes doubt is that you want to see it first before you believe and when you don't see it you then believe that it does not exist or it is not true. As a matter of fact unseen things are more real than physical things and as a Christian unseen things should be more real to you than physical things. But it is only with faith that such can be possible.

For you to be able to have faith it is important that you must realize that faith is a fight. That is why you are advised by God through Paul in 1Timothy 6:12 to fight the good fight of faith. If faith involves a fight then it means that it must have some form of opposition. There must be things that can hinder it. In order to find out those things that can oppose or hinder faith that we have to fight we must first try to find out how we get faith. Actually according to Romans 10:17 faith comes by hearing the Word of God. So in order to get faith it is the knowledge of the Word of God that we need.

> *Fight the good fight of faith, lay hold on eternal life, whereunto thou art also called, and hast professed a good profession before many witnesses.*
>
> **1 Timothy 6:12**

Be Patient

> *So then faith cometh by hearing, and hearing by the word of God.*
> **Romans 10:17**

If faith comes by hearing the Word of God then it follows that the greatest enemy of faith must be the lack of knowledge of the Word of God. That is the enemy of faith that you have to fight in the good fight of faith that God has called you to engage in. This is the bane of the problem that most Christians have; they lack the knowledge of the Word and as a result their faith is weak. Your faith can only be as great as the knowledge that you have of the object of your faith. Since God is the object of your faith it follows that the knowledge that you have of God determines the strength of your faith.

For example when we consider righteousness most Christians cannot see themselves as righteous because they have no work of righteousness. They believe that righteousness has to do with good works. But that is not what God says in His Word. Look at what God said in Romans 10:10 and Romans 5:17.

> *For with the heart man believeth unto righteousness; and with the mouth confession is made unto salvation.*
> **Romans 10:10**

> *For if by one man's offence death reigned by one; much more they which receive abundance of grace and of the gift of righteousness shall reign in life by one, Jesus Christ.*
> **Romans 5:17**

Living a Supernatural Life (Volume 2)

He said with the heart we ***believe unto righteousness;*** we don't ***work unto righteousness*** with our hands. When we receive Christ and we are born again ***we receive righteousness as a gift.*** We have to accept this in our heart and believe that we now have righteousness. Once we accept this then we know that all the promises that God made to the righteous are now true for us.

If you want to live a supernatural life and be an overcomer then doubt must be done away with and faith embraced because you already have victory but it is with faith that you will take hold of it. That is what we are made to see in 1 John 5:4.

> *For whatsoever is born of God overcometh the world: and this is the victory that overcometh the world, even our faith.*
> **1 John 5:4**

Note that He said, **"This is THE victory"**, not **"This is A victory"** Therefore we are talking here about the ultimate victory and it is your faith that will give it to you. I know that some Christians will say that this is meant for people with faith. But He is talking of people born of God and you are now born of God. Therefore your faith is what will give you victory.

But we are all given an equal measure of faith to start with. I say this because of what is written by Paul the Apostle in Romans 12:3 where we are told that every man is given the measure of faith.

Be Patient

For I say, through the grace given unto me, to every man that is among you, not to think of himself more highly than he ought to think; but to think soberly, according as God hath dealt to every man the measure of faith.
Romans 12:3

Note that He said, **"THE measure of faith"** not **"A measure of faith"**. This means that we are all given an equal measure. The major difference is that just like in the parable of the talents some Christians develop the measure that they are given by exercising it while others do not develop their own beyond the measure that they are given. God's language is faith; if you don't speak it or if you don't understand it then you cannot talk to God or hear Him.

With the measure of faith that you have been given you should now be able to walk by faith as we are directed to do in 2 Corinthians 5:7. You should not only walk by faith but you should now also be able to live by faith as we are directed to do in Romans 1:17 by Paul. This means that you should no longer be directed by your feeling, your seeing, your hearing, your tasting and your smelling. You should only be directed by what the Word of God says. Finally, remember that even if you believe, you have not exercised faith until you speak out what you believe. That is the spirit of faith as we are told in 2 Corinthians 4:13.

For we walk by faith, not by sight:
2 Corinthians 5:7

Living a Supernatural Life (Volume 2)

> *For therein is the righteousness of God revealed from faith to faith: as it is written, The just shall live by faith.*
> **Romans 1:17**

> *We having the same spirit of faith, according as it is written, I believed, and therefore have I spoken; we also believe, and therefore speak;*
> **2 Corinthians 4:13**

In the next Chapter we are going to show that God expects you to be His battle-axe but if you are to be then apart from all the conditions that we have discussed in the previous Chapters your faith must also be strongly in place, doubt must be thrown away and patience must be your companion at all times.

CHAPTER 15

YOU ARE GOD'S BATTLE AXE

With your new birth and redemption, you have not only been blessed; you have been made a saviour and a deliverer of the order of Christ. Some people will call that blasphemy. But I did not say it; Jesus Christ Himself said it. Look at what He said in John 17:18 and John 20:21. Jesus said that it is as His Father has sent Him that He Jesus has now sent you also into the world. You have been sent to do what He did. It may sound far-fetched, but I did not say it. That is the essence of what Jesus said in both verses as written below.

> *As thou hast sent me into the world, even so have I also sent them into the world.*
> **John 17:18**

> *Then said Jesus to them again, Peace be unto you: as my Father hath sent me, even so send I you.*
> **John 20:21**

From what Jesus said above you can see that you are also meant to be a saviour.

Living a Supernatural Life (Volume 2)

This is so because we know that the Father sent Jesus to this earth to be a Saviour of the world. That is what God told us through Apostle John in 1 John 4:14.

> *And we have seen and do testify that the Father sent the Son to be the Saviour of the world.*
> **1 John 4:14**

Therefore if He was sent by the Father to be the Saviour of the world, and He has now sent you just as He had been sent, by the Father then it follows that He has sent you to be a type of saviour and deliverer for mankind of the order of Christ. It is not that you are going to do the work of redemption all over again. No! Christ has already done that. But you are supposed to help your fellow human beings when you see them in the bondage into which Satan has put them. In order for you to be able to achieve that objective, you can see from what He said in John 14:12 that He has empowered you to do the work necessary for you to be a saviour and deliverer of your fellow human beings.

> *Verily, verily, I say unto you, He that believeth on me, the works that I do shall he do also; and greater works than these shall he do; because I go unto my Father.*
> **John 14:12**

He said that you would do the works that He did. Not only that, He said that you will even do greater works than He did. We have seen above that the totality of the works that He did was that He was a Saviour of this world.

You are God's Battle Axe

Therefore you are also supposed to work for the salvation and deliverance of your fellow human beings and you have been fully equipped to be able to do this. Jesus was slain and having gone through the ordeal of crucifixion He obtained power and riches and wisdom and strength and honour and glory and blessing. That is what we are told in Revelation 5:12.

> *Saying with a loud voice, Worthy is the Lamb that was slain to receive power, and riches, and wisdom, and strength, and honour, and glory, and blessing.*
> **Revelation 5:12**

He did not need these things that He took from Satan. He took them so that He can give them to you. But He is not giving them to you so that you can use them just to satisfy your own pleasure. You have not been given these so that you can use them just for any purpose. No! You have been given the power, riches, wisdom, strength, honour, glory and blessing that He took from Satan so that you can use them to help your fellow human beings and to deliver them from the oppression of Satan.

For this purpose God has made you a god. You are a god. That is what Jesus said in John 10:34. God has made you a god to your circumstances and to your enemies just like He made Moses a god to Pharaoh as He said in Exodus 7:1.

> *Jesus answered them, Is it not written in your law, I said, Ye are gods?*
> **John 10:34**

Living a Supernatural Life (Volume 2)

> *And the LORD said unto Moses, See, I have made thee a god to Pharaoh: and Aaron thy brother shall be thy prophet.*
> **Exodus 7:1**

Note that just like God gave Moses the staff of authority a ***Rod*** with, which to tackle Pharaoh, as stated in Exodus 4:17, He has also given you a ***Rod***, to use for bringing your enemies to submission and setting the people free. Christ, the Word of God, is actually called the ***Rod*** through Isaiah in Isaiah 11:1. Therefore you can use the Word of God as the ***Rod*** to do miracles, signs and wonders in the Name of Jesus Christ just like Moses used his ***Rod***.

> *And thou shalt take this rod in thine hand, wherewith thou shalt do signs.*
> **Exodus 4:17**

> *And there shall come forth a rod out of the stem of Jesse, and a Branch shall grow out of his roots:*
> **Isaiah 11:1**

Christ who is the Word of God is the Rod, which God has given us in this dispensation with which we are supposed to tackle all the problems that the enemy brings to our lives. And we are supposed to tackle all in the Name of Jesus. That is why it is extremely important that you get yourself soaked in the Word of God by meditating in it all the time. Jesus Himself confirmed in Mark 16:17-18 that you can use this Rod Jesus Christ that you have been given to do miracles signs and wonders.

You are God's Battle Axe

And these signs shall follow them that believe; In my name shall they cast out devils; they shall speak with new tongues;

They shall take up serpents; and if they drink any deadly thing, it shall not hurt them; they shall lay hands on the sick, and they shall recover.

Mark 16:17-18

And you do this by giving commands in the Name of Jesus. Commanding in Jesus' Name using the Word as a **Rod** can make you a saviour and deliverer of the order of Christ.

Using the Word of God and the Name of Jesus as the **Rod** you can do signs and wonders and go into the entire world to preach the good news of salvation to all nations, making them to become believers and redeemed Christians so that you can free them from the clutches of the enemy. That is what Jesus commanded us to do.

Using this **Rod**, you are not only to bring people to God, but as a battle-axe for God you are also to use it to inflict judgment on those who have refused to bow to the Word.

Just as God made Jeremiah His battle-axe and weapons of war, as written in Jeremiah 51:20, which is written below, you are now also supposed to be His battle-axe and weapons of war to be used by God here on earth in this dispensation.

> *Thou art my battle axe and weapons of war: for with thee will I break in pieces the nations, and with thee will I destroy kingdoms;*
> **Jeremiah 51:20**

The first thing that I want you to note in this Scripture is that God said *weapons of war* not just one *weapon*. Hence there are many different functions that you will have to perform in order to achieve the objective of being a saviour and a deliverer of the order of Christ. As His battle-axe and weapons of war, to achieve the objective of being a deliverer of the order of Christ, God is going to use you in different roles to act as different types of weapons. This is because you are supposed to root out some things, to pull down some things, to destroy some things, to throw down some things, to build some things and to plant some things. That is what God told Jeremiah in Jeremiah 1:10. He is telling you the same thing today. Definitely, you will need different types of weapons to achieve these because the weapon that will throw down, root out, pull down or destroy things will not necessarily be the weapon that will build or plant things.

> *See, I have this day set thee over the nations and over the kingdoms, to root out, and to pull down, and to destroy, and to throw down, to build, and to plant.*
> **Jeremiah 1:10**

This means that in order to achieve that purpose of God, there are many different types of functions that you will have to perform.

You are God's Battle Axe

God will use you as different types of *weapons* to tackle different types of problems. Each of these functions will require a different type of *weapon* to deal with it. Therefore for each function you will be required to act as the *weapon* best able to cope with that type of function. That is why God called you *weapons* of war instead of a *weapon* of war. This means that the power of God will be manifested in many different ways through you. In some situations you will have to pull down while in others you will have to build. In some situations you will have to plant while in others you will root out. As God's *weapons of war* He has also made you a threshing instrument having teeth so that you can thresh the mountains and beat them small and so that you can make the hills as chaff. That is what God made us to see through Isaiah in Isaiah 41:15.

Behold, I will make thee a new sharp threshing instrument having teeth: thou shalt thresh the mountains, and beat them small, and shalt make the hills as chaff.
Isaiah 41:15

What are the mountains of your life? You have to thresh them down and beat them small by applying the Word of God to them. *What are the hills of your life?* You have to thresh them to become as chaff by applying the Word of God to them on a continuous and incessant basis. God has given you teeth; do not be like a toothless bulldog. Apply the teeth that you have been given to thresh the mountains and the hills of your life. God has made you His battle axe and weapons of war.

Living a Supernatural Life (Volume 2)

You should therefore find out what God wants to use you to root out, what He wants to use you to pull down, what He wants to use you to destroy, what He wants to use you to throw down, what He wants to use you to build and what He wants to use you to plant. If you can find the answer to these questions, then you will know for what purpose God wants to use you as ***His battle-axe and weapons of war***. In ***Volume 1*** of this ***"Living a Supernatural life"*** book series written by the same author we showed how the Word in your mouth can be used in different ways as a weapon such as fire, a hammer, a sword, a mirror, sunlight, rain and even God's wisdom to achieve these various objectives for God. Let us now look at each case.

WHAT GOD WANTS YOU TO ROOT OUT

This is not very difficult to find out. Jesus Christ Himself answered this when He was here on earth. He said every plant, which our Heavenly Father has not planted, would be rooted up. Jesus Himself was the One who said this in Matthew 15:13.

> *But he answered and said, Every plant, which my heavenly Father hath not planted, shall be rooted up.*
> **Matthew 15:13**

So you now know what the Father wants to root up, for which He wants to use you as a weapon to achieve. He wants you to root up whatever He has not planted. The mind takes center stage in this battle.

Because it is the mind that takes the decision for the body and the spirit of man, it is in the mind that the devil attempts to plant whatever he wants to plant in man. Whatever Satan wants to plant in your body or in your life he first plants it as a thought in your mind. If you allow the thought to take root in your mind by thinking about it in fear and meditating on it then it will eventually manifest physically in your life. Any thought that the Heavenly Father has not planted in your mind must be violently rooted up.

Therefore whatever the Father has not planted, if you come across it, as a thought in your mind or physically in your body you are supposed to uproot it out. If that is the case what then is that disease doing in your body? Did the Father plant it there? If He did not, then you have the power and the authority to root it out. You should root out whatever the enemy has planted in your body, in your mind or in anybody's body or mind for that matter, whenever you come across it. You cannot be toying with the enemy. If the enemy attempts to plant anything in your body or mind, you should root it out with immediate effect. Every covenant of sorrow in your life must be rooted out. All pollutions working against your destiny must be rooted out and cleansed with the Blood of Jesus. Whatever wants to put your destiny to shame must be rooted up. Whatever wants to destroy the divine purpose of God for your life must be rooted up. There are some deep-rooted traditional thoughts of impossibilities that have been planted into the mind of some Christians. Such thoughts stand between them and the destiny that God has ordained for them. Such thoughts must be rooted up.

Living a Supernatural Life (Volume 2)

Anything that tries to make you move backwards instead of forward in your Christian adventure and making it unfruitful, you must root it up. There are other things that God wants to root out and you are the one that He wants to use to root them out. God said through David in Psalm 52:2-6 that every tongue that deviseth mischief, that lies and the deceitful tongue shall all be destroyed, plucked out and rooted out.

> *Thy tongue deviseth mischiefs; like a sharp razor, working deceitfully.*
>
> *Thou lovest evil more than good; and lying rather than to speak righteousness. Selah.*
>
> *Thou lovest all devouring words, O thou deceitful tongue.*
>
> *God shall likewise destroy thee for ever, he shall take thee away, and pluck thee out of thy dwelling place, and root thee out of the land of the living. Selah.*
>
> *The righteous also shall see, and fear, and shall laugh at him:*
>
> **Psalm 52:2-6**

Therefore whatever comes to you and tells you any thing contrary to what the Word of God says you know that it is telling lies. It must therefore be rooted out. Whatever comes to you pretending to have power and authority over you and putting such thoughts into your mind is not only lying but is also devising mischief.

This is so because you now know that God has given you power over all the power of the enemy. Jesus said in Luke 10:19 that He has given you power above your enemy. He said that no power of the enemy would be able to overcome you. Therefore thoughts of weakness and whatever brings them must be rooted out of your mind. God has given you the power to do this.

> ***Behold, I give unto you power to tread on serpents and scorpions, and over all the power of the enemy: and nothing shall by any means hurt you.***
> **Luke 10:19**

God also said through King Solomon in Proverbs 2:22 that the transgressors shall be rooted out.

> ***But the wicked shall be cut off from the earth, and the transgressors shall be rooted out of it.***
> **Proverbs 2:22**

Who are the transgressors? The transgressors are all those who transgress the laws of God and who keep not the Word of God. Now in 1 Peter 2:24 the Word of God says that you have been healed by the stripes that Jesus took. Anything that opposes this Word of God in your life is a transgressor and must be rooted up.

> ***Who his own self bare our sins in his own body on the tree, that we, being dead to sins, should live unto righteousness: by whose stripes ye were healed.***
> **1 Peter 2:24**

Now whatever disease comes to your body is not obeying that Word of God. Therefore it is a transgressor and must be rooted up. For example, God has given the order and laid down the laws for the growth and lifespan of the cells of your body. Therefore any cell that grows contrary to that order and to the laws laid down by God is a transgressor. Basically cancer and fibroid are the result of cells that have decided to grow contrary to the laws and order laid down by God for cell growth in the body.

Such cancer or fibroid cells are transgressors of the laws of God and must be rooted out. You have every right to root out all such transgressing cells. I am sure that you know of many situations in which the thoughts that came into your mind were contrary to what the Word of God says. Whenever such thoughts come into your mind they must be rooted out of your mind. Take for example the Word of God as written by Paul in Ephesians 1:3. There the Word of God says that you have been blessed with all spiritual blessings in heavenly places.

> ***Blessed be the God and Father of our Lord Jesus Christ, who hath blessed us with all spiritual blessings in heavenly places in Christ:***
> **Ephesians 1:3**

Therefore any thought that comes into your mind telling you that you are poor is a transgressor of the Word of God and must be rooted up out of your mind before it becomes a strong hold, which you will have to pull down and this is what we shall discuss in the next section.

WHAT GOD WANTS YOU TO PULL DOWN

In 2 Corinthians 10:4-6 God through Apostle Paul said that we have weapons of warfare that are not carnal but are mighty through God. God talked of things that we are supposed to use such weapons of warfare to pull down, to cast down and to bring into captivity.

For the weapons of our warfare are not carnal, but mighty through God to the pulling down of strong holds;

Casting down imaginations, and every high thing that exalteth itself against the knowledge of God, and bringing into captivity every thought to the obedience of Christ;

And having in a readiness to revenge all disobedience, when your obedience is fulfilled.
2 Corinthians 10:4-6

From the Scripture above, we can see that we are supposed to use the weapons of our warfare to pull down strong holds. We are also supposed to use them to cast down imaginations and every high thing that exalts itself against the knowledge of God, which means anything that exalts itself against the knowledge of the Word since Christ is the Word and is God. We are supposed to use the weapons to bring into captivity every thought that contradicts the Word *to the obedience of Christ* who, according to John 1:1,14 is the Word. What God is saying then is that you must bring such thoughts into captivity *to the obedience of what the Word of God says.*

Living a Supernatural Life (Volume 2)

In the beginning was the Word, and the Word was with God, and the Word was God.

And the Word was made flesh, and dwelt among us, and we beheld his glory, the glory as of the only begotten of the Father, full of grace and truth.
John 1:1, 14

So you have weapons of war as a Christian, which are not carnal but are very strong and, which you are supposed to use against the enemy. Note again that He said weapons not weapon. Therefore they are more than one. One of the spiritual weapons that you have with which you can fight the enemy is the Word of God. Remember what Jesus said in John 6:63 about the Word? He said that the Word is Spirit and is life. So the Word of God is not carnal. The Word of God is Spirit. Therefore if you use the Word in any situation you should realize that you are using a spiritual weapon.

It is the spirit that quickeneth; the flesh profiteth nothing: the words that I speak unto you, they are spirit, and they are life.
John 6:63

In *Chapter 8* of the *Volume 1* of this *"Living a supernatural life"* book series we discussed in detail the use of the Word of God as a weapon of warfare against the enemy. We showed how the Word of God was likened to different things. We showed that the Word can be used as fire to burn up all enemy deposits and as a hammer to break down every mountain.

You are God's Battle Axe

It can also be used as a sword to fight the enemy with, as God's wisdom to get insight into every problem, as a soothing balm to heal, as rain to bring life into anything, as light to brighten up any gloomy situation, as a mirror to be able to see a true picture of what is happening, as sunlight to bring energy into any situation, as a seed that can be planted to become a tree that can yield fruits and as a general weapon of war that can be used for various situations.

We tried to show the power that is in the Word. To see the power that is in the Word of God look at what God told us through Paul in Hebrews 4:12 concerning the Word of God. He said,

"For the word of God is quick, and powerful, and sharper than any twoedged sword, piercing even to the dividing asunder of soul and spirit, and of the joints and marrow, and is a discerner of the thoughts and intents of the heart."
Hebrews 4:12

Those thoughts that have stayed in your mind, which have been put there either by Satan, or by the effects of your traditions and environment, which many times has led you to all sorts of evil imaginations are what become the strong holds of Satan that you need to pull down. Such strong holds are what Satan uses to gain a hold on your thought pattern. The method of pulling them down is to cast down such thoughts and imaginations by bringing them captive and putting them in subjection to the Word of God.

Living a Supernatural Life (Volume 2)

Once you do this, they have to bow to the Word of God and be in obedience to the Word. But note that they will only subject themselves to what the Word says through your command, provided your own obedience of the Word is completely in place. So your own obedience of the Word of God must first be in place and fully established if you want such thoughts, imaginations and spirits to obey any command that you give them based on what the Word of God says. From what is written in 2 Corinthians 10:6 written previously you can see that if you are not fully in obedience to the Word of God, then you cannot expect the evil thoughts or imaginations to be obedient to the words that you speak to them.

It is a war and it is being fought for the control of your mind. The thoughts that you allow into your mind will decide who will have the control over your mind. In the next Chapter we shall discuss how Satan attempts to build strong holds in our minds with his thoughts that he tries to plant there and how to use the Word of God as a weapon to pull down such strong holds.

WHAT GOD WANT'S YOU TO DESTROY

God said through David in Psalm 9:5 and Psalm 73:27 that the wicked and all they that go whoring will be destroyed.

> *Thou hast rebuked the heathen, thou hast destroyed the wicked, thou hast put out their name for ever and ever.*
> **Psalm 9:5**

For, lo, they that are far from thee shall perish: thou hast destroyed all them that go a whoring from thee.
Psalm 73:27

As a battle-axe and weapons of war of God therefore, one of your functions is to destroy wickedness and all whoring and prostituting nature whenever you come across them. These are some of the things that God wants to destroy. Because you are now His battle-axe and weapons of war for His use on earth to achieve His purpose, it follows therefore that these are the things that you must be out to destroy whenever you come across them. From Psalm 37:38 we can see that anything that transgresses against the laws of God will be destroyed. The wicked and the workers of iniquities will be destroyed according to Psalm 92:7 as well as Psalm 145:20. Those are the people and things that God wants to destroy and you are the one He wants to use to do this. It is not that you are to kill them but you are to render them powerless.

But the transgressors shall be destroyed together: the end of the wicked shall be cut off.
Psalm 37:38

When the wicked spring as the grass, and when all the workers of iniquity do flourish; it is that they shall be destroyed for ever:
Psalm 92:7

The LORD preserveth all them that love him: but all the wicked will he destroy.
Psalm 145:20

Who are the transgressors? All those wicked spirits that refuse to obey the Word of God, which says that you have been healed, blessed and victorious are transgressors and must be destroyed. Some other things that must be destroyed are the high places and altars that have been built in the minds of the people that have become strong holds. That is what we are told in Leviticus 26:30, Deuteronomy 7:5 and Isaiah 23:11.

> *And I will destroy your high places, and cut down your images, and cast your carcases upon the carcases of your idols, and my soul shall abhor you.*
> **Leviticus 26:30**

> *But thus shall ye deal with them; ye shall destroy their altars, and break down their images, and cut down their groves, and burn their graven images with fire.*
> **Deuteronomy 7:5**

> *He stretched out his hand over the sea, he shook the kingdoms: the LORD hath given a commandment against the merchant city, to destroy the strong holds thereof.*
> **Isaiah 23:11**

Some of the altars that have been built in the minds of most Christians today include such thoughts that have been planted in their minds and which as a result of their environmental situations and traditions they have accepted as truths.

These include the belief that Satan is an evil equivalence of God and that he has power just as God has power but the only difference is that while God uses His own power for good Satan uses his own for evil. Nothing can be further from the truth!

You must destroy such strong holds in the minds of the people and show them that Satan has no power, that all power now belongs to Jesus as proved in *Volume 1* of this *"Living a supernatural life"* book series. You must also destroy all the despisers of the Word of God. That is what we are told in Proverbs 13:13. Not only that, you are also supposed to destroy the lies of all that speak leasing or lies, falsity and deceit. That is what we can see from Psalm 5:6. Every face of covering cast over the people that blinds them from seeing the truth of the Word of God must be destroyed. That is what we are told in Isaiah 25:7. And it is our responsibility to make sure that the truth of the Word is known.

> *Whoso despiseth the word shall be destroyed: but he that feareth the commandment shall be rewarded.*
> **Proverbs 13:13**

> *Thou shalt destroy them that speak leasing: the LORD will abhor the bloody and deceitful man.*
> **Psalm 5:6**

> *And he will destroy in this mountain the face of the covering cast over all people, and the vail that is spread over all nations.*
> **Isaiah 25:7**

Living a Supernatural Life (Volume 2)

Any disease or situation to which you speak the Word of God, which refuses to obey the Word is a despiser of the Word and must be destroyed. Situations that speak words contrary to what the Word of God says to you are speaking lies to you. Such situations must be destroyed. For example when you see cancer or any disease on your body, it is speaking lies to you because in 1 Peter 2:24 what the Word of God says is that you have been healed by the stripes that Jesus took.

> ***Who his own self bare our sins in his own body on the tree, that we, being dead to sins, should live unto righteousness: by whose stripes ye were healed.***
> **1 Peter 2:24**

Another example is this. You are now justified so you are the one the Scriptures refer to as the just. If you are the just therefore it means that from what is written in Proverbs 4:18 your path must be shining more and more every day.

> ***But the path of the just is as the shining light, that shineth more and more unto the perfect day.***
> **Proverbs 4:18**

This means that your today must be better than your yesterday for every day of your life. If you therefore come across a situation in which you are stagnant or your situation is getting worse rather than getting better then such a situation is speaking lies to you and it is despising the Word of God written above. You must destroy such a situation.

You are God's Battle Axe

There are some stubborn, obstinate and intractable situations that you command and they refuse to yield, that you pray about and they refuse to bulge. They just would not listen. They have become a yoke round your neck. As an anointed child of God you are supposed to destroy and uproot such situations because the yoke shall be destroyed because of the anointing. That is what we are made to understand from Isaiah 10:27. If it has also become a sort of persecution then note that whatever persecutes you is to be destroyed. That is what we understand from Jeremiah 17:18.

> *And it shall come to pass in that day, that his burden shall be taken away from off thy shoulder, and his yoke from off thy neck, and the yoke shall be destroyed because of the anointing.*
> **Isaiah 10:27**

> *Let them be confounded that persecute me, but let not me be confounded: let them be dismayed, but let not me be dismayed: bring upon them the day of evil, and destroy them with double destruction.*
> **Jeremiah 17:18**

Every work of the devil must be destroyed. That was what Jesus came to the world to do as we can see from what is written in 1 John 3:8. We are supposed to enforce Satan's defeat and demonstrate his defeat to the world. If Satan's defeat is not demonstrated to the world he will be demonstrating his fake power all over the place deceiving the people.

Living a Supernatural Life (Volume 2)

> *He that committeth sin is of the devil; for the devil sinneth from the beginning. For this purpose the Son of God was manifested, that he might destroy the works of the devil.*
>
> **1 John 3:8**

All the things that are not working in your life you must see them as works of the devil. Those are the things that Jesus Christ came to destroy. Now that He has left, He has given you the power of attorney to act on His behalf. Therefore it is now left for you to enforce Satan's defeat wherever he rears up his head. In particular, this body of sin that you carry about must be destroyed so that you will not have to serve sin anymore. That is what we are told in Romans 6:6 by God.

> *Knowing this, that our old man is crucified with him, that the body of sin might be destroyed, that henceforth we should not serve sin.*
>
> **Romans 6:6**

Before we were born again sin was reigning over us and we were in bondage to sin. We were servants of sin, which means that we were serving sin. But after our regeneration we are no longer under the bondage of sin. It is not that we can no longer sin, No! We can still be tempted by sin but we no longer have to yield to sin or indulge in it willfully. We now have the choice as to whether to yield to sin or not. The choice is ours. As a Christian we know that when we sin we have to pay a very heavy price for our sin.

This is so because every time that we sin we know that it amounts to our crucifying the Lord Jesus Christ afresh. It amounts to our siding with the ones that crucified Jesus Christ. What we are really doing when we sin, even though we may not know this, is that we are opposing the redemption work that Jesus came into the world to do.

WHAT GOD WANT'S YOU TO THROW DOWN

If you look at Judges 2:2 and Micah 5:11, you will see there what God wants to throw down. God wants to throw down the altars and the strong holds of the heathen. These include the things that have been built up as strong holds in the minds of such heathens.

> *And ye shall make no league with the inhabitants of this land; ye shall throw down their altars: but ye have not obeyed my voice: why have ye done this?*
> **Judges 2:2**

> *And I will cut off the cities of thy land, and throw down all thy strong holds:*
> **Micah 5:11**

From the language used by God to give these instructions, we can say that when Satan is trying to build strong holds in your mind as a believer God expects you to pull them down. You don't have to wait for God to come and do that for you.

But when you are dealing with strong holds, which Satan has already built in the minds of heathens and which have already been firmly rooted, you don't just pull them down you are supposed to throw them down. That was why Jesus said that you have been given power to go into the whole world and preach the Gospel to all people and convert them from their heathen and ungodly ways. That is God's objective. Throwing down is of a more forceful nature than pulling down. Therefore with altars that have already taken roots in the minds of people you have to be violent with the devil to throw them down. But please note that this battle is a spiritual battle not a physical battle. You are now God's battle-axe and weapons of war with which He wants to fight spiritually to achieve His objectives. Therefore it is now your duty to throw down all the altars built in people's mind that are not of God as well as the strong holds that have been built in their minds to protect those altars by using the Word in prayer and violent confessions.

When you try to preach the Gospel to most unbelievers they already have some other things that they believe and which they are worshipping or serving. Those are the altars that they have in their minds. They also already have some reasons, which they have built up in their minds over the years why they will not change. Those are the strong holds that Satan has built and has firmly established in their minds to protect such altars. As a battle-axe and weapons of war for God, you are supposed to attack these altars and strong holds and throw them down. You can achieve this by using the Word of God to attack such altars that they have already built in their minds.

You are God's Battle Axe

You have to throw down the altars that Satan has built in the minds of such unbelievers by preaching the Word of God to them and using the Word to attack and throw down the altars. You will be surprised what many people have in their minds which Satan has built there over the years.

WHAT GOD WANT'S YOU TO BUILD

Again we can find out what God wants to build from the Bible. If we look at Psalm 102:16, Zechariah 6:12, Ezekiel 36:36, Jeremiah 31:4 and Deuteronomy 27:5-6, we shall see there some of the things that God wants to build. You are supposed to build up Zion. You are supposed to build the temple of God that you are. You are supposed to build the ruined places. You are supposed to build the altar of the Lord.

> *When the LORD shall build up Zion, he shall appear in his glory.*
> **Psalm 102:16**

> *And speak unto him, saying, Thus speaketh the LORD of hosts, saying, Behold the man whose name is The BRANCH; and he shall grow up out of his place, and he shall build the temple of the LORD:*
> **Zechariah 6:12**

> *Then the heathen that are left round about you shall know that I the LORD build the ruined places, and plant that that was desolate: I the LORD have spoken it, and I will do it.*
> **Ezekiel 36:36**

Living a Supernatural Life (Volume 2)

> *Again I will build thee, and thou shalt be built, O virgin of Israel: thou shalt again be adorned with thy tabrets, and shalt go forth in the dances of them that make merry.*
> **Jeremiah 31:4**

> *And there shalt thou build an altar unto the LORD thy God, an altar of stones: thou shalt not lift up any iron tool upon them.*

> *Thou shalt build the altar of the LORD thy God of whole stones: and thou shalt offer burnt offerings thereon unto the LORD thy God:*
> **Deuteronomy 27:5-6**

Some other things that God wants to build include Zion the city of God, the ruined places, the altar of the Lord God and His people Israel. These are some of the things that God wants to build up. You are now His battle-axe and weapons of war. Therefore God wants to use you as His weapon to build these things up. According to what God said in 1 Corinthians 3:16 and 1 Corinthians 6:19 your body is now the temple of God.

> *Know ye not that ye are the temple of God, and that the Spirit of God dwelleth in you?*
> **1 Corinthians 3:16**

> *What? know ye not that your body is the temple of the Holy Ghost which is in you, which ye have of God, and ye are not your own?*
> **1 Corinthians 6:19**

This means that the temple of God, which He wants to build up, is the body of the saints in which His Spirit lives. In order to build up the body you have to put it under the control of the spirit. To do this we need to feed our spirits with the Word of God if we want them to grow and be strong enough to resist our bodies in the fight for the control of our minds. The way to build ourselves up is given in Acts 20:32 by God. This shows that it is the Word of God that will build us up as also confirmed by what Jesus said in Matthew 4:3-4 that the Word of God is the spiritual food that caters for our spirit just as the physical food that we eat caters for our body.

And now, brethren, I commend you to God, and to the word of his grace, which is able to build you up, and to give you an inheritance among all them which are sanctified.
Acts 20:32

And when the tempter came to him, he said, If thou be the Son of God, command that these stones be made bread.

But he answered and said, It is written, Man shall not live by bread alone, but by every word that proceedeth out of the mouth of God.
Matthew 4:3-4

God wants to build you up and He has commanded that you build yourself up in faith. The way to do this is to be constantly feeding on the Word by studying and meditating on the Word and also by praying in the Holy Ghost as written in Jude 1:20.

Living a Supernatural Life (Volume 2)

> *But ye, beloved, building up yourselves on your most holy faith, praying in the Holy Ghost,*
> **Jude 1:20**

That way you will be built up. You will become strong, and Satan will not be able to toss you around by putting thoughts, which are not of God into your mind. You will be able to eject his thoughts from your mind. As Christians under the New Covenant, God has called you to be the spiritual Israelite. The totality of believers under the New Covenant forms the new spiritual Israel of the Lord that we can call the Israelites after the spirit. That is what we can infer from what God told us through Apostle Paul in 1 Corinthians 10:18.

> *Behold Israel after the flesh: are not they which eat of the sacrifices partakers of the altar?*
> **1 Corinthians 10:18**

God wants to build up His people, the new spiritual Israel just like He did with His people the physical Israelites; the physical descendants of Abraham through Jacob. You are now one of the spiritual Israelites of God and you are God's battle-axe and weapons of war that He wants to use to build His new Israel up. How do you build up God's new-Israel? You build up God's new-Israel by building up the members that make up the nation. You build each individual member up spiritually by feeding him with the Word of God so that he can grow and become fruitful for the kingdom. Not only that, you should also contribute to their growth financially and economically.

You should make sure that you empower them business wise financially and economically. As each member of the nation grows, the nation as a whole grows. In whatever congregation of Christians you may find yourself therefore, your role there must be such that it contributes positively to the spiritual growth, physical growth, financial growth and economic growth of that congregation. That way you are actually building up the entire Body of Christ.

When new souls are won to become members of the Church and therefore a part of the Body of Christ, they must be fed continuously with the Word of God to build them up so that they can also stand against all the wiles of the enemy, Satan.

As a Christian, one of the things that God expects you to do is to feed His sheep with the Word of God. That is what God expects from you as a believer judging by what the Lord Jesus Christ told Peter in John 21:15-17. To show just how important this is to God you can see that Jesus Christ repeated that instruction to Peter three times as is shown below.

> *So when they had dined, Jesus saith to Simon Peter, Simon, son of Jonas, lovest thou me more than these? He saith unto him, Yea, Lord; thou knowest that I love thee. He saith unto him, Feed my lambs.*
>
> *He saith to him again the second time, Simon, son of Jonas, lovest thou me? He saith unto him, Yea, Lord; thou knowest that I love thee. He saith unto him, Feed my sheep.*

Living a Supernatural Life (Volume 2)

> *He saith unto him the third time, Simon, son of Jonas, lovest thou me? Peter was grieved because he said unto him the third time, Lovest thou me? And he said unto him, Lord, thou knowest all things; thou knowest that I love thee. Jesus saith unto him, Feed my sheep.*
> **John 21:15-17**

What Christ told Peter then is also applicable to you today. One of your prime responsibilities as a Christian is to make sure that you feed the people of God with the Word of God. Since the Word of God is the food for their spirit you know that you are contributing to their spiritual growth by doing this. This is therefore an essential responsibility for you as a Christian. You are now born-again. Therefore you are now born of God. You have become a member of the family of God. You are not born of the blood, or of the will of the flesh nor of the will of any man but of God. That is what you can see from what God said through John the Apostle in John 1:12-13.

> *But as many as received him, to them gave he power to become the sons of God, even to them that believe on his name:*
>
> *Which were born, not of blood, nor of the will of the flesh, nor of the will of man, but of God.*
> **John 1:12-13**

Because you are now a child of God and you belong to the family of God, you must strive to make sure that everybody in the family is built up.

When you do this then you are actually building up the entire Body of Christ since all believers are members of the Body of Christ. This is what is lacking in many Christians. They have no plan to build up other saints. That is why they find that in times of opposition they are on their own. And we all know the adage that in unity lies strength. Apart from building up the saints that are already planted God also wants you to plant some things. That is what we shall discuss in the next section.

WHAT GOD WANT'S YOU TO PLANT

Some of the things that God wants to plant are given in these Scriptures, Ezekiel 36:36, Daniel 11:45, also in Isaiah 17:10, as well as Psalm 44:2, Jeremiah 12:2, Psalm 92:13, Amos 9:15 and Jeremiah 32:14. God wants to plant that which was desolate. He wants to plant pleasant plants and His people on their lands. He also wants to plant the tabernacles of His palace between the seas in the glorious holy mountain but for this one He does not require our contribution or help.

> *Then the heathen that are left round about you shall know that I the LORD build the ruined places, and plant that that was desolate: I the LORD have spoken it, and I will do it.*
> **Ezekiel 36:36**

> *And he shall plant the tabernacles of his palace between the seas in the glorious holy mountain; yet he shall come to his end, and none shall help him.*
> **Daniel 11:45**

Because thou hast forgotten the God of thy salvation, and hast not been mindful of the rock of thy strength, therefore shalt thou plant pleasant plants, and shalt set it with strange slips:
Isaiah 17:10

How thou didst drive out the heathen with thy hand, and plantedst them; how thou didst afflict the people, and cast them out.
Psalm 44:2

Thou hast planted them, yea, they have taken root: they grow, yea, they bring forth fruit: thou art near in their mouth, and far from their reins.
Jeremiah 12:2

Those that be planted in the house of the LORD shall flourish in the courts of our God.
Psalm 92:13

And I will plant them upon their land, and they shall no more be pulled up out of their land which I have given them, saith the LORD thy God.
Amos 9:15

Thus saith the LORD of hosts, the God of Israel; Take these evidences, this evidence of the purchase, both which is sealed, and this evidence which is open; and put them in an earthen vessel, that they may continue many days.
Jeremiah 32:14

You are God's Battle Axe

As you can see from all the Scriptures above, the things that God wants to plant, which He will use you as a battle-axe and weapons of war to plant, are the followings. You are supposed to plant that which is desolate. Plant the Word of God in the people that you come across. You are supposed to plant pleasant plants and plant people in the House of God. You now know what God wants to use you as a battle-axe and weapons of war to root out, to pull down, to destroy, to throw down, to build and to plant. But *there are two things that you must note* about your role as His battle-axe and weapons of war.

The first thing that you must know and note is that the axe does not boast of itself against the one that is using it. That is what God said through Prophet Isaiah in Isaiah 10:15. God is the One using you therefore you cannot boast or magnify yourself before God.

> *Shall the axe boast itself against him that heweth therewith? or shall the saw magnify itself against him that shaketh it? as if the rod should shake itself against them that lift it up, or as if the staff should lift up itself, as if it were no wood.*
> **Isaiah 10:15**

God has given you all the necessary power that you need and the authority to back the power up. But you must not glory in that power that you now have or in the functions that you have been given by God. Instead make your boast in the Lord.

Living a Supernatural Life (Volume 2)

Boasting in yourself will be tantamount to pride and God hates pride. This is further confirmed by what God said through the Prophet Jeremiah in Jeremiah 9:23-24.

> *Thus saith the LORD, Let not the wise man glory in his wisdom, neither let the mighty man glory in his might, let not the rich man glory in his riches:*
>
> *But let him that glorieth glory in this, that he understandeth and knoweth me, that I am the LORD which exercise lovingkindness, judgment, and righteousness, in the earth: for in these things I delight, saith the LORD.*
> **Jeremiah 9:23-24**

But boasting and glorying is allowed, provided you are boasting or glorying not in yourself, but in the Lord and in the fact that you know the Lord. When you do this people will say that you are proud but boasting in the Lord is permitted.

This is confirmed by what God said above and through Paul in 1 Corinthians 1:31, and 2 Corinthians 10:17 as well as through David in Psalm 34:2. You can boast in the Lord. You can also boast in what the Lord is capable of doing through you.

> *That, according as it is written, He that glorieth, let him glory in the Lord.*
> **1 Corinthians 1:31**
>
> *But he that glorieth, let him glory in the Lord.*
> **2 Corinthians 10:17**

My soul shall make her boast in the LORD: the humble shall hear thereof, and be glad.
Psalm 34:2

However, you should know that there is a thin line between self-acclaim and pride, so be very careful. Do not say that you are glorifying God when what you are really doing is showing off your own achievements. You are not supposed to boast in what you can do but in what God can do through you. You should realize that you cannot do anything on your own for it is God that works in you. That is what God said through Apostle Paul in Philippians 2:13.

For it is God which worketh in you both to will and to do of his good pleasure.
Philippians 2:13

Any good thing that you did it was Christ that strengthened you to do it. That in essence is what God is telling us through Apostle Paul in Philippians 4:13.

I can do all things through Christ which strengtheneth me.
Philippians 4:13

The second thing that you must know and note is that God has made available to you through the Holy Spirit that is now resident in you, certain gifts that should help you to perform your functions as a battle-axe and weapons of war for God. Some of these gifts of the Holy Spirit that you can have, with which you can tackle your job as God's battle-axe and weapons of war are listed by Paul the Apostle in 1 Corinthians 12:4-12.

Now there are diversities of gifts, but the same Spirit.

And there are differences of administrations, but the same Lord.

And there are diversities of operations, but it is the same God which worketh all in all.

But the manifestation of the Spirit is given to every man to profit withal.

For to one is given by the Spirit the word of wisdom; to another the word of knowledge by the same Spirit;

To another faith by the same Spirit; to another the gifts of healing by the same Spirit;

To another the working of miracles; to another prophecy; to another discerning of spirits; to another divers kinds of tongues; to another the interpretation of tongues:

But all these worketh that one and the selfsame Spirit, dividing to every man severally as he will.

For as the body is one, and hath many members, and all the members of that one body, being many, are one body: so also is Christ.
1 Corinthians 12:4-12

You are God's Battle Axe

The ones that you will need to use mainly for this purpose are the gifts of the word of wisdom, word of knowledge, faith, healing, the working of miracles and discerning of spirits.

The Holy Spirit that you have living in you is supposed to be a comforter for you that should see you through difficult times. That is what Jesus told us in John 14:16, John 14:26, John 15:26 and John 16:7.

> *And I will pray the Father, and he shall give you another Comforter, that he may abide with you for ever;*
> **John 14:16**

> *But the Comforter, which is the Holy Ghost, whom the Father will send in my name, he shall teach you all things, and bring all things to your remembrance, whatsoever I have said unto you.*
> **John 14:26**

> *But when the Comforter is come, whom I will send unto you from the Father, even the Spirit of truth, which proceedeth from the Father, he shall testify of me:*
> **John 15:26**

> *Nevertheless I tell you the truth; It is expedient for you that I go away: for if I go not away, the Comforter will not come unto you; but if I depart, I will send him unto you.*
> **John 16:7**

Living a Supernatural Life (Volume 2)

The Holy Spirit is the Spirit of truth who abides with you and who teaches you all things and brings all things that Jesus had said to your remembrance. He guides you into all truths and shows you the things to come. He shows you the things that are of God. He is with you all the time as your helper and advocate to give you help and advice especially when you want to defend yourself against the wiles and trials from the enemy. When you are delivered for trial either by accusation or through a burden, an ordeal or adversity you don't have to think of what to say. What you will say will be given to you that same hour because you are not the one really speaking. The Spirit of your Father in you is the one that will speak through you.

These gifts and the role that the Holy Spirit plays in your supernatural living are discussed in detail in *Volume 4* of this *"Living a supernatural life"* book series by the same author.

CHAPTER 16

PULLING DOWN SATAN'S STRONG HOLDS

The battlefield for the warfare for pulling down strong holds is your mind. It is your mind that Satan wants to take control of by planting his thoughts there. You can see that the more of the Word of God you have in you, the more the likelihood of your pulling down those strong holds becomes, because as we have seen in the previous chapter from 2 Corinthians 10 4-6 you are supposed to pull them down with the Word of God. That was what Jesus did when Satan came to test Him. The way He handled those temptations by using the Word of God has been put in the Bible so as to be an example to us of the method that we should use to handle such temptations.

> *For the weapons of our warfare are not carnal, but mighty through God to the pulling down of strong holds;*
>
> *Casting down imaginations, and every high thing that exalteth itself against the knowledge of God, and bringing into captivity every thought to the obedience of Christ;*

Living a Supernatural Life (Volume 2)

And having in a readiness to revenge all disobedience, when your obedience is fulfilled.
2 Corinthians 10:4-6

Everything that was said to have been done by Satan in the temptation of Jesus Christ was done via the thoughts and imaginations that he brought into the mind of Jesus Christ. He expected Jesus to act on them. The thoughts and imaginations that you have are what eventually lead the actions that you take, if a stop is not put to them at the thought and imagination stage. If you do not stop them and pull them down at the thought or imagination stage and you allow them to progress to the action stage, they will become more difficult to pull down. Jesus Christ put a stop to those thoughts and imaginations that Satan brought into His mind by using the Word of God. What Jesus did there was written in the Scriptures so that it could be an example for us to follow. For example when you are sick and doctors tell you that there is no cure for your disease and there is no hope for you do not entertain such a thought in your mind. Know that it is an attempt by Satan to build a strong hold in your mind. Therefore expunge such a thought from your mind with the Word of God before it can be built up into a strong hold of Satan. If you entertain it and start thinking about or meditating on it Satan will turn it into a strong hold in your mind. You will then find it difficult to pull down that strong hold. When Satan comes with thoughts to build strong holds in your mind, you are supposed to do like Jesus did, which is tackling Satan with the Word of God. Satan will resist it. He will even quote the Word of God to also buttress his own points. But if you stand firm in the Word Satan must bow to it.

Pulling Down Satan's Strong Holds

I will now give you some examples of the type of thoughts and imaginations that Satan had in time past brought into my mind for processing, to try and build strong holds in my mind. I will also give for each case the Word of God which I used to pull it down.

These Scriptures that I used are by no means the only ones that you can use for these or similar cases. I am only saying that these are the ones that I used and that they worked for me. There may be better Scriptures that will work even faster for this purpose, but these were the ones that came to my mind or that I could remember quickly as at the times that the needs arose.

Living a Supernatural Life (Volume 2)

HERE THEN ON THE NEXT FEW PAGES ARE SOME THOUGHTS THAT CAN BECOME STRONG HOLDS

THOUGHTS OF GUILT-CONSCIENCE FOR SIN

When things are not working for you as they ought to, and you are going through some hard times, Satan can put into your mind, a guilt-conscience for sins that you have committed some long time before, for which you have already asked for forgiveness and been forgiven. But Satan will keep judging you of the sin and putting thoughts of guilt in your mind to give you the feeling that you have not been forgiven making you feel unworthy and giving you a guilt-complex. He will try to plant a guilt-conscience in you to make you feel that you have no right to ask for anything from God. He will be telling you that it is because of your sins that you are now going through the hard times. But if you reply him with what God said through John in 1 John 1:9 and tell him that **It is written,**

> *"If we confess our sins, he is faithful and just to forgive us our sins, and to cleanse us from all unrighteousness."*
>
> **1 John 1:9**

Then he will leave you alone for some time.

THAT GOD WILL NOT HELP YOU

Many times if things still continue to be a little hard for you and things seem not to be working the way they should for you, Satan will then come back with the thoughts that you will not be able to get out of that hard situation because God has forgotten all about you.

He may even ask, *"How do you know that God will help you?"* But if you reply him with what God said in Lamentation 3:31 and 2 Chronicles 15:7 and tell him that it is written that the Lord will not cast you off forever and your work will be rewarded. Tell him that **it is written,**

"For the Lord will not cast off for ever:
Lamentation 3:31

Be ye strong therefore, and let not your hands be weak: for your work shall be rewarded."
2 Chronicles 15:7

He will take those thoughts away from your mind. He will not be able to plant them in your mind.

THAT GOD WILL NOT GIVE YOU SOMETHING THAT BIG

But he will only leave you for some time. Sooner or later he will come back. Sometimes later, may be days, weeks or even some months afterwards you may be asking God for some things in prayer, and Satan will start trying to plant the thought in your mind that what you are asking for is too much and therefore God will not do them for you.

He may even tell you that if God is to give you what you want you will have to pay dearly for it. But when you reply him with what God told us through Paul in Romans 8:32 and tell him that **it is written,**

> *"He that spared not his own Son, but delivered him up for us all, how shall he not with him also freely give us all things?"*
> **Romans 8:32**

Then he will again leave you for sometime when he sees that you have beaten him to that.

THAT YOU WILL NOT GET ALL YOU ASKED OF GOD

But he may return and put a modification of the thought in your mind by stating that you will get some of the things you asked of God but not everything that you asked for. When you reply him with what God said through His Apostles in 1 John 3:22, Matthew 7:9-10 and also in Ephesians 3:20 that God is able to do exceeding abundantly above all that you can ask or even think. Tell him that **it is written,**

> *"And whatsoever we ask, we receive of him, because we keep his commandments, and do those things that are pleasing in his sight."*
> **1 John 3:22**

That **it is also written,**

> *"Or what man is there of you, whom if his son ask bread, will he give him a stone?*
>
> *Or if he ask a fish, will he give him a serpent?*
> **Matthew 7:9-10**

Living a Supernatural Life (Volume 2)

> *Now unto him that is able to do exceeding abundantly above all that we ask or think, according to the power that worketh in us,"*
> **Ephesians 3:20**

Then those thoughts of Satan will disappear from your mind and he will again leave you alone for sometime. He will not be able to build those thoughts into a strong hold in your mind.

THE THOUGHT THAT YOU ARE FINISHED

However, that does not mean that he has left you for good. No! He will come back again. Despite all your resistance to Satan, if you have not been able to get what you asked from God, you may come to a point where you find that some things are going wrong and it looks like your world is falling apart.

Then Satan will come into your mind boasting, putting in your mind the thoughts that you've had it this time. He will tell you that you are finished. He will start to ask you, "Did I not tell you that you cannot get all those things that you asked of God? Have I not told you so?" If you reply him with what God said the Scriptures in Lamentation 3:37 and tell him that **it is written,**

> *"Who is he that saith, and it cometh to pass, when the Lord commandeth it not?"*
> **Lamentation 3:37**

Then he will leave you alone and those thoughts will leave your mind.

SATAN TEMPTS YOU TO COMPLAIN OR MURMUR

But Satan will only leave you alone just for a while because if things remain unchanged he will come back into your mind putting the thoughts that things ought not to be the way that they are. He will want to get you to start thinking, complaining and murmuring in your mind. Instead of accepting his thoughts and imaginations, you should reply him right there with what God said in Ecclesiastes 7:10, also through Paul in 1 Corinthians 10:10, through Luke in Luke 7:23 and through David in Psalm 67:5-6. Tell him that **it is written,**

> *"Say not thou, What is the cause that the former days were better than these? for thou dost not enquire wisely concerning this.*
> **Ecclesiastes 7:10**

> *Neither murmur ye, as some of them also murmured, and were destroyed of the destroyer.*
> **1 Corinthians 10:10**

> *And blessed is he, whosoever shall not be offended in me.*
> **Luke 7:23**

> *Let the people praise thee, O God; let all the people praise thee.*
>
> *Then shall the earth yield her increase; and God, even our own God, shall bless us."*
> **Psalm 67:5-6**

You should then start to praise and worship God instead of complaining and murmuring. When you praise God He will bless you. Satan will be sad and he will leave you alone and take his thoughts away from your mind.

BRINGS THE THOUGHT THAT GOD IS FAR FROM YOU

But despite all the steadfastness of your stand against Satan, you may find that even though you have cried and sang praises to the Lord sometimes over some of those things that have been challenges in your life or somebody else's life, there may still be no answer forthcoming. If such challenges persist and you are not very conversant with God's methods, Satan may come again into your mind with his thought to set you into thinking that God is very far from you. He will tell you that if God cares so much for you He would have answered you. He will try to put it in your mind that God is not as near to you as you had believed. You reply him with what God said in Matthew 28:20, in Psalm 119:151 as well as in Psalm 145:18 and let him know that it is written, that God is near to you and is with you always. Then Satan will know that he has failed in his effort to establish that thought as a strong hold in your mind and he will leave you alone for that period and take his evil thought away from your mind. Tell him that **it is written,**

> *"Teaching them to observe all things whatsoever I have commanded you: and, lo, I am with you alway, even unto the end of the world. Amen.*
> **Matthew 28:20**

Pulling Down Satan's Strong Holds

Thou art near, O LORD; and all thy commandments are truth.
Psalm 119:151

The LORD is nigh unto all them that call upon him, to all that call upon him in truth."
Psalm 145:18

BRINGS THOUGHTS OF RESTLESSNESS

He may come back and start to put other thoughts in your mind that will begin to make you feel restless about your situation. If you allow his thoughts of restlessness to stay in your mind, you will become agitated.

But when he comes with such thoughts, uproot them from your mind by replying him with what the Word of God says in Psalm 46:10 and Isaiah 26:3. Tell him that you refuse to be restless and you will not be agitated since you know that God will keep you in perfect peace and it is when you are still that you will see Him fight your battles because **it is written,**

"Be still, and know that I am God: I will be exalted among the heathen, I will be exalted in the earth".
Psalm 46:10

"Thou wilt keep him in perfect peace, whose mind is stayed on thee: because he trusteth in thee."
Isaiah 26:3

Then he will leave you alone and take that thought away from your mind.

BRINGS THE THOUGHT THAT WHAT YOU DECREED WILL NOT BE ESTABLISHED

During your prayers to God you probably have been decreeing what you want because you know that as a believer, you have been given the authority to decree things and have them established.

Therefore you have probably been decreeing the changes that you want but you may find that your situation still has not changed. You will therefore start shouting your decrees even the more. Satan will also use this.

When you decree things like that, Satan will come and put in your mind the thought that what you have decreed will not be established and therefore will not come to pass. He will put doubt in your mind. You just reply him with what God promised in Mark 11:23, Matthew 17:20, Job 22:28 and also in Romans 10:10. Tell him that you will have whatever you decree and God will establish it because **it is written,**

> *"For verily I say unto you, That whosoever shall say unto this mountain, Be thou removed, and be thou cast into the sea; and shall not doubt in his heart, but shall believe that those things which he saith shall come to pass; he shall have whatsoever he saith.*
> **Mark 11:23**

And Jesus said unto them, Because of your unbelief: for verily I say unto you, If ye have faith as a grain of mustard seed, ye shall say unto this mountain, Remove hence to yonder place; and it shall remove; and nothing shall be impossible unto you.
Matthew 17:20

Thou shalt also decree a thing, and it shall be established unto thee: and the light shall shine upon thy ways.
Job 22:28

For with the heart man believeth unto righteousness; and with the mouth confession is made unto salvation."
Romans 10:10

If you do that, Satan will leave you alone for that time and the thought of doubt that he tried to plant in your mind will go.

THOUGHT THAT WHAT YOU DECREED WILL NOT BE ESTABLISHED BECAUSE IT IS NOT GOD'S WORD

But Satan never stops trying to plant thoughts in the mind of the believer therefore he will come back again sooner or later with new thoughts and new schemes. Such new thoughts and schemes will probably be made to be more appealing for you to accept into your mind.

Living a Supernatural Life (Volume 2)

He may come back to put thoughts into your mind that explains why what you have decreed cannot be established. He will tell you that what you decreed will not be established by God for you. He may tell you that the promise says if you have faith and then ask you whether you think that you have the necessary faith. He can also put it in your mind that the words that you have decreed are your own words and not God's Word.

He will then put it in your mind that if you had spoken God's Word alone to the situation in your decree, then it would have worked. By so doing he is trying to build a strong hold in your mind. Yes! God's Word will be established if you speak them out. But God will also establish your own words that you speak out. God did not say whosoever shall speak my Word to this mountain.

God did not say if ye shall speak my Word to this mountain. God did not say thou shalt decree my Word and I will establish it. However Satan will try to put it in your mind that if what you decreed had been God's Word it would have been established. If you want him to leave you alone then you reply him with what God said in His Word in Luke 21:15, Matthew 17:20, Proverbs 18:21, Job 22:28 and Isaiah 44:24-26 and tell him that you have a mouth and wisdom, which he cannot resist and the Lord will confirm your words because **it is written,**

> *"For I will give you a mouth and wisdom, which all your adversaries shall not be able to gainsay nor resist.*
> **Luke 21:15**

Pulling Down Satan's Strong Holds

And Jesus said unto them, Because of your unbelief: for verily I say unto you, If ye have faith as a grain of mustard seed, ye shall say unto this mountain, Remove hence to yonder place; and it shall remove; and nothing shall be impossible unto you.
Mathew 17:20

Death and life are in the power of the tongue: and they that love it shall eat the fruit thereof.
Proverbs 18:21

Thou shalt also decree a thing, and it shall be established unto thee: and the light shall shine upon thy ways.
Job 22:28

Thus saith the LORD, thy redeemer, and he that formed thee from the womb, I am the LORD that maketh all things; that stretcheth forth the heavens alone; that spreadeth abroad the earth by myself;

That frustrateth the tokens of the liars, and maketh diviners mad; that turneth wise men backward, and maketh their knowledge foolish;

That confirmeth the word of his servant, and performeth the counsel of his messengers; that saith to Jerusalem, Thou shalt be inhabited; and to the cities of Judah, Ye shall be built, and I will raise up the decayed places thereof:"
Isaiah 44:24-26

Let Satan know that God did not say, "Whosoever shall speak my Word to this mountain." God did not say, "Ye shall speak my Word unto this mountain." God did not say, "Thou shalt decree my Word and I will establish it unto you."

So you can root out the idea that Satan is putting in your mind that if what you decreed had been God's Word it would have been established. Once you do that, Satan will leave you alone, because he will not be able to establish that thought as a strong hold in your mind.

QUESTIONS THE TRUTH OF GOD'S WORD

But do not think that this will be the end of the attempt of Satan to build a strong hold in your mind. He will continue to try to find thoughts that he can bring into your mind, which you can accept and, which he can build into strong holds in your mind.

For example, if the answer to what you decreed is still not forthcoming, Satan may come into your mind and start to put thoughts to create further doubts in your mind by questioning you about your assurance of the Word of God.

He may say, *"Yes! The Word said that whatever you decree will be established for you, but how are you sure that what the Word says will always work? Do you not think that it is too simple if all you have to do is to just decree and it will come to pass?"*

Pulling Down Satan's Strong Holds

This is one of Satan's most frequent questions that he brings into the mind of man. He wants to test your resolve concerning the truth of the Word of God. Satan will even go into the minds of other people and use them to come and speak to you to persuade you to see things his own way. You can reply him with what the Word of God says in Psalm 119:89, in Mark 10:27, in John 10:35, Hebrews 12:1, Judges 2:1, Psalm 89:34 and in 2 Corinthians 11:3 and tell him that it is written that God's Word is settled for ever, that the Scripture cannot be broken, that God will never break His covenant and that you will not underestimate the Gospel of Christ because of its simplicity. Emphasize to him that the Word of God cannot be broken since it is settled for ever in heaven. Tell him that **it is written,**

"For ever, O LORD, thy word is settled in heaven.
Psalm 119:89

And Jesus looking upon them saith, With men it is impossible, but not with God: for with God all things are possible.
Mark 10:27

If he called them gods, unto whom the word of God came, and the scripture cannot be broken;
John 10:35

Wherefore seeing we also are compassed about with so great a cloud of witnesses, let us lay aside every weight, and the sin which doth so easily beset us, and let us run with patience the race that is set before us,
Hebrews 12:1

> *And an angel of the LORD came up from Gilgal to Bochim, and said, I made you to go up out of Egypt, and have brought you unto the land which I sware unto your fathers; and I said, I will never break my covenant with you.*
> **Judges 2:1**

> *My covenant will I not break, nor alter the thing that is gone out of my lips.*
> **Psalm 89:34**

> *But I fear, lest by any means, as the serpent beguiled Eve through his subtilty, so your minds should be corrupted from the simplicity that is in Christ."*
> **2 Corinthians 11:3**

When you do this, Satan will once again carry his thought that questions the truth of God's Word away and leave you alone.

BRINGS THE THOUGHT THAT YOU WILL HAVE TO WAIT LONG TO GET AN ANSWER

But if the answer to what you decreed still delays and takes much longer in coming or being established for you, Satan will come back to your mind to plant new thoughts that will erode your confidence in the truth that what you decreed will be established. He may tell you that if God will answer you He should have done so by now.

He will tell you that you will wait long and even despite your long wait you may not get your answer from God. He may even bring some facts that he can use to show you that the truth of the Word of God will not always come to pass.

Tell him that those are just facts, not the truth. The truth is what the Word says in Luke 21:19 as well as in Jeremiah 1:12 and Hebrews 10:35-36 that through patience you will win. Tell him that **it is written,**

> *"In your patience possess ye your souls.*
> **Luke 21:19**

> *Then said the LORD unto me, Thou hast well seen: for I will hasten my word to perform it.*
> **Jeremiah 1:12**

> *Cast not away therefore your confidence, which hath great recompence of reward.*
>
> *For ye have need of patience, that, after ye have done the will of God, ye might receive the promise."*
> **Hebrews 10:35-36**

Satan will immediately carry his thought away, because he will realize that you are willing to wait for God and that he cannot establish that thought to deviate from God's plan as a strong hold in your mind. He knows that with your resolve you will eventually get what you have decreed because your decree will be established if you are steadfast in your faith.

Living a Supernatural Life (Volume 2)

BRINGS THE THOUGHT THAT YOUR VICTORY WILL NOT LAST

When what you decreed now comes to pass and you have victory, or in any situation where you have victory over Satan's forces of darkness, do not think that is the end of the combat with Satan. He will go for another strategy. Satan may come back into your mind to plant the thought that your victory is just for a short while. He will try to build a strong hold in your mind with this thought. He may tell you that things may still change back and that your victory cannot last long. You should reply Satan with what the Word of God says as written in Ecclesiastes 3:14, in 1 John 4:4, in 1 John 5:4-5 and also through Paul in 2 Corinthians 2:14 that whatever God does is for ever, that the greater one than is in the world is living in you and that you have overcome the world and your faith in God is what has given you the victory. Let him know that you know that your victory is not a fluke. Let him know that God will always cause you to triumph in every situation that you can ever come across. Tell him that **it is written,**

> *"I know that, whatsoever God doeth, it shall be for ever: nothing can be put to it, nor any thing taken from it: and God doeth it, that men should fear before him.*
> **Ecclesiastes 3:14**

> *Ye are of God, little children, and have overcome them: because greater is he that is in you, than he that is in the world.*
> **1 John 4:4**

For whatsoever is born of God overcometh the world: and this is the victory that overcometh the world, even our faith.

Who is he that overcometh the world, but he that believeth that Jesus is the Son of God?
1 John 5:4-5

Now thanks be unto God, which always causeth us to triumph in Christ, and maketh manifest the savour of his knowledge by us in every place."
2 Corinthians 2:14

Satan will leave immediately with his thought. He will later come with other thoughts that may not even have to do with what you have just gone through.

BRINGS THE THOUGHT THAT YOU WILL GO DOWN WITH OTHERS

For example, the economic and trade situation in your country may suddenly take a downturn, and your country may start to go through a recession or even a depression that could be tough and damaging to your financial position. In such situations Satan may come back into your mind with thoughts of the fear of what may happen to you. He may say, *"Now you've had it. I will want to see how you will escape this economic crunch."* He will further tell you, "In particular I will want to see how you will cope with your family responsibilities." Tell him that you are really no longer of this world you are only living in this world. You don't have to fear what the world fears.

Living a Supernatural Life (Volume 2)

Tell him that as written in Philippians 4:19 God will supply all your needs according to His riches in glory by Christ Jesus. Tell him that **it is written,**

> *But my God shall supply all your need according to his riches in glory by Christ Jesus.*
> **Philippians. 4:19**

BRINGS THOUGHTS OF FEAR

He may leave but he may also put it in your mind that this time you cannot be exempted from this and that you are really going to suffer so as to create fear in you. Just reply Satan with what God said in 2 Timothy 1:7 and Romans 8:15. Tell him that you no longer have the spirit of fear. Tell him that the Spirit in you is no longer that of bondage to fear but that of power, and of love, and of a sound mind. Tell him that **it is written,**

> *"For God hath not given us the spirit of fear; but of power, and of love, and of a sound mind.*
> **2 Timothy 1:7**

> *For ye have not received the spirit of bondage again to fear; but ye have received the Spirit of adoption, whereby we cry, Abba, Father."*
> **Romans 8:15**

If you do this Satan will take his thoughts of fear away from your mind. Satan cannot plant fear in your mind as a Christian unless you agree with him. You no longer have the spirit of fear.

The Spirit living in you is a Spirit of power, of love and of a sound mind. You are no longer under any bondage to fear. Therefore Satan should no longer be able to succeed in using fear against you if you know that you no longer have that spirit.

BRINGS THE THOUGHT THAT YOU WILL SUFFER

If the economic crunch still persists and Satan brings the thought that you will suffer into your mind you must quickly let him know that whatever is happening in this world system cannot hold you down because you are no longer of this world. God's Kingdom that you now represent here on earth as an ambassador will always supply your needs. The Kingdom is rich in all things and there is nothing that you can ever want that cannot be supplied by that Kingdom.

Therefore tell him what God said in Isaiah 60:2 as well as in 1 Peter 2:9-10, also in Psalm 37:18-19 and in Roman 8:28 that you are called to show forth God's praises and He will satisfy you even in famine. Tell him that you belong to a chosen generation that is meant to show forth the praises of God not Satan's woes. Tell him that **it is written,**

> *"For, behold, the darkness shall cover the earth, and gross darkness the people: but the LORD shall arise upon thee, and his glory shall be seen upon thee.*
>
> **Isaiah 60:2**

> *But ye are a chosen generation, a royal priesthood, an holy nation, a peculiar people; that ye should shew forth the praises of him who hath called you out of darkness into his marvellous light:*
>
> *Which in time past were not a people, but are now the people of God: which had not obtained mercy, but now have obtained mercy.*
> **1 Peter 2:9-10**
>
> *The LORD knoweth the days of the upright: and their inheritance shall be for ever.*
>
> *They shall not be ashamed in the evil time: and in the days of famine they shall be satisfied."*
> **Psalm 37:18-19**
>
> *And we know that all things work together for good to them that love God, to them who are the called according to his purpose.*
> **Romans 8:28**

Satan will know that you have the right knowledge that can see you through the recession and he will therefore also leave you alone and take along his thought of fear about what may happen from your mind.

But he will not leave you for long he will come back again because he will continue to probe you looking for a weakness that he can take advantage of to plant his thoughts in your mind as strong holds.

BRINGS THE THOUGHT THAT YOU CANNOT MAKE IT WHERE MR. X HAS FAILED

But your situation may not necessarily change immediately. If the economic situation is still biting you hard, he will come back again at an opportune time. He will look for an appropriate time to throw another thought into your mind. If as a result of this economic downturn of your country, or for some other reasons your work or business continues steeply on the downward trend and you start to run at a loss, you may even find that all your labour seem to be yielding no returns. All the policies that the Government is bringing up seem to be making things worse for you. At such times Satan may come back with his thoughts into your mind to tell you once again that you've had it but he will support himself with more convincing reasons this time. He may say to you, *"Didn't I tell you that you've had it? Now you know that you've really had it this time. Let me see how you will get out of this situation now."* Satan may start to use some people you know very well as examples to you. He may say, *"Look at Mr. X who is much richer than you. He is suffering and unable to bear the crunch. Do you think you can bear the crunch? Do you think that you will be able to cope?"* He will say that no matter how hard you work you will not get anything. You can reply him with what God said through Apostle Paul in 2 Timothy 2:6 and through Solomon in Proverbs 14:23, to let him know that you will profit from your labour even if the economy is worse than it is. Tell him that **it is written,**

Living a Supernatural Life (Volume 2)

> *"The husbandman that laboureth must be first partaker of the fruits.*
> **2 Timothy 2:6**

> *In all labour there is profit: but the talk of the lips tendeth only to penury."*
> **Proverbs 14:23**

Satan will leave you alone and take those thoughts away from your mind to wait for a more opportune time to attack your mind. But it may be sooner than later.

BRINGS WORRY TO YOUR MIND

If the situation still persists he will again bring thoughts of anxiety and worry into your mind. He will bring such thoughts to make you to worry about how you may not be able to cope with your financial and other responsibilities as a father or mother, and get your mind agitated. You can reply him with what the Word says in Matthew 6:34, Philippians 4:19, Philippians 4:6-7, Psalm 5:12 as well as in 1 Peter 5:7. Tell him that God will supply all your needs and you know that He will bless you. Whatever God will not supply, it means that you don't need it because God will always supply whatever you need since **it is written,**

> *"Take therefore no thought for the morrow: for the morrow shall take thought for the things of itself. Sufficient unto the day is the evil thereof.*
> **Matthew 6:34**

But my God shall supply all your need according to his riches in glory by Christ Jesus.
Philippians 4:19

Be careful for nothing; but in every thing by prayer and supplication with thanksgiving let your requests be made known unto God.

And the peace of God, which passeth all understanding, shall keep your hearts and minds through Christ Jesus.
Philippians 4:6-7

For thou, LORD, wilt bless the righteous; with favour wilt thou compass him as with a shield.
Psalm 5:12

Casting all your care upon him; for he careth for you."
1 Peter 5:7

Satan will leave you alone and take his thoughts of worry and anxiety away from your mind.

SATAN TEMPTS YOU TO OFFER BRIBE

However if the situation still persists he will come back with some new thoughts into your mind. He will watch out for the right time when you may be vulnerable and likely to accept his thoughts into your mind. For example if your work involves taking contract jobs, he may tell you that it may be judicious for you to bribe some people so that you can be awarded a particular contract job.

Living a Supernatural Life (Volume 2)

He will tell you that the situation that you now are warrants that you bend the rules if you want to succeed. He can even go into the minds of some of your friends and plant the thoughts in them to come and advise you along that line. He may even use people that you have considered to be spiritually upright including even your Pastor or your spiritual mentor to come and convince you to do so. He will pile the pressure on you from all directions urging you to give what he has said a place in your mind so that he can build the thought into a strong hold in your mind. He will turn the screw on you and bombard your mind so much that you will start to feel that everything around you is crumbling and that bribing may be your only way out. You should reply him by telling him what the Word says as written in Psalm 127:1-2 and Zechariah 4:6. Tell him that it is not your struggling that matters but the Spirit of the Lord will do the job because **it is written,**

"Except the LORD build the house, they labour in vain that build it: except the LORD keep the city, the watchman waketh but in vain.

It is vain for you to rise up early, to sit up late, to eat the bread of sorrows: for so he giveth his beloved sleep."
Psalm 127:1-2

Then he answered and spake unto me, saying, This is the word of the Lord unto Zerubbabel, saying, Not by might, nor by power, but by my spirit, saith the Lord of hosts.
Zechariah 4:6

Satan will leave you alone when he hears this because he will realize that you know that your success depends only on God and not on the circumstances that you may create or find yourself. So he knows that you won't worry yourself.

SHOWS YOU EXAMPLES OF PEOPLE WHO HAVE BRIBED AND SUCCEEDED

However if the situation still persists, he may come back to your mind showing you physical signs of some people who have bribed, and have been given contracts. He will then buttress his thoughts, which he has put in your mind with these physical proofs. He may even make sure that tempting offers of big contracts for which bribes are demanded come your way at that point in time.

At such times he will bring pictures of some of your peers that have bribed to become very prosperous so as to tempt you and make you envious. He will show you and let you know that the prosperity of such people came as a result of the bribes that they paid. You should reply him with what God said through King David in Psalm 37:1-2, 5, 7-10 and also in Psalm 37:16, 22. Tell him that **it is written,**

> *"Fret not thyself because of evildoers, neither be thou envious against the workers of iniquity.*
>
> *For they shall soon be cut down like the grass, and wither as the green herb.*

Living a Supernatural Life (Volume 2)

Commit thy way unto the LORD; trust also in him; and he shall bring it to pass.

Rest in the LORD, and wait patiently for him: fret not thyself because of him who prospereth in his way, because of the man who bringeth wicked devices to pass.

Cease from anger, and forsake wrath: fret not thyself in any wise to do evil.

For evildoers shall be cut off: but those that wait upon the LORD, they shall inherit the earth.

For yet a little while, and the wicked shall not be: yea, thou shalt diligently consider his place, and it shall not be.
Psalm 37:1, 2, 5, 7, 8, 9, 10

A little that a righteous man hath is better than the riches of many wicked.

For such as be blessed of him shall inherit the earth; and they that be cursed of him shall be cut off."
Psalm 37:16, 22

He will then leave with his thoughts. But should he still tarry you can reply him with what God said through Paul in 2 Corinthians 5:7, and also what is written in the Second Book of kings in 2 Kings 6:16. Tell him that you do not walk by sight and that you know that those that are with you are more than those that are with him because **it is written,**

"For we walk by faith, not by sight:
> **2 Corinthians 5:7**

And he answered, Fear not: for they that be with us are more than they that be with them."
> **2 Kings 6:16**

When you tell Satan these he will leave with his thoughts. But if the situation still persists, he may come back through a new line of thoughts, hoping to plant them in your mind as strong holds.

BRINGS THOUGHTS THAT YOU ARE SUFFERING FROM AN ANCESTRAL CURSE

For example, if the economic situation of your country has improved, but your own personal situation has not improved, he may put it in your mind directly or through some people that what is happening to you is not a normal situation and that you are suffering as a result of some curse that have been operating in your family from the time of your ancestors.

He will tell you that what you are going through has come as a result of some evil thing that one of your ancestors did. He may use some people even those that you believe are prophets of God to also tell you this.

You may even find that your own Pastor will suddenly preach about ancestral curses and Satan will put it to you that he is talking about you. He will bring back the bribery thoughts.

Living a Supernatural Life (Volume 2)

People that you have a lot of respect for may even come to you trying to persuade you that it is not wrong or unchristian to give a bribe. He will even give examples of some of your older living or dead family members that have suffered as a result of that curse. In fact, when you look at the conditions in which such people are your faith may shake.

But you can reply Satan with what God said through Prophet Ezekiel in Ezekiel 18:20, and through Paul in Galatians 3:13-14 as well as in Colossians 2:13-14. Tell him that you don't have to carry the sins of anybody; it is the soul that sinneth that will carry his blame. You have been redeemed from the curse of the law so you don't have to suffer from any curse anymore. Tell him that you have been forgiven all your sins and Christ has taken out of the way all the handwriting of ordinances that were against you and contrary to you and nailed them to the Cross and that you will not take a bribe. Tell him that **it is written,**

> *"The soul that sinneth, it shall die. The son shall not bear the iniquity of the father, neither shall the father bear the iniquity of the son: the righteousness of the righteous shall be upon him, and the wickedness of the wicked shall be upon him.*
>
> **Ezekiel 18:20**

> *Christ hath redeemed us from the curse of the law, being made a curse for us: for it is written, Cursed is every one that hangeth on a tree:*

> *That the blessing of Abraham might come on the Gentiles through Jesus Christ; that we might receive the promise of the Spirit through faith.*
> **Galatians 3:13-14**

> *And you, being dead in your sins and the uncircumcision of your flesh, hath he quickened together with him, having forgiven you all trespasses;*

> *Blotting out the handwriting of ordinances that was against us, which was contrary to us, and took it out of the way, nailing it to his cross;"*
> **Colossians 2:13-14**

Once you can reply Satan with these verses from the Scriptures Satan will know that you have once again defeated him and he will take his thoughts that you are suffering as a result of a family curse or an ancestral curse and leave you alone. But do not think that he is gone for good; he will still come back again. He will look for an opportune time to strike back at you.

THOUGHTS THAT GOD IS THE ONE AFFLICTING YOU

Yes! He may come back to put in your mind that strange thought that since you have waited so long on God and you have not turned to either the left or right, yet God did not give you the answer that you want then it is possible that your affliction must have come directly from God.

Living a Supernatural Life (Volume 2)

Now, that has deceived many Christians and has been the knock-out blow that Satan used against many Christians. He will even try to prove his point to you in your mind. He will bring examples such as Job's affliction into your mind to prove this. In such a situation you should reply him with what the Word of God says in 3 John 2, also in Jeremiah 29:11, as well as in 1 Corinthians 10:13 and in John 10:10. Tell him that what God wants for you is prosperity and peace. Tell him that God's thoughts towards you are thoughts of peace and not of evil. Tell him that God may allow, but He is not the One bringing trials to you and in any case whatever trials may come to you it is because God knows that you can cope with it. That is why He allowed it. Tell him that Christ came so that you can live an abundant life. Tell him that **it is written,**

> *"Beloved, I wish above all things that thou mayest prosper and be in health, even as thy soul prospereth.*
> **3 John 2**

> *For I know the thoughts that I think toward you, saith the LORD, thoughts of peace, and not of evil, to give you an expected end."*
> **Jeremiah 29:11**

> *There hath no temptation taken you but such as is common to man: but God is faithful, who will not suffer you to be tempted above that ye are able; but will with the temptation also make a way to escape, that ye may be able to bear it.*
> **1 Corinthians 10:13**

The thief cometh not, but for to steal, and to kill, and to destroy: I am come that they might have life, and that they might have it more abundantly.

John 10:10

Satan will immediately take that thought away from your mind but he will come back sometimes again with other thoughts.

THOUGHTS THAT EVERYBODY IS AGAINST YOU

However another scenario may then develop in this form. Your business has once again picked up, and you are doing well once again. But then you may suddenly start to get verbal attacks from all directions, even from those people that you have considered as being your friends. You find that such people have suddenly changed and taken positions against you and on the side of your enemies. Some of these friends may become envious of your success and just change suddenly against you.

Satan may then come with his thoughts into your mind telling you that practically everybody is now your enemy and your enemies are just too many for you to cope with. He will try to prove to you that there is no way you can win against them. You should reply him with what God said in Nahum 1:12-13, in 2 Kings 6:16, Isaiah 8:10, Isaiah 50:8 in Isaiah 54:17 as well as also in 1 John 4:4. **Tell him that it is written,**

"Thus saith the LORD; Though they be quiet, and likewise many, yet thus shall they be cut down, when he shall pass through. Though I have afflicted thee, I will afflict thee no more.

For now will I break his yoke from off thee, and will burst thy bonds in sunder.
Nahum 1:12-13

And he answered, Fear not: for they that be with us are more than they that be with them."
2 Kings 6:16

Take counsel together, and it shall come to nought; speak the word, and it shall not stand: for God is with us.
Isaiah 8:10

He is near that justifieth me; who will contend with me? let us stand together: who is mine adversary? let him come near to me.
Isaiah 50:8

No weapon that is formed against thee shall prosper; and every tongue that shall rise against thee in judgment thou shalt condemn. This is the heritage of the servants of the LORD, and their righteousness is of me, saith the LORD."
Isaiah 54:17

Ye are of God, little children, and have overcome them: because greater is he that is in you, than he that is in the world.
1 John 4:4

Tell him that the Lord will break their yoke, whatever they speak against you shall not stand, every counsel of theirs will come to nothing; that every weapon they fashion against you shall not prosper and that you have the host of Heaven with you and these host of heaven that are with you are greater than anything that your enemies can put up. Not only that, tell him that the greater One than those that are in the world is in you and you have already overcome them

If you give these Scriptures above as your reply, Satan will quickly leave you alone and take those thoughts away from your mind. No matter how many enemies may come against you God has said that they will never overcome you. In fact no matter what you may be going through God has said that you have already won the battle. Therefore you don't have to allow Satan to give you the impression that the size or strength of the enemy forces are of any effect in the battle that you are involve in or fighting.

THOUGHTS THAT GOD DID NOT HEAR YOUR PRAYER

But even if you have prayed to God concerning the reproaches that these enemies are sticking on you, they may not disappear immediately. They might have implicated you with their words to the extent that people start to believe their words.

The afflictions and torments that come as a result of such reproaches from your enemies may still continue for a while before the answer to your prayer manifests physically. If that happens, Satan may come back into your mind with the thought that God has not heard your prayer. Like he did to Jesus, Satan may even quote the Scriptures to tell you what God said through John telling you that **it is also written in 1 John 5:14-15,**

> *"And this is the confidence that we have in him, that, if we ask any thing according to his will, he heareth us:*
>
> *And if we know that he hear us, whatsoever we ask, we know that we have the petitions that we desired of him."*
>
> **1 John 5:14-15**

BRINGS THOUGHTS THAT YOU HAVE NOT ASKED ACCORDING TO GOD'S WILL

He will then tell you that the reason why you have not got what you asked for is either because you have not asked according to God's will or because you were not sure that He heard you. He may even insinuate that he knows that God has not even heard you and therefore you cannot be confident that you will get what you asked for. He will quote the above Scripture to put doubt in your mind as to whether what you have been saying to God ever got to Him. He will bring into your mind pictures of people and situations where you have seen that people that you consider upright cried and cried to God and did not get a reply.

Pulling Down Satan's Strong Holds

He may even put the same thought into somebody's mind to pass the same message to you. But you just reply him with what God said in Psalm 66:19. Tell him that God has heard you and He has attended to the voice of your prayer. Tell him that **it is written,**

> *"But verily God hath heard me; he hath attended to the voice of my prayer."*
> **Psalm 66:19**

He will then leave you alone for some time. But if your prayer still remains unanswered and the affliction does not stop, despite the fact that you have said that you know that God has heard you, Satan will come back with a new plan against you. He will look for the appropriate moment to do this.

THOUGHTS THAT YOU ARE POWERLESS

Satan may come back and start boasting to you, putting in your mind the thoughts that he and his forces could be the ones stopping your prayers from being answered and that your prayers will not go to God because he has the power to stop them. He may even tell you that you are powerless and very weak against his own forces of darkness. He will also try to put it in your mind and also show you that his forces that you see as enemies are smarter than you are and therefore you stand no chance against them. He will tell you that these enemies will destroy you and that it is just a matter of time for your end to come. Reply him with what God said in Philippians 2:13, and Psalm 119:98. Tell him that **it is written,**

Living a Supernatural Life (Volume 2)

> *"For it is God which worketh in you both to will and to do of his good pleasure.*
>
> **Philippians 2:13**

> *Thou through thy commandments hast made me wiser than mine enemies: for they are ever with me."*
>
> **Psalm 119:98**

Tell him that it is God that works in you both to will and to do His good pleasure therefore you are smarter and wiser than your enemies.

Satan will leave you alone for a while. But if your prayer still remains unanswered he will come back.

BRINGS THOUGHTS THAT YOU ARE A LAME DUCK

He may come back boasting the more and putting the thoughts in your mind that since you have tried so much and God has refused to answer then you must be very weak. He will tell you that you are a lame duck and you are powerless against him. He will tell you that you have no option but to accept his ways so as to get what you want. You should reply him by saying that you are strong because even if you look weak it is written in Joel 3:10 that the weak should say that he is strong. Tell him that **it is written,**

> *"Beat your plowshares into swords, and your pruninghooks into spears: let the weak say, I am strong."*
>
> **Joel 3:10**

BRINGS THOUGHTS THAT YOU ARE VERY WEAK

When you tell him this thinking that you have got him Satan will obviously laugh at you and say that you must be stupid otherwise how can you in your situation say that you are strong when you look and feel so weak? He will ask, "Do you really believe that?" He will taunt you and let you see all your weaknesses. But if you now tell him that you are strong since you can do anything through Christ who strengthens you as written down in Philippians 4:13. Tell him it is obvious that Christ's strength is now your strength therefore you cannot be weak. Tell him **it is written,**

> *"I can do all things through Christ which strengtheneth me."*
> **Philippians 4:13**

He will leave you alone for a while but when you think that you are free from him he will come back again to buttress his points.

THOUGHTS ASKING YOU TO PROVE YOUR STRENGTH

When you are getting confident He will now start to taunt you. He will ask you, "How can you be so naive to believe that you can do all things?"

He may even tempt you and ask you to show him what you can do. He will even give you a test and say, *"If you know that you can do all things then do this."*

Living a Supernatural Life (Volume 2)

But you just reply him by telling him what the Word of God says in Philippians 2:13 that whatever you want to do you are not really the one going to do it but it is God Himself who will work in you. Tell him that **it is written,**

> *"For it is God which worketh in you both to will and to do of his good pleasure."*
> **Philippians 2:13**

Satan will go for a while but he will come back to taunt you the more. He will tell you that if you are so sure that it is God that works in you why then are you still so weak? If you have refused to or unable to do what he said that you should do he will ask, "Why then could you not do the thing that I asked you to do?" You should now reply him by letting him know that you don't have to do what he directs because it is written in Matthew 4:7 that we are not supposed to tempt the Lord our God and in any case, in 2 Corinthians 12:9-10 it is written that the strength of Jesus that you now use is made perfect in weakness therefore when you are weak it is then that you are really strong. Tell him that **it is written,**

> *Jesus said unto him, It is written again, Thou shalt not tempt the Lord thy God.*
> **Matthew 4:7**

> *"And he said unto me, My grace is sufficient for thee: for my strength is made perfect in weakness. Most gladly therefore will I rather glory in my infirmities, that the power of Christ may rest upon me.*

Therefore I take pleasure in infirmities, in reproaches, in necessities, in persecutions, in distresses for Christ's sake: for when I am weak, then am I strong."
                                  2 Corinthians 12:9-10

On this issue of who is the stronger, you or the devil, this last answer should give the devil a knockout punch. This is so because he will now realize that he cannot use your weakness to taunt you or harass you anymore. But this does not mean that he will go and leave you alone completely. He will still try to flex his muscle against you through another route pretending that he has some power.

THOUGHT THAT HE WILL EVENTUALLY DEFEAT YOU

He may even go to the extent of putting it in your mind that your words cannot do anything to him. Satan has seen the glorious destiny that God has for you. That is the reason why he will keep on piling the pressure on you so that you will accept his own words in your mind and he can then turn them into strong holds with which to manipulate you and your life.

He has seen many people even strong Christians fall to his antics. Therefore he will become boastful and continue to put thoughts in your mind to convince you to see things his own way. He will tell you that he will eventually get you; it is just a matter of time.

Living a Supernatural Life (Volume 2)

But you can reply him with what the Word said as written in John 3:8, John 6:63 and in 2 Peter 1:3-4 making him to realize that since you are now born of the Spirit, you are a spirit being and your ways can no longer be figured out by him therefore you are no longer vulnerable. Tell him also that because you now have the divine nature of God the Words of God that you speak are spirit and they are life, and no matter what he does you know that he cannot overcome you in any way. Tell him that you know that God has given you all things that pertain unto life and godliness. He will leave you when you tell him that **it is written,**

> *"The wind bloweth where it listeth, and thou hearest the sound thereof, but canst not tell whence it cometh, and whither it goeth: so is every one that is born of the Spirit.*
>
> **John 3:8**
>
> *It is the spirit that quickeneth; the flesh profiteth nothing: the words that I speak unto you, they are spirit, and they are life.*
>
> **John 6:63**
>
> *According as his divine power hath given unto us all things that pertain unto life and godliness, through the knowledge of him that hath called us to glory and virtue:*
>
> *Whereby are given unto us exceeding great and precious promises: that by these ye might be partakers of the divine nature, having escaped the corruption that is in the world through lust."*
>
> **2 Peter 1:3-4**

BRINGS THE THOUGHT THAT GOD'S PROMISES ARE NOT MEANT FOR YOU

If you are still suffering from any type of oppressions and afflictions, and your prayer seemed not to have been answered yet, he will come back again and put some new thoughts in your mind. For example he may put it in your mind that you should not expect all the promises that Jesus made to work for you because they were mainly meant for His disciples. You should reply him with what Jesus said in Mark 13:37 and remind him that Jesus said that what He was saying to His disciples He was saying unto us all therefore whatever He said to them applies to you also. Tell him that **it is written,**

> *"And what I say unto you I say unto all, Watch."*
>
> **Mark 13:37**

When you tell him this he will leave you alone for a while and remove his thoughts from your mind. But there is no extent that Satan will not go and there is nothing beyond him, which he cannot use to try and convince you so that he can derail your glorious destiny as a son of God.

THAT YOU MUST DIVORCE YOUR SPOUSE

For example this can happen if you are a single, unmarried believer trying to get married, or you are already married but you are going through some rough times with your marriage.

Living a Supernatural Life (Volume 2)

Satan may deviate from his usual antics and try to tackle you at the social level by bringing thoughts into your mind about your social standing. He may come into your mind in such a situation and put the thought in you that it may be better for you to stay single or get a divorce. He may even prove it to you. As you can see the incidence of divorce among Christian couples all over the world is increasing at an alarming rate. This is one of the things that Satan is using to derail many Christians.

It is part of his grand plan to derail your destiny. You should reply Satan with what God said through king Solomon in Ecclesiastes 4:9-12, and what the Word of God says in Genesis 2:18 and Deuteronomy 32:30 that two are better than one because they will have a good reward for their labour. Also tell him that the Word of God says that it is not good that you should be alone. Tell him that **it is written,**

> *"Two are better than one; because they have a good reward for their labour.*
>
> *For if they fall, the one will lift up his fellow: but woe to him that is alone when he falleth; for he hath not another to help him up.*
>
> *Again, if two lie together, then they have heat: but how can one be warm alone?*
>
> *And if one prevail against him, two shall withstand him; and a threefold cord is not quickly broken.*
> **Ecclesiastes 4:9-12**

And the LORD God said, It is not good that the man should be alone; I will make him an help meet for him.
Genesis 2:18

How should one chase a thousand, and two put ten thousand to flight, except their Rock had sold them, and the LORD had shut them up?"
Deuteronomy 32:30

When you resist him with these Words of God he will leave you alone but again he will do so only for a while. He will try to come back again if you have not settled the matter of who to marry in your mind.

THOUGHT THAT YOU CAN MARRY AN UNBELIEVER

He may not tackle you this time by saying that you should not marry anymore. He may change his tactics and he may now try to convince you as to whom you should marry. For example, if you are a young man, when you come into contact with a very beautiful lady who may not even be a Bible-believing, born-again Christian he may put the thought in your mind that she will be an ideal partner for you despite the fact that the Holy Spirit in you may be telling you otherwise.

He may tell you that there is nothing wrong with marrying such a woman, that her beauty will always appeal to you and that you can always get her converted after you have married her.

In that situation, you should reply him with what God said through Solomon in Proverbs 31:30 that favour is deceitful, that beauty is vain and the woman that feareth the Lord is the one God recommended for you. Tell him that **it is written,**

> *"Favour is deceitful, and beauty is vain: but a woman that feareth the LORD, she shall be praised."*
> **Proverbs 31:30**

When you say this Satan will know that you know what the Word says and he will leave you alone and take that thought away from your mind for that time.

BRINGS THE THOUGHT THAT THE HOLY SPIRIT IS NOT FOR THIS DISPENSATION

But if you still have not chosen a partner after some time he will come back into your mind with some other thoughts. For example he may start to question your dependence on the Holy Spirit's guidance on that matter. He may put it into your mind that the Holy Spirit was meant to manifest just during the times of the disciples of Christ and shortly after that. He may put it in your mind that the Holy Spirit is not meant to be working with us today. But you can reply him with what God said through Apostle Peter in Acts 2:38-39 that the promise of the Holy Spirit extends beyond the disciples. It was not meant for them alone. It was meant for the people at that time and their children but it was also meant for those of us from afar off.

It was meant for anybody that God calls. When you say this to him he will leave you alone and take that thought along with him Therefore tell him that concerning the Holy Spirit, **it is written,**

Then Peter said unto them, Repent, and be baptized every one of you in the name of Jesus Christ for the remission of sins, and ye shall receive the gift of the Holy Ghost.

"For the promise is unto you, and to your children, and to all that are afar off, even as many as the Lord our God shall call."
Acts 2:38-39

TEMPTS YOU TO PROVE THAT YOU ARE A SON OF GOD

Let us now look at one of Satan's greatest struggle against the Christian. This is the struggle to get the Christian to believe that those things written in the Scriptures about him are not true. Where the Christian believes that they are true he will ask the Christian to do some things to prove that they are true. This is not unusual. After all that was what he did to Jesus.

He told Jesus as written in Matthew 4:3, *"They have said that you are the Son of God. If it is true that you are truly the Son of God then command these stones that they become bread."* He knew that Jesus was hungry so he wanted Jesus to prove that He is the Son of God by tempting him to use His power to get the food.

Living a Supernatural Life (Volume 2)

> *And when the tempter came to him, he said, If thou be the Son of God, command that these stones be made bread.*
> **Matthew 4:3**

He also said in Matthew 4:6, *"If you are truly the Son of God then cast yourself down from the pinnacle of the temple. After all it is written that He will give His angels charge concerning you and in their hand they shall bear you up lest at any time you dash your feet against a stone."* He brought these temptations to Jesus to create fear and doubt in Him as to whether He is truly the Son of God.

> *And saith unto him, If thou be the Son of God, cast thyself down: for it is written, He shall give his angels charge concerning thee: and in their hands they shall bear thee up, lest at any time thou dash thy foot against a stone.*
> **Matthew 4:6**

We all know how Christ solved this problem. We have discussed this in detail in *Chapter 8* of *Volume 1* of this *"Living a Supernatural life"* book series. What concerns us now however is to show that Satan also does the same thing to us Christians today. From what is written in John 1:12-13 we can see that once you are born-again you are born of God and you are given the power to become a son of God. You don't have to do anything to prove this to Satan. He knows that you are a son of God. All he is doing is to convince you to believe that you are not.

But as many as received him, to them gave he power to become the sons of God, even to them that believe on his name:

Which were born, not of blood, nor of the will of the flesh, nor of the will of man, but of God.
John 1:12-13

ASKS, ARE YOU REALLY WHAT GOD SAYS YOU ARE?

Satan will come and test your stand on these truths. He will come to your mind and say, "If you are truly born of God and you are a son of God then command that your problems go right now. After all it has been written in 1 John 5:4 concerning you that whatsoever is born of God overcometh the world therefore show me now that you have overcome the world."

For whatsoever is born of God overcometh the world: and this is the victory that overcometh the world, even our faith.
1 John 5:4

In that case you should let Satan know that you will not command anything to satisfy him but that as written in the Scriptures in Revelation 5:10 you are not only a son of God but God has even made you a king and a priest unto Himself and it is written in Ecclesiastes 8:4 that where the word of a king is no body can oppose it and say no. Therefore you know that if you command anything it must obey you because **it is written,**

"And hast made us unto our God kings and priests: and we shall reign on the earth.
Revelation 5:10

Where the word of a king is, there is power: and who may say unto him, What doest thou?"
Ecclesiastes 8:4

You should let Satan know that it is also written in Luke 21:15 you have been given a mouth and wisdom which none of your adversaries can resist or gainsay. Let Satan know that you don't have to do what he says he cannot resist whatever you say. Tell him that **it is written,**

"For I will give you a mouth and wisdom, which all your adversaries shall not be able to gainsay nor resist."
Luke 21:15

You can now see how Satan comes into the mind of the believer to plant all kinds of thoughts bringing different types of temptations to suite the different situations that the believer comes across in life.

He wants to bring fear and doubt into your mind because as written in Job 3:25 Satan knows that whatever you fear will eventually come upon you and whatever you are afraid of will eventually come unto you.

For the thing which I greatly feared is come upon me, and that which I was afraid of is come unto me.
Job 3:25

Pulling Down Satan's Strong Holds

If you are not clued-up in the Word of God, you may find it difficult to bring the thoughts that Satan brings into your mind under subjection. It is with the Word of God that you will bring those thoughts into captivity. Therefore you can see why it is important that you must have the Word of God in you. Satan's objective is to bring doubt and fear into your mind and control it. Once he can do so, he has taken control of you. This is because whatever actions you will take in life first starts from the thoughts that you allow into your mind. But remember that like God said of the people of old in Psalm 53:5 they were in fear where there was no fear. Do not be in fear under any circumstance since you have already overcome the enemy. You have the greater One living in you than is in the world. You should let Satan realize that there is no fear for you anymore.

> *There were they in great fear, where no fear was: for God hath scattered the bones of him that encampeth against thee: thou hast put them to shame, because God hath despised them.*
> **Psalm 53:5**

Let him know that you will not compromise with fear because as a son of God you no longer have the spirit of fear. The Holy Spirit that you now have as you can see in 2 Timothy 1:7 is not a Spirit of fear but that of power, of love and of a sound mind.

> *For God hath not given us the spirit of fear; but of power, and of love, and of a sound mind.*
> **2 Timothy 1:7**

Living a Supernatural Life (Volume 2)

Therefore you don't have to fear in any situation anymore. Fear will not solve any problem for you; it is just the devil's trick and illusion and you don't have to fall for it. It is very important that you use the Word of God to pull down all the strong holds that Satan attempts to build in your mind with the thoughts that he attempts to plant there. We have shown in *Volume 1* of this *"Living a supernatural life"* book series written by the same author that the mind is the decision taker for man. That is why it is written in Proverbs 23:7 that as a man thinks in his heart, so is he. Therefore what you think in your heart is what will determine what you become in life. That is why it is such a priority for the devil to get his thoughts planted in your mind. Therefore watch out for the thoughts that you allow into your mind. That is why you are advised to gird the lions of your mind in 1 Peter 1:13.

> *For as he thinketh in his heart, so is he: Eat and drink, saith he to thee; but his heart is not with thee.*
> **Proverbs 23:7**

> *Wherefore gird up the loins of your mind, be sober, and hope to the end for the grace that is to be brought unto you at the revelation of Jesus Christ;*
> **1 Peter 1:13**

Sometimes Satan will come into your heart and put pointing questions there also some of which are written in the next section. These will be pointing questions that will test your stand on the Word of God. And if you are not careful he will make you to fall. Such questions as "Can you do what God says you can do?"

CAN YOU DO WHAT GOD SAYS YOU CAN DO?

ARE YOU WHERE GOD SAYS THAT YOU ARE?

You must reply him by what is written by Paul in Phillippians 4:13 and what is written in Ephesians 2:6.

> *I can do all things through Christ which strengtheneth me.*
> **Philippians 4:13**

> *And hath raised us up together, and made us sit together in heavenly places in Christ Jesus:*
> **Ephesians 2:6**

Tell him that *it is written that,*
"I can do all things through Christ which strengtheneth me."

Tell him that *it is written that,*
"He hath raised us up together, and made us sit together in heavenly places in Christ Jesus:"

Now then, we have shown you what God means by **the strong holds of Satan,** which He wants you to pull down and how God expects you to pull them down.

Strong holds are thoughts that Satan has planted in your mind, which you have allowed to take strong roots in your mind to the extent that they can even sometimes become your strong beliefs.

Living a Supernatural Life (Volume 2)

Most of the strong holds of Satan that he has planted in our minds come through our traditions and those things we have seen and learnt by our personal experience. We have depended on our senses to judge what we see, what we taste, smell and heard and we just follow the decisions taken through what we got from our senses. But God warned us through Paul the Apostle in Colossians 2:8 to beware of the tradition of men and their philosophies.

> *Beware lest any man spoil you through philosophy and vain deceit, after the tradition of men, after the rudiments of the world, and not after Christ.*
> **Colossians 2:8**

CHAPTER 17

YOU MUST BE BORN AGAIN

Now that you have read this book up to this point, I want you to know that what I have written in this book is just a tip of the iceberg of the power and ability that is available to you once you are born again. What I have shared with you in this book is how to make sure that this power and ability is demonstrated in your life once you are born again. If you can imbibe what is written in this book and act accordingly, your life will never be the same again. It will revolutionize your life. But as you can see it all starts with your being born-again.

If you have not believed Christ and accepted Him as your Saviour, or you are not absolutely sure that you have done so then you can see what you have been missing. But it is also quite possible that you may be saying that those things that you have read in this book cannot be true because they may not make sense to you. This is so because you cannot possibly understand these things using your innate, inborn or natural knowledge.

Living a Supernatural Life (Volume 2)

However, God has also recognized that until you become saved these will be foolishness to you because the things of God are spiritually discerned. That is what God said through Apostle Paul in 1 Corinthians 1:18-19 and in 1 Corinthians 2:14.

> *For the preaching of the cross is to them that perish foolishness; but unto us which are saved it is the power of God.*
>
> *For it is written, I will destroy the wisdom of the wise, and will bring to nothing the understanding of the prudent.*
> **1 Corinthians 1:18-19**
>
> *But the natural man receiveth not the things of the Spirit of God: for they are foolishness unto him: neither can he know them, because they are spiritually discerned.*
> **1 Corinthians 2:14**

That is why God is calling you today. Therefore if you are hearing the still small voice of God calling on you today to believe in Christ and accept Him as your Saviour, do not say, "No" to that voice because it is God Himself talking to you.

Jesus Himself said this in John 6:44. He said that it is not possible for you to come to Him unless God the Father draws you to Him.

> *No man can come to me, except the Father which hath sent me draw him: and I will raise him up at the last day.*
> **John 6:44**

You must be Born-again

You have probably been living a life that has little or no meaning to you. Take a bold step today to move into this new life in Christ. Do not delay today. Seize this opportunity to come to Jesus. It is a great opportunity for you to also become a son of God, an opportunity to have a Father-son relationship with the God who is the creator of the entire universe.

It is an opportunity for you to also become a partaker of God's divine nature. It is an opportunity for you to share in God's power and demonstrate God's power to the world. That you should have His power and demonstrate it to the world is God's plan for your life. It is a great privilege to be the son of the Almighty.

I know that you have seen and you know many people who call themselves Christians and who have accepted Christ as their Saviour but who do not have this power of God demonstrated in their lives. Yes! This is true, but this is so because most people who have accepted Christ as their Saviour lack this knowledge and do not know that they have this power available to them.

Even many of those that do know this do not know how to get this power demonstrated in their lives. So, even after they became born-again Christians, they continue to live their normal natural life, unable to demonstrate the power of God or the supernatural life that is now their portion. God Himself recognized this truth. That is why He said through the Prophet Isaiah in Isaiah 5:13 and through the Prophet Hosea in Hosea 4:6 that His people are destroyed and gone into captivity because of their lack of knowledge.

> *Therefore my people are gone into captivity, because they have no knowledge: and their honourable men are famished, and their multitude dried up with thirst.*
> **Isaiah 5:13**

> *My people are destroyed for lack of knowledge: because thou hast rejected knowledge, I will also reject thee, that thou shalt be no priest to me: seeing thou hast forgotten the law of thy God, I will also forget thy children.*
> **Hosea 4:6**

It is a lack of knowledge that has not allowed such Christians to demonstrate the power of God, which they now have in their lives. But you now know better. Having read this book, you have now been given the foundation knowledge that God wants you to have of the power that is made available to you once you become a born-again Christian and you also now know to some extent what you require to, and how you can, demonstrate this power in your life. As soon as you are born again this immense power is yours.

Knowing these therefore, I know that you will not like to miss the opportunity to demonstrate this type of power and the ability that we have talked about in this book in your life.

However, as I have earlier said, this power and ability can only be made available to you after you have accepted Jesus Christ as your Saviour and get born again.

You must be Born-again

You must have been told before that you have to change, clean up yourself and leave those things that you have been doing, which do not make your life compatible with a Christian life before you can be saved or become a born-again Christian. This is the obstacle that stops most people from changing. But I want you to know that this is not a pre-requisite for your being saved or born-again. Just accept that you are a sinner and agree to change. Once you receive Christ into your life, the change will come. God Himself will be the One who will clean you up. He will give you a new heart and a new spirit. He will also give you His Spirit who will guide you and direct you into all truths. Once you have this Spirit, your desires will change and the change in your attitudes and orientation will follow.

The process of accepting Jesus Christ as your Saviour is not difficult. It is actually a very simple thing. Just follow the four instructions listed below.

1

Accept that you are a sinner because we are all sinners before God. God Himself made this known to us through Apostle Paul in Romans 3:23 and also through Apostle John in 1 John 1:8, which is written below.

> *For all have sinned, and come short of the glory of God;*
> **Romans 3:23**

> *If we say that we have no sin, we deceive ourselves, and the truth is not in us.*
> **1 John 1:8**

Living a Supernatural Life (Volume 2)

2

Confess your sins and believe that God has forgiven you of those sins. God Himself has told us through John that if we confess our sins He is faithful and just to forgive us our sins and to cleanse us from all forms of unrighteousness. That is what He told us through Apostle John in 1 John 1:9 as written below.

> ***If we confess our sins, he is faithful and just to forgive us our sins, and to cleanse us from all unrighteousness.***
>
> **1 John 1:9**

3

Believe in your heart that Jesus Christ died for your sins and that God raised Him up from the dead. Confess this with your mouth. Then accept Jesus Christ as your Lord and your Saviour and confess this with your mouth also. Finally believe and confess with your mouth that as a result of this your confession with your mouth of His death for your sins and His resurrection you have now received your salvation as God made us to know through Apostle Paul in Romans 10:9-10.

> ***That if thou shalt confess with thy mouth the Lord Jesus, and shalt believe in thine heart that God hath raised him from the dead, thou shalt be saved.***
>
> ***For with the heart man believeth unto righteousness; and with the mouth confession is made unto salvation.***
>
> **Romans 10:9-10**

4

Finally, pray out loud with your mouth and from the depth of your heart the prayer written below. It must be a prayer resulting from a deep conviction in your heart.

"My God who is in Heaven, I have read your Word and I have heard what you have spoken to me. I desire to give my life to you today.

I now confess to you that I am a sinner and ask that you forgive me my sins and cleanse me from all my unrighteousness. I know that having confessed my sins and asked you to forgive me; you have forgiven me and cleansed me from all my sins. God, give me the strength of will not to go back to those sins. I believe in my heart and I now confess with my mouth that Jesus Christ died for my sins and that you raised Him up the third day from the dead. I have confessed this my belief with my mouth therefore I now believe that I am born-again and saved because your Word says that once I do so I am born again. I know that your Holy Spirit has now come to live in me and will be directing me from now on. Thank you Father for giving me this free salvation. Thank you Jesus for offering yourself to save me from my sins. Thank you Holy Spirit for coming to live in me to direct me from now on."

"I pray in the Name of Jesus Christ. AMEN"

Now that you have made the above confessions and prayed the above prayer from the depth of your heart, the Word of God says that once you do this you are saved and you have become a son of God.

Living a Supernatural Life (Volume 2)

I can now boldly tell you that you are now a born-again child of God. I therefore welcome you into the family of God. You have to believe this and move forward from this point on in faith. Your interaction with God can only be on the basis of faith in His Word. That is the only way you can please Him. He told us in Hebrews 11:6 that without faith we cannot please Him. Therefore you must have faith in God.

> *But without faith it is impossible to please him: for he that cometh to God must believe that he is, and that he is a rewarder of them that diligently seek him.*
> **Hebrews 11:6**

Start living your life from now based on faith in what the Word of God says. He has said that you are now saved and born-again, therefore believe and have the faith that you are now saved and that you are born-again. You must also note that a man of faith speaks out what he believes. That is how to know that you have the Spirit of faith according to what is written by Apostle Paul in 2 Corinthians 4:13. Therefore boldly speak out and let others know that you are now saved.

> *We having the same spirit of faith, according as it is written, I believed, and therefore have I spoken; we also believe, and therefore speak;*
> **2 Corinthians 4:13**

Because you have made the above confessions of your faith in Christ, in addition to your new birth, the Word of God also says the following have also happened to you: Please read the Bible to confirm these statements of truth.

You must be Born-again

(2 Corinthians 5:17)
You are now a new creation.

(Romans 5:17)
You have now been given the gift of righteousness.

(John 1:12), (Galatians 4:7)
You are now a son of God and an heir of God.

(1 Corinthians 3:16) (Romans 8:9)
You are now a temple of God. The Spirit of God lives in you.

(Ephesians 2:6) (Ephesians 1:19-23)
You are now spiritually translated to be far above all things.

(Revelation 5:10)
You are now a king and priest unto God.

(2 Corinthians 5:20)
You are now an ambassador for Christ here on earth.

(1 Corinthians 2:16)
You now have the mind of Christ.

From this point on, all the above statements are true of you. Therefore believe these and start acting and living your life accordingly. You have to live your life based on faith in God believing these truths.

Stop seeing by sight. Stop acting based on what you see, on what you feel, on what you hear, on what you taste, on what you smell, and on what you think.

Living a Supernatural Life (Volume 2)

Let all your actions be based on what the Word of God says that you are even where everything point to the opposite. Find a Bible believing place of worship near to you that you can join so that you can be having fellowship with other Saints of God where you can be fed with the Word of God from time to time so that you can continue to grow in the Word.

Read the Bible, which is the Word of God often to find out more about God's plan for your life. Read this book over again and in particular read *Volume 3* of this *"Living a supernatural life"* book series. You will find in that volume what God says about who you are now in Christ, what you are now in Christ, what you now have in Christ, what you can now do in Christ and where you are now in Christ. Believe these and continue to confess them. They are all true for you. They are all yours in Christ. As you continue to do these you will be growing from strength to strength in faith and in the Word. You will then become a vessel of honour to be used by God for this end time.

If you want more information on what has just happened to you and what you have now become with this new birth then read the remaining volumes of this book series written by the same author and titled *"Living a supernatural life" Volumes 1, 3 and 4.* Also read the companion book series to this series written by the same author and titled, *"You are a New Creature" Volumes 1, 2, 3 and 4.*

If you have just accepted Christ as your Saviour through the reading of this book or you find the book useful and have seen or learn new things that can help your Christian life's journey or help you concerning the challenges that you have the author will like to hear from you so that you can gain more from his experience and others can also gain from your own experience. Contact the author to share your testimonies. The author Pastor Olumbo also holds from time to time healing and counselling seminars. Please contact the author to find out when the next healing and counselling seminar will hold at the following e-mail address or telephone numbers or both so that you can take advantage of this opportunity to know more about who you have just become or who you really are in-Christ:

<u>*michaelolumbo@outlook.com*</u>
or
+234 816 526 5668
+234 802 310 3275

I look forward to hearing from you.

Living a Supernatural Life (Volume 2)

THE OTHER VOLUMES OF THIS BOOK SERIES

In *Volume 1* we showed what the make-up of man is. We showed that man is basically created as a spirit being and therefore ought to be more sensitive to the spiritual things, which are unseen than he is to the physical things that are seen. Then we talked about a law of the spirit, which is operating in man's life on a continuous basis and, which most men have not taken cognizance of. This law is very important in the scheme of things and any man that wants to live a supernatural life here on earth must not only be very conversant with the law but must also make use of it. We tried to show you that it is not only possible but also essential to live a supernatural life right now here on earth and we believe that to a great extent we were able to do this. Every Christian, nay every human being needs the information that is in this book to be able to live as God created man. This book can be considered to be an explanation of *The Secret* that people did not know which was claimed to have been discovered some years ago. *The Secret* has always been an open *Secret*. This book gives a Scriptural explanation for how the Laws discovered in **THE SECRET** works. Read the *Volume 1* of this *"Living a Supernatural Life"* if you want to know this *Secret*

In *Volume 3* we give you the right Scriptural view, perspective and image that you should have of yourself if you are to be able to live a supernatural life. This is a detailed discussion of who you are in Christ, what you are in Christ, what you now have in Christ, what you can now do in Christ and where you now are in Christ.

You will find in this Volume how Jesus Christ developed a Scriptural perspective and image of Himself. You will also find how you can follow His footsteps in order to develop the right Scriptural perspective and image of yourself. Once you do this living a Supernatural life becomes very cheap. Jesus lived a Supernatural life when He was on earth. You too can do the same by following His footsteps. Certain practical problems were considered as examples with a detailed exposition of how we should now reason to overcome the problems or challenges based on our new understanding of who we are in-Christ and what we are now capable of in-Christ.

In *Volume 4* we discuss two of the major requirements for living a supernatural life here on earth. These are the Holy Spirit and a willing mind. The roles that both the Holy Spirit and the mind play in living a supernatural life are examined in detail. The ways to submit to the Holy Spirit and harness the mind so as to live in the supernatural realm are also discussed. Finally we look at the various hindrances and obstacles that must be avoided if one is to live in this miracle realm.

OTHER BOOKS BY THE SAME AUTHOR
You Cannot Be Barren Series

Barrenness is a disease which can be very painful to whoever suffers from it. Yet the pain is difficult to express. The shame barrenness brings can lead to a deplorable and miserable life which makes the person become isolated.

Living a Supernatural Life (Volume 2)

While trying to solve this problem you will meet with all kinds of trials and insults. As a Christian you need not go through all these problems.

You Cannot Be Barren book series is written to uplift the minds of every individual who is suffering from dearth in all human aspects, be it fruitfulness, or any other pressing needs. The book series makes you understand that barrenness is not of God and that every trial and tribulation has its expiration if only one is born-again. The Book series ***You Cannot Be Barren*** is written in six volumes and they are written to show you how you can conquer barrenness.

In Volume 1 we discussed in a simple way the various causes of barrenness looking first at what medical sciences say about the human reproductive system. We also look at what they say about the human reproductive process and about barrenness and its causes. Then we looked at what the Word of God has to say about the causes of barrenness, giving the root cause as mainly spiritual even though it manifests physically. We showed how important it is not to have a sin-complex but a righteousness-complex if one is to approach God for the solution to the barrenness challenge. One must also be God-conscious, and God-focused if one is to solve the barrenness problem based on the Word of God. We also discussed briefly some of the things that the Word of God gives as the main causes of barrenness. These include sin, lack of forgiveness, taking the Communion unworthily and what one eats or drinks.

In Volume 2 we discussed the Covenant rights that you have to ask for healing from barrenness as a Christian. We first looked at your rights to healing as a result of the Covenant and showed that you have an unquestionable right as provided by God for your deliverance from anything that may be causing you to be barren. We discussed the terms of the Covenant that you must fulfill if you are to be able to claim your rights via the Covenant as well as how to use the Word of God to claim those rights. What we have done is to make sure that by the time that you would have gone through this *Volume 2* you would have gotten such a good understanding of the Covenant to the extent that there will be no doubt in your mind that it is your right to be fruitful and nothing can stop your fruitfulness.

In Volume 3 we looked at your New-Birth rights to being fruitful in detail. With your new-birth we showed that both spiritual and physical healing has been packaged with your salvation. Not only that, we also showed that as a result of your new-birth God's life was imparted to you. With this God's life that was imparted to you we showed that if you are conscious of this new life, which you now have which is God's life then it is impossible for any disease that can lead to barrenness or unfruitfulness to attack your body and inhabit it or win against you.

Our aim in *Volumes 2 and 3* is to try to develop and increase your faith to the point where you can see yourself in the light of the Scriptures by discussing your Old Covenant rights and your New Covenant and New-birth rights to fruitfulness.

Living a Supernatural Life (Volume 2)

In Volume 4 After discussing how important your confessions are and how to stand firm we looked at the various ways that the enemy uses to attack people with barrenness and give the Scriptures that can be used in confessions against it in each case. For each case we also gave sample Scripturally-based confessions that you can use. If you truly believe in your confessions and have processed them through meditation long enough for them to become revealed words of God to you embedded in your spirit then getting over any form of barrenness will be very easy for you. You will not have to struggle with barrenness.

In Volume 5 we discussed the various reasons why people don't generally receive their healing from diseases and in particular from barrenness. You will do well to look at these so that your healing will not be hindered.

Finally **in the *Volume 6*** of this, ***"You Can Not Be Barren"*** book series we looked at and discussed the various barrenness strong holds of the devil that he usually builds in the minds of the people who suffer from this scourge of barrenness. We looked at how these strong holds are developed in the mind in stages and discussed the Word of God to use to counter the strong holds at each stage.

REFERENCES

BROWN R. 1987. *Unbroken Curses.* New Kensington: Whitaker House.

CLARK J. 2003. *Exposing Spiritual Witchcraft.* Florida: Spirit of Life Publishing.

Grace Notes. *Bitterness.* Website. http://www.realtime.net/~wdoud/topics/bitterness.html. 20 August 2013

HICKEY M. 1987. *Breaking Generational Curses.* Oklahoma: Harrison House.

KENNETH E. HAGIN 1979. *What to do when Faith seems weak and Victory lost.* Kenneth Hagin Ministries.

NORI D. 1999. *Breaking Generational Curses.* Skippensburg: Destiny Image Publishers.

OLUMBO M. F. 2005. *Living A Supernatural Life. Volume 1.* Lagos: The Apostolic Church LAWNA Printing Press.

OLUMBO M. F. 2008. *Living A Supernatural Life. Volume 2.* Lagos: Extra Time Communications Ltd.

OLUMBO M. F. 2008. *Living A Supernatural Life. Volume 3.* Lagos: Extra Time Communications Ltd.

ORAL ROBERTS 1987. *When you see the invisible You can do the impossible.* Destiny Image Publishers Inc.

Living a Supernatural Life (Volume 2)

SHERMAN D. 1990. *Spiritual Warfare: How to live in Victory and Retake the Land. Seattle:* YWAM Publishing.

TOM MARSHALL 1977. *Free Indeed.* Sovereign World Publications.

WRIGHT H.W. 2005. *A More excellent way Be in Health.* Pleasant Valley Publications.

INDEX

A Living Proof **345**
A major key of the Kingdom **105**
A Parable of the Rich man and his Son **254**
Abide in Christ **355**
Ask in Jesus' Name and Jesus will do it **155**
Ask the Father in Jesus' Name and He will give it **152**
At the call of Jesus' Name Satan trembles **119**
Be Bold **449**
Be filled with the Holy Spirit **457**
Be patient **465**
Be sensitive to the Holy Spirit **403**
Be violent against the devil **411**
Be violent with your confessions **431**
Believe in His Name to get your benefits **122**
Believe on His Name to be saved **122**
Beware of the tradition of men **307**
Boast in the Lord **309**
Casting out a spirit of divination **170**
Confess your way to your Salvation **441**
Contend for your possessions **421**
Dealing with a serpent bite **190**
Devils are subject to you through the Name **127**
Do not let your past failures bother you **219**
Everything is put under Jesus Feet **117**
Everything you want is in Jusus's Name **139**
Expunge Bitterness **86**
Fight evil don't sympathize with it **428**
Four steps to being born-again **591**
Frame your world with your words **92**
Gathering in Jesus' Name brings His presence **128**
Gives examples of people who bribed and won **560**
God is a Spirit **71**
God is above you **327**

Living a Supernatural Life (Volume 2)

God is around you **328**
God is behind you **326**
God is Eternal **71**
God is Holy **76**
God is in front of you **324**
God is in you **329**
God is Omnipotent **72**
God is Omniscient **73**
God is Righteous **78**
God is underneath you **327**
God is with you **331**
God's Word is God's Power **436**
Have a good knowledge of God **452**
Have a righteousness-complex **399**
Have a stable mind **480**
Have holy anger **425**
Have love in your heart **460**
Have no sin-complex **383**
Have Wisdom **460**
Healing a lame man **166**
Healing a man of Palsy **175**
Healing the sick of fever **192**
How did the disciples obey Jesus' commands? **165**
How do you develop faith in Jesus' Name? **215**
How to use the Name of Jesus **147**
Ignore people's opinion of you **216**
Imprisoned and requiring freedom **171**
Is any sick among you? **196**
It is the only Name through which we can be saved **122**
Jesus authorized you to use His Name **135**
Jesus is heir of all things **116**
Jesus wants you to live in the Supernatural Realm **443**
Jesus' Name gives power to become a son of God **125**
Jesus' Name is a Strong Tower of Protection **106**
Jesus' Name is above every other name **114**

Jesus' Name is more excellent than angel's name **117**
Let him call the elders **196**
Live and walk in the spirit **36**
Live Right **450**
Maintaining your union with Christ **360**
Miracles are wrought through faith in Jesus' Name **120**
Never confess anything out of fear **85**
No oppression can subdue you **362**
Practice is the main issue **100**
Practicing Supernatural Living **299**
Praying for Boldness **168**
Praying the Prayer of Confession to Salvation **593**
Preach the Gospel of Christ **299**
Proclaim what you want **304**
Pulling down Satan's strong holds **533**
Raising of a cripple **184**
Raising of the dead **178**
Releasing the Supernatural **83**
Repetitive call of Jesus' Name is not necessary **141**
Satan asks if you are what God says that you are **582**
Satan asks you to prove your strength **572**
Satan asks, "Are you where God says you are?" **586**
Satan asks, "Can you do what God says?" **586**
Satan brings guilt-conscience for sin **536**
Satan brings the thought of fear **553**
Satan brings the thoughts of restlessness **542**
Satan brings the thoughts that God is far from you **541**
Satan brings the thoughts that you are finished **539**
Satan brings the thoughts that you will suffer **554**
Satan brings worry to your mind **557**
Satan questions the truth of God's Word **547**
Satan tempts you to complain or murmur **540**
Satan tempts you to offer bribe **558**
Satan tempts you to prove you are a son of God **580**
See beyond the natural **319**

Living a Supernatural Life (Volume 2)

See your words as seeds **478**
Send God's Angels **240**
Some thoughts that can become strong holds **535**
Speak God's Word to your situations **346**
Speak out the Word of God **239**
Speak to your Mountains **250, 423**
That God will not give you something that big **537**
That God will not help you **536**
That the Holy Spirit is not for this times **579**
That you did not ask according to God's will **569**
That you have to wait long to get answers **549**
That you will not get all you asked of God **538**
That your decree is not God's Word **544**
The fulfillment of your command is immediate **283**
The God-conscious attitude **370**
The Holy Spirit was sent in Jesus' Name **129**
The Name of Jesus **105**
The two instructions of Jesus about His Name **147**
There is power in the Name of Jesus **210**
There will be wilderness experience **375**
Thoughts that everybody is against you **566**
Thoughts that God did not hear your prayer **568**
Thoughts that God is the One afflicting you **564**
Thoughts that God's promises are not for you **576**
Thoughts that it is an ancestral curse **562**
Thoughts that Satan will defeat you **574**
Thoughts that you are a lame duck **571**
Thoughts that you are powerless **570**
Thoughts that you are very weak **572**
Thoughts that you can marry an unbeliever **578**
Thoughts that you can't make it where Mr. X failed **556**
Thoughts that you should divorce your spouse **576**
Thoughts that you will go down with others **552**
Thoughts that your decree will not stand **543**
Thoughts that your victory will not last **551**

Use both LOGOS and RHEMA to fight **437**
What are the works that Jesus did? **157**
What God wants you to Build **519**
What God wants you to Destroy **510**
What God wants you to Plant **525**
What God wants you to pull down **507**
What God wants you to root out **502**
What God wants you to throw down **517**
What makes the Name Unique? **106**
What then is the prayer of faith? **199**
Whatever you cannot proclaim you cannot possess **306**
Why don't we follow Jesus's Instructions? **194**
Why fear when you have already won the battle? **458**
You are a god **41**
You are a Member of Christ's Body **130**
You are a spirit-being **34**
You are a Supernatural Being **33**
You are an Ambassador for Christ **47**
You are an ambassador of His Name **137**
You are baptized into Jesus' Name **134**
You are born into God's family **132**
You are capable of a higher anointing **469**
You are for Signs and Wonders **49**
You are God's Battle Axe **495**
You are in God **330**
You are meant to reign in life **423**
You are Peculiar **44**
You are sent as Jesus was sent **56**
You are stronger than a Witch **69**
You are to function by Faith **94**
You can live your own heaven here on earth **337**
You can pass through any situation **363**
You have a Hedge of Protection around you **87**
You have a Rod for doing Signs and Wonders **50**
You have life through the Name of Jesus **126**

Living a Supernatural Life (Volume 2)

You have remission of sin through Jesus' Name **129**
You must be born-again **587**
You now partake of God's divine nature **70**
You too can do what Jesus did **58**
You will be God-conscious **364**
Your mouth creates your future **91**
Your mouth is the vehicle **221**
Your rights to the use of Jesus' Name **130**
Your victory is already guaranteed **351**

www.ingramcontent.com/pod-product-compliance
Lightning Source LLC
Chambersburg PA
CBHW070712160426
43192CB00009B/1161